REPRESENTING CLIENTS IN IMMIGRATION COURT

AILA TITLES OF INTEREST

AILA's OCCUPATIONAL GUIDEBOOKS

Immigration Options for Artists and Entertainers

Immigration Options for Essential Workers

Immigration Options for Physicians

*Immigration Options for Nurses
& Allied Health Care Professionals*

Immigration Options for Religious Workers

Immigration Options for Academics and Researchers

Immigration Options for Investors and Entrepreneurs

STATUTES, REGULATIONS, AGENCY MATERIALS & CASE LAW

Immigration & Nationality Act (INA)

Immigration Regulations (CFR)

*Agency Interpretations of Immigration Policy
(Cables, Memos, and Liaison Minutes)*

CORE CURRICULUM

Navigating the Fundamentals of Immigration Law

Immigration Law for Paralegals*

*AILA's Guide to Technology and Legal Research for
the Immigration Lawyer*

TOOLBOX SERIES

AILA's Immigration Practice Toolbox

AILA's Litigation Toolbox

FOR YOUR CLIENTS

Client Brochures (10 Titles)

*U.S. Tax Guides for Foreign Persons and Those
Who Pay Them, 4 volumes—
(H-1Bs, L-1s, J-1s, B-1s)**

AILA's FOCUS SERIES

EB-2 & EB-3 Degree Equivalency
by Ronald Wada

Waivers Under the INA
by Julie Ferguson

Private Bills & Pardons in Immigration
by Anna Gallagher

The Child Status Protection Act
by Charles Wheeler

Immigration Practice Under AC21
by A. James Vazquez-Azpiri & Eleanor Pelta

TREATISES & PRIMERS

Kurzban's Immigration Law Sourcebook
by Ira J. Kurzban

Professionals: A Matter of Degree
by Martin J. Lawler

AILA's Asylum Primer
by Regina Germain

*Immigration Consequences
of Criminal Activity*
by Mary E. Kramer

Representing Clients in Immigration Court
by CLINIC

Essentials of Immigration Law
by Richard A. Boswell

Litigating Immigration Cases in Federal Court
by Robert Pauw

Immigration Law & the Family
edited and written by Charles Wheeler

Immigration Law & the Transgender Client
by Transgender Law Center
& Immigration Equality

OTHER TITLES

*AILA's Guide to Worksite Enforcement
and Corporate Compliance*

David Stanton Manual on Labor Certification

Going Global: Trends in Outbound Immigration

*AILA's Global Immigration Guide:
A Country-by-Country Survey*

Immigration & Nationality Law Handbook

*The Visa Processing Guide
& Consular Posts Handbook*

*Immigration Practice Under NAFTA
and Other Free Trade Agreements*

The International Adoption Sourcebook

GOVERNMENT REPRINTS

BIA Practice Manual

Immigration Judge Benchbook

Citizenship Laws of the World

CBP Inspector's Field Manual

EOIR Immigration Court Practice Manual

Affirmative Asylum Procedures Manual

ONLINE RESEARCH TOOLS

AILALink Online

Tables of Contents and other information about these publications
can be found at *www.ailapubs.org*. Orders may be placed at that site or
by calling 1-800-982-2839.

*An AILA-distributed title

REPRESENTING CLIENTS

IN IMMIGRATION COURT

Contributed to and edited by CLINIC staff

Website for Corrections and Updates

Corrections and other updates to AILA publications
can be found online at: *www.aila.org/BookUpdates.*

If you have any corrections or updates to the information in this book,
please let us know by sending a note to the address below, or e-mail us at
books@aila.org.

This publication is designed to provide accurate and authoritative information in regard to the subject matter covered. It is distributed with the understanding that the publisher is not engaged in rendering legal, accounting, or other professional service. If legal advice or other expert assistance is required, the services of a competent professional should be sought.

—from a Declaration of Principles jointly adopted by a Committee of the American Bar Association and a Committee of Publishers

Proceeds from the sales of AILA publications are reinvested in the association to help support member programs and services in the areas of federal and state advocacy, government liaison, practice assistance, ethics education, media outreach, and timely dissemination of members-only information via InfoNet. In addition, contributions are made to the American Immigration Law Foundation (AILF).

Printed in the United States of America

ISBN 978-1-57370-272-0
Stock No. 52-72

FOREWORD

When I began practicing immigration law 30 years ago, deportation hearings were conducted in relatively informal settings by a handful of administrative law judges who typically learned on the job. The legacy INS trial attorney would meet with practitioners shortly before proceedings began and negotiate plea deals. The majority of the respondents, particularly the detained, were unrepresented and summarily deported in a group proceeding that followed those who had counsel. Most of the respondents I represented pled to the allegations in exchange for 90 days of voluntary departure, which they could later seek to extend. Many of these clients, in turn, simply left the country then returned illegally. Those who were eligible filed for suspension of deportation, adjustment of status, or relief under INA §212(c). Formal procedures for seeking asylum and withholding of removal came later, as did legalization and an updated registry.

In certain ways, much has changed since those days. Deportation and exclusion proceedings have now merged into removal proceedings. Whether the grounds of inadmissibility or deportability control depends on the manner of the respondent's last entry. The proceedings are held in settings that more closely resemble state or federal courtrooms. They are governed by uniform procedures and rules, and often apply evidentiary standards used in federal judicial proceedings. The immigration judges and trial attorneys now work for separate agencies. Video conferencing allows immigration judges to hold hearings and make decisions in cases where the respondent is being held in a remote detention facility. Gone are many of the defenses and forms of relief that were available up until the mid-1990s. A large percentage of proceedings are now conducted with the respondent "in absentia." Many foreign nationals are subjected to expedited removal, stipulated removal, and reinstatement of removal, and never even see the inside of these new courtrooms.

In other ways, very little has changed. Most respondents are still unrepresented, and an increasing number are detained. If you are unrepresented, the likelihood of your avoiding deportation is much smaller than it is for those who have the resources to retain counsel. And the strongest factor in measuring your chances of winning an asylum or cancellation of removal claim is the name of the judge assigned to hear your case. Former trial attorneys and political cronies still represent the majority of immigration judges now serving on the bench. Only a small percentage of respondents actually challenge their deportability; most concede it and request voluntary departure, if they qualify. While the representation of clients in removal proceedings may still be the most heartbreaking and frustrating part of an immigration law practice, it also holds the potential of being the most meaningful and rewarding.

The authors want to thank the many immigration practitioners who advised us during the creation and revision of this book. Their practical experience has proved invaluable. We also want to thank their clients and their clients' families for the lessons in fortitude, determination, and hope they have demonstrated.

Charles Wheeler
March 2009

SUMMARY TABLE OF CONTENTS

Foreword v

Acknowledgments ix

Table of Decisions..355

Index 367

Chapter 1: Removal Proceedings 1

Chapter 2: Grounds of Deportability...35

Chapter 3: Grounds of Inadmissibility 61

Chapter 4: Contesting Removability 97

Chapter 5: Adjustment of Status 125

Chapter 6: Waivers of Inadmissibility and Deportability in Removal Proceedings........155

Chapter 7: INA §212(c) and Cancellation of Removal for Lawful Permanent
Residents 179

Chapter 8: Cancellation and Suspension for Non-Permanent Resident Aliens..............195

Chapter 9: Asylum, Withholding of Removal, and Protection Under the Convention
Against Torture 233

Chapter 10: Voluntary Departure 269

Chapter 11: Naturalization as a Defense to Removal..279

Chapter 12: Administrative Review of Removal Orders 287

Chapter 13: Judicial Review of Removal Orders...297

Appendices

Appendix 1: Notice to Appear 313

Appendix 2: Order to Show Cause..317

Appendix 3: Sample I-122 323

Appendix 4: Criminal Record Check..325

Appendix 5: Court Instructions..327

Appendix 6: Summary Order of Removal 329

Appendix 7: Order of Expedited Removal..331

Appendix 8: Administrative Order of Removal...335

Appendix 9: Naturalization Charts...337

Appendix 10: Motion to Suppress Evidence...349

ACKNOWLEDGMENTS

This book began as the text for a series of trainings on relief from removal conducted during 2001 by staff from the Catholic Legal Immigration Network, Inc. (CLINIC). Various staff contributed information or wrote most of the chapters to these training materials. They were substantially updated and revised in subsequent years by the following current or former CLINIC staff: Evangeline Abriel, Sarah Bronstein, Margaret Gleason, Mary Holper, Susan Schreiber, Tom Shea, and Jill Sheldon. Portions of this book that originally appeared in other publications cited below are used by permission.

Chapter 1 was adapted from CLINIC's Basic Law Training materials, written by Margaret Gleason. Chapters 2 and 11 were adapted from Chapter 7 of the *Immigrants' Rights Manual*, which was co-authored by CLINIC and the National Immigration Law Center (NILC). That chapter was originally written and updated by NILC's Linton Joaquin. The following CLINIC staff wrote all or portions of the original chapters: Chapter 3 (Helen Morris); Chapter 4 (Mark von Sternberg and Lauren Gilbert); Chapter 5 (Pat Malone); Chapter 6 (Margaret Gleason and Jack Holmgren); Chapter 7 (Evangeline Abriel, Charles Wheeler, Anne Marie Gibbons, and Laurie Joyce); Chapter 8 (Evangeline Abriel, Mario Russell, Marisol Zequiera-Burke, and Charles Wheeler); Chapter 9 (Helen Morris); and Chapter 10 (Laurie Joyce and Jack Holmgren). Alice Brown from Justice for our Neighbors in Omaha contributed one of the appendices. The materials were first compiled and edited by Charles Wheeler.

Charles Wheeler
March 2009

TABLE OF CONTENTS

Foreword v

Acknowledgments ix

Table of Decisions 355

Index 367

Chapter 1: Removal Proceedings 1

    Introduction to Basic Concepts 1

        Congressional Power to Deport 2

        Changes in the Law Impacting Removal Proceedings 2

    How People Get Placed in Removal Proceedings 3

    Inadmissibility or Deportability—Which Concept Applies? 5

    Commencement of Removal Proceedings in Immigration Court 6

        Charging Documents 6

            Notice to Appear 6

            Order to Show Cause 7

            Form I-122 7

        Proper Service 8

            Notice to Appear 8

            Order to Show Cause 8

    Notice of Address Change 8

    Burden of Proof in Removal Proceedings 8

    Rights in Proceedings 9

        Representation by Counsel 9

        Legal Services 10

        Contacting Consulates 10

        Translation 10

        Right to Examine Evidence 10

        Right to Be Advised of Eligibility for Relief 11

        Right to Due Process 11

        Special Rules for Juveniles 11

    Pre-Hearing Procedures 12

        Bond 12

            Ineligible for Bond: Persons Subject to Mandatory Detention 12

            Joseph Hearings 14

            Ineligible for Bond—Arriving Aliens 14

            Eligible for Bond 15

            Bond Hearings 15

Pre-Hearing Motions 16
Discovery Through FOIA and Criminal Record Checks....................18
Pre-Hearing Statement..21
Master Calendar Hearings and Individual Hearings 21
In Absentia Orders 23
Immigration Judge Decisions/Appeals 25
Consequences of Being in Removal Proceedings..................................25
Jurisdiction...25
Penalties for Noncompliance with Court Orders 26
Anatomy of a Removal Hearing 27
Types of Removal Orders..28
Expedited Removal Under INA §235(b)..28
Administrative Removal Orders Under INA §238(b) 29
Judicial Removal Order Under INA §238(c) 30
Reinstatement of Removal, INA §241(a)(5)......................................31
Practice Tips for Non-Court Advocates..32
Chapter 2: Grounds of Deportability 35
Grounds of Deportability: Generally 35
Aliens Inadmissible at the Time of Entry or Adjustment of Status 36
Inadmissible Aliens 36
Aliens Present in the United States in Violation of Law 37
Failure to Maintain Status...38
Termination of Conditional Permanent Residence 38
Alien Smuggling..39
Marriage Fraud 40
Criminal Grounds of Deportability 41
General Crimes..41
Crime of Moral Turpitude (CMT) 41
Multiple Criminal Convictions..47
Aggravated Felony 48
High-Speed Flight 51
Failure to Register as a Sex Offender..51
Drug Offenses...52
Controlled Substance Convictions 52
Drug Abusers and Addicts...52
Firearm Violations..53
Miscellaneous Crimes...53
Crimes of Domestic Violence, Stalking, or Violation of a Protection Order ...54
Domestic Violence, Stalking, and Child Abuse 54
Violators of Protection Orders...54
Document-Related Grounds of Deportability 55
Change-of-Address Requirement 55

Criminal Convictions Relating to Failure to Register and Falsification of
    Documents...55
Document Fraud Violations...55
Falsely Claiming Citizenship..56
Security and Related Grounds of Deportability...56
Espionage, Sabotage, and Other Illegal Activities 56
Terrorist Activities..57
Foreign Policy Considerations..57
Participation in Genocide or Nazi-Sponsored Persecution..................................57
Public Charge Grounds of Deportability 57
Unlawful Voting Ground of Deportability..58

Chapter 3: Grounds of Inadmissibility **61**
Overview of the Inadmissibility Grounds...61
Who Bears the Burden of Proof Under INA §212? 62
Evaluating the Charges of Inadmissibility 62
Grounds of Inadmissibility 63
Health-Related Grounds 63
    Communicable Diseases..64
    Lack of Vaccination 65
    Physical or Mental Disorders 66
    Drug Abusers or Addicts 67
Criminal Grounds 68
    Overview 68
    Required Standards of Proof 68
    Obtaining Necessary Records and Analyzing a Criminal Conviction..........69
    "Conviction," "Admission," and "Sentence" 69
    Crimes Involving Moral Turpitude 70
    Multiple Criminal Convictions...71
    Controlled Substance Violations 71
    Traffickers in Controlled Substances 72
    Prostitution and Commercialized Vice...73
    Immunity from Prosecution..74
    Particularly Serious Violations of Religious Freedom 74
    Significant Traffickers in Persons 75
    Money Laundering 75
    Aggravated Felonies 75
National Security Grounds 76
    Espionage, Sabotage, Export Control Violations, and Other Unlawful
        Activities 76
    Terrorist Activity..77
    Potential for Serious Adverse Consequences for Foreign Policy 78
    Membership in the Communist or a Totalitarian Party 78
    Participant in Genocide or Nazi Persecution..79
Public Charge 80

Public Charge Standard 80
Bonds...82
Previous Immigration Violations..82
Foreign Nationals Present Without Permission or Parole 82
Failure to Attend Removal Proceedings......................................83
Fraud or Willful Misrepresentation 83
False Claim to U.S. Citizenship 85
Stowaways...86
Smugglers and Encouragers of Unlawful Entry 86
Final Civil Document Fraud Order...86
Foreign Students...87
Not in Possession of Immigration Document 87
Ineligible for Citizenship 87
Prior Removal Orders or Periods of Unlawful Presence 88
Having Been Removed Previously..88
Unlawful Presence Bars 90
Determining Unlawful Presence 91
Reentering the United States Without Authorization 94
Miscellaneous Grounds 95

Chapter 4: Contesting Removability **97**
Three Preliminary Considerations in Removal Proceedings 97
Is the Individual a U.S. Citizen?..97
Acquisition of Citizenship..98
Even if the Respondent Is Not a USC, Are They Actually Subject to Removal?.100
Prosecutorial Discretion..100
Prosecutorial Discretion to Decline to Institute Removal Proceedings......101
Prosecutorial Discretion During Removal Proceedings: Joining or Not
Opposing Motions to Administratively Close or Motions to
Terminate 101
Motions to Close Administratively 102
Motions to Terminate 102
The Decision to Concede or Contest Removability.............................103
Challenging the NTA...104
Burden and Standard of Proof in INA §240 Proceedings....................105
Removal Proceedings Based on Inadmissibility.............................105
Removal Proceedings Based on Deportability 106
Special Issues Where Respondent Is Charged with Being Removable on
Criminal Grounds 107
Requirements of Evidence to Establish a Criminal Ground of
Inadmissibility or Deportability 107
Does the Conviction Meet All Necessary Elements for Immigration
Consequences? 108

Do the records submitted by ICE establish that there was a conviction for
  immigration purposes? 108
If the ground of removability requires that a certain sentence have been
  ordered or that a certain amount of damages be involved, does the
  evidence reflect the minimum sentence or damages? 109
Is the conviction really for a crime involving moral turpitude, aggravated
  felony, or other criminal ground of inadmissibility or deportability?...110
Has the conviction been pardoned, expunged, or otherwise ameliorated
  so as to remove or diminish immigration consequences? 111
Constitutional Violations and Motions to Suppress..112
  Overview 112
  Motions to Suppress Evidence: A Case Study..113
  The Right to Be Free of Unreasonable Searches and Seizures Under the
    Fourth Amendment..113
  The Exclusionary Rule in Removal Proceedings 114
  When Is a Warrant Required?...115
  What Constitutes a Seizure? 117
  What Is an Arrest? 117
  What Is Mere Questioning? 118
  What Is Detentive Questioning? 119
  Preparing the Motion to Suppress..120
  The Right to Remain Silent 121
Conclusion 123
Chapter 5: Adjustment of Status 125
  Various Modes of Adjustment...125
  Readjustment of Status 126
  Arriving Aliens and Adjustment in Proceedings 126
  Termination to Proceed with Adjustment Before USCIS...............................128
Family-Based Adjustment of Status 129
  Overview of Eligibility Requirements..129
  Obtaining Benefits Under §245(i) 130
  Procedure 131
    When to Assert the Defense 132
    Motions to Continue...132
  Submitting Proof of Prima Facie Eligibility and Filing the Application.........135
  The Merits Hearing..136
Removal of Conditional Residence 137
  Overview 137
  Failure to Comply with Procedural Requirements 138
  Denial of Joint Petition or Waiver Application 138
  Immigration Court Jurisdiction...139
NACARA §202 and HRIFA..140

Introduction 140
NACARA §202 140
Haitian Refugee Immigration Fairness Act (HRIFA)..............................143
Registry...146
Eligibility Requirements...146
Residence...147
Good Moral Character 148
Not Ineligible to Citizenship 148
Grounds of Inadmissibility..148
Exercise of Discretion 149
The Application Process..149
Adjustment of Status for Certain Foreign Nationals from Vietnam, Cambodia,
and Laos..150
Cuban Adjustment Act of 1966 (CAA) 153
Spouses and Children of Cubans 154
How to Apply 154

Chapter 6: Waivers of Inadmissibility and Deportability in Removal
Proceedings 155
The Exercise of Discretion...156
Extreme Hardship 157
Definition...157
Documenting Extreme Hardship 161
Waivers of Inadmissibility Grounds in Removal Proceedings 163
INA §212(g) Waivers for Health-Related Inadmissibility Grounds................163
Waivers for Communicable Disease of Public Health Significance 163
Waivers for Physical or Mental Disorders with Associated Harmful
Behavior 164
Waivers of the Vaccination Requirement...164
INA §212(h) Waivers for Criminal Inadmissibility Grounds...........................165
What Criminal Inadmissibility Grounds Does INA §212(h) Waive? 165
What Are the Eligibility Requirements for §212(h) Waivers?...................166
INA §212(i) Waivers for Fraud or Misrepresentation 167
INA §212(a)(9)(B)(v) Waiver for Unlawful Presence....................................168
The VAWA Waiver for the "Permanent Bar" 169
The INA §212(d)(3) Nonimmigrant Waiver 169
Waivers for Refugees and Asylees 169
Waivers Under Special Forms of Relief..170
Strategy and Procedure for Waivers of Inadmissibility Grounds in Removal
Proceedings...171
Form I-212 Consent to Reapply for Admission...172
Eligibility and Strategy 172
Procedure 174

Waivers of Deportation Grounds in Removal Proceedings 175

    INA §237(a)(1)(H) Deportability Waiver for Fraud or Misrepresentation 175

    Waiver of Deportability Ground of Crimes of Domestic Violence,
        Stalking, or Violation of a Protection Order... 176

Conclusion 177

**Chapter 7: INA §212(c) and Cancellation of Removal for Lawful Permanent
Residents 179**

    Cancellation for LPRs—Cancellation of Removal Part A............................... 179

        LPR for Five Years.. 180

        Seven Years Continuous Residence After Lawful Admission 180

        Bars to Cancellation Eligibility 183

        Discretionary Factors... 185

        Where and How to File 186

    INA §212(c) Relief 186

        Relief Under §212(c) 186

        Background.. 187

        Eligibility Under Former INA §212(c).. 188

            Comparable Ground of Inadmissibility or Exclusion for Those Charged
               with Deportability 190

        Motions to Reopen to Apply for INA §212(c) Relief.................................... 191

        The Application for INA §212(c) Relief 191

            Persons Not Covered in the §212(c) Regulations................................... 192

        Looking Ahead 192

    Proposed Repapering Rule.. 193

Chapter 8: Cancellation and Suspension for Non-Permanent Resident Aliens.......195

    Former Suspension of Deportation 195

        Overview 195

        IIRAIRA Changes 195

        Current Standard and Procedure for Suspension Applicants......................... 196

            Eligibility.. 197

            Continuous Physical Presence 197

            Proposed Rule on Repapering 198

            Good Moral Character 199

            Extreme Hardship... 200

            Discretion 201

    Cancellation of Removal for Non-LPRs.. 201

        Introduction 201

        Eligibility... 202

        Continuous Residence or Physical Presence 202

        Exceptional and Extremely Unusual Hardship... 204

        Grounds of Ineligibility 207

        The 4,000 Annual Cap... 208

Cancellation of Removal for Abused Immigrant Women and Children..............208
  Background..208
  Requirements..208
    Marital Relationship..209
    Children...209
    Battery or Extreme Cruelty...210
    Three-year Continuous Physical Presence..211
    No Residence with Abuser...212
    Where Abuse Took Place...212
    Good Moral Character..212
    Inadmissible or Deportable...214
    Extreme Hardship..215
    Evidence...216
    Intake Interview...217
    Self-Petitions...217
    Laws of Other Countries...218
    VAWA Cancellation Cap...218
NACARA §203...218
  Introduction..218
  Beneficiaries of NACARA...219
    Eligibility to Apply...219
    Dependent Spouses and Children..220
    Unmarried Sons and Daughters...220
    Other Requirements...220
  Jurisdiction of NACARA Application...221
    Asylum Office..221
    Executive Office for Immigration Review..222
  Requirements for NACARA Suspension of Deportation or Cancellation of
    Removal..222
    Continuous Physical Presence...222
    Good Moral Character..223
    Extreme Hardship..224
    Presumption of Extreme Hardship for Certain NACARA Beneficiaries...225
  Statutory Bars to NACARA..226
    Bars Relating to Immigration Violations..226
    Bars Relating to Failure to Comply with Immigration Proceedings..........227
  Process for Applying in Removal Proceedings...228
    Application...228
    Unmarried Sons and Daughters...229
    Motions to Reopen...229
    Burden of Proof...230
    Types of Evidence...230
  Reinstatement of Removal Does Not Bar NACARA Application..................231
  Deadline for Applications...231

**Chapter 9: Asylum, Withholding of Removal, and Protection Under the
    Convention Against Torture** **233**
    Asylum vs. Withholding..233
    Standards of Proof, Evidentiary Considerations, and the REAL ID Act of
        2005 236
    The REAL ID Act of 2005..238
    Elements of Persecution..239
        Economic Refugee...239
        Persecution by Groups That the Government Cannot Control 239
        Internal Flight Alternative 240
        Persecution vs. Prosecution 240
        Coercive Family-Planning Programs..240
        Neutrality and Imputed Political Opinion...242
        Conscription by the Government...243
        Membership in a Particular Social Group..244
            The Proposed Regulations...249
    Exercise of Discretion..251
    Ineligible Classes 253
        Ineligible for Asylum..253
        Persons Inadmissible on Security Grounds or Removable as Terrorists 253
            Firm Resettlement 255
            Safe Third Country 255
            Particularly Serious Crime in the Asylum Context 256
        Ineligible for Withholding...256
            Particularly Serious Crime in the Withholding Context..........................257
    Termination of Asylum or Withholding 258
    Credible Fear Process 259
    Overview...260
    Definitions 260
    Establishing Eligibility..264
        Burden of Proof 264
        Article 3 Withholding or Deferral of Removal...264
    Procedures..265
        Persons Arriving at a Port of Entry..265
        Persons in Removal Proceedings..266
        Persons Who Apply Affirmatively for Asylum and Withholding..................266
        Persons Ordered Removed or Those Who Had Final Orders of Removal
            Before March 22, 1999..266
        Persons Who Had CAT Cases Pending with Legacy INS on or Before
            March 22, 1999..266
        Persons Whose Previous Removal Order Is Reinstated and Persons Who
            Are Not LPR Aggravated Felons 267

Persons Who Are Subject to Administrative Removal per INA §235(c) 268
Diplomatic Assurances 268

Chapter 10: Voluntary Departure..**269**
   Requirements 269
      Prior to the Conclusion of Removal Proceedings..270
      At the Conclusion of Removal Proceedings...270
   Negative Consequences for Failure to Timely Depart Under a Grant of
      Voluntary Departure 271
      Arguments to Avoid the Consequences of a Failure to Depart 274
   Appeals While the Voluntary Departure Clock Is Ticking...................................274
   The Effect of a Motion to Reopen Upon a Grant of Voluntary Departure 274
   The Application for Voluntary Departure..276
   Establishing Compliance with Voluntary Departure 277
   Conclusion 277
Chapter 11: Naturalization as a Defense to Removal **279**
   Prima Facie Eligibility for Naturalization...279
   Bars to Establishing Good Moral Character 280
   Aggravated Felony Convictions 280
   Naturalization as a Defense to Removal 281
      Procedure..281
         Prosecutorial Discretion 282
         Termination of Proceedings Under 8 CFR §1239.2(f) 283
         After Termination of Proceedings 285
   Final Finding of Deportability Bars Naturalization 286
Chapter 12: Administrative Review of Removal Orders............................**287**
   Overview...287
   Appeals to the BIA 287
   Motions to Reopen and Motions to Reconsider...289
      Purpose 289
      Time and Number Limits...289
      Content, Format, and Filing Requirements for Motions to Reopen and
         Motions to Reconsider...291
   Motions to Reopen in Absentia Removal Orders 293
   Conclusion 296
Chapter 13: Judicial Review of Removal Orders.......................................**297**
   Judicial Review Before 1996 Changes 297
   Judicial Review Under the Transitional Rules...298
   Judicial Review of Removal Orders After Passage of REAL ID 298
      Overview 298
      Habeas Corpus in District Courts 299

Habeas Corpus Prior to REAL ID 299
Habeas Petitions Pending Prior to REAL ID.............................299
Habeas Challenges to Detention...300
Petitions for Review in the Courts of Appeals 300
Petitions for Review After REAL ID 300
Bars to Judicial Review in the Court of Appeals........................301
Procedural Rules Regarding Petitions for Review 304
Judicial Review of Particular Types of Removal Orders.....................306
Expedited Removal of Aliens Arriving at Ports of Entry...............306
Treatment of Nationality Claims 307
Challenges to the Validity of Removal Orders in Criminal Proceedings 307
Judicial Review of Certain Administrative Removal Orders 308
Judicial Review of Judicial Orders of Removal 308
Mandamus and Other Types of Petitions.....................................309

Appendices

Appendix 1: Notice to Appear 313

Appendix 2: Order to Show Cause...317

Appendix 3: Sample I-122 323

Appendix 4: Criminal Record Check..325

Appendix 5: Court Instructions..327

Appendix 6: Summary Order of Removal 329

Appendix 7: Order of Expedited Removal.....................................331

Appendix 8: Administrative Order of Removal...............................335

Appendix 9: Naturalization Charts...337

Appendix 10: Motion to Suppress Evidence...................................349

IMMIGRATION FORMS[*]

Department of Homeland Security

- AR-11; AR-11-SR

- ER-398

- G-14; G-28; G-325; G-325-A; G-325-B; G-325-C; G-639; G-646; G-652; G-731-C; G-731-N; G-731-T; G-731-V; G-845; G-845-S; G-884; G-942; G-1020; G-1041

- IAP-66

- I-20-AB; I-20-MN; I-68; I-246; I-352; I-361; I-395; I-407; I-408; I-468; I-485-B; I-485-C; I-485-D; I-539-A; I-539-S1; I-604; I-687; I-690; I-693; I-694; I-765-DH; I-765-DL; I-817; I-823; I-829; I-847; I-850; I-854; I-864; I-864-P; I-866; I-876; I-901; I-905; I-914; I-918; I-9; I-90; I-102; I-129; I-129-F; I-129-S; I-130; I-131; I-134; I-140; I-191; I-192; I-193; I-212; I-290-B; I-360; I-485; I-485-A; I-508; I-526; I-538; I-539; I-566; I-589; I-590; I-600; I-600-A; I-601; I-602; I-612; I-643; I-698; I-730; I-751; I-765; I-821; I-824; I-864; I-864-A; I-864-EZ; I-864-W; I-865; I-881; I-907

- J-1 Waiver

- N-4; N-25; N-300; N-426; N-336; N-400; N-470; N-565; N-600/N-643-A; N-644; N-648; N-600; N-600-K

- WR-702; WR-703

Department of State

- DS-10; DS-11; DS-19; DS-60; DS-64; DS-71; DS-82; DS-86; DS-117; DS-1173; DS-1648; DS-1858; DS-1981; DS-2013; DS-2029; DS-2053; DS-2060; DS-3053; DS-3077; DS-4024; DS-4034; DS-4035; DS-4047; DS-4080; DS-4081; DS-4082; DS-4083; DS-4085; DS-5504; DS-156; DS-156-E; DS-156-K; DS-157; DS-158; DS-169; DS-230; DS-3032; DS-3035; DS-3052

- DSL-1083; DSP-122

Executive Office of Immigration Review

- EOIR-26-A; EOIR-26; EOIR-27; EOIR-28; EOIR-29; EOIR-30; EOIR-31; EOIR-33; EOIR-40; EOIR-44; EOIR-45; EOIR-42-A; EOIR-42-B

---

[*] All forms listed here can be found on AILA*Link* as fillable PDFs. AILA*Link* is AILA Publications' online immigration law research library (see *www.ailalink.org*). You must have Adobe Acrobat 6.0 or higher, or Adobe Reader 8.0 or higher (Reader is a free download).

Department of Labor

- ETA-9033; ETA-9033-A; ETA-9035; ETA-9081; ETA-9089; ETA-750-A; ETA-750-B

State Workforce Agencies

- SWA AZ; SWA CA; SWA IL; SWA MI; SWA MN; SWA NV; SWA NY; SWA OH; SWA PA; SWA TN; SWA TX; SWA VA

Social Security Administration

- HA-501; HA-520; HA-4608
- SS-5

ABOUT AILA

The American Immigration Lawyers Association (AILA) is a national bar association of more than 11,000 attorneys who practice immigration law and/or work as teaching professionals. AILA member attorneys represent tens of thousands of U.S. families who have applied for permanent residence for their spouses, children, and other close relatives for lawful entry and residence in the United States. AILA members also represent thousands of U.S. businesses and industries who sponsor highly skilled foreign workers seeking to enter the United States on a temporary or permanent basis. In addition, AILA members represent foreign students, entertainers, athletes, and asylum-seekers, often on a pro bono basis. Founded in 1946, AILA is a nonpartisan, not-for-profit organization that provides its members with continuing legal education, publications, information, professional services, and expertise through its 36 chapters and over 50 national committees. AILA is an affiliated organization of the American Bar Association and is represented in the ABA House of Delegates.

American Immigration Lawyers Association
www.aila.org

CHAPTER ONE

REMOVAL PROCEEDINGS

Introduction to Basic Concepts

A removal proceeding is an immigration court hearing to determine whether a noncitizen will be removed from the United States. Any person in the United States who is not a citizen of the country may be removed if he or she falls within one of the grounds of inadmissibility or deportability contained in the Immigration and Nationality Act (INA).[1] Even a legal permanent resident (LPR) may lose his or her residency status and be removed from the United States if he or she violates certain immigration law provisions.

- Luca entered the United States with a tourist visa and has remained beyond her authorized stay. Luca may be placed in removal proceedings because she has violated her tourist status. Luca's sister, Marie, an LPR, was recently convicted of misdemeanor possession of drug paraphernalia. She may be placed in removal proceedings for having been convicted of a law relating to a controlled substance.

The term *removal proceedings* applies to all immigration court cases commenced on or after April 1, 1997. Before this date, immigration court hearings were called *deportation hearings* or *exclusion hearings*, depending on whether the individual in proceedings was charged with violating a ground of deportability or a ground of inadmissibility. This distinction is discussed in more detail below.

It is important to understand the agencies involved and terminology used in removal proceedings. Under the Homeland Security Act of 2002,[2] the Immigration and Naturalization Service (legacy INS) ceased to exist on March 1, 2003. Its functions were taken over by three new agencies, each a part of the Department of Homeland Security (DHS):

- U.S. Citizenship and Immigration Services (USCIS), which performs all immigration service functions, such as adjudication of visa petitions, naturalization petitions, and affirmative asylum applications;

- U.S. Customs and Border Protection (CBP), which performs all border inspection functions;

- U.S. Immigration and Customs Enforcement (ICE), which carries out interior enforcement responsibilities. While all three agencies can issue Notices to Ap-

---

[1] Immigration and Nationality Act of 1952 (INA), Pub. L. No. 82-414, 66 Stat. 163 (codified as amended at 8 USC §§1101 *et seq.*).

[2] Homeland Security Act of 2002, Pub. L. No. 107-296, 116 Stat. 2135 (Nov. 25, 2002).

pear (NTAs), ICE is in charge of prosecuting individuals in removal proceedings.

The immigration court is under the Executive Office for Immigration Review (EOIR), which is an agency within the Department of Justice. The *prosecuting* attorney from the government is a trial attorney for the assistant chief counsel of ICE. Your client is the *respondent* in removal proceedings. Under immigration law, all persons who are not citizens or nationals of the United States are termed "aliens."[3]

Congressional Power to Deport

Although the U.S. Constitution does not specifically authorize the deportation of persons found to be in the United States without required permission or documentation, the U.S. Supreme Court has determined this authority to be inherent in the federal government's sovereign power.[4] Moreover, congressional power over matters of admission and deportation has been held to be plenary—that is, absolute or unqualified.[5] Federal control over U.S. immigration policy and law is so complete, in fact, states are excluded from taking any independent actions in this area.

Courts have found that Congress has absolute authority concerning the grounds of removal, and have determined that judicial scrutiny of Congress's determinations in this area is inappropriate because of the political issues involved. Rarely, if ever, has Congress been held to have exceeded its authority in establishing substantive grounds for removing individuals from the United States. However, congressional legislation establishing procedures for the deportation of removable individuals must comport with due process under the Fifth Amendment of the Constitution. The concept of due process means procedures that ensure fairness to all people under the law.

Changes in the Law Impacting Removal Proceedings

The grounds of deportability and inadmissibility, and the forms of relief from removal that may be available, were substantially revised by the Illegal Immigration Reform and Immigrant Responsibility Act of 1996 (IIRAIRA).[6] IIRAIRA added new grounds of inadmissibility and deportability, and narrowed many forms of relief from removal, making many more noncitizens subject to expulsion. IIRAIRA also modified the application of the grounds of deportability. Prior to IIRAIRA, the factor that determined whether an individual was subject to the grounds of deportability, as opposed to the grounds of inadmissibility, was whether the individual had made an entry into the United States. After the changes enacted by IIRAIRA, the key question became whether the individual was lawfully admitted into the United States. Foreign nationals who seek admission at the border or a port of entry are subject to the

---

[3] INA §101(a)(3).

[4] *Fong Yue Ting v. U.S.*, 149 U.S. 698 (1893).

[5] *Kleindienst v. Mandel*, 408 U.S. 753 (1972).

[6] Illegal Immigration Reform and Immigrant Responsibility Act of 1996 (IIRAIRA), Division C of the Omnibus Appropriations Act of 1996 (H.R. 3610), Pub. L. No. 104-208, 110 Stat. 3009 (Sept. 30, 1996).

grounds of inadmissibility rather than the grounds of deportability. Similarly, foreign nationals who are apprehended inside the United States, and who were not lawfully admitted to the country, are deemed to be applicants for admission subject to the grounds of inadmissibility rather than the grounds of deportability. The grounds of deportability may be applied only to foreign nationals who were admitted lawfully to the United States.

As a result of the 1996 changes, the general rule now is that the new provisions regarding removal proceedings do not apply to individuals who are in deportation or exclusion proceedings that commenced prior to April 1, 1997. The provisions of the prior law apply in such proceedings, unless the attorney general (AG) takes further action to bring these individuals under the new rules.[7]

Though not as sweeping as the changes brought by IIRAIRA, the Uniting and Strengthening America by Providing Appropriate Tools Required to Intercept and Obstruct Terrorism Act of 2001 (USA PATRIOT Act),[8] the REAL ID Act of 2005,[9] and the Violence Against Women and Department of Justice Reauthorization Act of 2005[10] also changed some parts of the law impacting removal proceedings.

How People Get Placed in Removal Proceedings

While anyone in the United States in violation of an immigration law is vulnerable to being placed in removal proceedings, some of the most common ways that DHS identifies and places individuals believed to be in the United States unlawfully are:

- Picking up a person from jail or prison after an arrest or after the individual has completed his or her sentence

- Placing someone in proceedings who has unsuccessfully applied for some type of immigration benefit

- Workplace raids

- Arresting a person at or near a border point just after he or she has entered

To illustrate, the eight case scenarios below describe some of the more common situations that expose noncitizens to being placed in removal proceedings. Each example is given in light of new, post–September 11, 2001, security initiatives:

- Paulo, from Argentina, entered the United States on a student visa in 1998 but dropped out of school after one year. He works at a factory, using a fake green card. ICE conducts a workplace raid at his job site and he is placed in removal proceedings.

- Georgette, from Ireland, is an LPR who is about to complete her three-year prison term for selling cocaine. She receives notice from ICE that it has

---

[7] IIRAIRA §309(c)(2).

[8] Pub. L. No. 107-56, 115 Stat. 272 (Oct. 26, 2001).

[9] Pub. L. No. 109-13, 119 Stat. 231, Division B (May 11, 2005).

[10] Pub. L. No. 109-162, 119 Stat. 2960 (Jan. 5, 2006).

placed a detainer on her. Instead of being released at the end of her term, she will be transferred to ICE custody and placed in removal proceedings.

- Ali, from Egypt, applied for adjustment of status. At the interview, the USCIS office learns that Ali made a false claim to U.S. citizenship last year by showing a U.S. citizen (USC) birth certificate to qualify for a Social Security number. He is placed in removal proceedings.

- Marco, from Honduras, crossed the border into Texas without documents and met up with a smuggler, who agreed to drive him to Florida. A few miles from the border, their car was stopped by border patrol and Marco was placed in proceedings.

- Said, from Lebanon, reported as required for special registration. At the interview with ICE, he explained that he overstayed his tourist visa but he is now engaged to be married to a USC, who plans to petition for him. His wife attended the interview, too. Said is placed in removal proceedings.

- Charles, from the United Kingdom, applied for naturalization. While he had two old convictions for check fraud (for which he was just sentenced to probation), he had never experienced any trouble with immigration and still qualified for naturalization. However, instead of granting his application for naturalization, USCIS initiated removal proceedings.

- Rina, from India, an LPR since 1990, was convicted in 2001 of one count of retail theft. While she had returned from trips abroad several times without incident since this conviction, on her last return, she was detained by CBP and placed in removal proceedings.

- Marisol, a B-2 visa overstay, boarded a Greyhound bus in Miami on her way back to her home in Georgia. As the bus was leaving, armed border patrol agents got on the bus, blocked the aisles and demanded to see proof of immigration status from everyone on the bus. Feeling she had no choice but to answer the agents' questions, Marisol admitted that her B-2 visa had expired, and she was taken into custody and placed in proceedings.

As these examples show, the typical enforcement priorities for removal proceedings target foreign nationals who have:

- Been arrested for a crime;
- Applied for an immigration benefit that is not approved;
- Worked without authorization;
- Requested admission without valid documents; and
- Fallen within a group of individuals targeted for special scrutiny since the attacks on the World Trade Center on September 11, 2001. These new security measures included special registration requirements for noncitizens from designated countries, and new background checks on persons who are seeking admission to the United States or some type of immigration benefit. When these new checks produce a hit—a match between the person undergoing the

check and some record of an immigration or criminal violation—this may trigger removal proceedings if the violation corresponds with a ground of inadmissibility or deportability.

Inadmissibility or Deportability—Which Concept Applies?

The grounds of *inadmissibility*, formerly called the grounds of exclusion, are contained in INA §212(a). These are the reasons why an individual can be refused admission to the United States or removed from the United States after entering without inspection by an immigration officer. These grounds apply at the border and in removal proceedings for persons who have never been lawfully admitted to the United States. Establishing admissibility is also a requirement for many immigration applications, such as adjustment of status.

The grounds of *deportability* are contained in INA §237(a). These grounds apply to individuals who are in the United States after inspection by an immigration officer.

A person who is placed in removal proceedings will be charged as being either inadmissible under INA §212(a) or deportable under INA §237(a). As noted above, one of the most important changes made by IIRAIRA in 1996 was its altering of to whom these two sets of grounds could apply.

The law prior to 1996 relied on the concept of entry to determine who would be subject to grounds of deportation and who would be subject to the grounds of exclusion. An entry meant a physical crossing into the territorial limits of the United States, but not necessarily a legal entry with inspection by an immigration officer. Due to the 1996 changes, however, the law now discards entry and instead requires that an individual be lawfully admitted to be subject to the grounds of deportation. Otherwise, an individual is subject to the grounds of inadmissibility. An admission is an entry to the United States that is lawful, after inspection by an immigration officer.[11] This often places persons who entered the United States without inspection or admission at a disadvantage. Under current law, even if a person who entered without inspection or admission has lived in the United States for years, they are considered to be seeking admission, and thus, are subject to the grounds of inadmissibility.

– Susan came to the United States on a B-2 visa in 2003 and remained longer than her authorized stay. She is now married to a USC. If Susan is arrested by ICE she will be charged with a ground of deportability because she is in the United States unlawfully after an inspection and admission by an immigration officer. However, if Susan applies for adjustment of status based on her marriage to a USC as a defense to removal, she will also be looked at under the grounds of inadmissibility and she will have to prove that she is admissible.

– Lorena entered the United States by sneaking across the border in October 1995. Even though she has now lived in the United States for 10 years, if

---

[11] INA §101(a)(13).

she is placed in removal proceedings, Lorena will be charged with a ground of inadmissibility because she was never inspected by an immigration officer when she first entered the United States.

Under IIRAIRA, there is, in addition, a special rule regarding admission for LPRs who are returning to their home in the United States. Such returning LPRs are not regarded as seeking admission (and therefore are not required to establish admissibility under the INA §212(a) inadmissibility grounds) unless the person:

- Has abandoned or relinquished his or her LPR status;
- Has been absent from the United States for a continuous period of more than 180 days;
- Has engaged in illegal activity after leaving the United States;
- Has departed from the United States while under legal process seeking his or her removal;
- Has committed a criminal inadmissibility ground, unless he or she has obtained a waiver or relief from removal under INA §240A(a) (Cancellation of Removal Part A); or
- Is attempting to enter at a time or place other than as designated by immigration officers, or has not been admitted to the United States after inspection and authorization by an immigration officer.[12]

A returning LPR who falls within one of the above-listed categories is subject to being placed in removal proceedings and charged with a ground of inadmissibility, even if the LPR wouldn't have been subject to removal proceedings if he or she hadn't left the country.

> – Tom has been an LPR since 1992. In 1998, Tom was convicted of the fraudulent use of a credit card involving $150 and received a two-year probation term that he satisfactorily completed. Even though Tom is not deportable for this offense, he is likely inadmissible for the same crime. If Tom travels outside the United States, even just to see his family for a few weeks, he will be treated as an individual seeking admission to the United States, and he may be detained and placed in removal proceedings upon his return to the United States.

Commencement of Removal Proceedings in Immigration Court

Charging Documents

Notice to Appear

Removal proceedings under INA §240 are initiated by a charging document called a Notice to Appear (NTA). The NTA must specify the following:

- The nature of the proceedings against the person;

---

[12] INA §101(a)(13)(C).

- The legal authority for the proceedings;
- The acts or conduct that allegedly violate the law;
- The formal charges and the statutory provisions allegedly violated;
- The person's right to representation, including time to secure counsel, and a list of available pro bono counsel;
- The requirement that the person charged provide, in writing, his or her address and telephone number (if any), and changes of same so that the government can contact the person, and the consequences of failing to do so, including the consequences of failing to appear at the hearing; and
- The time and place of the hearing and the consequences of failing to appear, including the entry of a removal order in absentia.[13]

The NTA need only be in English, and need only give 10 days notice of the hearing. The person against whom the NTA is issued is called the respondent—the person who must respond to the charges. By regulation, proceedings commence when the NTA is filed in court, and not when the NTA is served on the individual.[14] A sample NTA appears as Appendix 1 in the appendix section of this book.

Order to Show Cause

The Order to Show Cause (OSC) is the document used in cases commenced before April 1, 1997, charging an individual with being deportable. The OSC requires that:

- Notice be given of the charges and of the time and place of the hearing at least 14 days before the hearing date;
- Notice be written in Spanish and in English;
- The respondent be advised of the consequences of failure to appear; and
- The respondent be advised of address change requirements.[15]

A sample OSC appears as Appendix 2.

Form I-122

Form I-122 was the document used to commence *exclusion proceedings*, the name for the pre–April 1, 1997, immigration court proceedings charging an individual with being inadmissible to the United States. A sample I-122 appears as Appendix 3.

---

[13] INA §239(a); 8 CFR §§1003.15 (b), (c).

[14] 8 CFR §1003.14.

[15] 8 CFR §1003.15.

Proper Service

Notice to Appear

Under Code of Federal Regulations (CFR) Title 8 §1003.13, the NTA shall be served on the respondent in person; or if personal service is not practicable, the NTA shall be served by regular mail to the individual or his or her counsel of record. If the respondent does not receive the NTA and the notice of hearing it contained, and for this reason was never notified of the initiation of proceedings and the change of address requirements, then the immigration judge (IJ) may not enter an in absentia order.[16]

Order to Show Cause

For the OSC, service must be by personal service or certified mail to the respondent or to his or her counsel of record.[17]

Notice of Address Change

The law requires that the respondent inform the immigration court of any address change on Form EOIR-33 within five days.[18] It is critical to educate clients regarding this requirement to avoid the severe consequences of in absentia deportation/removal orders.

Burden of Proof in Removal Proceedings

An individual in removal proceedings will be labeled either as an arriving alien, an alien present in the United States who has not been admitted or paroled, or an alien who has been admitted but is deportable.

Arriving aliens bear the burden of proving that they are beyond a doubt entitled to be admitted and are not inadmissible under INA §212.[19] There is an exception to this for returning LPRs. The Supreme Court has held that returning LPRs are entitled to have the government bear the burden of proof in establishing their inadmissibility.[20]

For individuals charged with being in the United States without admission or parole, ICE must first establish the person's alienage.[21] If alienage is established, unless the respondent demonstrates by clear and convincing evidence that he or she is lawfully in the United States pursuant to a prior admission, the respondent must prove

---

[16] *Matter of G–Y–R*, 23 I&N Dec. 181 (BIA 2001).

[17] 8 CFR §1003.13.

[18] 8 CFR §1003.15(d).

[19] INA §§240(c)(2), 291; 8 CFR §1240.8(b).

[20] *Landon v. Plasencia*, 459 U.S. 21 (1982); *see also: Katebi v. Ashcroft*, 396 F.3d 463 (1st Cir. 2005); *Khodagholian v. Ashcroft*, 335 F.3d 1003 (9th Cir. 2003), citing *Landon, supra*; and *Matter of Huang*, 19 I&N Dec. 749 (BIA 1988) ("When an applicant has a colorable claim to returning resident status ... the INS has the burden of proving he is not eligible for admission to the United States").

[21] 8 CFR §1240.8(c).

that he or she is beyond a doubt entitled to be admitted to the United States and is not inadmissible under INA §212 as charged.[22]

If the individual is charged with deportability, ICE has the burden of establishing by clear and convincing evidence that the respondent is deportable under INA §237.[23] This standard is lower than the "beyond a reasonable doubt" standard used in criminal proceedings, but higher than the "preponderance of the evidence" standard used in civil proceedings. In deportation proceedings, commenced prior to April 1, 1997, ICE is required to prove that the alien is deportable by "clear, convincing, and unequivocal evidence."[24]

Where ICE has the burden of proof, it is important that representatives hold them to it. In removal proceedings, this is initially done by denying the charge(s) and corresponding ground(s) of removability set out in the NTA. If ICE does not meet its burden of proof, the representative should move to terminate the proceedings.

- Hang, an LPR from Korea, is charged with being deportable for a conviction for embezzlement, which ICE is calling a crime of moral turpitude. At the hearing, ICE has the burden of proving that the conviction occurred, and that the crime as defined by the statute is a crime of moral turpitude. It is not Hang's burden to show that the crime is not a crime of moral turpitude.

In all applications for relief from removal, the burden of proof is on the individual.[25]

Rights in Proceedings

Representation by Counsel

Respondents in proceedings have the privilege of being represented by counsel at their own expense.[26] It should be noted, however, that this is very limited in expe-

---

[22] INA §§240(c)(2), 291; 8 CFR §1240.8(c).

[23] INA §240(c)(3); 8 CFR §1240.8(a).

[24] *Woodby v. INS*, 385 U.S. 276 (1966).

[25] 8 CFR §1240.8(d).

[26] INA §§239(a)(1)(E), 240(b)(4)(A). Note: Until very recently, the Board of Immigration Appeals (BIA) and federal courts have operated under the assumption that immigrants have rights, under statute or the Constitution, to representation by a lawyer before they can be ordered deported. This assumption was based, in part, on the ruling in *Matter of Lozada*, 19 I&N Dec. 637 (BIA 1988), where the BIA responded to an individual's constitutional claim of ineffective assistance of counsel by assuming that a constitutional right to effective assistance of counsel (under the Due Process Clause of the Fifth Amendment) existed in the first place. On January 7, 2009, however, in the waning hours of a departing presidential administration, Attorney General (AG) Michael Mukasey declared that henceforth, immigrants, asylum-seekers, and all others in removal proceedings do not have any right under statute or the Constitution to representation by a lawyer before they can be ordered deported. In his decision in *Matter of Compean*, 24 I&N Dec. 710 (A.G. 2009), Mukasey stressed that INA §240(b)(4)(A) gives individuals in removal proceedings merely the "privilege" to be represented by counsel, not the right, thereby reversing many years of precedent and operation with a single stroke of his pen.

dited removal proceedings—the law only allows consultation with counsel that is deemed not to delay the process.

By regulation, respondents may be represented in court by attorneys, law students, and law graduates who meet certain requirements specified in the regulations. Respondents also may be represented by accredited representatives who have received full accreditation by the Board of Immigration Appeals (BIA).[27] The requirements for obtaining accredited representative status are found at 8 CFR §292.2. An attorney or representative in an immigration court proceeding must file a Notice of Appearance on Form EOIR-28 with the immigration court and serve a copy on ICE.[28]

Legal Services

Respondents in proceedings also have a right to be given a list of available legal services, and these lists are to be updated quarterly.[29] But note that in removal proceedings, unlike in criminal cases, counsel is not appointed for an individual who cannot find free services and cannot pay for private counsel. Respondents can find out about free legal services in their area on the immigration court website at *www.usdoj.gov/eoir*.

Contacting Consulates

Section 1236.1(e) of 8 CFR provides that a detained foreign national must be notified that he or she may communicate with the consul or diplomatic officer of the country of his or her nationality, where the country is on the treaty list. This right is also based on Article 36 of the Vienna Convention on Consular Relations.[30] In addition, ICE must immediately notify diplomatic officers of the countries listed in the regulation, whenever a national from a designated country is detained in removal proceedings.

Translation

Under 8 CFR §1240.5, a person in removal proceedings who does not understand English has an absolute right to a translator as part of the right to present evidence and cross-examine witnesses. This regulation does not, however, give respondents the right to translation of documents at the expense of the government.

Right to Examine Evidence

Under INA §240(b)(4)(B), an individual in proceedings shall have a reasonable opportunity to examine the evidence against him or her, to present evidence on his or her own behalf, and to cross-examine government witnesses.

---

[27] 8 CFR §292.1.

[28] 8 CFR §1003.17(a).

[29] 8 CFR §1003.61.

[30] 21 U.S.T. 77, 100–1; 596 U.N.T.S. 261.

Right to Be Advised of Eligibility for Relief

Pursuant to 8 CFR §1240.11(a)(2), the IJ "shall inform the alien of his or her apparent eligibility to apply for any of the benefits enumerated in this chapter and shall afford the alien an opportunity to make application during the hearing."

Right to Due Process

Individuals in removal proceedings are entitled to due process, which can be accomplished only by providing the opportunity for a full and fair hearing.[31] However, an individual also must demonstrate prejudice to prevail on a due process challenge.[32] In *Rodriguez Galicia v. Gonzalez*,[33] the U.S. Court of Appeals for the Seventh Circuit found that an IJ's decision to bar expert testimony that had the potential of affecting the outcome of the case on account of a time constraint imposed by the IJ was a due process violation that prejudiced the respondent and necessitated a new hearing. Furthermore, in an unpublished decision, a BIA panel concluded that a removal hearing where the IJ failed to consider arguments presented by respondent's counsel, and suggested to ICE alternative grounds of removal, was not full and fair and resulted in substantial prejudice to the respondent.[34]

Evidence also can be excluded or suppressed on due process grounds in removal proceedings if its use is not fundamentally fair.[35] For example, evidence can be suppressed if gained from an illegal search or seizure that is so egregious that it amounts to a violation of the due process clause of the Fifth Amendment.[36] Evidence that was obtained through an egregious violation of the Fourth Amendment also may be suppressed.[37] Moreover, evidence can be suppressed if it is gained in violation of an agency's own regulations.[38]

Special Rules for Juveniles

Special provisions apply where the individual in proceedings is under age 18. Pursuant to 8 CFR §1240.10(c), the IJ should not accept an admission of removability from an unrepresented juvenile individual who is not accompanied by a relative, friend or guardian. When the IJ does not accept an admission under this provision, a hearing must be scheduled to determine the matters at issue.

---

[31] *Matter of M–D–*, 23 I&N Dec. 540 (BIA 2002), *citing Landon v. Plasencia*, 459 U.S. 21 (1982).

[32] *See, e.g., Singh v. Gonzales*, 432 F.3d 533 (3d Cir. 2006); *Arellano-Garcia v. Gonzales*, 429 F.3d 1183 (8th Cir. 2005); *Rodriguez Galicia v. Gonzales*, 422 F.3d 529 (7th Cir. 2005).

[33] *Rodriguez Galicia, supra* note 32.

[34] *Matter of Chun*, A45 246 969 (BIA 2005) (unpublished), *available at www.lexisnexis.com/ practiceareas/immigration/immigration_cases.asp.*

[35] *Matter of Toro*, 17 I&N Dec. 340 (BIA 1980).

[36] *Id.*

[37] *INS v. Lopez-Mendoza*, 468 U.S. 1032 (1984).

[38] *Matter of Garcia*, 17 I&N 325 (BIA 1980).

Pre-Hearing Procedures

Bond

Upon issuance of an NTA, a foreign national may be kept in custody, released under a bond of a minimum of $1,500, or released on conditional parole into the community.[39]

Ineligible for Bond: Persons Subject to Mandatory Detention

Foreign nationals with certain types of criminal histories are subject to "mandatory detention," which means they cannot be released pending removal proceedings, even if they are permanent residents. Pursuant to INA §236(c)(1), the following persons are subject to mandatory detention:

- Those who are inadmissible by reason of having committed any offense covered in INA §212(a)(2) (the criminal inadmissibility grounds).

- Those who are deportable by reason of having committed any offense covered in INA §237(a)(2)(A)(ii) (multiple crimes of moral turpitude), §237(a)(2)(A)(iii) (aggravated felonies), §237(a)(2)(B) (controlled substances), §237(a)(2)(C) (certain firearms offenses), or §237(a)(2)(D) (miscellaneous espionage and sabotage crimes).

- Those who are deportable under INA §237(a)(2)(A)(i) (one crime involving moral turpitude) if the individual was sentenced to a term of imprisonment of at least one year.

- Those who are inadmissible under INA §212(a)(3)(B) (terrorist activities) or deportable under INA §237(a)(4)(B) (terrorist activities). After the passage of the REAL ID Act of 2005,[40] which expanded the definitions of "engaged in terrorist activity" and "terrorist organization," as well as the ground of deportability at INA §237(a)(4)(B), more individuals are potentially subject to removal, and thus, mandatory detention under these grounds.

Individuals who fall under these mandatory detention provisions must be taken into detention when released from their criminal sentence on parole, supervised release, or probation.[41] In *Matter of Kotliar*,[42] the BIA decided that an individual may be subject to mandatory detention for charges that are not listed on the NTA. However, mandatory detention only applies to those who were last released from criminal custody after October 8, 1998.[43]

---

[39] INA §236(a).

[40] REAL ID Act of 2005, *supra* note 9.

[41] INA §236(c)(1).

[42] *Matter of Kotliar*, 24 I&N Dec. 124 (BIA 2007).

[43] *Matter of Adeniji*, 22 I&N Dec. 1102 (BIA 1999).

In *Matter of West*,[44] the BIA held that "released from" means released from actual physical restraint. Many ICE offices and IJs read dicta in *Matter of West*[45] to mean that a release from the physical restraint of an arrest after October 8, 1998, is sufficient to trigger mandatory detention, even if the individual was never again in any physical custody for that offense but was instead, for example, sentenced to a period of probation. Moreover, in *Matter of Rojas*,[46] the BIA held that an individual is subject to mandatory detention even if DHS does not immediately detain him or her upon release from criminal custody.[47]

The BIA has held that the mandatory detention rules apply to someone who was released from criminal custody prior to October 8, 1998, yet was detained on an unrelated matter or a non–mandatory detention offense after October 8, 1998.[48] However, three district courts have decided that this was a wrongful interpretation of INA §236(c) and the transitional period custody rules.[49]

The Supreme Court, in *Demore v. Kim*,[50] held by a 5–4 vote that the mandatory detention provisions are constitutional, even as applied to LPRs. This decision came after many federal courts, including the U.S. Third, Fourth, Ninth, and Tenth Circuit Courts of Appeals, had held that the mandatory detention provisions were unconstitutional, particularly as applied to LPRs. Still, challenges to mandatory detention continue to be filed, specifically because the Supreme Court's decision was based, in part, on an understanding that removal proceedings for detained respondents are typically concluded within 90 days. Some of these challenges have been successful.[51]

Moreover, persons subject to mandatory detention may still be released if the AG decides that release from custody is necessary to provide protection to a witness or potential witness, a person cooperating with an investigation into a major criminal activity, or an immediate family member of such a person. Before any release takes place, however, the AG must also decide that persons subject to mandatory detention

[44] *Matter of West*, 22 I&N Dec. 1405 (BIA 2000).

[45] *Id.*

[46] *Matter of Rojas*, 23 I&N Dec. 117 (BIA 2001).

[47] *But see Zabadi v. Chertoff*, No. C 05-03335 WHA, 2005 WL 3157377 (N.D. Cal Nov. 22, 2005) (unpublished), *Quezada-Bucios v. Ridge*, 317 F. Supp. 2d 1221 (W. D. Wash. 2004).

[48] *Matter of Saysana*, 24 I&N Dec. 602 (BIA 2008).

[49] *Hy v. Gillen*, No. 08-11699-JLT, 2008 WL 5077820 (D. Mass. Dec. 3, 2008); *Saysana v. Gillen*, No. 08-11749-RGS (D. Mass. Dec. 1, 2008) (unpublished); *Thomas v. Hogan*, No. 1:08-CV-0417, 2008 U.S. Dist. LEXIS 88169 (M.D. Pa. Oct. 31, 2008) (unpublished); *Cox v. Monica*, No. 1:07-CV-0534, 2007 U.S. Dist. LEXIS 44660 (M.D. Pa. June 20, 2007) (unpublished); *Cavazos v. Moore*, No. M-03-347 (S.D. Tx. Jan. 07, 2005) (unpublished).

[50] *Demore v. Kim*, 538 U.S. 510 (2003).

[51] *See, e.g. Tijani v. Willis*, 430 F.3d 1241 (9th Cir. 2005), *Ly v. Hansen*, 351 F.3d 263 (6th Cir. 2003), *Diomande v. Wrona*, No. 05-73290, 2005 WL 3369498 (E.D.Mich., Dec. 12, 2005) (unpublished), *Parlak v. Baker*, 374 F. Supp. 2d 551 (E.D. Mich. 2005).

will not pose a danger to the safety of other persons or property and is likely to appear for any scheduled proceeding.[52]

Joseph Hearings

While the IJ does not have jurisdiction to release foreign nationals subject to mandatory detention, the IJ does retain jurisdiction to determine whether the person is, in fact, properly included in the mandatory detention provisions.[53] Individuals who think that have been improperly characterized as subject to mandatory detention should request a "*Joseph* hearing" before the IJ; the name for this hearing derives from the BIA's decision in *Matter of Joseph*.[54] To succeed at a *Joseph* hearing, the individual must demonstrate to the IJ that it is substantially unlikely that the charge of removability triggering mandatory detention will be upheld. If the judge decides that the respondent is not properly classified as a mandatory detainee, the judge will hold a bond hearing immediately.

Ineligible for Bond—Arriving Aliens

The IJ also does not have jurisdiction to consider release from detention for "arriving aliens" in removal proceedings. Arriving aliens are those applicants for admission who are either trying to enter the United States at a port of entry or are interdicted at sea and brought to the United States.[55] As mentioned above, LPRs returning from a trip abroad can be deemed to be making an admission and placed in proceedings as arriving aliens if they fit within one of the exceptions listed in INA §101(a)(13)(C), which includes those who have committed an offense identified in INA §212(a)(2), the criminal inadmissibility grounds.

Unlike the IJ, ICE does have the authority to release those characterized as arriving aliens on parole, under 8 CFR §212.5. However, parole is discretionary and parole practices vary greatly from district to district.

In certain circumstances, an individual may be able to mount a challenge to his or her designation as an arriving alien. For example, it may be possible in some cases to argue that DHS has not met its burden of proof in establishing that the returning LPR fits into one of the exceptions listed in INA §101(a)(13)(C).[56] In other instances, an individual might have reason to argue that §101(a)(13)(C) is impermissibly retroactive. For example, in *Olatunji v. Ashcroft*,[57] the U.S. Court of Appeals for the Fourth Circuit held that §101(a)(13)(C) is impermissibly retroactive as applied to LPRs who pled guilty to offenses before IIRAIRA altered the rules relating to returning LPRs,

---

[52] INA §236(c)(2).

[53] 8 CFR §1003.19(h)(2)(ii); *see also Matter of Joseph*, 22 I&N Dec. 799 (BIA 1999).

[54] *Matter of Joseph*, 22 I&N Dec. 799 (BIA 1999).

[55] 8 CFR §1.1(q).

[56] *Matter of Huang*, 19 I&N Dec. 749 (BIA 1988).

[57] *Olatunji v. Ashcroft*, 387 F.3d 383 (4th Cir. 2004).

and who would have been able to return from a trip abroad under the prior law without incident.[58]

Eligible for Bond

Other foreign nationals in custody and subject to INA §240 proceedings, besides arriving aliens and those subject to mandatory detention, may request custody redetermination hearings (bond hearings) before the IJ. Pursuant to the BIA's decision in *Matter of X–K–*,[59] this also includes individuals, other than arriving aliens, who were initially placed in expedited removal but who subsequently passed credible fear interviews and were placed in INA §240 removal proceedings. For example, people who are in expedited removal because they have been in the United States less than 14 days and are caught within 100 miles of a land border are eligible for bond under *Matter of X–K–*[60] once they have passed a credible fear interview.

Bond Hearings

Custody redetermination hearings are governed by 8 CFR §1003.19 and §1236.1. A foreign national in custody may request a bond hearing even if DHS has not yet filed the NTA with the immigration court.[61]

Bond redetermination hearings are separate from and form no part of removal proceedings.[62] This means that the IJ cannot consider evidence presented in the bond removal proceedings for purposes of determining removability or relief from removal.

In the past, when deciding on an appropriate bond, the IJ was limited to considering whether the individual posed a danger to the community and whether the individual posed a flight risk. In *Matter of D–J–*,[63] however, the AG concluded that in cases where individuals are attempting to enter the United States illegally, IJs and the BIA now must also consider national security interests whenever the government offers evidence from executive branch sources (with relevant expertise) establishing that significant national security interests are implicated.

In *Matter of Guerra*,[64] the BIA reiterated that IJs have broad discretion in deciding which factors to consider in bond redetermination hearings. In this case, the BIA upheld an IJ's decision to deny bond to a foreign national who had been charged but not yet convicted in a controlled substance trafficking scheme, based on a finding that the individual posed a danger to the community.[65]

---

[58] *See also Camins v. Gonzales*, 500 F.3d 872 (9th Cir. 2007).

[59] *Matter of X–K–*, 23 I&N Dec. 731 (BIA 2005).

[60] *Id.*

[61] 8 CFR §1003.14.

[62] 8 CFR §1003.19(d).

[63] *Matter of D–J–*, 23 I&N Dec. 572 (AG 2003).

[64] *Matter of Guerra*, 24 I&N Dec. 237 (BIA 2006).

[65] *Id.*

Note that bond hearings are scheduled quickly, and there will be little time to prepare. The more the respondent can present on paper prior to the hearing, the easier it will be for the judge to determine the equities. Specific factors to be considered in a bond redetermination hearing include:

- Family ties;
- Ties to the community;
- Employment history;
- Criminal record;
- The manner of entry and length of time in the United States;
- Membership in community organizations;
- Likelihood of obtaining permanent residency; and
- Any other discretionary factors.[66]

As mentioned above, national security interests also may be considered in certain cases.[67] Helpful bond documentation includes:

- Letters from family members and evidence of their USC or LPR status;
- Letters from community members and organizations, such as churches and service organizations; letters of recommendation from current and past employers;
- Documentation of good behavior, work record, program and counseling participation while incarcerated, if applicable;
- Payment of taxes and child support;
- A showing of eligibility for relief; and
- Any other evidence showing that the applicant is deserving of a favorable exercise of discretion.

The respondent may have only one bond hearing before the IJ. A request for a second bond hearing must be made in writing, and will only be considered if the respondent demonstrates that his or her circumstances have changed materially since the prior bond hearing.[68]

Pre-Hearing Motions

The rules governing these motions are found in the regulations, at 8 CFR §§1003.12–1003.41, and in the *Immigration Court Practice Manual*, which are obtained from the clerk of your local immigration court or online at *www.usdoj.gov/eoir*.[69] In many cases, counsel should consult with the ICE assistant district counsel assigned to the case to see if ICE will agree not to oppose the motion. If ICE so agrees, this should be indicated in the motion (*e.g.*, "The ICE Assistant Dis-

---

[66] *See Matter of Patel*, 15 I&N Dec. 666 (BIA 1976); *Matter of Daryousch*, 18 I&N Dec. 352 (BIA 1982).

[67] *Matter of D–J–*, 23 I&N Dec. 572 (AG 2003).

[68] 8 CFR §1003.19(e).

[69] See also AILA's Online Bookstore at *www.ailapubs.org* to purchase a bound copy of the manual.

trict Counsel has advised undersigned counsel that ICE does not oppose an order granting this motion."). Always be sure to include a certificate of service with any motion or filing, showing that a copy has been sent to the ICE district counsel.

Advocates must comply with the timing requirements for filing of any motions. For example, any motion must be filed 15 days in advance of the hearing if requesting a ruling prior to the hearing.[70] If it is not possible to meet this deadline, advocates must submit a motion to accept an untimely filing that includes evidence explaining the reasons for untimely filing (*i.e.*, affidavit of counsel). If a motion is untimely, it is denied.[71]

The following is a non-exhaustive list of motions that may be filed in removal proceedings:[72]

- Motions to continue the hearing date. These should be filed in writing as far in advance of the hearing as possible, and should provide a very good reason for the continuance.[73]

- Motions for extension of time to submit documents, memoranda, or applications. These should be filed only when absolutely necessary, and should provide a very good reason for granting the extension. This reason must be detailed in evidence (*i.e.*, affidavit of counsel).[74] The rules regarding motions to accept untimely filings are at chapter 3.1(d)(iii) of the *Immigration Court Practice Manual*.

- Motions to change venue. A basis for this motion might be that the respondent and witnesses live far from the scheduled site of the removal proceedings. If possible, the motion should indicate that the individual is represented in the new jurisdiction, and should include as an attachment an EOIR-28 notice of appearance from the new counsel. It is necessary to give a detailed explanation of the reasons for the request.[75] The regulations regarding motions to change venue are found at 8 CFR §1003.20. The *Immigration Court Practice Manual*, effective July 1, 2008, requires that the respondent admit or deny the factual and legal allegations in the NTA.[76] A respondent or his or her representative should not concede removability unless it is absolutely certain that a respondent is in fact removable, because this concession will govern the respondent's case and may greatly affect the outcome of the case and the relief available.

---

[70] *Immigration Court Practice Manual*, ch. 5.2(c), 3.1(b).

[71] *Immigration Court Practice Manual*, ch. 3.1(d)(iii).

[72] A list of motions and the corresponding section discussing such motions are at *Immigration Court Practice Manual*, ch. 5.10.

[73] *Immigration Court Practice Manual*, ch. 5.10(a).

[74] *Immigration Court Practice Manual*, ch. 3.1(c)(iv).

[75] *Immigration Court Practice Manual*, ch. 5.10(c).

[76] *Id.*

- Motions to terminate the proceedings. A motion to terminate may be appropriate in several types of situations, and certainly when the allegations of the NTA do not support the charge of removability. For example, if the charge is deportability because of conviction for a crime of moral turpitude occurring within five years of admission, and the crime was actually committed more than five years after admission, or the statute under which the client was convicted does not reflect a crime involving moral turpitude, the advocate should file a motion to terminate. A motion to terminate also might be appropriate when the NTA does not clearly state the charges of removability, so that the respondent cannot tell with what he or she is being charged. This would be the case if the respondent is charged with conviction of an aggravated felony, but the NTA fails to specify which of the aggravated felony definitions under INA §101(a)(43) is at issue.

- Motions for deposition of a witness or for issuance of a subpoena or subpoena duces tecum.[77] The regulations give the IJ authority to order depositions of witnesses who are not "reasonably available" at the time and place of the hearing and whose testimony is essential.[78] The regulations also give the IJ authority to issue subpoenas requiring the attendance of witnesses and subpoenas duces tecum, ordering the production of books, papers, and other documentary evidence. In an application for a subpoena or subpoena duces tecum, the applicant must state in writing or at the proceeding what he or she expects to prove by the witnesses or documentary evidence, and show affirmatively that he or she has made diligent effort without success to produce the same.[79] This opportunity to request subpoenas and depositions is an invaluable aid to presenting an effective case before the immigration court, and advocates should take advantage of it whenever needed. Getting the IJ to issue a subpoena duces tecum for documents can be especially important given the long delays in getting documents in response to Freedom of Information Act (FOIA) requests, discussed below.

- Motion for a pre-hearing conference. The regulations provide for pre-hearing conferences, which can be held to narrow issues, obtain stipulations between the parties, exchange information voluntarily, and otherwise simplify and organize the proceedings.[80]

Discovery Through FOIA and Criminal Record Checks

There is no provision in the statute or regulations for discovery as it is generally understood in civil and criminal proceedings. Though they are invaluable if it is known what is being sought, the provisions for requesting that the IJ order depositions and grant subpoenas, described above, are aids to produce evidence in court, not

---

[77] *Immigration Court Practice Manual*, ch. 4.20.

[78] 8 CFR §1003.35 (a).

[79] 8 CFR §1003.35(b).

[80] 8 CFR §1003.21(a); *Immigration Court Practice Manual*, ch. 4.18.

to discover what evidence is available. Some ICE district counsel trial attorneys allow counsel for respondents to view documents in their files, or are forthcoming concerning documents and evidence in their possession. However, the most reliable, albeit problematic, method of discovery in immigration proceedings is through a FOIA request.

Unfortunately, the FOIA system is in flux, and it often takes many, many months to get a response to a FOIA request. While the system was always slow, when legacy INS split into ICE, USCIS, and CBP, the system became even slower as jurisdictional issues between the agencies arose over documents in a single individual file, and FOIA requests were being batted around between these component agencies.

To clarify, there is only one alien file, or A-file, per foreign national. That file could be in the possession of USCIS, ICE, or CBP. However, within that single file, there could be documents controlled by different agencies. To complicate matters further, while there is only one A-file per foreign national, the A-file does not necessarily contain all the information these agencies have on a particular individual. For example, ICE might have an investigation file on an individual that would not be included in an individual's A-file. Also, some foreign nationals do not have an A-file, but only receipt files. However, all foreign nationals in proceedings will have an A-file.

In response to the growing confusion, in summer 2005, DHS informally announced that, from then on, *all* FOIA requests for USCIS, ICE, and CBP records would go directly to USCIS's National Records Center (NRC) for processing. The NRC became charged with getting the relevant information from CBP and ICE, and with responding in a timely manner. All pending FOIA requests with ICE and CBP were supposed to be delivered to USCIS for response. Practitioners report, however, that ICE is still processing some FOIA requests at its Washington, D.C., headquarters. CBP also reports that the process for having all its FOIA requests processed by USCIS has not yet been finalized, though USCIS and practitioners report that USCIS is processing some FOIA requests for CBP records.

In this period of flux, what is certain is that the NRC is now processing almost all FOIA requests for USCIS records.[81] What is less clear is which records it also is processing for CBP, including Border Patrol, and ICE. According to one official at the NRC, when the NRC receives a FOIA request and finds that some of the records in a file are under another agency's purview, the process works as follows:

- If the A-file or receipt file is in USCIS possession, NRC will take that file, process the request, and determine if any documents in the file belong to ICE or CBP.

- If any documents in the file do belong to ICE or CBP, the NRC will send the agency those documents and ask them to process that part of the FOIA request.

---

[81] *See* USCIS FOIA office directory at *http://uscis.gov/graphics/aboutus/foia/address.htm.*

- The NRC then will send a letter to the FOIA requester informing him or her that it has referred part of the request to ICE or CBP.

In 2007, for respondents in removal proceedings, DHS instituted a "fast track" FOIA process, which is called a "Track 3 FOIA request."[82] In order to place a FOIA request on this fast track, it is necessary to submit an NTA or Notice of Hearing in Removal Proceedings with the FOIA request. Respondents who already have been ordered removed or deported, but who are attempting to reopen their cases, cannot benefit from this fast track FOIA processing. Representatives should submit an E-28 with the FOIA request, Form G-639, and the NTA or Notice of Hearing.

For almost all USCIS records, FOIA requests should be sent to:

National Records Center FOIA Division
P.O. Box 648010
Lees Summit, MO 64064-8010

Or, by overnight delivery, send to:

National Records Center FOIA Division
150 Space Center Loop, Suite 300
Lees Summit, MO 64064

Or, via facsimile, send to:

National Records Center FOIA Division at (816) 350-5785, and then place a copy with an original signature in the mail to the P.O. Box address listed above.

Practitioners report that it takes at least six months to get requested records back from the NRC. For fast-track Track 3 FOIA requests for respondents in removal proceedings, practitioners report receiving records back in approximately three months. A requester can call the NRC FOIA division at (816) 350-5570 between 7:00 am and 3:15 pm (central time) to check on the status of the request or to ask questions. Representatives should have the capability to read a CD on their computers, as most FOIA responses are returned on a CD and not in hard copy.

For ICE records, requests should be sent to:

FOIA Office
U.S. Immigration and Customs Enforcement
800 North Capitol St., NW
5th Floor, Suite 585
Washington, DC 20536

For FOIA requests for documents controlled by CBP, send the form to:

U.S. Customs and Border Protection
FOIA Division
799 9th Street NW, Mint Annex
Washington, DC 20001-4501

---

[82] 72 Fed. Reg. 9017–18 (Feb. 28, 2007).

FOIA requests are processed on a first-come, first-served basis. Note that it is *not* necessary to make a FOIA request on the G-639 form, and it may be advisable to make your request in a letter if you do not wish to respond to particular questions on the form.

In addition to the FOIA request, advocates also should obtain criminal record checks from the Federal Bureau of Investigation (FBI) and from any state in which the client has resided or in which the client has been arrested. Information about requesting a criminal record check from the FBI appears in Appendix 4.

Pre-Hearing Statement

Under 8 CFR §1003.21, an IJ may require the parties to file a pre-hearing statement, containing such items as:

- A statement of the facts to which the parties have stipulated;

- A list of proposed witnesses and a summary of their anticipated testimony;

- A list of exhibits, with copies attached, and the purpose of their introduction; and

- A statement of unresolved issues.

All statements and evidence must be submitted at least 30 days prior to the scheduled individual hearing for nondetained respondents.[83]

Master Calendar Hearings and Individual Hearings

Master calendar hearings are preliminary hearings for pleading and scheduling, where a respondent answers the charges against him or her and may file his or her application for relief from removal. At the conclusion of the master calendar hearing, the IJ will set a trial date for the hearing on the application for relief. Typically, several foreign nationals will be scheduled to appear before the IJ at the same date and time on the judge's master calendar call, and each case will be expected to last just minutes.

It is a fairly common practice at master calendar hearings for advocates and their clients to admit the factual allegations contained in the NTA, concede the charge(s) of removability against the respondent, and concentrate their energies on the next stage of the removal proceedings (*i.e.*, the applications for relief from removal). However, advocates should think very carefully before admitting allegations and conceding removability. There may be cases where an admission and concession is still in order (*e.g.*, if the advocate is certain that ICE can bear its burden of proof, and there is a strong case for relief from removal).

Denying the allegations and charges in an NTA is not lying to the immigration court. Rather, it is a means of putting ICE to its burden of proof when a client is charged with deportability. If a foreign national or his representative admits the allegations and concedes deportability when pleading to the NTA, ICE likely will not

---

[83] *Immigration Court Practice Manual*, ch 3.1(b)(ii).

have to fulfill any burden it may have had. Indeed, under 8 CFR §1240.10, an IJ can determine that removability has been established if, during pleading to the NTA, the respondent admits the allegation and concedes removability, so long as the IJ is satisfied that no issues of law or fact remain. Even when a client is charged with inadmissibility and it is the client's burden to show that he or she is admissible, charges should be denied when there is any colorable argument that the client is, in fact, not inadmissible as charged, and all arguments against the charges should be made on the record.

In addition to denying the allegations and the charges of deportability or inadmissibility, advocates should scrutinize the NTA and any evidence offered by ICE, and make all appropriate arguments against the charges and objections against proffered evidence.

In some situations, the case may be concluded at the master calendar hearing without further hearings. For example, when a person is planning to admit the charges in the NTA, and is just seeking permission to depart the United States voluntarily within a certain period of time, the judge typically will rule on that request at the master calendar hearing. A foreign national attending the master calendar hearing without counsel can request a continuance to have time to seek counsel.

The individual hearing, also known as the merits or regular calendar hearing, is typically scheduled for a block of time long enough to consider the respondent's case in detail. A case may be set for an entire morning or afternoon, and additional individual hearings may be scheduled if the hearing isn't completed in that time period.

At the individual hearing, the IJ will consider evidence relating to the matter at issue, which may include challenges to the charges in the NTA, or a request for relief from removal. The different forms of relief from removal are discussed in several chapters of this manual, and each form of relief has separate eligibility requirements defined by statute and regulation. A foreign national in proceedings is not limited to applying for one form of relief, and may request all remedies for which he or she may be eligible. Note that the IJ cannot consider relief from removal until making a finding on the charge of inadmissibility or deportability. If the IJ finds that the charge of inadmissibility or deportability has not been established, the case will be terminated, and the issue of relief from removal will not be reached.

Evidence presented at a removal hearing typically consists of applications and supporting documents filed in advance of the hearing. The testimony of witnesses, usually including the respondent, also is presented. If the respondent or a witness will be testifying in a language other than English, the court will provide an interpreter. If the respondent's counsel does not speak and understand the language in which the respondent or witness will be testifying, it is helpful to bring along someone who can let counsel know if there is a problem with the translation; it is not uncommon for advocates to object to incorrect translations by the court-appointed interpreters.

Court proceedings are recorded on a tape-recorder, and if an appeal of the judge's decision is filed, the proceedings will be transcribed. If a case already has commenced when counsel is retained to represent a respondent, he or she can ask the court to listen to the tape of the proceedings to learn what has happened in court to date.

Note that the law allows removal proceedings to go forward by video or telephonic conference. Consent of the respondent is needed to proceed by telephone. The respondent must be advised of his or her alternative right to proceed in person or through videoconference.[84]

The respondent must submit required biometrics. EOIR regulatory changes in 2005 mandated certain security checks before the grant of any relief from removal.[85] The courts require that a respondent mail copies of the application for relief, proof of application fee payment, and payment for biometrics to a designated USCIS service center address in Mesquite, TX. After a receipt is produced, the respondent is supposed to be scheduled for a fingerprint appointment at an application support center.[86] The EOIR regulations allow for dismissal of cases where applicants are deemed to have failed to provide in a timely manner the needed biometrics and biographical information. Note that ICE is responsible for competing biometrics for detained respondents.

In Absentia Orders

Respondents who have received the required notices under INA §§239(a)(1) or (2) and do not attend an INA §240 proceeding will be ordered removed in absentia, if ICE establishes by clear, convincing, and unequivocal evidence that written notice was provided and that the foreign national is removable.[87] A foreign national may be removed in absentia even absent the INA §§239(a)(1) or (2) written notices; however, if the foreign national has failed to provide ICE with his or her address as required under INA §239(a)(l)(F).[88]

The BIA has held that if ICE elects to serve the NTA with its required warnings to the last address it has for the respondent, this service constitutes the required §239(a) notice if the respondent actually received the notice or can be charged with receiving the notice. The respondent can be charged with receiving the notice if it is sent to the correct address, but fails to reach the respondent through some failure in the internal workings of the household. If the respondent actually received or can be charged with receiving the notice, then in absentia proceedings may be held.[89]

If the respondent did not actually receive the NTA and the notice of hearing it contains, and cannot be charged with having received the notice, then the respondent cannot be on notice of either removal proceedings or the address obligations particu-

---

[84] 8 CFR §1003.25(c).

[85] 70 Fed. Reg. 4743 (Jan. 31, 2005).

[86] The instructions distributed by the courts are *published on* AILA InfoNet at Doc. No. 05040472 (*posted* Apr. 4, 2005), and appear in this book as Appendix 5.

[87] INA §240(b)(5).

[88] INA §240(b)(5)(B).

[89] *Matter of G–Y–R–*, 23 I&N Dec. 181 (BIA 2001); *Matter of M–D–*, 23 I&N Dec. 540 (BIA 2002).

lar to removal proceedings. In this case, the entry of an in absentia order is precluded.[90] The government in *Matter of G–Y–R–* had argued that the INA §265(a) requirement of notification to the AG of address changes meant that an NTA sent to the last address provided by the foreign national supports an in absentia removal order. The BIA did not agree, noting that an in absentia removal order is not one of the penalties imposed for failure to comply with that registration requirement.[91] If the respondent who fails to appear for a hearing, however, does not argue that the notice was sent to the incorrect address or that the postal service did not deliver it, service of the NTA to the last address provided is sufficient to satisfy the INA §239(a) notice requirements.[92]

In *Matter of M–R–A–*,[93] the BIA held that a respondent did not receive proper notice of his hearing. The BIA held that because notices of hearing need not be sent by certified mail, there was a weak presumption of delivery of the notice, which the respondent overcame. The BIA distinguished its holdings in *Matter of Grijalva*[94] and *Matter of M–D–*[95]; these cases were decided when all notices of hearings were required to be sent by certified mail, which created a stronger presumption of delivery. In contrast, the BIA in *Matter of M–R–A–*[96] held that a respondent can rebut the weaker presumption of delivery by regular mail by presenting evidence that could include, but is not limited to, the following:

- Respondent's affidavit;

- Affidavits from family members or others knowledgeable about the facts relevant to whether notice was received;

- Respondent's actions upon learning of the in absentia order and whether due diligence was exercised to redress the situation;

- Any prior affirmative application for relief, indicating that respondent had an incentive to appear;

- Any prior application for relief filed with the immigration court or prima facie evidence of eligibility for such relief;

- Respondent's previous attendance at immigration court hearings, if applicable; and

- Any other circumstances or evidence indicating possible nonreceipt of notice.

---

[90] *Matter of G–Y–R–*, 23 I&N Dec. 181 (BIA 2001). (NTA sent to address given by respondent in a change of address form that was several years old and predated removal proceedings).

[91] *Id.*

[92] *Matter of M–D–*, 23 I&N Dec. 540 (BIA 2002). (NTA sent by certified mail, which was not claimed by respondent; no argument that address was incorrect or that postal service did not notify him that he had a certified letter).

[93] *Matter of M–R–A–*, 24 I&N Dec. 665 (BIA 2008).

[94] *Matter of Grijalva*, 21 I&N Dec. 27 (B(A 1995).

[95] *Matter of M–D–, supra* note 92.

[96] *Matter of M–R–A–, supra* note 93.

Individuals ordered removed in absentia, other than because of exceptional circumstances or a notice error, are ineligible for various forms of relief—voluntary departure; cancellation of removal; registry; and adjustment or change of status—for a period of 10 years after the date of the final removal order.

Because of these drastic consequences of a failure to appear, counsel must emphasize to each client that he or she must keep USCIS, ICE, the immigration court, the BIA (if the case is on appeal), and counsel apprised of his or her current address. If a client is in removal proceedings before the IJ, notices of change of address should be submitted to the immigration court on Form EOIR-33/IC. If the matter is on appeal, notices of change of address should be submitted to the BIA on Form EOIR-33/BIA via certified mail, return receipt requested. In each case, a copy must be sent to ICE district counsel.

In certain limited circumstances, an in absentia order may be reopened. The requirements for filing a motion to reopen an in absentia order are discussed in more detail in chapter 12 of this manual.

Immigration Judge Decisions/Appeals

At the conclusion of the case, the IJ will issue an order determining the respondent's alleged inadmissibility or deportability, and deciding on any requested relief from removal. The order may be in summary form, where the IJ just checks off boxes and fills in blank spaces to indicate what order was made (A sample summary removal order appears at Appendix 6). In cases where the IJ believes there may be an appeal on his or her order, the judge will prepare a more detailed narrative decision, giving the reasoning for the decision. The decision may be read at the hearing, or the hearing may be adjourned after the presentation of evidence, giving time for the IJ to prepare a written decision.

Either side may appeal the IJ decision to the BIA within 30 days of the decision.[97] To protect the right to appeal, the respondent must tell the judge that he or she is reserving appeal. The appeal form and fee, or the fee waiver request, must then be received by the BIA within the 30-day period, or it will be rejected as untimely.[98] If no appeal is taken, the decision of the IJ is final.

Appeal procedures are discussed in more detail in chapter 12 of this manual.

Consequences of Being in Removal Proceedings

Jurisdiction

Jurisdiction is the concept describing who has authority to decide a matter. When an individual has a case pending in immigration court, the IJ has jurisdiction over that individual's case until he or she departs the United States, and the individual is not eligible to apply for most forms of immigration benefits before USCIS.

---

[97] 8 CFR §1003.3.
[98] 8 CFR §§1003.38(b), 1240.15.

- Jill never attended her immigration court hearing and the judge ordered her removed in absentia. Jill, who never departed the United States, is now married to a USC and wants to apply for adjustment of status. Jill cannot file her application with the local USCIS office because the IJ still has jurisdiction over her case. Jill can apply only for adjustment of status if she is eligible to file a motion to reopen her case in immigration court.

Penalties for Noncompliance with Court Orders

There are harsh consequences for failure to attend an immigration court hearing or comply with an order of departure. As mentioned above, a foreign national ordered removed in absentia is barred for 10 years from most forms of relief from removal and from adjustment of status, if the foreign national's failure to appear was not due to exceptional circumstances and the foreign national was given oral notice of the time and place of the hearing and the consequences of failure to appear.[99] In addition, a foreign national who fails to attend a hearing without reasonable cause is inadmissible for five years after his or her subsequent departure or removal.[100] Further, for those foreign nationals granted time to voluntarily depart the United States and who fail to leave within the time specified, there is a civil penalty of $1,000 to $5,000 that may be imposed, and the foreign national also is ineligible for most forms of relief from removal, including adjustment of status, for a 10-year period.[101] Voluntary departure is discussed in more detail in chapter 10 of this manual.

---

[99] INA §240(b)(7).

[100] INA §212(a)(6)(B).

[101] INA §240B(d).

PUTTING THE PIECES TOGETHER

Anatomy of a Removal Hearing

Based on the stages of the removal hearing described above, here is a sample case scenario to illustrate how a case might proceed:

Laura entered the United States with a tourist visa in 1998, and remained longer than her authorized stay. She got a job working at a factory and used a fake green card to get hired. Laura was arrested in a factory raid in January 2004, and ICE tried to get her to leave voluntarily instead of having a hearing. Laura did not want to do this because she had just married a USC who was planning to petition for her.

Laura was served with an NTA and held in custody on a bond of $5,000, which neither she nor her husband could afford to pay. Two weeks later, Laura finally had a bond hearing, at which her husband testified. Laura also presented proof of her steady employment, her volunteer work at a local community center, and her joint ownership of a home she just purchased with her husband. Laura was released on a bond of $1,500, which her husband paid.

Laura received a hearing notice in February 2004, setting her case for a master calendar hearing in June. Meanwhile, Laura hired a lawyer, who assisted Laura's husband in filing a visa petition for Laura. At the master calendar hearing, Laura's counsel admitted the charges in the NTA, and conceded that Laura was deportable as charged. The lawyer explained to the judge that a visa petition was pending and that Laura would be eligible to adjust status once the petition was approved. The IJ granted a three-month continuance.

At the next master calendar hearing in September, Laura's counsel sought another continuance because the visa petition was still not approved. The IJ reset the case for another master calendar hearing in six months, advising counsel that there would be no further continuances.

The visa petition filed for Laura was approved in January 2005. When Laura attended the third master calendar hearing in her case in March 2005, her lawyer advised the court that they were now ready to be scheduled for an individual calendar hearing. The judge set a hearing date in December 2005, and advised Laura's counsel about the EOIR biometrics procedures and deadlines for submitting the adjustment application and supporting documents.

Prior to the hearing and in accordance with the deadlines set by the IJ, Laura's counsel submitted the original adjustment application with all supporting documents to the immigration court, along with proof that Laura had paid all application fees and completed the biometrics process.

At the hearing in December, Laura appeared in court with her husband, and they each testified briefly about Laura's eligibility to adjust status. After a 30-minute hearing, the IJ granted the adjustment of status application, and both sides waived appeal. The decision of the IJ became final at the hearing.

Types of Removal Orders

Most of this manual addresses the removal orders issued by an IJ in removal proceedings under INA §240. However, it is important to know that there are some circumstances where someone other than an IJ can issue a removal order. These situations are described below.

Expedited Removal Under INA §235(b)

Certain arriving aliens who are determined by CBP or ICE to be inadmissible under INA §212(a)(6)(C) (fraud or willful misrepresentation of material fact) or INA §212(a)(7) (lack of valid entry documents) are subject to abbreviated removal procedures, called "expedited removal," under INA §235(b).

The scope of expedited removal has been expanded significantly since it was created in 1996 as a component of IIRAIRA,[102] with the most recent expansion announced in September 2005. In sum, there now are three general groups of foreign nationals who are subject to expedited removal:

- Those arriving at ports of entry seeking admission to or transit through the United States;

- Those interdicted at sea and brought to the United States, including foreign nationals paroled under such arrival; and

- Those encountered within 100 miles of the U.S./Mexican or U.S./Canadian border who cannot establish that they have been continuously present in the United States for 14 days or longer.

While the announcement that those encountered within 100 miles of the borders may be subject to expedited removal came in August 2004, this policy previously was only implemented in a few specified border patrol sectors. However, in September 2005, DHS announced that all southwest border patrol sectors would now subject all foreign nationals "other than Mexicans" apprehended within 100 miles of the southwest border within 14 days of arrival to expedited removal.

Expedited removal applies only to foreign nationals in the three listed categories above who are determined to be inadmissible under INA §§212(a)(6)(C) (false documents) or (7) (no valid documents). If CBP or ICE charges the arriving alien with inadmissibility under any other inadmissibility ground, even if coupled with INA §§212(a)(6)(C) or (7), the individual must be placed in regular INA §240 removal proceedings.[103]

     – Roberto, from Argentina, arrived in the United States with a passport and tourist visa that did not belong to him; he substituted his photo in a friend's passport. At the airport, Roberto admitted that the passport he used was not his, and he did not express a fear of returning to Argentina. Roberto will be

---

[102] IIRAIRA, *supra* note 6.

[103] 8 CFR §235.3(b)(3).

subject to expedited removal because he is inadmissible under INA §212(a)(6)(C).

If a foreign national subject to expedited removal indicates a wish to apply for asylum or expresses a fear of persecution, he or she must be referred to an asylum officer for an interview. Consultation with counsel is allowed only if it will not unduly delay the process. The asylum officer must keep a written record of the "credible fear" interview.[104] A foreign national found to have a credible fear will be placed in full §240 removal proceedings. In those proceedings, if found inadmissible by the IJ, the respondent may apply for asylum as a form of relief from removal. The respondent also may apply for any other form of relief from removal for which he or she may be eligible.

The term *credible fear* is defined as "a significant possibility, taking into account the credibility of the statements made by the alien in support of the alien's claim and such other facts as are known to the officer, that the alien could establish eligibility for asylum under Section 208."[105] It is important to note that a *credible fear of persecution* is a lower standard than that required for an actual grant of asylum. For a grant of asylum, the applicant must show that he or she has experienced past persecution, or that he or she has a well-founded fear of persecution in the future. The *well-founded* fear standard has been determined to mean that a reasonable person in the applicant's position would fear persecution.

If the asylum officer finds that the foreign national does not have a credible fear of persecution, the foreign national may request that the IJ review the asylum officer's decision. The IJ may review the asylum officer's decision either in person or telephonically, within seven days, and the foreign national must be detained during the review. If the IJ determines that the foreign national does have a well-founded fear of persecution, then that person is placed in regular INA §240 removal proceedings.

There is no other administrative review of CBP's decision that an arriving alien is inadmissible, except for foreign nationals who claim to be LPRs or USCs, or those who have been admitted as refugees or granted asylum.[106]

A sample expedited removal order is found at Appendix 7 to this chapter. For a more thorough discussion of expedited removal see "Immigration Policy on Expedited Removal of Aliens."[107]

Administrative Removal Orders Under INA §238(b)

No formal removal hearing is required for an individual charged with deportability as an aggravated felon under INA §237(a)(2)(A)(iii) who was not an LPR when proceedings were commenced against him or her. The individual must be given reason-

---

[104] INA §235(b)(1)(B)(II).

[105] INA §235(b)(1)(B)(v).

[106] INA §235(b)(1)(C).

[107] "Immigration Policy on Expedited Removal of Aliens," CRS Report for Congress (updated Jan. 24, 2007), *available* at *www.rcusa.org/uploads/pdfs/2007,0402-crs.pdf.*

able notice of the charges, may be represented by counsel at no expense to the government, and must have a reasonable opportunity to inspect the evidence and rebut the charges.[108] The immigration officer conducting the proceedings must keep a record of the proceedings and cannot be the same person who instituted the charges. The AG may not execute an order of removal under this section until 14 days after the issuance of the order, unless the individual waives this delay. The purpose of this delay in execution is to allow the individual to apply for judicial review under INA §242. An individual subject to administrative removal is not eligible for any discretionary relief from removal, but may seek withholding of removal or relief under the Convention Against Torture.[109]

- Leonardo, from Italy, entered the United States on a tourist visa several years ago and never left. Last year, he was convicted of delivery of cocaine and sentenced to a two-year prison term. Leonardo's offense will be considered an aggravated felony by ICE. Because Leonardo is not an LPR, he is subject to an administrative removal order, without an opportunity to appear before an IJ.

A sample administrative removal order is included in this chapter at Appendix 8.

Judicial Removal Order Under INA §238(c)

U.S. district court judges have the authority to enter judicial orders of removal when sentencing an individual who is deportable. The U.S. attorney must request that such an order be entered, DHS must concur, and the court must choose to exercise this jurisdiction. The U.S. attorney must file with the court and serve on the defendant a notice of intent to request judicial removal prior to commencement of trial or entry of guilty plea. At least 30 days before sentencing, the U.S. attorney must file a charge containing factual allegations regarding alienage and crimes that make the individual deportable under INA §§237(a)(2)(A) and 238(c)(2)(B). The U.S. attorney may enter into a plea agreement in which the individual waives the right to notice and hearing, and agrees to the entry of a judicial order of removal as a condition of the plea agreement, probation, or supervised release.

There are certain procedural safeguards for foreign nationals under this section. These include a reasonable opportunity to examine the evidence against him or her, present evidence of his or her own, and cross-examine government witnesses. The court may consider only evidence that would be admissible in a regular removal hearing under INA §240. The court also may consider relief from removal.

---

[108] 8 CFR §§238.1(b)(2), (c).

[109] INA §238(b)(5); 8 CFR §208.31. *See also* U.N. Convention against Torture and Other Cruel, Inhuman or Degrading Treatment or Punishment (CAT), Dec. 10, 1984, *opened for signature* Feb. 4, 1985, G.A. Res. 39/46, Annex, 39 U.N. GAOR Supp. No. 51, at 197, U.N. Doc. A/RES/39/708 (1984) (entered into force June 26, 1987), *reprinted in* 1465 U.N.T.S. 85, 23 I.L.M. 1027 (1984), *modified* 24 I.L.M. 535 (1985).

Reinstatement of Removal, INA §241(a)(5)

Under INA §241(a)(5), ICE has the authority to reinstate automatically a prior removal order against an individual who left the United States following a final order of removal and later reentered the United States illegally. This is known as reinstatement of removal. Based on this provision, if ICE finds an individual has reentered the United States illegally after having departed under an order of removal, the prior order is "reinstated" from its original date and the individual is not eligible for most forms of relief; the individual then is removed under the prior order. Note that an individual subject to reinstatement of removal is not barred from seeking adjustment of status under the Haitian Refugee and Immigrant Fairness Act,[110] or under §203 of the Nicaraguan Adjustment and Central American Relief Act,[111] withholding of removal, or relief under the Convention Against Torture.[112]

USCIS has interpreted this provision broadly to include (a) unlawful reentries after deportation or exclusion orders, not just orders of removal; and (b) unlawful entries prior to April 1, 1997, the effective date of this provision. This means, for example, that a person who was deported in 1990 and then reentered the United States without authorization in 1992 would face reinstatement if ICE became aware of his or her presence.

- Dinah was ordered removed from the United States in May 1999. She later reentered the United States without inspection and married a USC, who filed a visa petition on her behalf in June 2000. If Dinah applies for adjustment of status, she may be arrested by ICE and processed for reinstatement of her prior removal order.

In the last few years, this area of the law has been in a state of flux, with significant splits between the circuit courts on various points. The U.S. Supreme Court, in *Fernandez-Vargas v. Gonzales*,[113] resolved one of the more significant splits, regarding the retroactive application of INA §241(a)(5). Unfortunately, the Supreme Court held that INA §241(a)(5) can be applied to foreign nationals who last reentered the United States prior to April 1, 1997, and took no affirmative steps to obtain lawful status before that date. This decision effectively overturned decisions in the Ninth Circuit, in *Castro-Cruz v. INS*,[114] and the Sixth Circuit, in *Bejjani v. INS*.[115] However, the Supreme Court decision left several open issues, including whether INA §241(a)(5) can be applied to foreign nationals who last reentered the United States prior to April 1, 1997, and did take affirmative steps to obtain lawful status before

---

[110] Haitian Refugee and Immigrant Fairness Act of 1998, Pub. L. No. 105-277, 112 Stat. 2681 div. A, title IX.

[111] Nicaraguan Adjustment and Central American Relief Act, Pub. L. No. 105-100, 111 Stat. 2160, 2193.

[112] 8 CFR §§241.8(d), (e); 8 CFR §208.31. *See also* CAT, *supra* note 109.

[113] *Fernandez-Vargas v. Gonzales*, 548 U.S. 30 (2006).

[114] *Castro-Cruz v. INS*, 239 F.3d 1037 (9th Cir. 2001).

[115] *Bejjani v. INS*, 271 F.3d 670 (6th Cir. 2001).

that date. For example, the Seventh Circuit, prior to the Supreme Court's decision, had held that INA §241(a)(5) could not apply to someone who reentered before April 1, 1997, and also applied for relief before that date.[116] In addition, the Ninth Circuit has permitted foreign nationals with prior removal orders to apply for adjustment and a waiver of inadmissibility prior to the reinstatement of the prior order, notwithstanding the Supreme Court's decision in *Fernandez-Vargas*.[117] Note that other circuit courts have held that the filing of an adjustment of status application with a waiver does not protect someone from reinstatement.[118]

For an excellent discussion of reinstatement of removal and remaining issues and arguments after *Fernandez-Vargas v. Gonzales*, see the American Immigration Law Foundation's practice advisory entitled "Reinstatement of Removal."[119]

Practice Tips for Non-Court Advocates

Many immigration advocates work in offices at great distances from immigration court, and don't have the financial or legal resources to do immigration court advocacy. For those who can do court advocacy, several chapters in this manual describe in more detail challenges and defenses to removal proceedings, and requirements for various types of relief from removal. But even those advocates who don't do direct court representation can play a critical role in helping the individual who is or was in removal proceedings prepare for a pending case, or understand how a prior case now impacts on his or her status. Some practical steps that all immigration advocates can take are listed below:

- *Confirm the date, place and time of the hearing for all clients who have received an NTA.* You can do this by calling the EOIR information phone line at (800) 898-7180. When you call this number and punch in the foreign national's 9-digit case number that appears on the NTA and begins with the letter A, you can retrieve information listing the date, place and time of the next scheduled hearing in the case, and any decision information, if a decision was already rendered. (If your client's A-number has only 8 digits, press "0" before the 8 digits). This is particularly important if the client you are counseling has moved without informing the court of his or her new address. A new court date may have been set without the client knowing about the changed or new date; checking on the date may help avoid an in absentia court order.

- *Remind your client to advise the court of any change of address within five days of moving.* This will help protect the client from the consequences of an in absentia removal order.

---

[116] *Faiz-Mohammed v. Ashcroft*, 395 F.3d 799 (7th Cir. 2005).

[117] *Fernandez-Vargas, supra* note 113. *See also Duran-Gonzales v. DHS*, 508 F.3d 1227 (9th Cir. 2007); *Perez-Gonzalez v. Ashcroft*, 379 F.3d 783 (9th Cir. 2004).

[118] *See, e.g., Delgado v. Mukasey*, 516 F.3d 65 (2d Cir. 2008); *Lino v. Gonzales*, 467 F.3d 1077 (7th Cir. 2006).

[119] "Reinstatement of Removal," updated April 23, 2008, *published at www.ailf.org/lac/lac_pa_topics.shtml.*

- *Counsel the client on the consequences of missing the court date.* In other types of court hearings that your client may have experienced, the consequences of missing a court date are not necessarily drastic, and cases are routinely re-opened. This is not true for immigration court, and a client's simple confusion about the date or time of a scheduled hearing for which proper notice was received will not be an adequate basis for getting an in absentia removal order reopened. For this reason, it is very important to emphasize to a client the importance of arriving to court at the time designated for the hearing and of planning enough time to travel.

- *Review the allegations in the charging document and note if any facts are incorrect.* It is not unusual for ICE to misstate facts on the NTA, and this may have bearing on your client's removability as an inadmissible or deportable individual, and on his or her eligibility for relief. For example, the NTA may inaccurately describe a criminal conviction, or the list an incorrect entry date. Your client needs to know that these matters should be brought to the attention of the IJ, either through counsel, or by the respondent, if he or she will not be represented in court.

- *Assist client in obtaining records as necessary.* You may be able to help a client who is still seeking counsel for court representation, or who is going to represent him- or herself in court, by assisting the individual in securing records that may help contest inadmissibility or deportability charges, or that may help document eligibility for relief. For example, you may file a FOIA request to enable an individual in proceedings to get a copy of his or her immigration record; help an individual secure a copy of a court record of conviction; or help secure documents relating to community ties, family relationships, employment, and other issues that can support an application for bond reduction or for relief from removal.

- *Advise client on how to dress for court.* There is not one way to dress for immigration court, but a client should be encouraged to wear his or her more formal or conservative apparel. A person in removal proceedings who dresses very casually (*i.e.*, jeans or shorts and a t-shirt) may risk the disfavor of the judge, who may interpret that apparel as not taking the experience seriously.

- *Where a client has a pending criminal charge, make sure the criminal defense counsel partners with immigration counsel who can give advice on immigration consequences of crimes.* In many instances, criminal convictions have serious immigration consequences that may either create independent grounds of inadmissibility or deportability, or preclude a client from qualifying for an immigration benefit.[120] Many criminal lawyers are unaware of these issues and may recommend an outcome on a criminal charge that may seem advantageous

---

[120] For an in-depth discussion and practical advice on how to handle criminal charges against a foreign-born client, see M. Kramer, *Immigration Consequences of Criminal Activity*, 3rd Ed. (AILA 2008), *www.ailapubs.org*.

in terms of the criminal consequences (*e.g.*, probation instead of a jail term), but still have disastrous results in terms of immigration law. You can significantly help a client with pending criminal charges by counseling him or her to make sure that the criminal attorney is aware of immigration issues or consults with an immigration advocate who can assess these issues and appropriately advise the client.

- *Refer the client to an accredited representative or attorney who can provide in-court representation, or advise the client to seek a continuance while looking for court counsel.* Your client will be best served by having representation in court to respond to the charges and pursue any appropriate applications for relief from removal. You can assist your client in identifying legal services programs in the area that offer free or low-cost representation by attorneys or accredited representatives, or by referring your client to private attorneys. Many private attorneys are willing to have payment plans with clients to help make services more affordable.

- *Counsel the client on the consequences of noncompliance with an immigration court order.* As detailed above, failure to attend an immigration court hearing, or to comply with an order of voluntary departure, can have serious repercussions on future eligibility for relief. It is important for clients to understand that they may be disqualified from future immigration opportunities if they miss court or overstay an order of voluntary departure. Clients who do have voluntary departure orders should be counseled to report to ICE before they depart the United States, in order to obtain a travel document to turn in to the U.S. consulate in their home countries (which, in turn, is forwarded back to ICE as proof of the departure of the individual). Otherwise, ICE may not believe that a person subject to a voluntary departure order in fact complied with the order.

CHAPTER TWO
GROUNDS OF DEPORTABILITY

Grounds of Deportability: Generally

If a foreign national is charged with deportability in removal proceedings, Immigration and Customs Enforcement (ICE) has the burden of establishing by clear and convincing evidence that the respondent is deportable under Immigration and Nationality (INA) §237.[1] This standard is lower than the "beyond a reasonable doubt" standard used in a criminal proceeding, but higher than the "preponderance of the evidence" standard used in civil proceedings.[2]

This chapter describes the specific deportability grounds that correspond to the six general categories of "deportable aliens." The grounds of deportability are found at INA §237(a).

The six general categories of deportable individuals are:

- Non–U.S. citizen's (USC) who were inadmissible at the time they entered the United States or who have violated their immigration status;

- Those who have committed certain criminal offenses;

- Those who have violated laws relating to official documents;

- National security risks;

- Public charges; and

- Unlawful voters.

Under some of the deportability grounds corresponding to these six categories, foreign nationals may be found deportable for actions they committed after entry. Other grounds apply to these foreign nationals if an event occurs at any time after admission or within five years of admission. *Entry* as used here means generally the foreign national's physical entry into the United States, whether or not pursuant to a lawful admission; *admission* is defined in the INA as referring to a foreign national's lawful entry after inspection.[3] While adjustment of status is not deemed an entry (even though the grounds of inadmissibility apply to adjustment applicants),[4] the Board of Immigration Appeals (BIA) has held that adjustment is an admission in the context of determining deportability.[5]

---

[1] Immigration and Nationality Act of 1952 (INA), Pub. L. No. 82-414, 66 Stat. 163 (codified as amended at 8 USC §§1101 *et seq.*), §240(c)(3); 8 Code of Federal Regulations (CFR) §1240.8(a).

[2] *Woodby v. INS*, 385 U.S. 276 (1966).

[3] INA §101(a)(13).

[4] *Matter of Adetiba*, 20 I&N Dec. 506 (BIA 1992).

[5] *Matter of Rosas*, 22 I&N Dec. 616 (BIA 1999), *Matter of Shanu*, 23 I&N Dec. 754 (BIA 2005); *but see Shivaraman v. Ashcroft*, 360 F.3d 1142 (9th Cir. 2004), *Abdelqadar v. Gonzales*, 413 F.3d 668 (7th

- Sara entered the United States without inspection in 1979, and subsequently adjusted status through the amnesty program in 1989. In 1997, Sara was convicted of delivery of a controlled substance, and the government charged her with being deportable for conviction of an aggravated felony offense after admission. Even though Sara entered without inspection, and therefore wasn't admitted, under BIA case law, Sara's adjustment of status is considered an admission for purposes of determining her deportability for her criminal conviction.

Aliens Inadmissible at the Time of Entry or Adjustment of Status[6]

This ground of deportability contains six subcategories, each of which is described below.

Inadmissible Aliens[7]

This category of deportability amounts to a form of delayed inadmissibility, for it provides that "[a]ny alien who at the time of entry or adjustment of status was within one or more of the classes of aliens inadmissible by the law existing at such time is deportable."

The two most important aspects of this ground of deportability are:

- First, an individual may be deported as inadmissible at the time of entry even though he or she was examined and admitted by an immigration officer; and

- Second, to determine whether an individual is deportable under this ground, the grounds of inadmissibility are applied to the individual's circumstances as they existed at the time of each of the individual's entries.

  - Laura immigrated to the United States as the unmarried daughter of a lawful permanent resident (LPR). ICE later learns Laura was married when she obtained her residency status. Laura may be placed in proceedings and charged with being inadmissible at the time of entry.

Foreign nationals who obtained entry to the United States through material deception and those who committed crimes of moral turpitude prior to entry are the most likely to face deportability based on being inadmissible at the time of entry. But this deportability ground may be applied any time an individual was, at the time of entry, inadmissible under any of the other grounds.

A special discretionary waiver under INA §237(a)(1)(H) is available for curing deportability on this ground, where the foreign national was inadmissible for visa

---

Cir. 2005), *Aremu v. DHS*, 450 F.3d 578 (4th Cir. 2006) (for purposes of determining deportability for a crime involving moral turpitude within five years of admission, the five years begins from the initial admission and does not restart with any subsequent admission, including adjustment of status); *see also Zhang v. Mukasey*, 509 F.3d 313 (6th Cir. 2007).

[6] INA §237(a)(1).

[7] INA §237(a)(1)(A).

fraud, as in the example of Laura, described above. This waiver is discussed in more detail in chapter 6 of this manual.

As described in chapter 1 of this manual, special rules apply to determining when an LPR makes an application for admission. The INA specifies that an LPR returning to the United States after a departure of 180 days or less, and who meets certain other criteria, is not to be considered an applicant for admission.[8] Given this provision, LPRs returning from abroad who, under the statute, are not considered applicants for admission should not be subsequently subject to deportability for having been inadmissible at the time of their arrival.

> – Gloria, a 70-year-old LPR from Portugal, has been receiving Supplemental Security Income from the Social Security Administration for 10 years. Last year, her son paid for her two-week trip to Portugal to visit family. Gloria will not have to be concerned about being inadmissible on public charge grounds because, as a returning LPR, her return to the United States will not be treated as an admission.

In addition, persons who were inadmissible at the time of entry also are not deportable if they are Violence Against Women and Department of Justice Reauthorization Act of 2005[9] self-petitioners.[10]

Aliens Present in the United States in Violation of Law[11]

Before the April 1, 1997 effective date of the Illegal Immigration Reform and Immigrant Responsibility Act of 1996 (IIRAIRA),[12] this ground of deportability applied to any foreign national who entered the United States "without inspection or at any time or place other than as designated by the Attorney General or [who] is in the United States in violation of [the INA] or in violation of any other law of the United States."[13] Since April 1, 1997, however, foreign nationals who enter the United States without inspection are subject to the grounds of inadmissibility rather than the grounds of deportability. Entry without inspection remains a basis for a deportation charge for individuals in deportation proceedings that commenced prior to April 1, 1997.

> – Brothers Manuel and Javier entered the United States without inspection together in 1995. In 1996, Manuel was arrested by the Immigration and Naturalization Service (legacy INS) and placed in deportation proceedings, charged with entry without inspection. His brother Javier was picked up in a legacy INS work raid in 1998, and removal proceedings were commenced

---

[8] INA §101(a)(13)(C).

[9] Pub. L. No. 109-162, 119 Stat. 2960 (Jan. 5, 2006).

[10] INA §237(a)(1)(H)(ii).

[11] INA §237(a)(1)(B).

[12] Illegal Immigration Reform and Immigrant Responsibility Act of 1996 (IIRAIRA), Division C of the Omnibus Appropriations Act of 1996 (H.R. 3610), Pub. L. No. 104-208, 110 Stat. 3009 (Sept. 30, 1996).

[13] Former INA §241(a)(1)(B).

against him. Javier is charged with being inadmissible because he is present in the United States without admission or parole.

Foreign nationals who were lawfully admitted and subsequently violated their nonimmigrant status or remained beyond the period of authorized stay could fall within this deportability ground, but typically are charged with deportability for failure to maintain status (described below). For this reason, this ground now appears to be purely duplicative of other grounds of deportability.

Failure to Maintain Status[14]

The admission and stay of foreign nationals who enter the United States under the various nonimmigrant classifications are subject to many conditions imposed by the statute and regulations. Foreign nationals who fail to maintain their nonimmigrant status or to comply with the conditions of their stay in the United States are subject to deportation. Common violations of nonimmigrant status that may make a foreign national deportable include:

- Overstaying the prescribed period of admission;
- Accepting unauthorized employment; and
- Discontinuing studies (if the nonimmigrant is a student).

A nonimmigrant also may lose lawful status if he or she is convicted of *any* criminal offense punishable by a term of imprisonment of at least one year.[15]

- Lena enters the United States on a tourist visa, and is given an authorized stay of six months. During this period, Lena finds a job as a babysitter and starts working. Lena is deportable for violating her nonimmigrant tourist status, which does not permit employment.

Finally, note that most non-USCs who seek to be admitted to the United States have to undergo a medical examination to determine whether they are inadmissible on a medical ground. If the exam finds them to be inadmissible, they may obtain a waiver for any medical ground of inadmissibility but the drug-abuser ground. In granting this waiver, the Department of Health and Human Services may impose conditions upon the applicant, and failure to comply with these conditions also makes the foreign national deportable under the failure to maintain status ground of deportability.[16]

Termination of Conditional Permanent Residence[17]

Conditional permanent residency is a status that is granted to the spouse or child of a USC or LPR when the spouse or child obtains immigrant status through a marriage entered into less than two years before they are admitted for permanent residency. A sec-

---

[14] INA §237(a)(1)(C).

[15] INA §214(k)(1)(B).

[16] INA §237(a)(1)(C)(ii).

[17] INA §237(a)(1)(D).

ond category of foreign nationals who are given conditional permanent residence is that of entrepreneurs who obtain a visa as employment-creating investors.

If the conditional LPR fails to file a petition to remove the condition before the second anniversary of obtaining conditional status, or if it is found that the qualifying marriage was fraudulent or has been terminated, the foreign national's conditional status may be terminated. Foreign nationals who have their conditional permanent residency terminated are then subject to deportability. This ground of deportability does not apply to an individual granted a waiver of the petition requirement.

– Maku obtained conditional resident status in 1999, after immigrating through her USC spouse in 1998. Maku never filed the required joint petition or waiver to remove the condition on her residency. Maku may be charged with deportability under this section on the law.

Alien Smuggling[18]

This ground of deportability applies to any foreign national who, prior to entry, at the time of entry, or within five years of entry, knowingly encouraged, induced, assisted, aided or abettcd any othcr foreign national to enter or try to enter the United States. Deportability on this basis applies regardless of whether the person being smuggled is a close relative or whether the smuggling was for gain. Furthermore, this is not a criminal ground of deportability; the respondent's deportability may be established even if he or she has never been convicted of a criminal smuggling offense.

There are, however, two instances in which this ground of deportability is modified. First, the smuggling ground is inapplicable to foreign nationals who:

- Qualified for the family unity program; and

- Are applying for either family unity or for an immigrant visa as an immediate relative, or under the second preference.

To be eligible for this exemption, the foreign national must have aided the unlawful entry of his or her spouse, parent, son, or daughter, but no other foreign national.[19]

Second, this ground of deportatability may be waived for humanitarian purposes, to assure family unity, or when it is in the public interest. However, this waiver is available only to LPRs and only if the person smuggled was the LPR's spouse, parent, son, or daughter.[20] This provision was amended in 1996 to require that the smuggled person had to have the required relationship to the foreign national *at the time* the smuggling occurred. The LPR who smuggled the family member must ask the immigration judge (IJ) for this waiver during deportation or removal proceedings.

– Three years after he immigrated to the United States, LPR Eduardo assisted his fiancée, Sofia, to enter the United States unlawfully. After Sofia's arrival, they got married. ICE later learned how Sofia entered the United States,

---

[18] INA §237(a)(1)(E).

[19] INA §237(a)(1)(E)(ii).

[20] INA §237(a)(1)(E)(iii).

and Eduardo was charged with deportability as a smuggler. Eduardo will not qualify for a waiver because Sofia was not his spouse at the time the smuggling took place.

Marriage Fraud[21]

Two grounds of deportability provide the government with tools to investigate and deal with marriage fraud. First, INA §237(a)(1)(G)(i) provides that if a foreign national obtained LPR status through a marriage that took place within two years prior to the foreign national's gaining status, and the marriage was judicially annulled or terminated within two years after the foreign national gained LPR status, the marriage is presumed to have been fraudulent. The foreign national, whose burden it is to rebut this presumption, may overcome it by proving that he or she did not marry to evade the immigration laws. The issue to be proven is not whether the marriage is currently viable, but that it was not entered into with the intent of circumventing the immigration laws. The foreign national's burden is satisfied if he or she proves by the preponderance of the evidence that the marriage was bona fide.

This presumption is separate from the procedural requirement that after two years of conditional status a resident alien must file a petition to remove the condition in order to maintain permanent residency. The introduction of conditional permanent residency in 1986 has reduced the importance of the presumption of fraud ground of deportability. For the most part, this ground of deportability will only arise in connection with persons who immigrated to the United States on the basis of a marriage to a USC or LPR before 1986, when conditional residency status was established.

- Mika, from Romania, married USC Maureen in 1982, and immigrated to the United States in 1983. They divorced later that same year, and completely lost touch with each other. In 1998, Mika applied to become a USC, and had to list the dates of his marriage and divorce. Mika is at risk of being placed in removal proceedings and charged with deportability on this ground, based on a presumption of marriage fraud in his case.

The second weapon aimed at marriage fraud is the deportability ground in INA §237(a)(1)(G)(ii), which makes a foreign national deportable if the foreign national has failed or refused to fulfill the foreign national's marital agreement, which, in the opinion of the attorney general (AG), was made for the purpose of procuring the foreign national's admission as an immigrant. Apparently, Congress designed this rule to protect unwary USCs from foreign nationals who, with no other reason than obtaining immigration benefits, have deceived citizens by agreeing to marry them. However, this section does not make a foreign national deportable if that individual could not consummate the marriage because the USC spouse refused to fulfill his or her marital responsibility. This is because a foreign national cannot be deported under this ground unless the foreign national procured his or her immigrant visa by fraud.

---

[21] INA §237(a)(1)(G).

Criminal Grounds of Deportability

In the INA, the criminal grounds of deportability are divided into categories relating to:

- General crimes;
- Crimes involving controlled substances (*i.e.,* drugs);
- Crimes relating to firearms;
- Miscellaneous crimes; and
- Crimes of domestic violence, stalking, or violation of a protective order.

General Crimes

There are four general criminal grounds of deportability:

- Crimes of moral turpitude (CMTs);
- Multiple criminal convictions;
- Aggravated felonies; and
- High speed flight.

A detailed discussion on reviewing criminal records and analyzing the immigration consequences of a crime is found at chapter 4 of this manual.

Crime of Moral Turpitude (CMT)[22]

The CMT ground of deportability makes deportable any foreign national who was: (1) convicted of a crime; (2) where the crime was of moral turpitude; (3) the crime was committed within five years after the foreign national's admission into the United States; and (4) the crime was one for which a sentence of one year or more of confinement in prison may be imposed. Each of the four elements is discussed in detail below.

CONVICTION

The term *conviction* is defined in INA §101(a)(48)(A). Foreign nationals are considered to have been convicted if a court has adjudicated them guilty or has entered a formal judgment of guilt against them. In addition, even if the court has withheld such an adjudication, a person is considered to have been convicted for immigration purposes if:

- The person was found guilty or entered a plea of guilty or nolo contendere; and
- The judge ordered some form of punishment or restraint on the person's liberty.

Forms of punishment can include, but are not limited to, incarceration, probation, and a fine or restitution. Punishment also may include community-based sanctions such as a rehabilitation program, a work release or study release program, revocation or suspension of a driver's license, deprivation of nonessential activities or privileges, or

---

[22] INA §237(a)(2)(A)(i).

community service. The imposition of administrative court costs alone may constitute a punishment under INA §101(a)(48).[23]

Under INA §101(a)(48)(B), a *term of imprisonment* includes the period of incarceration or confinement ordered by the court, regardless of any suspension of the imposition or execution of the sentence. Thus, suspended sentences also are punishments and count as a period of incarceration even if no jail time is actually served. For example, if a foreign national has been sentenced to a one-year suspended sentence, for immigration purposes, that person has been sentenced to one year in jail.

Outcomes that *do not* constitute a conviction under immigration law include:

- An acquittal or finding of not guilty.

- A conviction that is not final.

- A conviction from which the defendant has taken an appeal as of right that is still pending or for which the time to file a notice of appeal has not expired is not final and should not constitute a conviction for immigration purposes.[24] While finality traditionally has been required in order to meet the definition of *conviction*, for immigration purposes, some circuit courts have reasoned that Congress eliminated the finality requirement when it defined *conviction* in IIRAIRA.[25] On the other hand, if the conviction is under collateral attack (*e.g.,* if a writ of coram nobis or a habeas corpus motion has been filed in the case), the conviction is considered final until the motion is finally decided.[26] If the collateral attack is decided in the defendant's favor, this may cure crime-based deportability.

- A nolle prosequi, or nol pros by the prosecutor, which means that the person was arrested and charged but that the prosecutor dismissed the charges before a determination.

- Refusal to prosecute, sometimes called declining of charges or no information. In this situation, the person has been accused of a crime and perhaps been arrested, but either the police do not bring charges or the prosecutor declines to prosecute those charges.

- *Certain pre-plea* or *diversionary* programs. These types of programs exist in many states and counties. The exact descriptions differ, but, generally, the accused agrees to participate in some sort of program or community service, without any admission or determination of guilt. If the program is successfully completed, the proceedings are dismissed. If the program is not successfully completed, the case is returned to court for a determination of guilt. The attorney must be careful in these cases to make sure that the client has not pled

---

[23] *Matter of Cabrera*, 24 I&N Dec. 459 (BIA 2008).

[24] *See Pino v. Landon*, 349 U.S. 901 (1955); *Matter of Thomas*, 21 I&N Dec. 20 (BIA 1995).

[25] *See Puello v. BCIS*, 511 F.3d 324 (2d Cir. 2007); *Abiodun v. Gonzales*, 461 F.3d 1210 (10th Cir. 2006); *Montenegro v. Ashcroft*, 355 F.3d 1035 (7th Cir. 2004); *Moosa v. INS*, 171 F.3d 994 (5th Cir. 1999).

[26] *Rohas Paredes v.AG of the United States*, 528 F.3d 196 (3d Cir. 2008).

guilty and has not admitted sufficient facts to establish guilt. If this has occurred, the client may be determined to have a conviction under INA §101(a)(48)(A).

- Convictions in proceedings in the United States that do not require proof of guilt *beyond a reasonable doubt* or otherwise comport with standard criminal proceedings.[27]

- Withholdings of adjudication where no criminal penalty or punishment is imposed (*e.g.*, according to at least one unpublished BIA decision, where only administrative court costs are imposed).

- A juvenile delinquency finding. A determination that a child is a delinquent is not a conviction for immigration purposes.[28] However, when a juvenile is tried and sentenced as an adult, this may be considered a conviction for immigration purposes, if the juvenile could have been transferred to adult court under the standards set forth in the Federal Juvenile Delinquency Act (FJDA).[29] In *Uritsky v. Gonzales*, the U.S. Court of Appeals for the Sixth Circuit held that a plea of guilty to third-degree sexual conduct under Michigan's Youthful Trainee Program, for which the respondent was sentenced to probation, did constitute a conviction under INA §101(a)(48)(A).[30] In reaching its decision, the Sixth Circuit agreed with the BIA that the Michigan program was distinguishable from both the FJDA and the New York law at issue in *Matter of Devison*,[31] and was more akin to a rehabilitative expungement than a finding of juvenile delinquency. However, an admission made by a minor or an adult about a CMT or controlled substances committed when the person was a minor does not trigger inadmissibility because the admission is of committing juvenile delinquency, not a crime.[32]

- Convictions vacated due to a substantive or constitutional flaw in the underlying proceeding instead of solely to alleviate immigration problems or other hardships.[33]

Moreover, the foreign national's conviction, if it is to make him or her deportable under INA §237(a)(2)(A)(i), must be for a CMT. Though the term *moral turpitude* is difficult to define, it has been held to involve acts demonstrating "baseness, vileness, or depravity" on the part of the perpetrator.[34] Moral turpitude does not exist simply because there has been a violation of the law. According to the BIA, "Neither the se-

---

[27] *Matter of Eslamizar*, 23 I&N Dec. 684 (BIA 2004).

[28] *Matter of Devison*, 22 I&N Dec. 1362 (BIA 2000).

[29] *Matter of Ramirez-Rivero*, 18 I&N Dec. 135 (BIA 1981); *but see Garcia v. INS*, 239 F.3d 409 (1st Cir. 2001). *See also Uritsky v. Gonzales*, 399 F.3d 728 (6th Cir. 2005).

[30] *Uritsky v. Gonzales*, 399 F.3d 728 (6th Cir. 2005).

[31] *Devison, supra* note 28.

[32] *Matter of MU*, 2 I&N Dec. 92 (BIA 1944).

[33] *Matter of Pickering*, 23 I&N Dec. 621 (BIA 2003).

[34] *Matter of Franklin*, 20 I&N Dec. 867 (BIA 1994).

riousness of the offense nor the severity of the sentence imposed is determinative of whether a crime involves moral turpitude. Instead, the characterization of the offense relates to the offender's evil intent or corrupt mind.[35] In an interesting discussion of the meaning—or rather lack of meaning—of the term *moral turpitude* in the immigration context, Judge Richard Posner, writing for the court in *Mei v. Ashcroft*[36] dismissed as unhelpful any notion that some sort of "evil intent" is required. He noted that both the BIA and the federal courts have failed to provide a clear meaning to the term *moral turpitude* and, before launching into a discussion whether the conviction at issue in the case was in fact a CMT, posited that perhaps the term has "outlived its usefulness."

In general, crimes that have fraud as an element usually are classified as CMTs, as are those involving permanent takings, sex offenses, and infliction of serious bodily injury.[37] Other CMTs include, for example, bribery,[38] robbery,[39] and arson.[40] A conviction for simple assault does not involve moral turpitude.[41] An assault offense that requires a mental state of criminal recklessness will not involve moral turpitude unless the statute also requires that the assault result in serious bodily injury.[42] Nonetheless, a conviction for an assault offense where injury to a spouse or child is an element of the offense may involve moral turpitude.[43] A conviction for assault with a deadly weapon also is a conviction for a CMT,[44] as is aggravated assault.[45] The BIA held that possession of child pornography under Florida law is a CMT,[46] as is retail theft when in violation of the Pennsylvania Code.[47] The BIA also found that trafficking in counterfeit goods or services is a CMT.[48] Simple driving under the influence, without other aggravating factors, is not considered a CMT.[49]

---

[35] *Matter of Lopez-Meza*, 22 I&N Dec. 1188 (BIA 1999); *but see Mei v. Ashcroft*, 393 F.3d 737 (7th Cir. 2004).

[36] *Mei v. Ashcroft*, 393 F.3d 737 (7th Cir. 2004).

[37] *See e.g. Matter of Adetiba*, 20 I&N Dec. 506 (BIA 1992) (fraud); *Matter of Beato*, 10 I&N Dec. 740 (BIA 1964) (sex offense).

[38] *Matter of H*, 6 I&N Dec. 358 (BIA 1954).

[39] *Matter of Frentescu*, 18 I&N Dec. 244 (BIA 1982).

[40] *Matter of S*, 3 I&N Dec. 617 (BIA 1949).

[41] *Matter of Short*, 20 I&N Dec. 136 (BIA 1989).

[42] *Matter of Fualaau*, 21 I&N Dec. 475 (BIA 1996).

[43] *Compare Matter of Tran*, 21 I&N Dec. 291 (BIA 1996) *with Matter of Sejas*, 24 I&N Dec. 236 (BIA 2007).

[44] *Matter of Logan*, 17 I&N Dec. 367 (BIA 1980).

[45] *Matter of Medina*, 15 I&N Dec. 611 (BIA 1976).

[46] *Matter of Olquin*, 23 I&N Dec. 896.

[47] *Matter of Jurado*, 24 I&N Dec. (BIA 2006).

[48] *Matter of Kochlani*, 24 I&N Dec. 128 (BIA 2007).

[49] *Matter of Torres-Varela*, 23 I&N Dec. 78 (BIA 2001); *Matter of Lopez-Meza*, 22 I&N Dec. 1188 (BIA 1999). A listing of BIA precedent decisions on CMTs can be found at Appendix E to *Immigration Law and Crimes*, a West publication that is updated semi-annually. Access to similar and regularly updated charts are available at *www.criminalandimmigrationlaw.com* for a monthly fee. These lists are

To determine whether a crime is one involving moral turpitude, the immigration judge (IJ) will examine what the elements are of the statute, and whether any offenses punishable under the statute involve moral turpitude. In practical terms, this means that regardless of what specific conduct led to the foreign national's conviction, the foreign national is not considered to have been convicted of a CMT if he or she was convicted under a penal code section that also would convict a person whose crime did not exhibit any moral turpitude.[50]

If the statute is divisible (*i.e.*, some offenses punishable involve moral turpitude and some do not), the IJ will be allowed to consult the record of conviction or any additional evidence deemed necessary or appropriate to resolve accurately the moral turpitude question.[51] The AG's decision in *Matter of Silva-Trevio*[52] represents a departure from the traditional categorical approach to divisible statutes, which prevented IJs from looking at any evidence outside of the record of conviction. Note that this approach applies only to moral turpitude determinations; the traditional categorical approach to divisible statutes applies to most other criminal grounds of removability.[53] This approach to divisible statutes is discussed more in chapter 4.

> – Corina was convicted of possession of a fake ID. The state statute that she violated makes no distinction between possessing the document with intent to use it, which is a CMT, and possession alone, which is not a CMT. Since moral turpitude cannot be determined from the statute itself, the IJ will consult her conviction record (*i.e.*, the criminal complaint, the plea, or the sentence) to see if her conviction was for possession with a fake ID with intent to use it. If the examination of the record of conviction is unclear, the IJ can consider any other evidence to determine whether her offense involved moral turpitude. If Corina were charged with another criminal ground of deportability, the IJ would not be able to consult documents outside of the record of conviction.

WITHIN FIVE YEARS OF ADMISSION

Another element that must be present for a foreign national to be deportable under this ground is that the CMT must have been committed within five years after the foreign national's admission to the United States. The BIA held that this five-year period can begin anew after each admission.[54] Relying in part on the reasoning set out in *Mat-*

---

very useful for seeing how the BIA and federal courts have ruled regarding criminal offenses similar to the offense at issue. Keep in mind, however, that it is the specific statute under which the foreign national was convicted that must be analyzed in determining whether the offense was one of moral turpitude.

[50] *Matter of Short*, 20 I&N Dec. 136 (BIA 1989).

[51] *Matter of Silva-Trevino*, 24 I&N Dec. 687 (A.G. 2008).

[52] *Id.*

[53] *See Matter of Velazquez-Herrera*, 24 I&N Dec. 503 (BIA 2008) (whether an alien is removable on the basis of a conviction for a "crime of child abuse" under INA §237(a)(2)(E)(i) is determined by the categorical approach).

[54] *Matter of Shanu*, 23 I&N Dec. 754 (BIA 2005).

ter of Rosas,[55] which held that adjustment of status to an LPR constitutes an *admission* for the purpose of the aggravated felony deportation ground, the BIA in *Matter of Shanu* held that even if a person was admitted at an earlier time, any subsequent admission—including an adjustment of status—will start the five-year period set out in INA §237(a)(2)(A)(i) anew. Thus, for example, under the BIA's interpretation, if a client was admitted on a student visa in 1998, adjusted his or her status to an LPR in 2002 and was convicted of a theft offense in 2005, he or she is still potentially subject to deportation under INA §237(a)(2)(A)(i) because, even though the conviction was seven years after his or her first admission in 1997, it was only three years after the subsequent admission when he or she adjusted status.

The Fourth, Sixth, Seventh, and the Ninth federal circuit courts of appeals have rejected the reasoning and holding in *Shanu.*[56] Indeed, before the *Shanu* decision was issued, the U.S. Court of Appeals for the Ninth Circuit already essentially had rejected the BIA's interpretation in *Shanu*, concluding that the clock starts with an initial admission and does not restart with a later adjustment of status.[57] A month after the BIA issued its decision in *Shanu*,[58] the Seventh Circuit, in a decision that made it apparent that it was unaware of the BIA's recent holding , also held that the five years begins from the initial admission and does not restart with any subsequent admission.[59] In *Aremu v. DHS*,[60] the U.S. Court of Appeals for the Fourth Circuit sided with the Seventh and the Ninth Circuits and explicitly rejected *Shanu.*[61]

For purposes of this time limit, a foreign national's departure and readmission to the United States also may start a new five-year period.[62] However, note that there is a special rule concerning admission for returning LPRs, found at INA §101(a)(13)(C). If an LPR is not considered to be making an admission upon reentering the United States, then the reentry should not start the five years running anew for this deportation ground. If, on the other hand, the reentry is deemed to be an admission, then the five-year period will start anew and a CMT committed within the new five-year period can make the LPR deportable.

SENTENCE OF ONE YEAR OR LONGER MAY BE IMPOSED

The final element that must be present for a foreign national to be deportable under this ground is that he or she must have been convicted of a crime for which a sentence of one year or longer may be imposed. Thus, to determine whether this element is satisfied, it is necessary to consider the possible sentence carried by the crime rather than the actual sentence received by the foreign national.

---

[55] *Matter of Rosas*, 22 I&N Dec. 616 (BIA 1999).

[56] *Shanu, supra* note 54.

[57] *Shivaraman v. Ashcroft*, 360 F.3d 1142 (9th Cir. 2004).

[58] *Shanu, supra* note 54.

[59] *Abdelqadar v. Gonzales*, 413 F.3d 668 (7th Cir. 2005).

[60] *Aremu v. DHS*, 450 F.3d 578 (4th Cir. 2006).

[61] *See also Zhang v. Mukasey*, 509 F.3d 313 (6th Cir. 2007).

[62] *But see Abdelqadar v. Gonzales*, 413 F.3d 668 (7th Cir. 2005).

– Margot was convicted of shoplifting but tells you that her conviction shouldn't be a problem because she didn't have any jail time and she just had to pay a fine. When you check Margot's criminal record you find out that she was convicted of a felony because of the value of the items she stole. In the state where Margot was convicted, this category of felony offense is punishable by up to three years in prison. Even though Margot didn't spend any time in jail, her offense qualifies as a conviction where a sentence of one year or more could have been imposed.

This ground was expanded by the Antiterrorism and Effective Death Penalty Act of 1996.[63] Foreign nationals who were placed in deportation proceedings prior to April 24, 1996, are subject only to the prior ground, which required that the foreign national have an actual sentence of one year or longer for the crime.

Multiple Criminal Convictions[64]

INA §237(a)(2)(A)(ii) states: "Any alien who at any time after admission is convicted of two or more crimes involving moral turpitude, not arising out of a single scheme of criminal misconduct, regardless of whether confined thereof and regardless of whether the convictions were in a single trial, is deportable."

The elements of this deportability ground are similar to those of the preceding ground. However, under this ground, *two* convictions will make a foreign national deportable if the convictions occurred after the foreign national entered the United States, regardless of how long after entry they occurred. Under this ground, a foreign national is deportable even, for example, if he or she was convicted of one CMT eight years after entering and of a second CMT 20 years later.

For a foreign national to be found deportable under this ground, the convictions must have been for two crimes that did not arise out of the same scheme of misconduct. The BIA says this single scheme exception refers to crimes "performed in furtherance of a single criminal episode, such as where one crime constitutes a lesser included offense of another or where two crimes flow from and are the natural consequences of a single act of criminal misconduct."[65] At least five circuit courts have accepted this definition.[66]

In *Abdelqadar v. Gonzales*,[67] the Seventh Circuit commented on the BIA's interpretation of *single scheme*, saying that:

---

[63] Pub. L. No. 104-132, 110 Stat. 1214.

[64] INA §237(a)(2)(A)(ii).

[65] *Matter of Adetiba*, 20 I&N Dec. 506 (BIA 1992).

[66] *See Abdelqadar v. Gonzales*, 413 F.3d 668 (7th Cir. 2005), *citing Balogun v. INS*, 31 F.3d 8 (1st Cir. 1994); *Akindemowo v. INS*, 61 F.3d 282 (4th Cir. 1995); *Iredia v. INS*, 981 F.2d 847 (5th Cir. 1993); *see also Nguyen v. INS*, 991 F.2d 621 (10th Cir. 1993) (conviction of possession of stolen vehicle and shooting with intent to kill when stopped a by police officer for speeding in stolen vehicle did not arise out of single scheme); *but see Gonzalez-Sandoval v. INS*, 910 F.2d 614 (9th Cir. 1990) (two robberies planned at same time and committed within two days of each other arose out of single scheme).

[67] *Abdelqadar v. Gonzales*, 413 F.3d 668 (7th Cir. 2005).

robbing six people at one poker game … would be a single scheme even if it led to multiple convictions … as would lesser included offenses of a criminal transaction. Likely the Board would treat conspiracy and its overt acts as a single scheme, even though the overt acts may be separate crimes as well. But the BIA would treat a series of securities frauds by a broker who finds a new *mark* daily as distinct offenses rather than aspects of a single scheme because the broker could stop after any of the frauds.

If the person is tried for both crimes in a single trial, the crimes usually will be considered separate if the foreign national was charged with the crimes under separate counts and the prosecution must prove separate facts to obtain each conviction. The burden of proving that the two crimes were not part of a *single scheme of criminal misconduct* is on the government.

The reason the government bears the burden of proving that the two crimes were not part of a single scheme of criminal misconduct is because ICE has the burden of proof on all grounds of deportability. However, for the government to establish that a foreign national is deportable under this ground, it only must show that the foreign national was convicted of two CMTs, not that the foreign national was sentenced to or served any time in confinement. Even if the foreign national was never confined for either of the crimes, he or she would still be deportable under this ground.

- Kevin, an LPR, was convicted of misdemeanor retail theft in 1997, six years after he became an LPR. This offense did not make Kevin deportable because it was committed more than five years after Kevin's admission, and because it was not punishable by a year or more. Three years later, Kevin is convicted of mail fraud. Kevin will be considered deportable for having two crimes of moral turpitude not arising out of a single scheme of criminal misconduct.

Aggravated Felony[68]

A foreign national is deportable if he or she has been convicted of an aggravated felony at any time after admission. The element in this deportability ground that has not been discussed previously in this chapter is the meaning of aggravated felony. Because foreign nationals subject to this ground are barred from nearly all relief, as discussed below, determining whether a foreign national is an aggravated felon is extremely important.

The INA contains a definition of aggravated felony that was first enacted in 1988, and that subsequently has been expanded by later amendments. As defined in INA §101(a)(43), the term *aggravated felony* now refers to a list of 21 categories of offenses, some of which are relatively minor. As noted below, several of these categories apply only if the term of imprisonment is at least one year. However, many foreign nationals who never actually served time in prison may be included within these categories, because of the INA's definition of *term of imprisonment*. Under this defi-

---

[68] INA §237(a)(2)(A)(iii).

nition, a term of imprisonment includes the period of incarceration or confinement ordered by the court, regardless of any suspension of the imposition or execution of the sentence.

Each category of aggravated felony is described briefly below:

- Murder, rape, or sexual abuse of a minor;

- Illicit trafficking in a controlled substance, including a drug trafficking crime;

- Illicit trafficking in firearms, destructive devices, or explosive materials;

- A money-laundering offense if the amount of the funds exceeded $10,000;

- Certain offenses concerning explosive materials or firearms;

- A crime of violence, not including a purely political offense, for which the term of imprisonment is at least one year;

- A theft offense, including receipt of stolen property, or burglary offense for which the term of imprisonment is at least one year;

- A crime relating to the demand for or receipt of ransom;

- A crime relating to child pornography;

- An offense related to racketeer-influenced corrupt organizations, or an offense described in 18 USC §1084 if it is a second or subsequent offense, or a gambling offense for which a sentence of one year or more of imprisonment may be imposed;

- An offense related to the owning, controlling, managing, or supervising of a prostitution business; or related to transportation for the purpose of prostitution if committed for commercial advantage; or an offense related to peonage, slavery, or involuntary servitude;

- An offense related to gathering, transmitting or disclosing national defense or classified information, or treason; or a violation of laws protecting the identity of undercover intelligence agents;

- An offense involving fraud or deceit in which the loss exceeds $10,000, or a tax evasion violation under §7201 of the Internal Revenue Code of 1986,[69] in which the loss to the government exceeds $10,000;

- A smuggling conviction under INA §§274(a)(1)(A) or (2), except for a first offense for which the foreign national has shown affirmatively that he or she committed the offense for the purpose of assisting his or her spouse, child, or parent (and no other individual);

- A conviction for entry without inspection or following deportation, where the foreign national was deported previously based on a conviction for an aggravated felony;

---

[69] The Tax Reform Act of 1986, Pub. L. No. 99-514, 100 Stat. 2085 (Oct. 22, 1986), redesignated the Internal Revenue Code of 1954, Pub. L. No. 83-591, 68A Stat. 3 (codified at 26 U.S.C. section 5848 (1954), as the Internal Revenue Code of 1986.

- An offense for falsely making, forging, counterfeiting, mutilating, or altering a passport or instrument, for which the term of imprisonment is at least 12 months, and except in the case for which the foreign national has shown affirmatively that he or she committed the offense for the purpose of assisting the his or her spouse, child, or parent (and no other individual);

- An offense relating to a defendant's failure to appear to serve a sentence, if the underlying offense is punishable by imprisonment for a term of five years or more;

- An offense relating to commercial bribery, counterfeiting, forgery, or trafficking in vehicles with altered identification numbers, for which the term of imprisonment is at least one year;

- An offense relating to obstruction of justice, perjury, or subornation of perjury, or bribery of a witness, for which the term of imprisonment is at least one year;

- An offense relating to a failure to appear before a court pursuant to a court order to answer or dispose of a felony charge for which a sentence of two years imprisonment or more may be imposed; and

- An attempt or conspiracy to commit any of these offenses.

Under the statute, these offenses are considered aggravated felonies whether the conviction was under state or federal law. Foreign convictions are considered aggravated felonies if the term of imprisonment was completed within the previous 15 years.

The most recent amendments to the definition of aggravated felony include an INA provision that states: "Notwithstanding any other provision of law (including any effective date), the term aggravated felony applies regardless of whether the conviction was entered before, on, or after the date of enactment of this paragraph."[70] This provision means that a conviction that was entered against a foreign national prior to the enactment of the 1996 changes to the immigration laws,[71] and at a time when the crime was not considered an aggravated felony, nonetheless now may come within the definition.

The INA contains many provisions specifying negative consequences for foreign nationals convicted of an aggravated felony. Under INA §238(b), noncitizens who are not LPRs may be ordered removed by an immigration official without a hearing, upon a determination that the foreign national is deportable because of a conviction for an aggravated felony. Further, as detailed in the subsequent chapters addressing eligibility requirements for various forms of relief from removal, an aggravated felony conviction is a bar to most immigration law remedies. For this reason, an advocate almost always should avoid conceding that an offense is an aggravated felony, and look for arguments to contest that characterization of the conviction. Where appropriate, a respondent whose offense is an aggravated felony by virtue of the sentence imposed should be counseled to investigate whether a sentence modification may be sought that will reduce the sentence below the one-year term required to meet an aggravated felony definition.

---

[70] INA §101(a)(43).

[71] IIRAIRA, *supra* note 12.

– Dzung Do, an LPR, was convicted of theft and sentenced to a term of one year in prison. The entire prison term was suspended and Dzung Do served a year on probation. USCIS learned of Dzung Do's conviction when he applied for citizenship, and ICE placed him in proceedings, charging him with deportability for an aggravated felony. Since a theft offense is only an aggravated felony if a sentence of one year or more is imposed, Dzung Do will not be deportable as an aggravated felon if he can file a post-conviction petition seeking a sentence reduction, and persuade the criminal court judge to reduce his sentence by even one day.

There is an increasing amount of case law in this complicated and developing area of the law, and practitioners dealing with a potential aggravated felony conviction need to thoroughly research applicable cases and talk to colleagues regarding potential arguments and strategies. Often, there is room to argue that an offense is in fact not an aggravated felony under immigration law. Because of the often severe immigration consequences of an aggravated felony conviction, it is critical that such arguments be made.

The U.S. Supreme Court has taken up circuit court splits on aggravated felony decisions frequently in the recent past. For example, in November 2004, the Court decided that a DUI offense that resulted in serious bodily injury was not a crime of violence, and therefore, was not an aggravated felony under INA §101(a)(43)(F).[72] In December 2006, the Court decided that a state felony offense for simple possession of drugs was not an aggravated felony under INA §101(a)(43)(B).[73] Finally, the Court decided in 2007 that a statute punishing aiding and abetting a theft offense was an aggravated felony under INA §101(a)(43)(G).[74]

High-Speed Flight[75]

In 1996, IIRAIRA[76] created a new federal crime for high-speed flight from an immigration checkpoint and a new ground of deportability for conviction of this crime. The crime consists of fleeing or evading at high speed a law enforcement checkpoint operated by ICE or any other agency. *High speed* is defined as any speed in excess of the legal speed limit.

Failure to Register as a Sex Offender[77]

A foreign national is deportable if he or she is convicted under 18 USC §2250, which punishes failure to register as a sex offender. This offense requires that the foreign national knowingly fails to register. This ground of deportability was added by amendments to the INA in 2006.

---

[72] *Leocal v. Ashcroft*, 542 U.S. 1 (2004).

[73] *Lopez v. Gonzales*, 549 U.S. 47 (2006).

[74] *Gonzales v. Duenas-Alvarez*, 548 U.S. 183 (2007).

[75] INA §237(a)(2)(A)(iv).

[76] IIRAIRA, *supra* note 12.

[77] INA §237(a)(2)(A)(v).

Drug Offenses

Controlled Substance Convictions[78]

This ground of deportability refers to:

Any alien who at any time after admission has been convicted of a violation of (or a conspiracy or attempt to violate) any law or regulation of a State, the United States, or a foreign country relating to a controlled substance (as defined in §102 of the Controlled Substances Act (21 USC §802), other than a single offense involving possession for one's own use of thirty grams or less of marijuana.

Unlike the deportability ground for a CMT, this ground contains no time limitation, as foreign nationals are subject to removal for a controlled substance conviction occurring at any time after admission.

A foreign national's violation of a state, federal, or foreign narcotics law or regulation is not sufficient in itself to render the foreign national deportable under this ground. The foreign national may be deported under this ground only if he or she has been convicted of a proscribed offense. Also, under the terms of the statute, a single conviction for simple possession of less than 30 grams of marijuana does not render the foreign national deportable.

Drug Abusers and Addicts[79]

Under this section of the law, any foreign national who is, or at any time after admission has been, a drug abuser or addict is deportable.

Prior to 1990, foreign nationals were deportable for drug use only if they were addicted to narcotic drugs. The Immigration Act of 1990[80] introduced the concept of deportability for drug abuse into immigration law for the first time. The Public Health Service's definition of drug abuse is very broad and includes any non-medical use of a controlled substance.[81]

The most important difference between how the drug abuse and drug addiction provisions are applied in the admissibility and deportability contexts is that the standard for establishing that a foreign national is deportable is stricter than for establishing that a foreign national is inadmissible. To find a foreign national deportable under this ground, ICE must prove by clear and convincing evidence that the person is a drug addict or abuser.

Because of the way the drug abuser/addict deportability ground is worded, having been cured of the drug addiction is not a defense against deportability under this ground.

---

[78] INA §237(a)(2)(B)(i).

[79] INA §237(a)(2)(B)(ii).

[80] Pub. L. No. 101-649, 104 Stat. 4978 (Nov. 29, 1990).

[81] See 42 CFR §34.2(g).

Firearm Violations[82]

The firearms deportability ground applies to "any alien who at any time after admission is convicted under any law of purchasing, selling, offering for sale, exchanging, using, owning, possessing, or carrying, or of attempting or conspiracy to purchase, sell, offer for sale, exchange, use, own, possess, or carry, any weapon, part, or accessory which is a firearm or destructive device ... in violation of any law." This is a severe ground of deportability, because even a minor firearm-related conviction can make a foreign national deportable.

LPRs in removal proceedings may apply for relief from this ground of deportability through cancellation of removal, discussed in chapter 7. Cancellation of removal is not available for non-LPRs who are deportable under this ground. However, foreign nationals who are deportable under this ground are not precluded from seeking asylum or withholding of removal.

Miscellaneous Crimes[83]

This ground makes foreign nationals deportable if they are convicted under specific subsections of certain federal statutes. The miscellaneous crimes that could make a foreign national deportable under this ground include offenses related to the following:

- Espionage;
- Sabotage (for which the potential term of imprisonment is five or more years);
- Treason and sedition (for which the potential term of imprisonment is five or more years);
- The Military Selective Service Act;[84]
- The Trading with the Enemy Act of 1917;[85]
- Sections of the U.S. Code dealing with threats against the president and against successors to the presidency;
- The law prohibiting expeditions against friendly nations;
- The section of the INA relating to importation of foreign nationals for immoral purposes;
- The section of the INA relating to travel documentation requirements.

---

[82] INA §237(a)(2)(C).

[83] INA §237(a)(2)(D).

[84] 50 USC App. 451 *et seq.*

[85] 12 USC §95a.

Crimes of Domestic Violence, Stalking, or Violation of a Protection Order[86]

Domestic Violence, Stalking, and Child Abuse[87]

In 1996, IIRAIRA[88] added a new ground of deportability that applies to foreign nationals convicted, at any time after entry, of a crime of domestic violence, stalking, or child abuse, child neglect, or child abandonment. A crime of violence (as defined in 18 USC §16) against a person is included under this ground if it is committed by:

- A current or former spouse of the victim;

- A foreign national with whom the victim shares a child in common;

- A foreign national who is cohabiting with or has cohabited with the victim as a spouse;

- A foreign national similarly situated to a spouse of the victim under the domestic violence laws of the jurisdiction where the offense occurs; or

- Any other foreign national against a victim who is protected from that foreign national's acts under the domestic or family violence laws of the United States or any state, Indian tribal government, or unit of local government.

This ground of deportability only applies to convictions occurring after September 30, 1996.[89] Convictions for a domestic violence offense on or before September 30, 1996, however, may still fall within the CMT deportability ground.[90]

Violators of Protection Orders[91]

Another ground of deportability added by IIRAIRA[92] applies to any foreign national who at any time after entry is enjoined under a protection order issued by a court, and whom the court determines has engaged in conduct that violates the portion of the order that involves protection against threats of violence, repeated harassment, or bodily injury. A protection order under this ground includes any injunction issued for the purpose of preventing violent or threatening acts of domestic violence, including temporary or final orders issued by civil or criminal courts, other than support or child custody orders or provisions. This ground applies to violations of court orders occurring after September 30, 1996.

---

[86] INA §237(a)(2)(E).

[87] INA §237(a)(2)(E)(i).

[88] IIRAIRA, *supra* note 12.

[89] *Matter of Gonzales-Silva*, 24 I&N Dec. 218 (BIA 2007).

[90] *Matter of Tran*, 21 I&N Dec. 291 (BIA 1996).

[91] INA §237(a)(2)(E)(ii).

[92] IIRAIRA, *supra* note 12.

Document-Related Grounds of Deportability[93]

Change-of-Address Requirement[94]

Under this deportability ground, foreign nationals who fail to comply with the change-of-address requirement imposed by INA §265 are deportable unless they establish to the AG's satisfaction that their failure to comply was reasonably excusable or was not willful. Changes of address must be reported within 10 days of the change by submitting Form AR-11 to the immigration office listed on the form. All foreign nationals are subject to this requirement except diplomats (nonimmigrant visa status A) and official government representatives to an international organization (nonimmigrant visa status G).

Criminal Convictions Relating to Failure to Register and Falsification of Documents[95]

Foreign nationals also are deportable under INA §237(a)(3)(B) if they are convicted under the sections of law that penalize violations of the Foreign Agents Registration Act,[96] fraud and misrepresentations in U.S. government registration forms, and fraud and misuse related to visas, permits, and other entry documents.

Document Fraud Violations[97]

Foreign nationals who are subject to an administrative law judge's (ALJ) final order for having violated the document fraud provisions of INA §274C also are deportable. These document fraud provisions authorize civil penalties for foreign nationals who make or use false documents, or who use documents issued to other persons, to satisfy any requirements imposed by the INA. To impose such a penalty, the ALJ must determine by only a preponderance of the evidence that the foreign national has committed a violation. There is no administrative appeal from an order by the ALJ; the order becomes final unless the AG vacates or modifies it.

There is a limited waiver available to eligible LPRs who are deportable under this ground. This waiver is available only to LPRs who establish that their use of false documents was committed solely in order to assist, aid, or support a spouse or child.[98]

In addition, long-time LPRs in removal proceedings may apply for relief from this ground of deportability through cancellation of removal, which is discussed in chapter 7. Cancellation of removal also is available for non-LPRs deportable under this ground who have lived in the United States continuously for 10 years. Foreign nationals who are deportable under this ground are not precluded from seeking asylum or withholding of removal. However, ICE may use the document fraud order to op-

---

[93] INA §237(a)(3).

[94] INA §237(a)(3)(A).

[95] INA §237(a)(3)(B).

[96] 22 USC §611 *et seq.*

[97] INA §237(a)(3)(C).

[98] INA §237(a)(3)(C)(ii).

pose applications for all these forms of relief (except withholding of removal) because they are discretionary.

Falsely Claiming Citizenship[99]

In 1996, IIRAIRA[100] added a new ground of deportability that is identical to the new ground of inadmissibility for a foreign national who falsely claims to be a USC for any purpose or benefit under the INA, or federal or state law. This new and severe ground applies to false claims of citizenship made on or after September 30, 1996.

A provision of the Child Citizenship Act of 2000[101] provides a limited exception to this ground of deportability to certain foreign nationals who innocently claimed U.S. citizenship. The law affects only foreign nationals who:

- Are children of USC parents (or former USC parents), including adopted children;

- Permanently resided in the United States before the age of 16; and

- Reasonably believed they were USCs.

The law is retroactive to the date of enactment of IIRAIRA—September 30, 1996.

Security and Related Grounds of Deportability[102]

The security grounds of deportability are virtually identical to the security grounds of inadmissibility. The following discussion lists these deportability grounds, then explains the differences between their application in the inadmissibility and deportability contexts.

Espionage, Sabotage, and Other Illegal Activities[103]

INA §237(a)(4)(A) provides:

Any individual who has engaged, is engaged, or at any time after entry engages in (i) any activity to violate any law of the United States relating to espionage or sabotage or to violate or evade any law prohibiting the export from the United States of goods, technology, or sensitive information, (ii) any other criminal activity which endangers public safety or national security, or (iii) any activity a purpose of which is the opposition to, or the control or overthrow of, the Government of the United States by force, violence, or other unlawful means, is deportable.

Because it incorporates the language *has engaged*, this ground apparently provides that offending foreign nationals are deportable regardless of whether they committed the relevant offenses before or after they entered the United States.

---

[99] INA §237(a)(3)(D).

[100] IIRAIRA, *supra* note 12.

[101] Child Citizenship Act of 2000, Pub. L. No. 106-395, 114 Stat. 1631 (Oct. 30, 2000).

[102] INA §237(a)(4).

[103] INA §237(a)(4)(A).

Unlike the parallel ground of inadmissibility, the *any other criminal activity* clause in this deportability ground is limited to activities that endanger public safety or national security. For this clause to apply, the foreign national need not have been convicted; having been or being engaged in the activity is enough. On the other hand, ICE has the burden of proving by clear and convincing evidence that the activity is criminal and that it endangers public safety or national security.

Terrorist Activities[104]

Under this provision, any foreign national who has engaged, is engaged, or at any time after admission engages in any terrorist activity (as defined in INA §212(a)(3)(B)(iii)) is deportable. This ground of deportability is not only virtually identical to the parallel ground of inadmissibility, but it also incorporates by reference the definition of terrorism in the inadmissibility provision at INA §212(a)(3)(B)(iv). In the inadmissibility context, a foreign national may be excluded if the consular officer or DHS knew or had reasonable ground to believe that the foreign national was likely to engage in terrorist activity after entry. In the deportability context, however, ICE must prove that the foreign national has engaged or is engaged in terrorist activity.

Foreign Policy Considerations[105]

Under INA §237(a)(4)(C)(i), a foreign national "whose presence or activities in the United States the Secretary of State has reasonable ground to believe would have potentially serious adverse foreign policy consequences for the United States is deportable." This deportability ground is identical to the parallel ground of inadmissibility, except that removal can take place only after a foreign national enters the United States. The deportability ground applies to foreign nationals whose presence or activities in the United States are undesirable. A foreign national is inadmissible, on the other hand, if his or her entry or proposed activities in the United States are undesirable.

Participation in Genocide or Nazi-Sponsored Persecution[106]

Any foreign national who has assisted in persecution perpetrated or sponsored by the Nazi party, or has engaged in genocide, is deportable. This ground is not only identical to the parallel ground of inadmissibility, but it also refers specifically to the ground of inadmissibility: any foreign national described in the parallel ground of exclusion is deportable.

Public Charge Grounds of Deportability[107]

Under this provision, a foreign national is deportable if he or she, within five years after the date of entry, has become a public charge from causes not affirmatively

---

[104] INA §237(a)(4)(B).

[105] INA §237(a)(4)(C).

[106] INA §237(a)(4)(D).

[107] INA §237(a)(5).

shown to have arisen since entry. In practice, very few foreign nationals are deported on this ground, since there are strict requirements for a foreign national to be considered a public charge in the deportation context. For a foreign national to be deportable under this ground, all the following elements must be present:

- The law must impose a debt for the services provided to the foreign national (*i.e.,* the law must provide that the state or other public entity can sue the foreign national or other designated foreign nationals for payment of services rendered).

- The public entity must demand payment of charges; and

- The foreign national must refuse to pay the charges imposed.[108]

Receiving benefits under such federal programs as Temporary Assistance to Needy Families, Aid to Families with Dependent Children, Supplemental Security Income, Medicaid, or the Food Stamp Program does not impose any legal debt on the foreign national. However, in some states, accepting state general relief or general assistance payments may create a liability.

Foreign nationals who become public charges as defined by this ground of deportability can rebut a charge that they are deportable by showing that the reasons for their condition arose after they entered the United States. For example, a foreign national should not become deportable for receiving unemployment insurance benefits if the foreign national lost his or her job after entry. In addition, foreign nationals are not subject to deportability on public charge grounds if they have been forced to accept public assistance because they have become physically disabled or because their spouse has abandoned them.

Unlawful Voting Ground of Deportability[109]

This ground of deportability encompasses "any alien who has voted in violation of any federal, state, or local constitutional provision, statute, ordinance, or regulation." The statute does not expressly require a showing of intent (*i.e.,* that the foreign national knew that voting was in violation of the requirement), but note that some local municipalities actually allow voting by non-USCs, and such voting would not violate this provision.

- Corina, an LPR, was asked to register to vote when she went to renew her driver's license. Corina thought this meant that she was eligible to vote, so when the next election period came around, she did vote in the state election. Even though Corina didn't know that she was not qualified to vote, she cannot now safely apply for citizenship. ICE, therefore, is likely to consider that Corina is deportable because of her voting, and there is no waiver ground available to her.

---

[108] *Matter of L*, 6 I&N Dec. 349 (BIA 1954).

[109] INA §237(a)(6).

The Child Citizenship Act of 2000[110] provides a narrow exception to the above deportability ground. If a foreign national:

- Is a child of USC parents or former USC parents, including adopted children;
- Resided in the United States before the age of 16; and
- Reasonably believed they were USCs.

Then there is a waiver available for innocent participation in the voting process. This law is retroactive to the IIRAIRA enactment date—September 30, 1996.

---

[110] Child Citizenship Act of 2000, *supra* note 101.

CHAPTER THREE
GROUNDS OF INADMISSIBILITY

Overview of the Inadmissibility Grounds

Prospective immigrants and nonimmigrants must establish that they are admissible to the United States. This means that they must not fall under any of the grounds of inadmissibility found in Immigration and Nationality Act (INA)[1] §212(a) or that, if they do, a waiver of inadmissibility applies. Foreign nationals who are found to be inadmissible by U.S. Citizenship and Immigration Services (USCIS), U.S. Immigration and Customs Enforcement (ICE), or U.S. Customs and Border Protection (CBP) may be placed in removal proceedings based on inadmissibility.

The inadmissibility grounds are distinguished from the grounds of deportability, set forth in INA §237(a), which are invoked to remove individuals already in the United States who have been admitted or paroled. However, grounds of inadmissibility also can come into play when a person is placed in removal proceedings based on the ground of deportability found at INA §237(a)(1)(A), making a foreign national deportable if he or she was inadmissible at the time of admission or adjustment of status, based on a ground of inadmissibility existing at that time.

Specifically, the inadmissibility grounds will apply in the following circumstances:

- When a person applies for a U.S. visa, either immigrant or nonimmigrant, at a U.S. consulate abroad.

- When a person applies for adjustment of status to lawful permanent resident (LPR) status or for a change of nonimmigrant status.

- If a prospective immigrant or nonimmigrant is found inadmissible upon inspection, at the U.S. border, or its functional equivalent.

- In removal proceedings:

  - When a person is found inadmissible upon inspection and referred to the immigration judge (IJ).

  - When a non-LPR who entered without inspection (EWI) is placed in removal proceedings.

  - When a person labeled an *arriving alien* is placed in proceedings (note that there is a special rule for returning LPRs).

  - When a person is placed in removal proceedings based on the ground of deportability found at INA §237(a)(1)(A), making a foreign national deportable if he or she was inadmissible at the time of his or her admission or ad-

---

[1] Immigration and Nationality Act of 1952 (INA), Pub. L. No. 82-414, 66 Stat. 163 (codified as amended at 8 USC §§1101 *et seq.*).

justment of status, based on a ground of inadmissibility existing at that time. In other words, the Department of Homeland Security (DHS) is not precluded or estopped from finding a person inadmissible in the future, even if the government erroneously granted a visa and/or admitted the person.

Who Bears the Burden of Proof Under INA §212?

A first-time applicant for admission must establish that he or she is "clearly and beyond a doubt entitled to be admitted."[2] A person returning to a status must establish by "clear and convincing evidence" that he or she is "lawfully present pursuant to a prior admission."[3]

For foreign nationals charged with being in the United States without admission or parole, ICE first must establish the person's *alienage*. If alienage is established, unless the respondent demonstrates by clear and convincing evidence that he or she is lawfully in the United States pursuant to a prior admission, the respondent must prove that he or she is clearly and beyond a doubt entitled to be admitted to the United States and is not inadmissible as charged.[4]

Arriving aliens bear the burden of proving that they are "clearly and beyond a doubt entitled to be admitted and are not inadmissible."[5] However, there is an exception to this rule for returning LPRs who are considered to be seeking admission under INA §101(a)(13)(c). For those foreign nationals, the U.S. Supreme Court has held that they are entitled to have the government bear the burden of proof in establishing their inadmissibility.[6]

Evaluating the Charges of Inadmissibility

An advocate should consider the following series of questions any time any potential grounds of inadmissibility are discovered or arise or appear on a Notice to Appear (NTA):

- Does the inadmissibility ground really apply to my client? In other words, are the alleged charges and facts they are based on correct? For example, if ICE asserts that the client has been convicted of a crime involving moral turpitude

---

[2] INA §240(c)(2)(A).

[3] INA §240(c)(2)(B).

[4] INA §§240(c)(2), 291; 8 CFR §1240.8(c).

[5] 8 CFR §1240.8(b).

[6] *Landon v. Plasencia*, 459 U.S. 21 (1982); *see also Katebi v. Ashcroft*, 396 F.3d 463 (1st Cir. 2005); *Khodagholian v. Ashcroft*, 335 F.3d 1003 (9th Cir. 2003), *citing Landon* and *Matter of Huang*, 19 I&N Dec. 749 (BIA 1988): "When an applicant has a colorable claim to returning resident status … the INS has the burden of proving he is not eligible for admission to the United States." In *Huang,* the BIA, *citing Woodby v. INS,* 385 U.S. 276 (1966), held that, where an applicant for admission has a colorable claim to returning resident status, "the burden is on the INS to show by clear, unequivocal and convincing evidence that the applicant should be deprived of his or her lawful permanent residence." 19 I&N Dec. 749, 754 (BIA 1988). *See also In re Luna Rubio*, A74 317 521 (BIA Index May 24, 2000), which states that it is the government's burden to establish that a returning LPR falls within one of the exceptions specified by INA §101(a)(13)(C) and, therefore, is an arriving alien.

(CMT), can I show that the disposition in the client's criminal case does not meet the definition of *conviction* or that the crime was not one of moral turpitude?

- Are there other grounds of inadmissibility that may potentially apply to my client? ICE may amend an NTA at any time, so be aware of any new charges that could arguably be added.

- Even if my client is inadmissible, is there a waiver for which he or she is eligible? We will mention those waivers in this chapter, and will discuss how to apply for them in chapter 6.

- Even if the client is inadmissible and no waivers apply, is there any form of relief from removal for which the client might be eligible? (Chapters 7 through 11 of this manual deal with forms of relief from removal).

Grounds of Inadmissibility

There are 10 general categories of inadmissibility grounds. They are:

1. Health-related grounds;
2. Criminal-related grounds;
3. National security grounds;
4. Public charge;
5. Labor protection grounds;
6. Fraud or other immigration violations;
7. Documentation requirements;
8. Grounds relating to military service in the United States;
9. Prior removals or unlawful presence in the United States; and
10. Miscellaneous grounds.

Each category comprises several grounds. This chapter will cover many of the more common grounds. Advocates should be careful to review all of the inadmissibility grounds when representing a client in removal proceedings, since the client may be inadmissible and therefore potentially removable under more than one ground.

Health-Related Grounds

There are four health-related grounds of inadmissibility:

- Exclusion of persons who "have a communicable disease of public health significance."[7]

- Exclusion of prospective immigrants who have not been vaccinated against certain diseases.[8]

---

[7] INA §212(a)(1)(A)(i).
[8] INA §212(a)(1)(A)(ii).

- Exclusion of those with physical or mental disorders and associated behavior that poses a threat to the property, safety, or welfare of the applicant or other persons.[9]
- Exclusion of drug abusers or addicts.[10]

There are waivers available for the first, second, and third health-related grounds. There is no waiver of the drug abuse or addiction ground.

In removal proceedings, inadmissibility under a health-related ground often is demonstrated through the medical examination that is required for all applicants for adjustment of status. This examination is conducted by a civil surgeon in the United States. These examinations are conducted pursuant to Public Health Service (PHS) regulations and the Technical Instructions for Medical Examination of Aliens, issued by the Centers for Disease Control and Prevention (CDC), a part of the U.S. Department of Health and Human Services (HHS). Thus, in this section, citations will be made sometimes to those regulations and technical instructions. The CDC's Technical Instructions for Medical Examination of Aliens (Technical Instructions) can be found at *www.cdc.gov.*

If the civil surgeon finds that a prospective immigrant falls under the communicable disease, physical or mental disorder, or drug abuse or addiction inadmissibility grounds, he or she will issue a "Class A" medical certificate, noting the condition.[11] The prospective immigrant may appeal this finding. If this is done, a medical review board is convened, and the applicant may bring his or her own medical experts to testify.[12]

In this section, we will discuss each of the health-related inadmissibility grounds in more detail and mention the waivers that are available.

Communicable Diseases

Under the first health-related ground, persons are inadmissible if they have "a communicable disease of public health significance," as determined by the secretary of HHS through one of its divisions, the PHS.[13] The diseases considered by the PHS to be communicable and of public health significance are:

- Active tuberculosis;
- Infectious leprosy;
- HIV infection; and
- Five venereal diseases:
  - chancroid,
  - gonorrhea,

---

[9] INA §212(a)(1)(A)(iii).

[10] INA §212(a)(1)(A)(iv).

[11] 42 CFR §34.2(d).

[12] 42 CFR §§34.8(a), (c).

[13] INA §212(a)(1)(A)(i).

- granuloma inguinale,

- lymphogranuloma venereum, and

- the infectious stage of syphilis.[14]

The list of diseases was expanded recently to include:

- Quarantinable, communicable diseases specified by presidential executive order, as provided under §361(b) of the Public Health Service Act;[15] and

- Any communicable disease that requires notification to the World Health Organization as an event that may constitute a public health emergency of international concern, pursuant to the revised International Health Regulations of 2005.[16]

On July 30, 2008, Congress passed the Global Leadership Against HIV/AIDS, Tuberculosis and Malaria Reauthorization Act of 2009.[17] Section 305 of this legislation amended INA §212(a)(1)(A)(i) so that HHS was not *required* to designate HIV infection as a "communicable disease of public health significance." However, HHS did not subsequently remove HIV infection from the list of communicable diseases of public health significance. Therefore, persons who have HIV still are inadmissible under INA §212(a)(1)(A)(i).

There is a general waiver of the communicable disease ground for foreign nationals who are parents, spouses, or unmarried sons or daughters of U.S. citizens (USCs), LPRs, or immigrant visa recipients.[18] There is a special waiver of the communicable disease ground for Violence Against Women Act and Department of Justice Reauthorization Act of 2005 (VAWA)[19] self-petitioners.[20] These waivers are discussed in more detail in chapter 6.

Lack of Vaccination

Intending immigrants must present evidence that they received vaccinations against mumps, measles, rubella, polio, tetanus and diphtheria toxoids, pertussis, influenza type B and hepatitis B, and any other vaccinations recommended by the Advisory Commission for Immunization Practices.[21]

There are three waivers available for prospective immigrants who are inadmissible because they cannot present proof of vaccinations. The vaccination requirement may be waived if:

---

[14] 42 CFR §34.2(b).

[15] 42 USC §242 (2001).

[16] 73 Fed. Reg. 58047 (Oct. 6, 2008).

[17] Pub. L. No. 110-293, 122 Stat. 2918 (2008).

[18] INA §§212(g)(1)(A), (B).

[19] Violence Against Women and Department of Justice Reauthorization Act of 2005 (VAWA 2005), Pub. L. No. 109-162, 119 Stat. 2960 (2006).

[20] INA §212(g)(1)(C).

[21] INA §212(a)(1)(A)(ii).

- The immigrant receives the vaccination;

- A civil surgeon or panel physician certifies that the vaccination would not be medically appropriate; or

- The vaccination would be contrary to the applicant's religious or moral beliefs.[22]

These waivers will be covered in more detail in chapter 6.

Physical or Mental Disorders

Persons are inadmissible under the physical or mental disorder ground if they have or had a condition with an associated behavior that poses a threat to the property, safety, or welfare of themselves or others. For this purpose, the presence of a physical or mental illness alone does not determine a person's inadmissibility. Instead, persons will be excluded only "if they have physical or mental disorders with a history of harmful behavior associated with the disorder."[23] *Harmful behavior* is defined as "a dangerous action or series of actions by the individual that has resulted in injury (psychological or physical) to the alien or another person, or that has threatened the health or safety of the alien or another person, or that has resulted in property damage."[24]

The CDC Technical Instructions list a series of disorders that may have harmful behavior associated with them. The Technical Instructions also list mental disorders for which harmful behavior is an element of the diagnosis. Diagnosing the applicant for any of these conditions automatically establishes his or her inadmissibility, unless the condition is in remission. Alcohol dependence and abuse are included as disorders for which harmful behavior is a necessary part of the diagnosis.

If the person no longer has the condition, it does not constitute an inadmissibility ground unless the behavior is likely to recur or the condition is likely to lead to other harmful behavior.[25] Generally, a physical or mental disorder with an associated history of harmful behavior will be considered in remission—and, therefore, not likely to recur—if no pattern of the behavioral element has manifested in the previous two years.[26] However, if the behavior is described under the categories of antisocial personality disorder, impulse control disorders, paraphilias, or conduct disorders (*i.e.,* the first four categories listed in Table 2 of the Technical Instructions), no remission will be found unless the behavior has been absent for five years.

---

[22] INA §212(g)(2).

[23] 42 CFR §§34.2(d)(2)(1), (2), 34.2(n), 34.2(p).

[24] "Physical and Mental Disorders with Associated Harmful Behavior," CDC Technical Instructions, §III(B)(2)(c).

[25] INA §212(a)(1)(A)(iii)(II).

[26] *See* CDC Technical Instructions, notes to Table 5.

Drug Abusers or Addicts

Persons who are determined to be drug abusers or addicts are inadmissible.[27] The PHS regulations contain very broad definitions of the terms *drug abuse* and *drug addiction*. The regulations define *drug abuse* as the "non-medical use of a substance listed in section 102 of the Controlled Substances Act[28] ... which has not necessarily resulted in physical or psychological dependence."[29] *Drug addiction* is defined as a non-medical use of a controlled substance "which has resulted in physical or psychological dependence."[30] Section 102 of the Controlled Substances Act lists hundreds of controlled drugs, arranged into five schedules, which determine the degree of a criminal offense involving a particular drug.[31] For example, marijuana is included on the list in Schedule I, the most severely penalized category.

Under the CDC Technical Instructions, applicants are not inadmissible for non-medical use of controlled substances if the use amounts to no more than experimentation with the substance.[32] A single use of marijuana or of other psychoactive substances is considered an example of experimentation. The instructions require that when a clinical question is raised as to whether use was experimental or part of a pattern of abuse, examining doctors should consult with other physicians who have experience in medically evaluating substance abusers.[33]

The CDC Technical Instructions also include a *remission* rule. They define *remission* as "no non-medical use of a [listed drug] for 3 or more years, or no non-medical use of any other psychoactive substance for 2 or more years."[34] Therefore, people who stopped using drugs more than three years before their medical examination should not be inadmissible.

The Technical Instructions' definition of the term *abuse* is the same as that of *use*.[35] They provide: "If it is determined that the applicant is using or has used a psychoactive substance, the physician must ... determine whether the applicant currently is using or has used the psychoactive substance in the last 3 years (for [controlled] substances ...)."[36]

There are no waivers for the drug abuse or addiction inadmissibility ground.

Chronic alcoholism is not specifically included as an inadmissibility ground, nor is it included under the definitions of drug user or drug abuser. The Technical Instruc-

---

[27] INA §212(a)(1)(A)(iv).

[28] Comprehensive Drug Abuse Prevention and Control Act of 1970, Pub. L. No. 91-513, title II, 84 Stat. 1236 (Oct. 27, 1970); 21 USC 801 *et seq.*

[29] 42 CFR §34.2(g).

[30] 42 CFR §34.2(h).

[31] Controlled Substances Act, §102; 21 USC §802.

[32] DOS Cable, 91-State-416180 (Dec. 24, 1991), *reprinted in* 61 *Interpreter Releases* 6 (Jan. 6, 1992).

[33] CDC Technical Instructions, §III(C)(2)(c).

[34] CDC Technical Instructions, §III(C)(2)(b).

[35] CDC Technical Instructions, Section III(C)(2)(a).

[36] CDC Technical Instructions, Section III(C)(3).

tions equate *drugs* with *controlled substances* as defined in §102 of the Controlled Substances Act, and this definition specifically excludes alcoholic beverages and tobacco from its coverage.[37]

The Technical Instructions do, however, instruct physicians to evaluate prospective immigrants for alcohol abuse as part of the evaluation for mental and physical disorders with associated harmful behavior.[38] Still, since there is a waiver available for the physical or mental disorders inadmissibility ground, a person found inadmissible because of chronic alcoholism may be eligible for a waiver.[39]

Criminal Grounds

Overview

Foreign nationals are inadmissible for the following:

- Conviction or admission of a CMT;
- Conviction or admission of a controlled substance violation;
- Conviction of multiple crimes;
- A consular or immigration officer's knowledge or reason to believe that the applicant has engaged in controlled substance trafficking;
- Having engaged in or coming to the United States to engage in prostitution and commercialized vice;
- Asserting diplomatic immunity from prosecution for serious crimes;
- Engaging in particularly serious violations of religious freedom;
- Being a significant trafficker in persons; and
- Money laundering.

Each of these grounds is discussed later below. A limited waiver is available for some of these criminal inadmissibility grounds, and some forms of relief also may cure inadmissibility.

Required Standards of Proof

The required standards of proof vary significantly for the criminal grounds of admissibility. As discussed below, some require proof of actual conviction, while others require only a valid admission. Remarkably, five grounds require neither a conviction nor an admission, but instead require lesser forms of proof for the charge to be sustained. These grounds are:

- Controlled substance trafficking;
- Prostitution and commercialized vice;
- Traffickers in persons;

---

[37] Controlled Substances Act, §102; 21 USC §802.
[38] CDC Technical Instructions, Notes to Table 5.
[39] INA §212(g).

- Money laundering; and
- Foreign government officials' engaging in severe violations of religious freedom.

Obtaining Necessary Records and Analyzing a Criminal Conviction

If DHS charges that your client is inadmissible on any of the above criminal grounds, you must first find out all the facts by obtaining and reviewing all pertinent records. You must then thoroughly analyze any criminal activity under immigration law. See chapter 4 for more details on how to obtain records and analyze criminal activity under immigration law.

"Conviction," "Admission," and "Sentence"

The criminal inadmissibility grounds use several terms that have special definitions. These include *conviction*, *admission*, and *sentence*. Some of the criminal grounds of inadmissibility require that to be inadmissible, the foreign national must have been convicted. Whether another ground applies depends at least in part on the length of any sentence(s) imposed. The definitions of *conviction* and *sentence* are contained in the INA and discussed in chapter 2.

Two of the criminal inadmissibility grounds—CMTs and controlled substance offenses—apply to foreign nationals who admit having committed either a crime or the essential elements of a crime, even though they were never convicted of the crime. There is no statutory provision regarding the meaning of an admission of a crime; instead, under case law, an admission of a crime is valid when:

- The act is considered criminal under the law in force where the act was alleged to have been committed;
- The person was advised in a clear manner of the essential elements of the alleged crime;
- The person has clearly admitted conduct constituting the essential elements of the crime; and
- The admission was made in a free and voluntary manner.

The three principal Board of Immigration Appeals (BIA) cases concerning admissions for purposes of the criminal inadmissibility grounds are *Matter of Winter*,[40] *Matter of K–*,[41] and *Matter of G–M–*.[42]

Guilty pleas are considered admissions for immigration purposes. However, the admission cannot have a greater effect than the criminal proceeding.[43] Thus, if after the guilty plea the accused is not convicted, neither DHS nor the immigration court can use the plea as an admission for purposes of inadmissibility.

---

[40] *Matter of Winter*, 12 I&N Dec. 638 (BIA 1968).

[41] *Matter of K–*, 7 I&N Dec. 594 (BIA 1957).

[42] *Matter of G–M–*, 7 I&N Dec. 40 (BIA 1955).

[43] *Matter of Seda*, 17 I&N Dec. 550 (BIA 1980); *Matter of Winter*, 12 I&N Dec. 638 (BIA 1968).

Crimes Involving Moral Turpitude

Persons are inadmissible if they are convicted of a CMT, or if they admit having committed a CMT.[44] The elements of a CMT are discussed in chapter 2.

Exceptions to Inadmissibility Due to CMT Conviction or Admission

The INA contains two exceptions for inadmissibility based on conviction or admission of a CMT. The first of these exceptions is for crimes that were committed when the foreign national was under the age of 18, while the second exempts petty offenses. Persons who have committed more than one CMT, however, cannot claim either of the exemptions.

THE "UNDER 18" EXCEPTION

Under INA §212(a)(2)(A)(ii)(I), a foreign national is not inadmissible for a CMT if the crime was committed while the foreign national was under age 18 and the foreign national both committed the crime and was released from prison more than five years before applying for a visa, other documentation, or admission to the United States. This provision is different from the rule that findings of juvenile delinquency are not considered convictions for purposes of immigration law. If the foreign national's acts were adjudicated under juvenile proceedings, or if the foreign proceedings are interpreted as falling within the federal juvenile type of proceedings, then this provision does not apply. In such a case, the foreign national would not have been convicted of any crime and would not be inadmissible. On the other hand, if the minor was convicted as if he or she were an adult, or, in the case of foreign convictions, if the minor's conviction does not fall within the type of proceedings that federal law considers necessarily as juvenile proceedings, then this exception comes into play.

 - In January 1997, at the age of 16, Jack was charged and convicted as an adult of burglary. He received a sentence of 90 days, which he successfully completed in 1997.

Jack is not inadmissible. Burglary is generally a CMT, but John appears to fall within the *under 18* exception because he committed the offense before the age of 18 and was released from confinement more than five years ago.

THE "PETTY OFFENSE" EXCEPTION

This second exception has two elements. First, the applicant qualifies for the exception only if the CMT of which he or she was convicted, or to which he or she admitted, had a maximum possible penalty of one year of imprisonment. Second, if the person was convicted, he or she must not have been sentenced to more than six months imprisonment, regardless of how much time he or she actually served.[45]

 - Joe and his brother, Sam, stole $100 from a store in California. Joe was arrested for the crime and convicted by a court. He was sentenced to four months in prison, suspended upon successful completion of probation. Sam

---

[44] INA §212(a)(2)(A)(i)(I).

[45] INA §212(a)(2)(A)(ii)(II).

was not arrested, but, overcome by guilt, he admitted his involvement in the crime to the police. Under California law, the maximum sentence for this offense is one year. This is a first offense for both Joe and Sam.

Neither Joe nor Sam should be inadmissible. While theft is often considered a CMT, both Joe and Sam appear to fall under the petty offense exemption. Joe was sentenced to less than six months imprisonment, and the offense of which he was convicted meets the exemption requirement of having a maximum sentence of one year or less. Sam was not convicted, but an admission could be enough to make him inadmissible. The advocate must examine Sam's admission carefully to see whether it meets the elements of an admission for purposes of the criminal inadmissibility grounds. Even if it does, Sam should fall under the exemption since the offense he admits committing carries a maximum sentence of one year or less.

Both of these exceptions are available only if the foreign national has committed only one crime. The BIA has interpreted the *only one offense* provision, however, as meaning "only one crime involving moral turpitude."[46] Thus, while a second offense involving moral turpitude will make a foreign national ineligible for the exceptions, a second offense that does not involve moral turpitude will not.

Multiple Criminal Convictions

A person convicted of two or more offenses (other than purely political offenses), for which the aggregate sentences to confinement were five years or more, is inadmissible. Under this ground, it is irrelevant whether the convictions occurred in a single trial, whether the offenses arose from a single scheme of misconduct, or whether they involved moral turpitude.[47]

Where a person is convicted of two or more crimes in one proceeding and given concurrent sentences, the aggregate sentence is the longer of the two concurrent sentences.[48] For example, if a person is convicted of two counts of theft in the same proceeding and sentenced to two years for one offense and four years for the other, to be served *concurrently* (as opposed to *consecutively*), then the aggregate sentence for immigration purposes is four years.

Controlled Substance Violations

Of the two grounds of inadmissibility relating to drug crimes, one is for persons who have been convicted or admit commission of drug-related crimes, while the other is for persons believed to be drug traffickers.

A person is inadmissible under the first of these grounds if he or she has been convicted of or makes a valid admission of having violated, or having conspired to violate, "any law or regulation of a State, the United States, or a foreign country relating to a controlled substance (as defined in §102 of the Controlled Substances Act)."[49]

---

[46] *Matter of Garcia-Hernandez,* 23 I&N Dec. 590 (BIA 2003).

[47] INA §212(a)(2)(B).

[48] *Matter of Aldebesheh*, 22 I&N Dec. 983 (BIA 1999).

[49] INA §212(a)(2)(A)(i)(II).

This ground covers virtually every type of drug. The words "any law or regulation ... relating to a controlled substance" have been interpreted as broad enough to encompass convictions for being under the influence of drugs and convictions for facilitating the unlawful sale of cocaine.[50]

The INA does not provide any waiver for a controlled substance violation, unless the violation was for simple possession of 30 grams or less of marijuana. It is important to note that a conviction dismissed under the Federal First Offender's Act (FFOA)[51] for first-time offenses of simple possession of a controlled substance arguably constitutes a removal of the conviction for immigration purposes. However, after the BIA's decision in *Matter of Roldan*,[52] it is unlikely that a conviction dismissed under a state counterpart to the FFOA will constitute a removal of the conviction for immigration purposes.

In *Roldan*, the respondent's drug possession conviction had been expunged under a state counterpart of the FFOA (for first-time convictions of simple possession of drug offenses). The BIA held that following the 1996 changes[53] to the law adding a definition of *conviction* to the INA, any state action that purports to expunge, dismiss, cancel, vacate, discharge, or otherwise remove a guilty plea or other record of guilt or conviction by operation of a state rehabilitative statute, such as the one under which Roldan's conviction was expunged, will be given no effect for immigration purposes. The BIA left open the question of the effect, for immigration purposes, of the new INA definition of *conviction* upon a dismissal and expungement under the FFOA.

The U.S. Court of Appeals for the Ninth Circuit reversed the BIA's *Roldan* decision in *Lujan-Almendariz v. INS*.[54] There, the court held that the new definition of *conviction* did not repeal the FFOA or the rule that a person cannot be deported based on an offense that could have been tried under the FFOA. The individual instead is prosecuted under state law, where the findings are expunged pursuant to a state rehabilitative statute. However, in all other circuits, the BIA's holding in *Roldan*[55] controls.

Traffickers in Controlled Substances

No conviction—or even valid admission—is necessary to exclude people believed to be drug traffickers. This ground applies to "[a]ny alien who the consular or immigration

---

[50] *Matter of Esqueda*, 20 I&N Dec. 850 (BIA 1994); *Matter of Hernandez-Ponce*, 19 I&N Dec. 613 (BIA 1988); *Matter of Del Risco*, 20 I&N Dec. 109 (BIA 1989); *see also Desai v. Mukasey*, 520 F.3d 762 (7th Cir. 2008) (holding that conviction for distribution of an imitation drug was a crime relating to a controlled substance).

[51] Federal First Offender Act (FFOA), 18 USC §3607 (Current version added by Sentencing Reform Act of 1984, Pub. L. No. 98-473, §212(a)(2), 98 Stat. 1837, 2003).

[52] *Matter of Roldan*, 22 I&N Dec. 512 (BIA 1999).

[53] Illegal Immigration Reform and Immigrant Responsibility Act of 1996 (IIRAIRA), Pub. L. No. 104-208, div. C, 110 Stat. 3009, 3009-546 to 3009-724.

[54] *Lujan-Almendariz v. INS*, 222 F.3d 728 (9th Cir. 2000).

[55] *Matter of Roldan, supra* note 52.

officer knows or has reason to believe is or has been an illicit trafficker" in any controlled substance. It also applies to persons who knowingly assist in the trafficking.[56]

Illicit trafficking refers to unlawful trading or dealing in a controlled substance.[57] An illicit trafficker includes not only persons who smuggle or attempt to smuggle drugs into the United States, but also to people who serve as conduits for the drug trade within the country.[58] A person can be an illicit trafficker even if he or she has committed only one transgression.[59]

The government's *reason to believe* determination must be supported by "reasonable, substantial, and probative evidence."[60] In the context of security and related grounds of inadmissibility under INA §§212(a)(3)(A), (B), (C), and (E), the BIA has equated the *reason to believe* standard with *probable cause.*[61]

The drug trafficking inadmissibility ground also makes inadmissible the spouse, son, or daughter of a drug trafficker, if the spouse, son, or daughter has obtained any financial or other benefit from the trafficking within the previous five years, and if he or she knew or reasonably should have known that the benefit was from illicit trafficking.[62]

Prostitution and Commercialized Vice

Unlike the other grounds included under INA §212(a)(2), prostitution and commercialized vice are not technically "criminal" inadmissibility grounds. They apply even to persons who come from countries where prostitution is legal, and presumably also to those who are coming to states of the United States where prostitution is legal. This ground's three subsections, found at INA §212(a)(2)(D), make the following persons inadmissible:

1. Persons who are coming to the United States to engage in prostitution or who have engaged in prostitution within 10 years of the date of application for a visa, adjustment of status, or entry into the United States.

2. Persons who are procurers of prostitutes, or who attempt to procure, or who receive the proceeds of prostitution, or people who have done any of these activities within 10 years of the date of application for a visa, adjustment of status, or entry into the United States.

3. Persons who are coming to the United States to engage in unlawful commercialized vice, whether or not it is related to prostitution.

---

[56] INA §212(a)(2)(C).

[57] *Matter of Davis*, 20 I&N Dec. 536 (BIA 1992).

[58] *Matter of R–H–*, 7 I&N Dec. 675 (BIA 1958).

[59] *Matter of Rico*, 16 I&N Dec. 181 (BIA 1977).

[60] *Lopez-Molina v Ashcroft*, 368 F.3d 1206 (9th Cir. 2004); *Alarcon-Serrano v. INS*, 220 F.3d 1116 (9th Cir. 2000); *Matter of Rico*, 16 I&N Dec. 181 (BIA 1977).

[61] *See Matter of U–H*, 23 I&N Dec. 355 (BIA 2002); *see also Yusupov v. AG*, 518 F.3d 185 (3d Cir. 2008); *Adams v. Baker*, 909 F.2d 643 (1st Cir. 1990).

[62] INA §212(a)(2)(C)(ii).

Immunity from Prosecution

This inadmissibility ground bars admission into the United States of "any alien ... for whom immunity from criminal jurisdiction was exercised with respect to [a serious criminal] offense."[63] This ground was intended to exclude former foreign diplomats who have escaped punishment for serious traffic offenses. The term *serious crimes*, for purposes of this inadmissibility ground, includes any felony, crime of violence, or reckless or drunk driving that injures another person.[64]

Particularly Serious Violations of Religious Freedom

Foreign government officials, who were responsible for or directly carried out particularly severe violations of religious freedom during the previous 24 months, and their spouse and children, are inadmissible.[65] The phrase "particularly severe violations of religious freedom" is defined to include arbitrary prohibitions on, restrictions of, or punishment for:

- Assembling for peaceful religious activities;
- Speaking freely about one's religious beliefs;
- Changing one's religious beliefs and affiliation;
- Possession and distribution of religious literature;
- Raising one's children in the religious teachings and practices of one's choice; or
- Any of the following acts if committed on account of an individual's religious belief or practice:
  - detention;
  - interrogation;
  - imposition of an onerous financial penalty;
  - forced labor;
  - forced mass resettlement;
  - imprisonment;
  - forced religious conversion;
  - beating;
  - torture;
  - mutilation;
  - rape;
  - enslavement;

---

[63] INA §212(a)(2)(E).

[64] INA §101(h).

[65] INA §212(a)(2)(G).

    – murder; and

    – execution.[66]

Significant Traffickers in Persons

Under §111(b) of the Trafficking Victims Protection Act of 2000,[67] the president must prepare a report to Congress publicly identifying foreign persons to be sanctioned under the act. Any foreign national who is listed in that report, or whom the consular officer or an immigration officer knows or has reason to believe is or has been a knowing aider, abettor, assister, conspirator, or colluder with such a trafficker in severe forms of trafficking in persons, is inadmissible.[68] Spouses, sons, and daughters (except unmarried children under 21) of traffickers also are inadmissible, if they have obtained any financial or other benefit from the trafficker's illicit activity, and they knew or should have known that the financial or other benefit was a product of such illicit activity.[69]

The phrase "severe forms of trafficking in persons" is defined as either:

- Sex trafficking in which a commercial sex act is induced by force, fraud, or coercion, or in which the person induced to perform the commercial sex act is under 18 years of age; or

- The recruitment, transportation, provision, or obtaining of a person for labor or services, through the use of force, fraud, or coercion, for the purpose of subjection to involuntary servitude, peonage, debt bondage, or slavery.[70]

Money Laundering

Any foreign national who a consular or immigration officer knows or has reason to believe has engaged, is engaging, or seeks to enter the United States to engage in an offense relating to laundering of monetary instruments under 18 USC §§1956 or 1957, or who has helped or conspired in money laundering, is inadmissible.[71]

Aggravated Felonies

There is no inadmissibility ground aimed specifically at aggravated felons, but the INA references them under many other provisions that entitle aggravated felons to fewer procedural protections and benefits than other inadmissible foreign nationals. For example, persons removed from the United States based on a conviction for an aggravated felony are permanently inadmissible under INA §212(a)(9)(A), and LPRs who have been convicted of an aggravated felony are ineligible for the INA §212(h)

---

[66] International Religious Freedom Act of 1998, Pub. L. No. 105-292, §3, 112 Stat. 2787; 22 USC §6402.

[67] Pub. L. No. 106-386, div. A, 114 Stat. 1464, 1466–91.

[68] INA §212(a)(2)(H).

[69] INA §§212(a)(2)(H)(ii), (iii).

[70] 28 CFR §1100.25.

[71] INA §212(a)(2)(I).

waivers of the criminal inadmissibility grounds.[72] Aggravated felonies are covered in more detail in chapter 2.

National Security Grounds

Persons inadmissible under the political/national security grounds are divided into five categories:

1. Persons seeking to enter the United States to engage in prejudicial and unlawful activities, including espionage, sabotage, "any unlawful activity," or the violation or evasion of "any law prohibiting the export from the United States of goods, technology or sensitive information;"[73]

2. Terrorists;[74]

3. Persons whose admission into the United States would bring about serious foreign policy consequences;[75]

4. Members of the Communist or any totalitarian party (this inadmissibility ground applies only to immigrants);[76] and

5. Participants in Nazi persecution or genocide.[77]

Espionage, Sabotage, Export Control Violations, and Other Unlawful Activities

Any foreign national is inadmissible if a consular officer, an immigration officer, or an IJ has reason to believe that the person will:

- Engage in espionage or sabotage;

- Attempt to violate or evade export control laws;

- Engage in activities with a view to overthrowing the U.S. government by unlawful means; or

- Engage in any other unlawful activity.[78]

For that person to be barred from admission, it is sufficient for the consular or immigration officer to have reasonable grounds to believe that the person intends to engage in the proscribed activities. The applicant is inadmissible even if he or she intends to engage only incidentally in the described activities.

The provision barring entry to those who seek to "violate or evade any law prohibiting the export from the United States of goods, technology, or sensitive information" was intended by Congress to forbid the entry not only of those whom the consular officer has reason to believe seek to violate the export control laws, but also of

---

[72] See INA §212(h).

[73] INA §212(a)(3)(A).

[74] INA §212(a)(3)(B).

[75] INA §212(a)(3)(C).

[76] INA §212(a)(3)(D).

[77] INA §212(a)(3)(E).

[78] INA §212(a)(3)(A).

those who have the intention to evade those laws. Thus, the ground covers activity not expressly forbidden by the export control laws. However, the legislative history indicates that this provision should be applied only to those cases "where such evasion would harm the national security."

Terrorist Activity

The reach and applicability of this ground has been greatly expanded by the recent passage of two acts: first by the Uniting and Strengthening America by Providing Appropriate Tools Required to Intercept and Obstruct Terrorism (USA PATRIOT) Act[79] and then, most recently, by the REAL ID Act of 2005.[80]

Specifically, the REAL ID Act, passed on May 11, 2005, further expanded provisions and definitions in this ground that had previously been greatly expanded by the USA PATRIOT Act. For example, it widened the definition of "terrorist organization" to include, among other things, any group that engages, or has a subgroup that engages in terrorist activity, including soliciting funds or otherwise providing material support. It also expanded the definition of a *non-designated* terrorist organization to include a group of two or more foreign nationals, whether organized or not, which engages in, or has a subgroup that engages in any form of terrorist activity.

The BIA issued a precedent decision, *Matter of S–K–*,[81] holding that this ground of inadmissibility applied regardless of whether the applicant gave such support intentionally and regardless of how substantial the support was. The BIA also held that it would not use a *totality of the circumstances* test to determine whether an organization engaged in terrorist activity, so factors such as the organization's goals and the nature of the regime it opposed would not matter. After significant bad press about the "material support bar" (particularly the effect that it had on asylum cases and processing of refugees into the United States), DHS Secretary Michael Chertoff made a statement on January 19, 2007, allowing for a totality of circumstances consideration to be used to consider the cases of those who provided material support under duress to "Tier III" organizations.[82] Later statements by Chertoff allowed this totality of the circumstances test to be used when considering the cases of those who provided material support under duress to "Tier I and II" organizations.

In a follow-up precedent decision, *Matter of S–K–*,[83] the BIA discussed INA §212(a)(3)(B) and the effect of the passage of the Consolidated Appropriations Act of 2008[84] on December 26, 2007, which stated that certain groups shall not be considered to be a terrorist organization on the basis of any act or event occurring before

---

[79] Uniting and Strengthening America by Providing Appropriate Tools Required to Intercept and Obstruct Terrorism (USA PATRIOT) Act of 2001, Pub. L. No. 107-56, 115 Stat. 272.

[80] REAL ID Act of 2005, Pub. L. No. 109-13, div. B, 119 Stat. 231, 302–23.

[81] *Matter of S–K–*, 23 I&N Dec. 936 (BIA 2006).

[82] 72 Fed. Reg. 9958 (March 6, 2007).

[83] *Matter of S–K–*, 24 I&N Dec. 475 (BIA 2008).

[84] Consolidated Appropriations Act, 2008, Pub. L. No. 110-161, §6, div. J, sec. 691, 121 Stat. 1844, 2364–66.

December 26, 2007. Since the respondent in the case was deemed to have provided material support to the CNF/Chin National Army, which the legislation deemed not to be a terrorist organization based on events occurring before December 26, 2007, the respondent was no longer ineligible for asylum based on the material support to terrorism bar. The BIA stated, however, that its decision in *Matter of S–K–*[85] was still the law with respect to the material support bar to asylum and withholding of removal. Therefore, persons who have given support to other organizations deemed terrorist organizations, regardless of the level of support, are inadmissible under this ground.[86]

Potential for Serious Adverse Consequences for Foreign Policy

Another ground bars the entry of a foreign national if the secretary of state has reasonable basis to believe that the foreign national's entry or proposed activities would have serious adverse foreign policy consequences.[87]

BELIEFS, STATEMENTS, AND ASSOCIATIONS EXCEPTION

Beliefs, statements, or associations that would be lawful within the United States do not make foreign nationals inadmissible under this ground. However, the secretary of state may override this exception if she or he "personally determines that the alien's admission would compromise a compelling United States foreign policy interest." The law provides that if the secretary of state makes such a determination, he or she must notify the chairs of the Judiciary and Foreign Affairs Committees of the House of Representatives, and of the Judiciary and Foreign Relations Committees of the Senate, regarding the foreign national's identity and the reasons for the determination.

EXCEPTION FOR FOREIGN POLITICIANS

Another exception to the adverse foreign policy effect inadmissibility ground specifically protects foreign politicians. No official of a foreign government or purported government, and no candidate in a foreign election during the period immediately preceding the election, may be excluded on the basis of beliefs, statements, or associations, if such beliefs, statements, or associations would be lawful in the United States. The secretary of state has no authority to override this exception.

Membership in the Communist or a Totalitarian Party

The INA bars the admission of immigrants who are, have been members of, or are affiliated with, the Communist party or any totalitarian party.[88] This inadmissibility ground does not apply to nonimmigrants. Membership must be a *meaningful associa-*

---

[85] *Matter of S–K–*, 23 I&N Dec. 936 (BIA 2006).

[86] For a detailed discussion of the changes in this ground, *see* Human Rights First, "Refugees at Risk Under Sweeping Terrorism Bars," available with other relevant information, including Secretary Chertoff's statements and other relevant documents, at *www.humanrightsfirst.org/asylum/asylum_refugee.asp*.

[87] INA §212(a)(3)(C).

[88] INA §212(a)(3)(D)(i).

tion to be the basis of inadmissibility. The term *totalitarian party* means an organization that advocates the establishment in the United States of a one-party system and that forcibly suppresses opposition.[89]

There are broad exceptions to this inadmissibility ground:[90]

- One exception is for persons whose membership or affiliation was involuntary, was solely when the person was under 16 years of age, was by operation of law, or was required in order to obtain employment, food rations, or other essentials of living.

- A second exception applies if the person's membership ended at least two years before the person applies for a visa (five years for persons who belonged to a Communist or totalitarian party that controlled the government).

- Finally, the third exception is one where this inadmissibility ground may be waived for immigrants who are the spouse, parent, son, daughter, brother, or sister of a USC or LPR, in order to assure family unity, or when it is otherwise in the public interest, as long as the immigrant is not a threat to the security of the United States.

Speech-related conduct—*i.e.*, "advocating or teaching totalitarian doctrine, or writing publishing, distributing, printing, or possessing totalitarian materials"—no longer constitutes a ground of inadmissibility. Also, foreign nationals no longer are inadmissible, as they once were, for being members of organizations proscribed by the Subversive Activities Control Act of 1950.[91]

Participant in Genocide or Nazi Persecution

The INA bars admission of foreign nationals who, as members of the Nazi government or its allies, participated in the persecution of others on account of race, religion, national origin, or political opinion. Another inadmissibility ground excludes foreign nationals who have engaged in genocidal conduct as defined by the International Convention on the Prevention and Punishment of Genocide.[92] The convention defines genocide as the commission of any of a number of specified acts with intent to destroy, in whole or in part, a national, ethnic, racial or religious group. The acts specified are:

1. Killing members of the group;

2. Causing serious bodily or mental harm to the members of the group;

3. Deliberately inflicting on the group conditions of life calculated to bring about its physical destruction;

4. Imposing measures intended to prevent births within the group; and

---

[89] INA §101(a)(37).

[90] INA §212(a)(3)(D).

[91] 50 USC §781 *et seq.*

[92] INA §212(a)(3)(E); *see also* International Convention on the Prevention and Punishment of Genocide, Dec. 9, 1948, 78 U.N.T.S. 277.

5. Forcibly transferring children of the group to another group.

Public Charge

Public Charge Standard

The public charge inadmissibility ground bars admission to anyone who, "in the opinion of the consular officer at the time of application for a visa, or in the opinion of an immigration officer or IJ at the time of application for admission or adjustment of status," is likely to become a public charge.[93]

A *totality of the circumstances* test is applied to determine whether a person is likely to become a public charge.[94] Under this test, the immigration officer or the consular officer considers such factors as the applicant's age, health, family status, vocation, assets, resources, financial status, education, and skills.[95] The applicant may also submit information concerning personal funds or property at his or her disposal in the United States to show that he or she will not become a public charge.

The mere possibility that the foreign national may become a public charge is not sufficient to find him or her inadmissible. Some specific circumstance—*i.e.*, mental or physical disability, advanced age, or some other fact reasonably tending to show that the burden of supporting the foreign national is likely to be cast on the public— must be present.[96] A healthy person in the prime of life cannot ordinarily be considered likely to become a public charge, especially if he or she has friends or relatives in the United States who have indicated their ability and willingness to provide help in case of emergency.[97]

Thus, the main emphasis in the public charge inadmissibility ground is not on existing economic factors but rather on "the alien's physical and mental condition as it affects ability to earn a living ...." The negative side of this approach is that the frail, the elderly and the sick are likely to be inadmissible from the United States under this standard. On the other hand, even though low earnings and past receipt of public assistance are factors that are considered, they do not automatically make a person "likely to become a public charge."

The term *public charge* is defined as "likely to become ... primarily dependent on the government for subsistence, as demonstrated by either the receipt of public cash assistance for income maintenance, or institutionalization for long-term care at government expense."[98] "Cash assistance for income maintenance" includes Supplemental Security Income, cash assistance from the Temporary Assistance for Needy Families

---

[93] INA §212(a)(4)(A).

[94] INS Memorandum, M. Pearson, "Subject: Public Charge: INA Section 212(a) and 237(a)(5)" (May 20, 1999), 64 Fed. Reg. 28686 (March 26, 1999), *reprinted at* 76 *Interpreter Releases* 873–877 (May 28, 1999).

[95] INA §212(a)(4)(B).

[96] *Matter of Martinez-Lopez*, 10 I&N Dec. 409 (AG 1964); *see also* Pearson Memo, *supra* note 94.

[97] Pearson Memo, *supra* note 94.

[98] *Id.*

(TANF) program, and state or local cash assistance programs for income maintenance, often called "General Assistance." In addition, public assistance, including Medicaid, that is used for supporting foreign nationals who reside in an institution for long-term care also will be considered as part of the public charge analysis. Past or current receipt of these forms of public cash assistance does not lead to an automatic determination that the person is inadmissible as a public charge. Instead, receipt of these benefits should be taken into account under the totality of the circumstances test.[99]

There are certain types of public benefits that will not be considered in determining whether a foreign national may become a public charge. Among these are any benefits that are not considered cash assistance for income maintenance. These include the following:

- Medicaid;
- Children's Health Insurance Program (CHIP);
- Food stamps;
- The Special Supplemental Nutrition Program for Women, Infants and Children (WIC);
- Immunizations;
- Prenatal care;
- Testing and treatment of communicable diseases;
- Emergency medical assistance;
- Emergency disaster relief;
- Nutrition programs;
- Housing assistance;
- Energy assistance;
- Child care services;
- Foster care and adoption assistance;
- Transportation vouchers;
- Educational assistance;
- Job training programs;
- Non-cash benefits funded under the TANF program; and
- In-kind, community-based benefits, such as soup kitchens, crisis counseling, and short-term shelter.[100]

Although some of these programs may provide cash benefits, their purpose is not for income maintenance but rather to avoid the need for ongoing cash assistance for income maintenance. Cash payments that have been earned, such as Title II Social

---

[99] *Id.*

[100] *Id.*

Security disability and retirement benefits, government pensions, and veteran's benefits, do not support a finding of public charge.

Generally, receipt of even cash benefits by members of the applicant's family is not attributed to the applicant for purposes of a public charge determination. However, if the family relies on the public benefits as its sole means of support, the applicant may be considered to have received public cash assistance.[101]

Note that on June 21, 2006, DHS published a final rule regarding affidavits of support (Form I-864), which are used to overcome the public charge ground of inadmissibility.[102]

Bonds

Foreign nationals seeking immigrant status who are inadmissible on economic grounds may be admitted to the United States at an immigration officer's discretion by posting a "public charge bond" or paying a cash deposit of at least $1,000.[103]

Previous Immigration Violations

INA §212(a)(6) covers certain immigration-related misconduct. These grounds of inadmissibility apply to the following categories of individuals:

- Foreign nationals present in the United States without being lawfully admitted or paroled;
- Foreign nationals who fail to attend removal proceedings;
- Foreign nationals who engage in fraud or misrepresentation;
- Foreign nationals who falsely claim U.S. citizenship;
- Stowaways;
- Smugglers;
- Foreign nationals who are subject to a final order for violation of civil document fraud under INA §274C; and
- Foreign students who study at public institutions.

Foreign Nationals Present Without Permission or Parole

This ground of inadmissibility applies to foreign nationals who are present in the United States without being admitted or paroled, or who arrive at a place other than a designated port of entry.[104] This ground took effect on April 1, 1997, and is a very common charge on an NTA. It does not apply to foreign nationals who were in exclusion or deportation proceedings initiated prior to that date, unless the government provides notice and exercises the option to proceed under the new law's provisions.

---

[101] Pearson Memo, *supra* note 94.

[102] *See* 71 Fed. Reg. 35732 (June 20, 2006).

[103] INA §213.

[104] INA §212(a)(6)(A).

There is an exception to this ground of inadmissibility for individuals who qualify for immigrant status under the INA's provisions for battered spouses and children. If such individuals entered before April 1, 1997, they need show only status as a VAWA self-petitioner.[105] If the entry was on or after April 1, 1997, however, these individuals must also show that there was a substantial connection between the entry without inspection and the abuse he or she suffered.[106]

Failure to Attend Removal Proceedings

Another bar to admissibility applies to persons who without reasonable cause fail to attend their removal proceedings.[107] They are inadmissible for a period of five years following their subsequent departure or removal from the United States. This ground applies only to foreign nationals who failed to attend removal proceedings—it does not apply to foreign nationals who failed to attend deportation or exclusion proceedings. In other words, the ground applies only to foreign nationals who fail to attend proceedings that were initiated on or after April 1, 1997, and who were served with the Form I-862 NTA. Moreover, this ground does not apply unless the person departed from the United States after failing to attend the removal hearing.

It also should be noted that persons who fail to attend removal proceedings after receiving notice may be ordered removed in absentia.[108] The BIA has provided guidance for determining when an in absentia order may be entered properly, and how persons may overcome the presumption of effective delivery by mail.[109] In absentia orders are covered in more detail in chapter 12.

Finally, in situations in which a foreign national: (1) has received oral notice of the time and place of proceedings and the consequences of failing to appear; (2) fails to appear for less than "exceptional circumstances;" and (3) is ordered deported in absentia, the person is ineligible for 10 years for cancellation of removal, voluntary departure, adjustment of status, change of status, and registry.[110]

Fraud or Willful Misrepresentation

A person is inadmissible if he or she commits fraud or willfully misrepresents a material fact in attempting to obtain, or in obtaining, a visa, other documentation, admission into the United States, or other benefit under the INA.[111] *Other documentation* refers to documents required at the time of the foreign national's admission to the United States, such as:

---

[105] Illegal Immigration Reform and Immigrant Responsibility Act of 1996 (IIRAIRA), Pub. L. No. 104-208, §301(c)(2), div. C, 110 Stat. 3009, 3009-546 to 3009-724.

[106] INA §212(a)(6)(A)(ii).

[107] INA §212(a)(6)(B).

[108] INA §240(b)(5).

[109] *Matter of M–R–A–*, 24 I&N Dec. 665 (BIA 2008); *Matter of G–Y–R–*, 23 I&N Dec. 181 (BIA 2001); *Matter of M–D–*, 23 I&N Dec. 540 (BIA 2002).

[110] INA §240(b)(7).

[111] INA §240(a)(6)(C).

- Reentry permits;
- Border crossing cards;
- U.S. Coast Guard identity cards; or
- U.S. passports.

Other benefit includes, among other things:

  - Adjustment of status applications;
  - All visa petitions;
  - Requests for extension of stay;
  - Change of nonimmigrant classification;
  - Requests for employment authorization; and
  - Voluntary departure requests.[112]

For the misrepresentation to be willful, intent to deceive is not necessary. It is sufficient that the person made the false statement deliberately and voluntarily, and that he knew the statement was false.[113]

Only misrepresentations of material facts will make a person inadmissible. In this context, a misrepresentation will be found to be material if: (1) the person was inadmissible on the true facts; or (2) the misrepresentation tended to shut off a line of inquiry that was relevant to the applicant's eligibility, and the line of inquiry might have resulted in a proper determination that he or she not be admitted.[114] When the true facts would not have made the applicant inadmissible, but it has been established that the misrepresentation tended to cut off a relevant line of inquiry, the applicant has the burden of persuasion and production to show that the inquiry would not have resulted in a proper determination that he or she was inadmissible.[115]

Under this ground, only misrepresentations to U.S. government officials (generally a consular officer or an immigration officer) can serve as the basis of inadmissibility.[116] Therefore, buying documents from a private individual does not make a foreign national inadmissible under the ground of procuring a document by fraud or misrepresentation; nor does using false documents to procure an entry into the United States make a foreign national inadmissible, unless they are presented to a U.S. official.[117] The possession, making, purchase, or use of false immigration documents, however, could subject the individual to criminal prosecution or to a civil order of document fraud. This, therefore, could lead to inadmissibility for either conviction or admission of a CMT, or for a final civil order of document fraud (discussed below).

---

[112] 9 FAM N7.1, N7.2 to 22 CFR §40.63.

[113] *Matter of Tijam*, 22 I&N Dec. 408 (BIA 1998).

[114] *Matter of Ng*, 17 I&N Dec. 536 (BIA 1980); *Matter of S and B–C–*, 9 I&N Dec. 436 (AG 1960).

[115] *Matter of Tijam*, 22 I&N Dec. 408 (BIA 1998).

[116] *Matter of Y–G–*, 20 I&N Dec. 794 (BIA 1994); 9 FAM NN 4.3 & 7.1 to 22 CFR §40.63.

[117] *Matter of D–L– & A–M–*, 20 I&N Dec. 409 (BIA 1991); *Matter of Shirdel*, 19 I&N Dec. 33 (BIA 1984).

A timely retraction of a misrepresentation sometimes may prevent it from being considered a basis for inadmissibility.[118] In general, a retraction should be made at the first opportunity.

> – Estella immigrated through her USC husband. During her adjustment interview, she told two lies to the USCIS examiner. First, she told the officer that she had no other relatives living in the United States. Second, she told the officer that she had never been arrested or convicted, when in fact she had been arrested for and convicted of theft and sentenced to a year's imprisonment. When USCIS discovers these lies, she is served with an NTA and charged with being inadmissible under the "willful misrepresentation of material fact" ground. Is this correct?

Yes. The first lie is not material. The fact that Estella has other relatives in the United States would not have made any difference in the outcome of her case. While it was a lie, it was not material and therefore was not fraud. The second lie, however, was material. If the officer had known that Estella had been convicted of theft, he might have determined that she was inadmissible under the criminal inadmissibility grounds. Estella's lie made a difference in the outcome of her case and is therefore material.

Estella may, however, be eligible for the INA §212(i) waiver of the misrepresentation inadmissibility ground.

There are both general and VAWA-specific waivers for the fraud or misrepresentation inadmissibility ground.[119] These waivers are discussed in chapter 6.

False Claim to U.S. Citizenship

A foreign national who falsely represents him- or herself to be a USC, at any time on or after September 30, 1996, and for any purpose or benefit under the INA or any other federal or state law, is inadmissible.[120] This could include false claims of citizenship to an immigration agent for purposes of gaining admission to the United States, as well as false claims of citizenship to a state employee for purposes of obtaining a driver's license or public benefit.

You may have a client who has checked the box marked "I am a citizen or national of the United States" on Form I-9, Employment Eligibility Verification Form. This should not constitute a false claim of citizenship for two reasons. First, checking "I am a citizen or national" may not constitute a specific claim to citizenship. Second, the advocate can argue that a statement made to an employer in order to obtain employment is not done for any purpose under the INA or state or federal law. However, circuit courts that have reviewed this issue have found that a person in this situation

---

[118] 9 FAM 40.63, N.4.6.

[119] INA §212(i).

[120] INA §212(a)(6)(C)(ii).

could not meet his burden of proving that he did not check the box because he believed himself to be a national of the United States.[121]

There is a narrow waiver for certain misrepresentations of U.S. citizenship. This waiver applies only to individuals who (1) are children of USC parents (or former USC parents), including adopted children; (2) resided in the United States before the age of 16; and (3) reasonably believed they were USCs.[122] The law is retroactive to the date of enactment of the Illegal Immigration Reform and Immigrant Responsibility Act of 1996 (IIRAIRA)[123]—September 30, 1996.[124]

Stowaways

Stowaways are inadmissible. There is no specific waiver available for this ground of inadmissibility.[125]

Smugglers and Encouragers of Unlawful Entry

Persons are inadmissible if they have at any time knowingly encouraged, induced, assisted, abetted or aided any other alien to enter the United States illegally.[126] There is no requirement that the smuggling have been for gain. Individuals who qualified for Family Unity *and* who are applying for either Family Unity or an immigrant visa under the immediate relative or the second preference family visa provisions of the INA are not subject to this ground.[127]

There is a waiver for persons who have smuggled immediate family members. This waiver is available to (1) LPRs who are returning from a visit abroad, and (2) applicants for permanent residence who are immediate relatives of USCs or fall under the family-based immigration preferences (other than brothers and sisters of USCs). Even for these individuals, the waiver is available only if the alien they encouraged or assisted to enter illegally was, at the time of the smuggling, their "spouse, parent, son or daughter (and no other individual). The waiver can be granted only if it is deemed to be for humanitarian purposes, to assure family unity, and when it is in the public interest.[128]

Final Civil Document Fraud Order

A foreign national is inadmissible if he or she is subject to a final order for violation of INA §274C, which authorizes civil penalties for making or using false documents, or using documents issued to other persons, for purposes of satisfying any re-

---

[121] *See, e.g., Kirong v. Mukasey*, 529 F.3d 800 (8th Cir. 2008); *Ateka v. Ashcroft*, 384 F.3d 954 (8th Cir. 2004).

[122] INA §212(a)(6)(C)(ii)(II).

[123] IIRAIRA, *supra* note 105.

[124] Child Citizenship Act of 2000, §201(b)(3), Pub. L. No. 106-395, 114 Stat. 1631 (Oct. 30, 2000).

[125] INA §212(a)(6)(D).

[126] INA §212(a)(6)(E).

[127] INA §212(a)(6)(E)(ii).

[128] INA §212(d)(11).

quirement imposed by the INA.[129] Many of these activities also are prohibited under criminal statutes and may be punished criminally. However, to impose civil penalties under INA §274C, an administrative law judge (ALJ) only needs to determine by a preponderance of evidence that the violations have been committed. There is no administrative appeal from an order by an ALJ under this section, and the order becomes final unless the attorney general vacates or modifies it within 30 days of the decision. Once the order becomes final, the affected person has 45 days to file a petition for review of the order with a federal court of appeals.[130]

There is a waiver for this ground of inadmissibility. The waiver is available only to the following: (1) LPRs who temporarily left the country voluntarily and are otherwise admissible; and (2) foreign nationals seeking admission or adjustment based on immediate relative or family-preference petitions who have not previously been fined under §274C and whose offense was committed solely to assist, aid, or support the foreign national's spouse or child and not another individual.[131]

Foreign Students

In 1996, IIRAIRA created a new ground of inadmissibility for foreign students who attend public schools in violation of the restrictions of INA §214(*l*).[132] These persons are inadmissible for a period of five years from the date of the violation. This provision is not retroactive, and applies only to students who obtain (or extend) F-1 student status after November 29, 1996.[133] There is no waiver of the five-year bar.

Not in Possession of Immigration Document

Immigrants are inadmissible if, at the time of application for admission, they are not in possession of a valid unexpired immigrant visa, reentry permit, border crossing identification card, or other required valid entry document, or if they have a visa that has been issued without compliance with the visa provisions of INA §203.[134] There is a waiver available for this ground of inadmissibility if the immigrant did not know of, and could not have known of, the invalid visa.[135]

Ineligible for Citizenship

Immigrants are inadmissible if they are *ineligible to citizenship*.[136] By *ineligible to citizenship*, the INA refers to persons who are permanently barred from becoming USCs because of laws relating to military service.[137] In addition, any person who has

---

[129] INA §212(a)(6)(F).

[130] INA §274C.

[131] INA §212(d)(12).

[132] INA §212(a)(6)(G).

[133] IIRAIRA §346.

[134] INA §212(a)(7)(A).

[135] INA §212(k).

[136] INA §212(a)(8)(A).

[137] INA §101(a)(19).

left or remained outside the United States to avoid or evade military training or service in a time of war or a period of national emergency is inadmissible.[138] This does not apply to a person who was a nonimmigrant at the time of departure and seeks to reenter the United States as a nonimmigrant.[139]

Prior Removal Orders or Periods of Unlawful Presence

Under INA §212(a)(9), persons are inadmissible based on certain immigration violations. The section is divided into three categories:

1. Foreign nationals previously ordered excluded, deported, or removed.[140]

2. Foreign nationals who were unlawfully present in the United States for specified periods of time and now seek admission following a voluntary departure or removal.[141]

3. Foreign nationals who enter or attempt to enter the United States without authorization after having been ordered removed previously.[142]

Each of these categories is discussed below.

Having Been Removed Previously

Persons who have been ordered removed are inadmissible for a certain period of time. The length of the inadmissibility period depends upon the section of law under which the person was ordered removed and on the person's immigration history. Persons ordered removed in INA §235(b) expedited removal proceedings, or ordered removed after INA §240 removal proceedings initiated on their arrival in the United States (in other words, the equivalent of exclusion proceedings under pre-IIRAIRA law) are inadmissible for five years after their removal. Other persons who have been ordered deported or removed or who departed the United States under an order of deportation or removal are inadmissible for 10 years. Individuals are inadmissible for 20 years after a second removal, and forever if they were convicted of an aggravated felony.[143]

> – Juan came to the United States, was caught at the airport, and unsuccessfully sought asylum before the IJ. He was deported to Colombia in 2007. He wants to know if it is possible that he will be allowed to return to the United States in the next few months, because he really wants to visit his 4-year-old USC daughter whom he had to leave behind and who is now ill. Will Juan be allowed to return to the United States this year?

The general rule is that Juan is inadmissible for five years after his removal in 2007, and thus would not be eligible for admission until at least 2012. However, it

---

[138] INA §212(a)(8)(B).

[139] INA §212(a)(8)(B).

[140] INA §212(a)(9)(A).

[141] INA §212(a)(9)(B).

[142] INA §212(a)(9)(C).

[143] INA §212(a)(9)(A).

may be possible for Juan to obtain a "consent [for the alien] to reapply" for admission under INA §212(a)(9)(A)(iii) (See discussion below).

This ground of inadmissibility took effect on April 1, 1997. The person must reside outside the United States for the required period (five, 10, or 20 years) before seeking admission again.[144] This rule applies retroactively, so that foreign nationals who were subject to the prior five-year bar based on a deportation must now wait 10 years.[145]

Not every person who has been apprehended by ICE will be subject to this inadmissibility ground. A person who was granted voluntary departure by either ICE or an IJ, and who left the United States on his or her own by the specified date, is not subject to this inadmissibility ground.[146] However, persons who leave the United States at their own expense after an IJ has entered a deportation or removal order against them are considered to have self-deported or self-removed and are subject to this ground.[147]

This ground of inadmissibility does not apply to persons who received a final order but who have not subsequently left the United States.[148] Those persons may be able to adjust their status before the IJ if they are successful in reopening their proceedings.

To ameliorate the harshness of this inadmissibility ground, an immigration officer is authorized to waive inadmissibility by granting, not a waiver, but a "consent [for the alien] to reapply" for admission.[149] If the person has entered the United States already, he or she may still request the government's consent to reenter with an I-212 waiver.[150] If granted, the consent is deemed to date back to before the reentry. However, if the person reentered illegally, ICE is required to *reinstate* the deportation or removal order, denying the person the opportunity to apply for adjustment or any other form of relief (except for withholding of removal).[151]

This area of the law is currently in flux, with the BIA, various circuit courts, and USCIS weighing in with various interpretations of when a foreign national who unlawfully reentered after removal can file an I-212 in conjunction with an application for adjustment of status.[152] Most circuit courts have decided that the filing of an adjustment of status application with a waiver does not protect someone from rein-

---

[144] INA §212(a)(9)(A).

[145] DOS Cable, 98-State-060539 (April 4, 1998), *reprinted in* 75 *Interpreter Releases* 791–794, 792 (May 12, 1997).

[146] INS Memorandum, L. Crocetti, "3/10 Year Bars and Section 245(i)" (May 1, 1997), *published on* AILA InfoNet at Doc. No. 97050191 (*posted* May. 1, 1997).

[147] 8 CFR §241.7.

[148] Crocetti Memo, *supra* note 146.

[149] INA §212(a)(9)(A)(iii); 8 CFR §212.2.

[150] 8 CFR §§212.2(e), (f).

[151] INA §241(a)(5).

[152] *See e.g.*, *Matter of Torres-Garcia*, 23 I&N Dec. 866 (BIA 2006).

statement of removal.[153] VAWA 2005[154] provisions also contain guidance on the I-212. In response to the issues raised by the Ninth Circuit's decision in *Perez-Gonzalez v. Ashcroft*,[155] which held that a foreign national who illegally reentered after removal could file for adjustment of status in conjunction with an I-212 application before the prior removal order was reinstated, USCIS issued a memorandum on I-212 applications.[156] See chapter 6 for a further discussion of the I-212 waiver.

Reinstatement itself is a complex issue and has been the subject of a number of recent decisions, including a decision by the Supreme Court. The Court, in *Fernandez-Vargas v. Gonzales*,[157] resolved one of the more significant splits that had developed between the circuits on this issue, regarding the retroactive application of the reinstatement provisions in INA §241(a)(5). Unfortunately, the Court held that INA §241(a)(5) can be applied to individuals who last reentered the United States prior to April 1, 1997, and took no affirmative steps to obtain lawful status before that date However, the decision left many issues unresolved. A more detailed discussion of reinstatement is in chapter 1.

Unlawful Presence Bars

Persons "Unlawfully Present." Departing the United States after being unlawfully present will make a person inadmissible. The length of the inadmissibility period depends on the duration of the unlawful presence, and there are special rules for calculating unlawful presence. Persons who are unlawfully present in the United States after April 1, 1997, for more than 180 days but less than one year and who then voluntarily depart the United States before commencement of removal proceedings, are inadmissible for a period of three years after their departure.[158] Persons who are unlawfully present after April 1, 1997, for one year or more and who depart are inadmissible for 10 years after their departure.[159]

The three-year bar provisions apply only to persons who voluntarily depart the United States before the commencement of removal proceedings. If removal proceedings have begun, the person will not be subject to the three-year bar, although he or she may be subject to the ten-year bar. This means that persons who leave the United States under voluntary departure granted by an IJ will not be subject to the three-year bar and will be subject to the ten-year bar only if they accumulated a year or more of unlawful presence. "Voluntarily departed" includes voluntary departure granted by

---

[153] *See, e.g., Delgado v. Mukasey*, 516 F.3d 65 (2d Cir. 2008); *Lino v. Gonzales*, 467 F.3d 1077 (7th Cir. 2006); *but see also Perez-Gonzalez v. Ashcroft*, 379 F.3d 783 (9th Cir. 2004) and *Duran-Gonzales v. DHS*, 508 F.3d 1227 (9th Cir. 2007).

[154] VAWA 2005, *supra* note 19.

[155] *Perez-Gonzalez v. Ashcroft*, 379 F.3d 783 (9th Cir. 2004).

[156] *See* USCIS Memorandum, M. Aytes, "Effect of *Perez-Gonzalez v. Ashcroft* on adjudication of Form I-212 applications filed by aliens who are subject to reinstated removal orders under INA §241(a)(5)" (March 31, 2006), *published on* AILA InfoNet at Doc. No. 06080967 (posted Aug. 9, 2006).

[157] *Fernandez-Vargas v. Gonzales*, 548 U.S. 30 (2006).

[158] INA §212(a)(9)(B)(i)(I).

[159] INA §212(a)(9)(B)(i)(II).

the IJ, as well as voluntary departure granted by ICE prior to the initiation of proceedings. It also may apply to persons who simply left the United States on their own initiative.

In contrast, the ten-year bar applies regardless of whether the person departed before or after commencement of removal proceedings. It also does not matter for the ten-year bar whether the person departed voluntarily or under removal.

If ICE charges a client with this ground of inadmissibility on the NTA, the advocate must look at the case to see whether the periods of stay actually qualify as unlawful presence. There are several special rules, set out below, for calculating unlawful presence. There also are two exceptions to this inadmissibility ground for VAWA self-petitioners. Finally, there is a general waiver at INA §212(a)(9)(B)(v), which is discussed in more detail in chapter 6.

Determining Unlawful Presence

The INA sets out very specific rules for calculation of periods of unlawful presence:[160]

1. Periods of unlawful presence in the United States are not counted in the aggregate; instead, each period is counted separately. Thus, this bar does not apply to a person with multiple periods of unlawful presence if no single period exceeded 180 days.[161]

2. Under this ground, *unlawfully present* means that the person is present after overstaying an authorized period of stay, or is present without being admitted or paroled.[162] For foreign nationals who entered with a nonimmigrant visa and then violate the terms of the visa (*e.g.*, by working without authorization), unlawful presence begins only after an immigration officer or an IJ determines that the person violated status.[163]

3. No period of time prior to April 1, 1997, (the effective date of IIRAIRA) counts as unlawful presence.[164]

4. No period of time in which the noncitizen is under 18 years of age is counted as unlawful presence.[165]

5. The three- and ten-year bars to admissibility apply only to persons "who have previously physically departed the United States and are now either seeking admission or have entered or attempted to enter the United States without being inspected." This

---

[160] INA §§212(a)(9)(B)(iii), (iv).

[161] INS Memorandum, P. Virtue, "Additional Guidance for Implementing Sections 212(a)(6) and 212(a)(9) of the INA" (June 17, 1997), *published on* AILA InfoNet at Doc. No. 97061790 (*posted* June 17, 1997).

[162] INA §212(a)(9)(B)(ii).

[163] INS Memorandum, P. Virtue, "Section 212(a)(9)(B) Relating to Unlawful Presence" (Sept. 19, 1997), *published on* AILA InfoNet at Doc. No. 97092240 (*posted* Sep. 22, 1997).

[164] IIRAIRA §301(b)(3).

[165] INA §212(a)(9)(B)(iii)(I).

means that the bars do not apply to persons applying for adjustment of status who have not left the United States after accumulating unlawful presence.[166] Even a departure under advance parole will trigger the unlawful presence bars.[167]

6. For purposes of the unlawful presence inadmissibility grounds, ICE and USCIS consider the following classes of persons to be present in the United States pursuant to a period of authorized stay:

- Persons with properly filed applications for adjustment of status under INA §§245(a) or 245(i), including foreign nationals who, in removal proceedings, renew adjustment applications that were denied by the, but not including foreign nationals who first apply for adjustment when in removal proceedings.[168]

- Foreign nationals admitted to the United States as refugees under INA §207.[169]

- Foreign nationals granted asylum under INA §208.[170]

- Foreign nationals granted withholding of deportation/removal under INA §241(b)(3) or its predecessor, INA §243(h).[171]

- Foreign nationals granted relief under the Convention Against Torture.[172]

- Foreign nationals under a current grant of deferred enforced departure (DED) pursuant to an order issued by the president.[173]

- Foreign nationals under a current grant of temporary protected status (TPS).[174]

- Cuban/Haitian entrants under Public Law 99-603 §202(b).[175]

- Foreign nationals granted voluntary departure, during the period of time allowed.[176]

- Foreign nationals who have filed an application for legalization under either of the two amnesty programs, excluding "late amnesty" applicants.[177]

---

[166] INS Memorandum, P. Virtue, *supra* note 161; INS Memorandum, P. Virtue, "Implementation of Section 212(a)(6)(A) and 212(a)(9) Grounds of Inadmissibility" (March 31, 1997), *reprinted at* 74 *Interpreter Releases* 578 (April 7, 1997).

[167] INS Memorandum, P. Virtue, "Advance Parole for Aliens Unlawfully Present in the United States for More than 180 Days" (Nov. 26, 1997), *reprinted at* 74 *Interpreter Releases* 1864 (Dec. 8, 1997).

[168] INS Memorandum, P. Virtue, *supra* note 161.

[169] *Id.*

[170] *Id.*

[171] *Id.*

[172] INS Memorandum, M. Pearson, "Period of Stay Authorized by the AG for Purposes of Section 212(a)(9)(B) of the INA," (March 3, 2000), *published on* AILA InfoNet at Doc. No. 00030774 (*posted* Mar. 7, 2000). *See also* Convention Against Torture and Other Cruel, Inhuman or Degrading Treatment or Punishment, Dec. 10, 1984, 1465 U.N.T.S. 85 (entered into force June 26, 1987).

[173] INS Memorandum, P. Virtue, *supra* note 161.

[174] *Id.*

[175] *Id.*

[176] INS Memorandum, P. Virtue, *supra* note 163.

[177] INS Memorandum, M. Pearson, *supra* note 172.

- Foreign nationals who have filed a bona fide asylum application during the pendency of the application, provided the foreign nationals did not work without authorization.[178]

- Persons who have applied for registry under INA §249 during the application period, including removal proceedings and BIA appeal.[179]

- Foreign nationals who have been granted Family Unity during the authorized period.[180]

- Applicants for adjustment of status pursuant to the Nicaraguan Adjustment and Central American Relief Act §202.[181]

- Conditional resident aliens who have had their status terminated by USCIS or ICE, but who have appealed that determination administratively, through the appeals process.[182]

- Nonimmigrants who have made a timely, nonfrivolous application for an extension of stay or change of status, and who have not been employed without authorization pending the adjudication during the pendency of the application.[183]

- Foreign nationals with deferred action status.[184]

7. Persons who are *not* considered to be in a period of authorized stay under this ground include the following:

- Foreign nationals under an order of supervision (pending removal).

- Foreign nationals with pending applications for cancellation of removal.

- Foreign nationals with pending applications for withholding of removal.

- Asylum applicants who have worked without employment authorization.

- Foreign nationals in removal or deportation proceedings, unless found to be not deportable. If I-94 expires while in proceedings, unlawful presence begins on date of deportation order. If the individual is granted relief from deportation by an IJ, unlawful presence ends on date of order.

- Foreign nationals present pursuant to pending federal court litigation.[185]

---

[178] INA §212(a)(9)(B)(iii)(II).

[179] INS Memorandum, J. Williams, "Unlawful Presence" (Jun. 12, 2002), *published on* AILA InfoNet at Doc. No. 02062040 (*posted* June 20, 2002).

[180] INA §212(a)(9)(B)(iii)(II).

[181] INS Memorandum, M. Pearson, *supra* note 172. *See also* Nicaraguan Adjustment and Central American Relief Act, Pub. L. No. 105-100, tit. II, 111 Stat. 2160, 2193–201 (1997).

[182] INS Memorandum, P. Virtue, *supra* note 163.

[183] INA §212(a)(9)(B)(iv); INS Memorandum, M. Pearson, *supra* note 172.

[184] Williams Memo, *supra* note 179.

[185] *See* INS Memorandum, P. Virtue, *supra* note 163.

There is a VAWA exception to the unlawful presence inadmissibility ground. Under that exception, a VAWA self-petitioner is not subject to the unlawful presence inadmissibility ground if he or she can show a substantial connection between the violation of the person's nonimmigrant visa and the abuse he or she suffered.[186] This exception has a severe limitation, however, because it applies only to persons whose status is unlawful because they have overstayed a visa. It does not apply to persons who entered without authorization.

Because of the unusual wording of the unlawful presence exceptions, advocates contend that there is a second possible exception, which applies to self-petitioners who entered before April 1, 1997. Under this exception, self-petitioners who entered before April 1, 1997, are completely exempt from the unlawful presence inadmissibility ground.[187] This is a broader exception, because it provides that the unlawful presence ground simply does not apply to VAWA self-petitioners who entered before April 1, 1997.

Not all self-petitioners who entered on or after April 1, 1997, will be able to show the required connection between the violation and the unlawful presence. For example, a self-petitioner may have become unlawfully present for more than one year prior to meeting his or her spouse. In this situation, it might not be possible to show the required connection. Instead, the advocate should carefully analyze the situation to verify that the client has really acquired unlawful presence in a sufficient amount to meet the elements of the inadmissibility ground and, if so, whether a waiver is available.

Reentering the United States Without Authorization

A more severe ground of inadmissibility applies to a foreign national who has been unlawfully present in the United States for an aggregate period of one year or more and who then enters or attempts to reenter the United States without authorization.[188] By definition, this applies to persons who enter or attempt to enter illegally on or after April 1, 1997.[189] In contrast to the three– and ten-year bars for unlawful presence, however, the one-year period of unlawful presence for purposes of INA

---

[186] INA §§212(a)(9)(B)(iii)(IV), (a)(6)(A)(ii).

[187] This unlawful presence exception at INA §212(a)(9)(B)(iii)(IV) is defined in terms of the VAWA exception to unlawful presence, found at INA §212(a)(6)(A)(ii). That provision was included in the INA by IIRAIRA and contained a special provision for persons arriving before April 1, 1997. IIRAIRA §301(c)(2) states: "(2) Transition for Battered Spouse or Child Provision. The requirements of subclauses (II) and (III) of section 212(a)(6)(A)(ii) of the Immigration and Nationality Act, as inserted by paragraph (1), shall not apply to an alien who demonstrate that the alien first arrived in the United States before the title III-A effective date (described in section 309(a) of this division [Sec. 309(a) of IIRAIRA]." As so described in IIRAIRA §309(a), the "title III-A effective date" is "the first day of the first month beginning more than 180 days after the date of the enactment of this Act [enacted Sept. 30, 1996]." The effective date of the INA §212(a)(9)(B)(iii)(IV) exception is thus determined by the effective date of the INA §212(a)(6)(ii) exception.

[188] INA §212(a)(9)(C)(i)(I).

[189] INS Memorandum, P. Virtue, *supra* note 161.

§212(a)(9)(C) requires only an *aggregate period* of one year or more.[190] Thus, if several periods of unlawful presence taken together equal one year, the person falls under this inadmissibility ground.

A similar ground of inadmissibility applies to a person who has been ordered removed under any provision of law and who then enters or attempts to reenter the United States without authorization.[191] This covers persons who were ordered removed, deported, or excluded at any time and who entered or attempted to reenter the United States unlawfully on or after April 1, 1997.[192]

Persons who are inadmissible under INA §212(a)(9)(C) are permanently inadmissible, with no relief available until 10 years after their last departure from the United States. Only at that time may DHS may consider a request for permission to reapply for admission.

There is a special waiver of the INA §212(a)(9)(C) inadmissibility ground for VAWA self-petitioners, if there is a connection between the abuse the self-petitioner suffered and the self-petitioner's:

- Removal;
- Departure from the United States;
- Reentry or reentries into the United States; or
- Attempted reentry into the United States.[193]

A more detailed discussion of the special INA §212(a)(9)(C) waiver is in chapter 6.

Miscellaneous Grounds

The *miscellaneous* inadmissibility grounds, found at INA §212(a)(10)(A), concern:

- Practicing polygamists;
- Guardians required to accompany excluded foreign nationals;
- International child abductors;
- "Unlawful voters;" and
- Former citizens who renounced their citizenship in order to avoid taxation.

Because these grounds arise only infrequently, this chapter will not provide an in-depth analysis of them.

---

[190] INS Memorandum, P. Virtue, "Implementation of Section 212(a)(6)(A) and 212(a)(9) grounds of inadmissibility" (March 31, 1997), *reprinted at* 74 *Interpreter Releases* 578 (April 7, 1997), and *published on* AILA InfoNet at Doc. No. 97033190 (*posted* Mar. 31, 1997).

[191] INA §212(a)(9)(C)(i)(II).

[192] INS Memorandum, P. Virtue, *supra* note 161.

[193] INA §212(a)(9)(C)(ii).

Removal proceedings in the immigration court fall into three basic stages: bond proceedings (covered in chapter 1); determination of removability; and, if the respondent is deemed removable, applications for one or more of the various types of relief from removal (covered in chapters 5 through 12). As can be imagined from the number of chapters devoted to it, relief from removal is often the focal point of a removal proceeding, and, not infrequently, the respondent simply will concede removability and proceed on to the relief from removal stage of the proceedings. Nonetheless, removability is not at all a foregone conclusion, and advocates should scrutinize the facts and charging document closely to determine whether removability itself can be contested.

This chapter explores ways to defend a respondent in removal proceedings, concentrating on removal proceedings under the Immigration and Nationality Act (INA)[1] §240. It begins by considering three preliminary considerations:

- Whether the respondent is a U.S. citizen (USC), in which case he or she is not subject to removability;

- Whether the respondent is removable; and

- Even if the respondent is possibly removable, whether U.S. Immigration and Customs Enforcement (ICE) might be willing to exercise prosecutorial discretion.

Following these preliminary considerations, the chapter will examine the burdens and standards of proof in removal proceedings, how to evaluate the sufficiency of ICE's evidence, and the possibility of raising a motion to suppress evidence obtained in violation of the U.S. Constitution.

Three Preliminary Considerations in Removal Proceedings

Is the Individual a U.S. Citizen?

The first question to ask in challenging deportability is whether the respondent could be a USC. USCs are not subject to removal, and a person might be a citizen without knowing it. As discussed below, a person can either acquire or derive citizenship. Bear in mind that one of the respondents' parents also may have obtained citizenship through a USC parent, so that neither the respondent nor his or her parent may realize that he or she is a citizen. This means that researching back one or more generations to determine whether the individual is a citizen sometimes is necessary.

---

[1] Immigration and Nationality Act of 1952 (INA), Pub. L. No. 82-414, 66 Stat. 163 (codified as amended at 8 USC §§1101 *et seq.*).

In removal proceedings, the burden is on the government to prove *alienage* by "clear, convincing, and unequivocal evidence of foreign birth."[2] However, a person born abroad is, prima facie, presumed to be an *alien* in the legal sense of the term.[3] Once foreign birth has been established, the burden then shifts and the suspected individual must overcome this presumption in order to establish that they are, in fact, a USC.[4] "If the deportee can produce substantial credible evidence in support of his or her citizenship claim;" however, "thereby rebutting the presumption, [the Department of Homeland Security's (DHS)] burden of proving deportability by clear and convincing evidence again comes into play."[5] While an immigration judge (IJ) is not permitted to declare an individual a citizen, he or she must terminate proceedings if ICE cannot prove alienage by clear and convincing evidence.

Acquisition of Citizenship

A person may have acquired U.S. citizenship either by birth in the United States or by birth abroad if at least one USC parent meets the relevant requirements of residence in the United States.[6] The law governing how long a citizen must have resided in the United States in order to convey citizenship to a child born abroad has changed over the years. The length of time the parent must have lived in the United States before his or her child born abroad will acquire citizenship depends on the law in effect on the date of the child's birth and whether the child was born in or out of wedlock. For example, for children born in wedlock on or after November 14, 1986, to one USC and one alien parent, the USC parent must have been physically present in the United States or its possessions for at least five years prior to the child's birth, two of which were after the parent turned 14 years of age. Charts setting out the requirements for acquisition of citizenship by children born abroad are included as Appendix 9.

- ICE has charged Maria, who was born in 1988, with being removable on the basis of being present in the United States without admission. Maria tells you that her mother was born in the United States, and that her father was born in Mexico. Maria's mother lived in the United States until she was 17, when she moved to Mexico and later met and married Maria's father. Maria has a Mexican passport.

Maria appears to be a USC. Her mother was born in the United States and appears to have lived there the required period of time to be able to confer her citizenship upon her child born abroad. Maria's counsel should file a motion to terminate the removal proceedings, since Maria is a citizen and therefore not subject to removability.

---

[2] *Woodby v. INS,* 385 U.S. 276 (1966); 8 CFR §1240.8(c).

[3] *Matter of A–M–,* 7 I&N Dec. 322 (1965).

[4] *Id.; Matter of Leyva,* 16 I&N Dec. 118 (BIA 1977).

[5] *Murphy v. INS,* 54 F.3d 605 (9th Cir. 1995).

[6] INA §§301, 309.

In addition, a child may obtain citizenship derivatively, upon the naturalization of his or her parent. In determining whether an individual derived citizenship, the law in effect when the last material condition is met is generally controlling.[7] Under the Child Citizenship Protection Act of 2001[8] (effective February 27, 2001), a child born outside the United States automatically becomes a citizen when all of the following conditions occur:

- At least one parent is a citizen, by birth or naturalization;

- The child is under 18 years of age; and

- The child is a lawful permanent resident (LPR) residing in the United States in the legal and physical custody of the citizen parent.[9]

It is not necessary that the parent have legal custody at the time of the parent's naturalization; it is sufficient that all of these factors occur before the child's 18th birthday.[10] Unfortunately, the act does not apply retroactively, and those who turned 18 before February 21, 2001 cannot derive citizenship under it.[11] However, such individuals may have derived citizenship under the provisions in effect before they turned 18.[12] If an individual born abroad has a claim to U.S. citizenship, a motion to terminate should be filed along with credible evidence that the individual has either acquired or derived citizenship under the applicable legal provisions. Solid evidence of citizenship (*e.g.*, a U.S. passport or a certificate of citizenship) can and should be submitted if obtainable, but other credible evidence indicating that all requirements for citizenship have been met also is acceptable.

– Harry was born in Haiti on Novem-

> **PRACTICE TIP**
> **Obtaining a Passport**
>
> A first-time passport applicant must appear in person at a passport office and submit an application, along with proof of identity and citizenship. A person may become a USC through any of several routes, and evidence must be presented to show that the requirements of the particular route in question are met. For example, proof of citizenship can be a birth certificate, certificate of citizenship, or the applicant's parents' naturalization certificates, birth certificates, or passports. Persons claiming citizenship through birth abroad to a USC also must submit evidence that the parents meet the physical presence requirements. This evidence could be an affidavit by the parents or other persons knowledgeable about the parents' stay in the United States, or documents such as the parents' school, employment, or medical records.
>
> **PRACTICE TIP**
> **Obtaining a Certificate of Citizenship**
>
> A certificate of citizenship establishes that a person who was born outside the United States was a citizen at birth or became a citizen through derivation. The application is filed on Form N-600, along with photographs, the filing fee, and proof of citizenship of the same type presented to support an application for a passport. The applicant will be examined under oath by U.S. Citizenship and Immigration Services (USCIS). However, there is no swearing-in, since the person only is seeking proof that he or she is already a USC.

---

[7] *Matter of Rodriguez-Tejedor*, 23 I&N Dec. 153 (BIA 2001).

[8] Child Citizenship Protection Act of 2001, Pub. L. No. 106-395, 114 Stat. 1631.

[9] INA §320.

[10] *Matter of Baires-Larios*, 24 I&N Dec. 467 (BIA 2008).

[11] *Matter of Rodriguez-Tejedor*, *supra* note 7.

[12] *See* the derivation charts included as appendices.

ber 1, 1983. He was admitted to the United States as an LPR in 1991. His father naturalized on April 1, 2001. Until the age of 18, he lived with both his parents. He was placed in removal proceedings after being convicted of a theft offense with a sentence of 16 months. In removal proceedings, Harry files a motion to terminate with a copy of his father's naturalization certificate, a copy of his birth certificate, a copy of his green card, a notarized letter from his father indicating that he always had legal and physical custody of his son until his son turned 18, and copies of his parents' 2001 tax return listing Harry as a dependent living in the same household. The IJ grants the motion to terminate, finding that Harry has submitted substantial credible evidence of citizenship and ICE cannot prove alienage by clear and convincing evidence.

Even if the Respondent Is Not a USC, Are They Actually Subject to Removal?

The advocate must not concede removability unless he or she is absolutely certain that the respondent is, in fact, removable. DHS often overreaches in its determinations that respondents actually are removable from the United States. If there is any argument that the respondent is not removable as charged, it is critical that the advocate make the argument. This is discussed in more detail below.

Prosecutorial Discretion

If an individual is detained by DHS or has been or will be placed in some sort of removal proceedings, the advocate may request that the government exercise prosecutorial discretion in his or her case. In its exercise of prosecutorial discretion, the government may decline to institute removal proceedings and/or may grant the individual deferred action status, allowing the individual to remain in the United States for a certain period of time, possibly with employment authorization. This is particularly helpful if the individual appears to be removable and if there is no form of relief from removal that would regularize his or her status immediately. The government's prosecutorial discretion does not allow it to grant permanent or lawful immigration status, however, to persons who otherwise are ineligible.

There are formal guidelines setting forth standards for the exercise of prosecutorial discretion. However, these guidelines make it clear that the government has the power to decide on a case-by-case basis whether to initiate removal proceedings against an individual, as well as conduct other law enforcement actions or investigations.

The factors that the government will use in determining whether to exercise prosecutorial discretion favorably for a foreign national include the following:

- Immigration status;
- Length of residence in the United States;
- Criminal history;
- Humanitarian concerns;
- Immigration history;

- Likelihood of ultimately removing the foreign national or achieving enforcement goal;

- Eligibility for other immigration relief;

- Effect of the action on future admissibility;

- Current or past cooperation with law enforcement authorities;

- Honorable U.S. military service;

- Community attention; and

- Resources available to the government.[13]

Prosecutorial Discretion to Decline to Institute Removal Proceedings

In its exercise of prosecutorial discretion, the government may decline to institute removal proceedings or some other procedure and/or may grant the individual deferred action status, allowing the individual to remain in the United States for a certain period of time, possibly with employment authorization. This is particularly helpful if the individual appears to be removable, and if there is no form of relief from removal that would regularize his or her status immediately. It is also particularly important in situations where a foreign national is statutorily eligible for and has already applied for some benefit—*i.e.,* adjustment of status or naturalization—but also is at least arguably removable. If the reviewing agency (often USCIS, but sometimes ICE or U.S. Customs and Border Patrol (CBP)) indicates that it believes the applicant is removable, practitioners should immediately ask the agency to exercise its prosecutorial discretion to approve the application instead of placing the applicant in removal proceedings.

A formal request for prosecutorial discretion and/or deferred action status is usually made by a letter to the local director of the agency handling the case (usually USCIS or ICE), with a copy going to the adjudicator or officer directly assigned to the case and to his or her supervisor. Evidence supporting the request should be attached to the letter. If the request is for deferred action status pending the foreign national's expected obtaining of a certain visa or status, the applicant should attach documentation of that status, such as a visa petition, an approval notice, or evidence that the person appears eligible for a particular visa or other relief and will be applying for it. The letters should be sent by certified mail, return receipt requested. Follow-up calls to discuss the request in more detail are almost always advisable.

Prosecutorial Discretion During Removal Proceedings: Joining or Not Opposing Motions to Administratively Close or Motions to Terminate

If a Notice to Appear (NTA) has been filed already with the immigration court and jurisdiction thus has shifted to the IJ, practitioners can ask ICE to exercise of its prosecutorial discretion by joining in or at least not opposing particular motions. This

---

[13] INS Memorandum, D. Meissner, "Exercising Prosecutorial Discretion" (Nov. 17, 2000), *published on* AILA InfoNet at Doc. No. 00112702 (*posted* Nov. 27, 2000),

is particularly critical when making a motion to terminate or a motion to administratively close when an individual is at least arguably removable.

Motions to Close Administratively

If the individual is in any sort of proceedings before the immigration court, it may be appropriate in certain circumstances to ask that such proceedings be administratively closed, particularly when a new form of relief has come into existence. However, a case may not be closed administratively if either party opposes closure.[14] Administrative closure effectively puts a case into *hibernation*—*i.e.,* the case is not terminated but is placed in inactive status. For example, after Congress passed the Nicaraguan Adjustment and Central American Relief Act,[15] the immigration court granted respondents' motions to close the case administratively in order to allow them to apply for relief under the new act with the Immigration and Naturalization Service (legacy INS). The regulations also provide that respondents who appear eligible for the V visa also should move to close their cases administratively in order to apply for the visa.[16] The proceedings may be reopened by either party filing a motion to re-calendar.

Motions to Terminate

An IJ can and must terminate proceedings when he or she finds that a respondent is not removable as charged on the NTA, even if ICE opposes termination. An IJ also may terminate proceedings to allow a respondent to proceed on a naturalization application if he or she finds that the requirements at 8 Code of Federal Regulations (CFR) §1239.2(f) have been met and a communication of prima facie eligibility for naturalization has been sent by DHS to the respondent.[17] In all other situations, however, an IJ will terminate proceedings only if both parties agree to termination.

While it is often difficult to get ICE to exercise its discretion to join or not oppose a motion to terminate in cases involving criminal issues, practitioners may have particularly strong arguments for prosecutorial discretion when an applicant is not eligible for a particular form of relief before the IJ but would be eligible for relief before USCIS if proceedings were terminated. For example, pursuant to the U visa regulations, applicants for a U visa may ask ICE to terminate removal proceedings while a petition for U nonimmigrant status is being adjudicated by USCIS.[18] As another example, practitioners might ask ICE to join in motions to terminate in cases involving abused spouses or children of LPRs with approved I-360s whose priority dates are not current and who either do not qualify for or have weak Violence Against Women and Department of Justice Reauthorization Act of 2005 (VAWA)[19] cancellation

---

[14] *Matter of Gutierrez*, 21 I&N Dec. 479 (BIA 1996).

[15] Nicaraguan Adjustment and Central American Relief Act, Pub. L. No. 105-100, tit. II, 111 Stat. 2160, 2193–201 (1997).

[16] 8 CFR §214.15.

[17] *See Matter of Acosta Hidalgo*, 24 I&N Dec. 103 (BIA 2007).

[18] 8 CFR §214.14(c).

[19] Violence Against Women and Department of Justice Reauthorization Act of 2005 (VAWA 2005), Pub. L. No. 109-162, 119 Stat. 2960 (2006).

cases. If proceedings are terminated these respondents could be given deferred action status while waiting for their priority dates to become current, a status that would allow them to work and qualify for certain public benefits until they are eligible to adjust status.

In 2005, ICE issued a memorandum indicating that it will exercise its prosecutorial discretion to join in or file a motion to terminate proceedings without prejudice in certain instances. The instances relate to cases where adjustment of status applications currently pending before the IJ are deemed by ICE to be approvable by USCIS (in order to allow for a focus on "priority" cases). However, the memorandum sets out that ICE will not move or agree to termination where an asylum application also is pending. The memorandum also states that in the absence of "unique or special circumstances," ICE will not join in a motion to terminate or move to terminate in cases involving threats to national security, human rights violators, criminal convictions, or cases requiring an INA §212(h) or §212(i) waiver.[20]

If the foreign national is in removal proceedings, a request for prosecutorial discretion is usually first made informally to the ICE trial attorney assigned to the case and/or his or her supervisor. If this informal request is denied, a formal written request should be sent to the head of the ICE district counsel's office and the ICE district director, with a copy to the same trial attorney and his or her supervisor. Evidence supporting the request should be attached to the written request. This written request should be sent by certified mail, return receipt requested, and followed up on via telephone to discuss the matter further.

The Decision to Concede or Contest Removability

It is a fairly common practice in proceedings before the immigration court for advocates and their clients to admit the factual allegations contained in the NTA, concede the charge against the respondent, and concentrate their energies on the next stage of the removal proceedings (*i.e.*, the applications for relief from removal). Advocates never should take this step, however, without carefully scrutinizing the NTA, assessing ICE's evidence and any rebuttal evidence available to the respondent, and evaluating the immigration consequences of the removal ground urged against the respondent.

> **PRACTICE TIP**
> **Procedural Rules**
>
> The procedural rules for the immigration court are found in four places: the EOIR *Immigration Court Practice Manual,* INA §240, 8 CFR §1003.12–1003.65, and 8 CFR §§1240.1–1240.13. Advocates must be familiar with these three sets of instructions in order to practice effectively before the immigration court.

For example, because of the dire immigration consequences of a criminal conviction, particularly a conviction for an aggravated felony, advocates should think very carefully before admitting and conceding removability based on a criminal conviction. An admission and concession may still be in order, however, if the criminal conviction is for a relatively minor offense, the advocate is certain that ICE can bear

---

[20] *See* ICE Memorandum, W. Howard, "Exercising Prosecutorial Discretion to Dismiss Adjustment Cases" (Oct. 6, 2005), *published on* AILA InfoNet at Doc. No. 05101360 (*posted* Oct. 13, 2005).

its burden of proof, and there is a strong case for relief from removal. Nevertheless, in general, the NTA allegations and charges should not be admitted for a respondent with a criminal conviction. Similarly, in part because of ICE's tendency to over-charge fraud and in part because of the narrowness of the fraud waiver (described in chapter 6), it is often wise to contest a fraud charge.

Remember that denying the allegations and charges in an NTA is not lying to the immigration court. Rather, it is a means of forcing ICE to meet its burden of proof. If it is the respondent's burden to meet, a charge should be denied whenever there is any possible ground to deny it, and any and all arguments should be made to support the denial.

Challenging the NTA

Removal proceedings commence with issuance and service of the NTA charging document. Procedural and content requirements concerning the NTA are addressed in chapter 1.

The advocate should scrutinize the NTA for facial defects and errors in service. If it does not contain all necessary information or if it was improperly served, counsel should consider filing a motion to terminate the proceedings. Although ICE may is-sue and serve a new NTA, the later date may be beneficial if the noncitizen has be-come eligible for some immigration benefit in the time since the original service. For example, since the issuance of the NTA stops the accumulation of residence in the United States for purposes of Cancellation of Removal Parts A and B, a later-filed NTA might allow the respondent to accumulate the necessary period of residence.

Nonetheless, there may be cases in which strategic considerations indicate that a motion to terminate for the NTA's insufficiency of content or notice would not be advisable. For example, if the defects are easily curable by ICE, and if there is little to gain for the respondent by the motion to terminate, an IJ might view the motion as frivolous or dilatory, and the resulting ill-will might have a detrimental effect on the respondent's case.

There are two principal questions in determining the sufficiency of the NTA:

- First, does the NTA state allegations sufficiently to inform the respondent of the facts upon which the charge is based? For example, if the respondent is charged with deportability for an aggravated felony, does the NTA state the exact provision of INA §101(a)(43) under which the respondent is charged?

- Second, do the allegations support the charge? For example, if the respondent is charged with deportability based on one conviction of a crime of moral turpi-tude (CMT), is the crime actually one of moral turpitude? Was the crime com-mitted within the first five years after the respondent's entry? If the respondent is charged with deportability because of conviction of an aggravated felony, was the offense really an aggravated felony under the definitions found at INA §101(a)(43)?

  - Diego is in removal proceedings based on the deportation ground of having committed an aggravated felony after admission. The NTA states that he was convicted of an aggravated felony, but cites to the general aggravated felony deportation ground, at INA §237(a)(2)(A)(iii), and does not specify which of the offenses included within the definition of *aggravated felony*[21] is at issue. Because of this, the NTA does not tell Diego exactly what he is being charged with, and a motion to terminate might be appropriate. The likely result of the motion to terminate, however, is that ICE will simply amend the NTA to reflect the exact aggravated felony offense on which it bases the charge of deportability.

– ICE serves an NTA on Susana, charging her with being removable based on conviction of a CMT committed within five years after her admission. Susana has been convicted of a crime, and it is arguably one of moral turpitude, but it is clear from the conviction records that this CMT actually was committed more than five years after her admission. Susan's advocate should file a motion to terminate.

ICE may lodge additional or substituted charges of removability at any time during the proceedings. However, the foreign national must be given a reasonable continuance to respond to the additional factual allegations and charges.[22] If proceedings have been completed or terminated, ICE can place a foreign national in removal proceedings again by simply filing a new NTA. However, if ICE does try to issue a new NTA to begin a new proceeding based on facts or arguments that it did or could have litigated in the prior proceeding, practitioners should consider invoking the principles of res judicata and/or estoppel to argue against ICE's attempt at a second bite of the same apple. While these principles are not highly developed in the immigration context at the administrative level and, thus, are largely arguments that will have to be pursued through to the federal court level, they have been applied by the BIA in certain limited contexts.[23]

Burden and Standard of Proof in INA §240 Proceedings

Removal Proceedings Based on Inadmissibility

Arriving foreign nationals bear the burden of proving that they are clearly and beyond doubt entitled to be admitted and are not inadmissible.[24] There is an exception to this for returning LPRs. For these foreign nationals, the Supreme Court has held that they are entitled to have the government bear the burden of proof in establishing their inadmissibility.[25]

---

[21] INA §101(a)(43).

[22] 8 CFR §§1003.30, 1240.10(e).

[23] *See e.g. Matter of Fedorenko*, 19 I&N Dec. 57 (BIA 1984) (applying the doctrine of collateral estoppel in a deportation proceeding). *See also Matter of Amaya-Saenz*, A90-897-254, (BIA Aug. 12, 2005) (unpublished), *available at www.lexisnexis.com/practiceareas/immigration/archive_cases.asp* (applying the doctrine of res judicata in a removal proceeding).

[24] INA §§240(c)(2), 291; 8 CFR §1240.8(b).

[25] *Landon v. Plasencia*, 459 U.S. 21 (1982); *see also Katebi v. Ashcroft*, 396 F.3d 463 (1st Cir. 2005); *Khodagholian v. Ashcroft*, 335 F.3d 1003 (9th Cir. 2003), *citing Landon, supra*, and *Matter of Huang*,

Removal proceedings based on being present in the United States without admission or parole are characterized by an unusual burden shifting rule. In such cases, ICE must first establish the person's alienage.[26] The government may establish a prima facie case of alienage by introducing Form I-213 (Record of Deportability), together with testimony or an affidavit of the officer who prepared it, confirming preparation of the form on the basis of the noncitizen's statements. If this is done, the burden shifts to the foreign national to show that he or she is in the United States lawfully. If the respondent bears that burden, the burden shifts back again to the government to show that the respondent is removable.[27] Consequently, if alienage is established and the respondent declines to testify, he or she may fail to meet the burden and may be found to be removable.

– Rosa has been placed in removal proceedings and charged with being inadmissible on the basis of being present without admission. ICE arrests Rosa and takes her to ICE offices, where one officer questions her and another writes down her answers on Form I-213. ICE does not have a birth certificate or a passport for Rosa, so in bearing its burden of establishing alienage, ICE introduces a copy of Form I-213, in which Rosa admitted that she did not possess a visa to come to the United States, together with the testimony of the officer who arrested Rosa. Rosa does not object to the introduction of the I-213. This evidence—Form I-213 and the officer's testimony—may be enough to establish Rosa's alienage. In that case, the burden then shifts to Rosa to show that she is in the United States pursuant to a lawful admission.

Removal Proceedings Based on Deportability

If the foreign national is charged with deportability under INA §237, ICE has the burden of establishing by *clear and convincing evidence* that the respondent is deportable.[28] This standard is lower than the *beyond a reasonable doubt* standard used in a criminal proceeding, but higher than the *preponderance of the evidence* standard used in civil proceedings.[29]

In some instances, the burden is on the noncitizen to prove his or her right to be or remain in the United States. For example, if a person is charged with reentry after deportation and ICE proves that he or she was deported previously, he or she must show that permission to reenter was granted.[30] If charged with entry to perform labor, he or she must show that a labor certification has been issued. If a person is charged with obtaining an immigrant visa through a fraudulent marriage, ICE must prove the marriage occurred less than two years before the immigrant's entry into the United

---

19 I&N Dec. 749 (BIA 1988) ("When an applicant has a colorable claim to returning resident status … the INS has the burden of proving he is not eligible for admission to the United States").

[26] 8 CFR §1240.8(c).

[27] INA §240(c)(3)(A).

[28] *Id.*

[29] *See Woodby v. INS*, 385 U.S. 276 (1966).

[30] INA §§212(a)(9)(A)(iii), (C)(ii).

States and that the marriage was terminated within two years after entry.[31] Once ICE establishes those facts, the burden is on the immigrant to rebut the presumption of marriage fraud by a preponderance of the evidence.

If ICE does not meet its burden of proving deportability, the advocate should move to terminate the proceedings at the conclusion of ICE's presentation of its case. The IJ may deny the motion, in which case the respondent must go forward with any evidence on his or her behalf.

If removability is established, the respondent then must apply for any and all available forms of relief. In all applications for relief from removal, the burden of proof is on the foreign national.

Special Issues Where Respondent Is Charged with Being Removable on Criminal Grounds

Requirements of Evidence to Establish a Criminal Ground of Inadmissibility or Deportability

Where the NTA asserts a criminal ground of inadmissibility or deportability, ICE may offer into evidence any of the following as proof of a criminal conviction:

- An official record of judgment and conviction;

- An official record of plea, verdict, and sentence;

- A docket entry from court records that indicates the existence of the conviction;

- Official minutes of a court proceeding or a transcript of a court hearing in which the court takes notice of the existence of the conviction;

- An abstract of a record of conviction prepared by the court in which the conviction was entered, or by a state official associated with the state's repository of criminal justice records, that indicates the charge or section of law violated, the disposition of the case, the existence and date of conviction, and the sentence;

- Any document or record prepared by, or under the direction of, the court in which the conviction was entered that indicates the existence of a conviction; and

- Any document or record attesting to the conviction that is maintained by an official of a state or federal penal institution, which is the basis for that institution's authority to assume custody of the individual named in the record.[32]

Notice that the police report is NOT one of the documents that can be admitted into evidence for the purpose of showing a criminal conviction.

In addition, the document purporting to establish the criminal conviction must be in one of three forms:

- The original document from the court;

---

[31] INA §237(a)(1)(G).

[32] INA §240(c)(3)(B), 8 CFR §1003.41.

- A copy of the document certified by the custodian of the document as being an authentic copy of an original record maintained in the entity's records (*e.g.*, the clerk of court); or

- A document received by ICE from a state or court by electronic means, if it bears two certifications:

    (1) a certification by a state official associated with the state's repository of criminal justice records that the document is an official record from its repository or by a court official from the court in which the conviction was entered that it is an official record from its repository (signature and statement of authenticity can be computer-generated), and

    (2) a certification by a DHS official that the document was received electronically from the state or court's record repository.[33]

Special rules apply for certification of foreign documents.[34]

Does the Conviction Meet All Necessary Elements for Immigration Consequences?

Each element of the inadmissibility or deportation ground or bar to relief in question must be satisfied in order for immigration consequences to attach.

Do the records submitted by ICE establish that there was a conviction for immigration purposes?

Advocates should scrutinize ICE's evidence carefully to verify whether the evidence establishes that a conviction has actually taken place. The term *conviction* is defined as:

[A] formal judgment of guilt of the foreign national entered by a court or, if adjudication of guilt has been withheld, where—

(i) a judge or jury has found the foreign national guilty or the foreign national has entered a plea of guilty or nolo contendere or has admitted sufficient facts to warrant a finding of guilt, and

(ii) the judge has ordered some form of punishment, penalty, or restraint on the foreign national's liberty to be imposed.[35]

What constitutes a *conviction* under this definition was discussed in depth in chapter 2. For example, a conviction from which the defendant has taken an appeal that is still pending, or for which the time to file a notice of appeal has not expired, is not final and does not constitute a conviction for immigration purposes.[36] While finality traditionally has been required in order to meet the definition of *conviction*, for immigration purposes, some circuit courts have reasoned that Congress eliminated the finality require-

---

[33] INA §240(c)(3)(C); 8 CFR §1287.6(a).

[34] 8 CFR §§1287.6 (b), (c),(d).

[35] INA §101(a)(48)(A).

[36] *See Pino v. Landon*, 349 U.S. 901 (1955); *Matter of Thomas*, 21 I&N Dec. 20 (BIA 1995).

ment when it defined conviction" in the Illegal Immigration Reform and Immigrant Responsibility Act of 1996.[37]

A determination that a child is a delinquent is not a conviction for immigration purposes.[38] A child tried and found guilty as an adult, however, may have a conviction.

If the ground of removability requires that a certain sentence have been ordered or that a certain amount of damages be involved, does the evidence reflect the minimum sentence or damages?

For certain convictions to form the basis of a ground of inadmissibility or deportability or a bar to immigration relief, the conviction must be accompanied by a minimum sentence of imprisonment or by a minimum amount of damage. For example, a theft offense is an aggravated felony only if a sentence of at least one year has been imposed, and a fraud offense is an aggravated felony only if the loss to the victim exceeds $10,000. Similarly, a person is inadmissible for multiple criminal convictions only if there was an aggregate sentence to confinement of five years or more. As a third example, an aggravated felony conviction is a statutory bar to applying for or obtaining asylum, but it is a statutory bar to withholding of removal only if there is a sentence of imprisonment of five years.

The INA defines the term *sentence* as follows:

Any reference to a term of imprisonment of a sentence with respect to an offense is deemed to include the period of incarceration or confinement ordered by a court of the law, regardless of any suspension of the imposition or execution of that imprisonment or sentence in whole or in part.[39]

This means that a person convicted of theft and given a sentence of "three years, suspended, upon successful completion of probation of five years" has a sentence of three years for immigration purposes, even though the person never spent a day in jail.

Remember that *sentence* under the immigration laws refers to a sentence to incarceration or confinement. It does not refer to other types of punishment, such as community service, payment of fines, completion of special programs, or probation. For concurrent sentences, the aggregate sentence is the longer of the concurrent sentences.[40]

---

[37] *See Puello v. BCIS*, 511 F.3d 324 (2d Cir. 2007); *Abiodun v. Gonzales*, 461 F.3d 1210 (10th Cir. 2006); *Montenegro v. Ashcroft*, 355 F.3d 1035 (7th Cir. 2004); *Moosa v. INS*, 171 F.3d 994 (5th Cir. 1999). *See also* Illegal Immigration Reform and Immigrant Responsibility Act of 1996, Pub. L. No. 104-208, div. C, 110 Stat. 3009, 3009-546 to 3009-724.

[38] *Matter of Devison*, 22 I&N Dec. 1362 (BIA 2000); *Matter of Ramirez-Rivero*, 18 I&N Dec. 135 (BIA 1981).

[39] INA §101(a)(48)(B).

[40] *Matter of Aldebesheh*, 22 I&N Dec. 983 (BIA 1999).

Is the conviction really for a crime involving moral turpitude, aggravated felony, or other criminal ground of inadmissibility or deportability?

Look at the crime as defined by the elements in the criminal statute, not the defendant's actual conduct.[41] Where, for example, moral turpitude is not an element of the offense, the conviction will not be deemed one involving moral turpitude.

Sometimes, the statute under which the individual was convicted is a broad or multi-sectioned one. These statutes are called *divisible* statutes. Some divisible statutes contain both crimes that involve moral turpitude and crimes that do not, or crimes that constitute aggravated felonies and crimes that do not. In these cases, the fact finder will examine the record of conviction (consisting of the charging document, the plea or verdict, the judgment and the sentence) to see under which section the defendant was convicted. For many grounds of removability based on convictions, if the record does not establish that the defendant was convicted under a section of the statute that renders him removable, then the conviction cannot be deemed to be a removable offense.[42] However, IJs are permitted to look outside of the record of conviction to determine if the loss to the victim is for a fraud aggravated felony and to determine whether a prostitution aggravated felony was committed for commercial advantage.[43]

The attorney general (AG) recently issued a precedential decision, *Matter of Silva-Trevino,*[44] which further eroded the categorical approach. The AG reversed and sent back for reconsideration a BIA decision that, in applying the categorical approach, had held that the foreign national's "indecency with a child" conviction in Texas did not constitute a CMT. He directed IJs and the BIA to determine first if the statute is divisible (*i.e.*, if some offenses involve moral turpitude and some do not). If the statute is divisible and the record of conviction is inconclusive, IJs should consider any additional evidence deemed necessary or appropriate to resolve accurately the moral turpitude question.[45] The AG pronounced that his opinion in *Matter of Silva-Trevino* establishes an administrative framework for determining whether a foreign national has been convicted of a crime involving moral turpitude. This decision is applicable only to CMTs; it does not apply when IJs determine other grounds of inadmissibility and deportability.[46]

---

[41] *Matter of Short*, 20 I&N Dec. 136 (BIA 1989).

[42] *Id.*; *Matter of Velazquez-Herrera*, 24 I&N Dec. 503 (BIA 2008).

[43] *See Matter of Babaisakov*, 24 I&N Dec. 306 (BIA 2007); *Matter of Gertsenshteyn*, 24 I&N Dec. 111 (BIA 2007); *but see Gertsenshteyn v. Mukasey*, 544 F.3d 137 (2d Cir. 2008) (remanding case to BIA because it had failed to explain why it was departing from its longstanding use of the categorical approach).

[44] *Matter of Silva-Trevino*, 24 I&N Dec. 687 (A.G. 2008).

[45] *See also Ali v. Mukasey*, 525 F.3d 497 (7th Cir. 2008) (holding that presentence report or any other evidence can be used to determine whether an offense was a CMT).

[46] *See Matter of Velazquez-Herrera*, 24 I&N Dec. 503 (BIA 2008) (whether an alien is removable on the basis of a conviction for a "crime of child abuse" under INA §237(a)(2)(E)(i) is determined by the categorical approach).

Advocates are very troubled by the AG's surprise decision in *Matter of Silva-Trevino*[47] and have filed a motion to reconsider the decision.[48] Advocates whose clients' cases are impacted by this ruling should continue to challenge it at the BIA and circuit courts.

Advocates should be prepared to conduct "mini-trials" on the issue of whether an offense involved moral turpitude. Such a hearing would include direct and cross examination of the complaining witness and arresting police officer. Although the AG in his decision in *Matter of Silva-Trevino*[49] reasoned that such retrials of the criminal case would not be required under this new approach to CMTs, he gave little guidance on how judges would resolve such issues. Moreover, a "mini-trial" on the issue of moral turpitude is consistent with a respondent's right to present evidence on his or her own behalf.[50] Should DHS attempt to admit police reports to prove that a respondent's offense involved moral turpitude, advocates should object because this report is hearsay evidence. Although the rules of evidence technically do not apply in immigration court, the BIA has reasoned that evidence submitted in removal hearings must be probative and its use must be fundamentally fair.[51] The use of hearsay evidence to prove the nature of the conviction is fundamentally unfair and violates the respondent's due process rights. In addition, if DHS bears the burden of proof, such evidence is insufficient to prove by clear and convincing evidence that the respondent was convicted of a CMT.[52]

Other types of divisible statutes include both misdemeanor and felony levels of the same offense; misdemeanor levels may carry a maximum sentence of one year, while felony levels carry longer sentences. This is important for determining whether a conviction is for an aggravated felony or whether a crime involving moral turpitude falls within the "petty offense exception" of the deportation grounds.

Has the conviction been pardoned, expunged, or otherwise ameliorated so as to remove or diminish immigration consequences?

A respondent is not deportable under the criminal grounds of deportability of one CMT, multiple CMTs, aggravated felonies, or high speed flight, if he or she has been granted a full and unconditional pardon from the president of the United States or the governor of a state.[53] Expungement of a first offense conviction for simple possession

---

[47] *Matter of Silva-Trevino*, *supra* note 44.

[48] *See* "Memorandum of Law of *Amici Curiae* American Immigration Lawyers Association, Florence Immigrant and Refugee Rights Project, Immigrant Defense Project of the New York State Defenders Association, Immigrant Legal Resource Center, National Immigration Project of the National Lawyers Guild, National Immigrant Justice Center, Refugio del Rio Grande, Inc. and Washington Defenders Association Immigration Project in Support of Reconsideration," filed December 5, 2008, *available at* bibdaily.com.

[49] *Matter of Silva-Trevino*, *supra* note 44.

[50] INA §240(b)(4)(B).

[51] *Matter of Barcenas*, 19 I&N Dec. 609 (BIA 1988).

[52] *See* INA §240(c)(3)(A).

[53] INA §237(a)(2)(A)(v).

of a controlled substance, under the Federal First Offender Act (FFOA),[54] will prevent deportation based on that conviction. The BIA held in *Matter of Roldan* that state counterparts of the FFOA do not erase convictions for immigration purposes,[55] although that decision was reversed by the Ninth Circuit in *Lujan-Almendariz v. INS.*[56]

Under *Matter of Roldan,*[57] state rehabilitative statutes that provide expungements or other relief from convictions as a matter of law will not erase a conviction for immigration purposes; vacating or amelioration of convictions based on constitutional or other flaws in the underlying criminal proceedings will serve to remove a conviction for immigration purposes.[58] A post-conviction sentence modification is valid for immigration purposes even if it is done solely for immigration purposes.[59]

In recognizing a sentence modification as valid for immigration purposes, the BIA distinguished such a modification from a vacation of a conviction, and held that while the latter is not valid if it is done solely for immigration or rehabilitative purposes as held in *Matter of Pickering,*[60] the former is valid without regard to the trial court's reasons for modifying the sentence.

Constitutional Violations and Motions to Suppress

Overview

As explained earlier in this chapter, ICE has the burden in removal proceedings of establishing alienage. Common types of evidence presented by ICE to establish alienage are the respondent's birth certificate, passport, or visa. Often, however, ICE will not have these documents and will attempt to establish alienage through statements made by the respondent and recorded on Form I-213, or through an ICE officer's testimony as to what the respondent told ICE. These statements may have been obtained through means that violate the constitutional protections against unreasonable searches and seizures in the Fourth Amendment to the U.S. Constitution and to the right of fundamental due process under the Fifth Amendment. If so, the IJ should not allow the statements into evidence. The respondent raises this issue through a motion to suppress the wrongfully-obtained evidence.

In addition, ICE may attempt to obtain evidence of alienage by asking the respondent questions in the removal hearing. It may be possible for the respondent to refuse to answer these questions, on the basis of the right against self-incrimination in the Fifth Amendment.

---

[54] 18 USC §3607.

[55] *Matter of Roldan*, 22 I&N Dec. 512 (BIA 1999).

[56] *Lujan-Almendariz v. INS,* 222 F.3d 728 (9th Cir. 2000).

[57] *Matter of Roldan, supra* note 55.

[58] *Matter of Pickering*, 23 I&N Dec. 621 (BIA 2003).

[59] *Matter of Cota-Vargas*, 23 I&N Dec. 849 (BIA 2005).

[60] *Matter of Pickering, supra* note 58.

Motions to Suppress Evidence: A Case Study

The following facts illustrate the type of situation in which a motion to suppress evidence in removal proceedings might be warranted.

Hilaria and her daughter Monica flew with several other family members from Phoenix to Chicago on America West Airlines flight 333. When they disembarked in Chicago, they began walking through the jetway connecting the plane with the terminal. At the end of the jetway, they saw three men blocking the entrance to the terminal. The men showed Hilaria and Monica ICE badges and said they were ICE agents.

Hilaria and Monica, along with other disembarking passengers, were ordered to step to one side if they did not have documents. The area was patrolled by several ICE officers, so Hilaria and Monica could not leave. Hilaria and Monica noticed that the ICE officers appeared to be detaining and questioning only passengers of Latino appearance. Passengers who appeared "anglo" or "American" were allowed to enter the terminal without questioning.

After some time, Hilaria and Monica and about 30 other persons who had been stopped by ICE were ordered to follow ICE officers to a bus, which they then were directed to board. The ICE agents did not show them any warrant for their arrests. The individuals were taken to ICE headquarters, where they waited for two or three hours until an ICE agent called them for questioning. They were not advised of their rights to make a telephone call or consult with an attorney prior to questioning. After being questioned and fingerprinted, they were allowed to leave on their own recognizance. Based on the information Hilaria and Monica provide during the questioning, the ICE agent prepares a Form I-213 and issues NTAs to Hilaria and Monica.

Hilaria and Monica file a motion to suppress all evidence obtained by ICE as a result of the ICE activity described above. The evidence they seek to suppress is the I-213 and any testimony as to information given to ICE by Hilaria and Monica. Without this evidence, ICE may not be able to establish its charge of deportability against Hilaria and Monica.

The result of a successful motion to suppress evidence, or of a successful assertion of the right against self-incrimination, is that ICE will not be able to present the suppressed evidence and, therefore, may not have sufficient evidence to meet its burden and standard of proof. If ICE does not meet this burden and standard, then the IJ must terminate the removal proceedings.

The area of law dealing with constitutional protections against unreasonable stops, arrests, searches, and seizures is a large and complicated one, and an extensive discussion of it is beyond the scope of this manual. The following, however, is a brief outline of the issues involved.

The Right to Be Free of Unreasonable Searches and Seizures Under the Fourth Amendment

The Fourth Amendment provides that "[t]he right of the people to be secure in their persons, houses, papers, and effects, against unreasonable searches and seizures, shall not be violated, and no Warrants shall issue, but upon probable cause ...." Thus, governmental searches and seizures must be reasonable, and warrants to conduct them must be based on probable cause.

We should take a moment to consider what the terms *search* and *seizure* mean. Although the Fourth Amendment uses the word *search*, the Fourth Amendment also protects people from unreasonable entry into a residence. For example, a law enforcement officer standing outside the door of a motel room orders the inhabitants to *open up*, and they comply by opening the door. At that point, before the officer steps into the room, an *entry* and *search* have been conducted.[61]

A person has been *seized* if an officer or officers has used physical force or his authority to stop or restrain a person.[62] The officer must show through force or show of authority that the person is not free to leave or refuse the officer's requests.[63] In contrast, an officer walking up to a person in a public place and asking a few questions, without more, is not making a seizure.[64] That sort of brief inquiry is sometimes called a *stop*.[65]

Whether a search or seizure is reasonable depends on the location and circumstances of an individual's encounter with law enforcement, including ICE. The rights are generally strongest in the home or another place where individuals have a recognized right of privacy. An individual's rights are more limited when he or she is traveling in a vehicle or on foot in a public place. They are most limited at an ICE or CBP checkpoint or when crossing an international border or the *functional equivalent* of a border, meaning the first place that an individual lands within a country, such as an international airport.

To analyze the constitutional reasonableness of a particular enforcement activity, the following tests are typically applied:

- In the case of a search, did the officer have a warrant and, if not, did one of the exceptions to the warrant requirement apply?

- In the case of a seizure, did a seizure occur, and, if so, was it legally justified by the appropriate level of suspicion?

The Exclusionary Rule in Removal Proceedings

The *exclusionary rule* is a court-made rule that prohibits the introduction in criminal proceedings of statements and evidence gathered in violation of the Fourth Amendment's prohibition on unreasonable searches and seizures. Evidence obtained subsequent to this illegal law enforcement conduct also may be subject to the exclusionary rule as *fruit of the poisonous tree*.

Unfortunately, the Supreme Court has determined that the Fourth Amendment exclusionary rule does not apply in deportation hearings, because they are civil rather than criminal proceedings. The rule applies to civil proceedings only where the benefits of not allowing the tainted evidence outweigh the costs of keeping it out. As a

---

[61] *U.S. v. Winsor*, 846 F.2d 1569 (9th Cir. 1988).

[62] *Terry v. Ohio*, 392 U.S. 1 (1968).

[63] *U.S. v. Mendenhall*, 446 U.S. 544 (1980) (opinion of Stewart, J.).

[64] *U.S. v. Sullivan*, 128 F.3d 126 (4th Cir. 1998).

[65] *Terry v. Ohio*, *supra* note 62.

result, noncitizens may raise Fourth Amendment arguments to suppress ICE's evidence in removal proceedings only where the ICE's violation was egregious.[66] However, results similar to those that otherwise would be achievable under the Fourth Amendment's exclusionary rule can sometimes be achieved in removal proceedings—particularly in cases of egregious misconduct by enforcement officers—by raising parallel arguments under the Fifth Amendment's due process clause.[67]

The Fifth Amendment states that the federal government may not deprive a person of life, liberty, or property without due process of law. It also states that individuals cannot be forced to testify against themselves in criminal matters.

Respondents in removal proceedings can challenge the admission of evidence by arguing that it was gathered in violation of the due process clause. Egregious violations—of the Fourth Amendment and of DHS regulations—that affect the fundamental fairness of a proceeding amount to violations of the Fifth Amendment. Evidence obtained pursuant to such violations therefore may be suppressed. Examples of due process violations include failure to make respondents aware of their rights, coerced confessions, repeated denial of access to counsel, and extremely intrusive searches and seizures that "shock the conscience." For example, a seizure based solely on a person's ethnic appearance or his or her name is an egregious violation of the Fourth Amendment.[68]

When Is a Warrant Required?

To be lawful, a search must be reasonable. This means that it must be conducted with a search warrant or pursuant to one of the exceptions to the warrant requirement.[69] In determining whether a search or seizure was reasonable, courts will examine whether, if there was a warrant, the officers exceeded its scope, and, if there was no warrant, whether one of the exceptions truly existed.

Under the Fourth Amendment, a search warrant must be based on probable cause to suspect that the place to be searched contains evidence that a law has been broken. The probable cause must be established through reliable affidavits submitted with the request for the warrant.

Warrants permit searches or seizures only to the extent specified in the warrant. A warrant to conduct a search must state specifically the person or thing to be searched. A warrant to inspect premises for undocumented individuals must indicate with sufficient specificity which persons on those premises ICE reasonably believes are in the United States unlawfully. A warrant is invalid if it would allow enforcement officers to search and seize "unnamed others," since there can be no probable cause to arrest unknown individuals.[70] However, if ICE officers enter a location to seize persons

---

[66] *INS v. Lopez-Mendoza*, 468 U.S. 1032 (1984).

[67] *Id.*; *Matter of Toro*, 17 I&N Dec. 340 (BIA 1980).

[68] *U.S. v. Brignoni-Ponce*, 422 U.S. 873 (1975).

[69] *Walter v. United States*, 447 U.S. 649 (1980); *Welsh v. Wisconsin*, 466 U.S. 740 (1984).

[70] *See Abel v. U.S.*, 362 U.S. 217 (1960).

named in a valid warrant that contains particularized information, they probably may question (but not seize) others not named in the warrant.

Note that if immigration agents present a warrant, it will often be an ICE-issued arrest warrant. Generally, an ICE arrest warrant alone will not give agents authority to enter a home. If agents come to the door with an arrest warrant alleging that a person in the residence is in the United States in violation of immigration laws, the warrant alone does not give the agents authority to enter the house.[71]

There are circumstances under which enforcement agencies are exempted from the requirement that they obtain warrants before conducting searches and making arrests. One such exception to the warrant requirement is where the officers have been given consent to enter or search. This consent may be given by any adult resident and people such as a baby-sitter or housekeeper, although the consent of a landlord or manager of a rented building is not sufficient.[72] The consent must be free and voluntary.[73]

Exceptions to the warrant requirement also arise in the following circumstances, as long as the officer has probable cause to suspect illegal activity:

- Incident to a lawful arrest;
- When officers are in hot pursuit of a felon;
- Where an immediate threat exists that evidence will be destroyed;
- When what is being searched is an automobile;
- When the items officers are searching for are in plain view or are held out to the public; and
- When the officer made the search believing in good faith that it was lawful to do so.

The strongest Fourth Amendment protections apply to homes and residences.[74] Places that count as residences include: apartments,[75] motel rooms,[76] and even a tent, if it is being used as a residence.[77] Advocates argue that homeless shelters and group homes also should be treated as residences under the law. Even the broad enforcement powers given to ICE by statute do not authorize the agency to conduct warrantless searches of private dwellings, and the warrant requirement protects farm labor housing to the same extent as other residences.[78] Absent exigent circumstances or

---

[71] See See v. City of Seattle, 387 U.S. 541 (1967).

[72] Chapman v. U.S., 365 U.S. 610 (1961).

[73] Colorado v. Connelly, 479 U.S. 157 (1986).

[74] Payton v. New York, 445 U.S. 573 (1980).

[75] U.S. v. Ramos, 12 F.3d 1019 (11th Cir. 1994).

[76] U.S. v. Albrekton, 151 F.3d 951 (9th Cir. 1998).

[77] U.S. v. Gooch, 6 F.3d 673 (9th Cir. 1993).

[78] Laduke v. Nelson, 762 F.2d 1318 (9th Cir. 1985).

the consent of the person whose home it is, a warrant is necessary to enter a private home.[79]

- Six officers with their guns drawn came onto the front porch of a house. They shone flashlights into the windows. One of the officers knocked on the front door and yelled, "Police. Open up or we'll knock the door down." If a resident opens the door in response to this show of authority, he or she has not given free and voluntary consent, but only complied with a show of authority by the police.[80]

What Constitutes a Seizure?

Under the Fourth Amendment, the term *seizure* refers to the forcible restraint of an individual's liberty or the taking of property.[81] The seizure of a person also is called a *detention*, a term used in the law to refer to a broad spectrum of intrusion into personal liberty. At one end of the spectrum, a detention is incarceration: a person incarcerated in an ICE prison is called a *detainee*. At the other end of the spectrum, a detention can be brief, consisting of a short inquiry or pat-down search, also called a *stop*.

The Fourth Amendment imposes a reasonableness standard on any detention, although what is considered reasonable varies depending on the severity or degree of detention (*i.e.,* it is easier to prove that a brief stop was reasonable than it is to prove that an arrest was). A government officer who has a *reasonable suspicion* that a person is engaging in or about to engage in illegal activity is justified in stopping the person. To do more than just stop and briefly question a person, however, the officer must have *probable cause* to suspect illegal activity.

What Is an Arrest?

To lawfully arrest someone, an enforcement officer must have probable cause to suspect that the person has broken a law.[82]

When possible, ICE officers must obtain arrest warrants before making an arrest and, when making a criminal arrest, must provide certain warnings. In addition, ICE officers cannot use threats, coercion, or physical abuse to induce a suspect to waive his or her rights and/or to make a statement.

For ICE officers to arrest a foreign national pursuant to a warrant, the warrant need not have been issued by a magistrate; foreign nationals may be arrested on administrative warrants issued by ICE itself. Certain ICE officials are authorized to issue warrants for the arrest of foreign nationals pending a determination of their deportability.[83]

---

[79] *Welsh v. Wisconsin*, 466 U.S. 740 (1984); *Payton v. U.S.*, 445 U.S. 573 (1980).

[80] *U.S. v. Winsor*, 846 F.2d 1569 (9th Cir. 1988).

[81] *Terry v. Ohio*, 392 U.S. 1 (1968).

[82] *Beck v. Ohio*, 379 U.S. 89 (1964).

[83] 8 CFR §287.5.

ICE and CBP officers can make a warrantless arrest of a foreign national already in the United States when they have a *reason to believe* the foreign national is guilty of a violation of the law and is likely to escape before a warrant can be obtained.[84] Courts have understood the phrase *reason to believe* to require arresting officers to have probable cause to arrest.[85]

ICE and CBP officers have the authority to make a warrantless arrest of any person believed to have committed a felony relating to immigration law, when the officer has probable cause to suspect that the person is guilty of such a felony and is likely to escape.[86] This gives ICE and CBP officers the power to arrest USCs whom they suspect have committed immigration-related felonies, which include crimes related to smuggling of foreign nationals, fraud, and perjury.

When an ICE or CBP officer arrests someone without having a warrant, an officer other than the one who made the arrest must determine within 48 hours whether ICE or CBP has prima facie evidence that the person arrested is deportable.[87] However, if "no other qualified officer is readily available" the arresting officer may conduct the questioning. ICE and CBP also must determine, within the 24 to 48-hour period, whether the arrested foreign national will be released on bond, except in the event of an emergency or other extraordinary circumstance in which case a determination will be made within an additional reasonable period of time.[88] If after this allotted period ICE or CBP has not been able to gather enough facts to establish that the detainee is deportable, it has no legal authority to hold the person. Detention by ICE or CBP that violates these rules can be challenged through a habeas corpus action filed in federal district court.

What Is Mere Questioning?

ICE and CBP efforts to apprehend and deport undocumented individuals depend heavily on officers' ability to question persons they suspect of being in the United States unlawfully. If, in a casual encounter on the street or at a workplace, an officer poses questions without demanding an answer, the officer is engaging in *mere questioning* (as opposed to *detentive questioning*, which is discussed below). An officer may *merely question* a person without having either a reasonable suspicion that the person is in the United States unlawfully or probable cause to suspect as much, so long as the person being questioned does not feel compelled to answer, and so long as a reasonable person would believe that the person being questioned was free to leave or refuse to respond.[89] When an ICE or CBP officer questions someone regarding his or her alienage without having any individualized suspicion about that person, the questioning must be brief and nondetentive.

---

[84] INA §287(a).

[85] *See U.S. v. Reyes-Oropesa*, 596 F.2d 399 (9th Cir. 1979).

[86] INA §287(a).

[87] 8 CFR §287.3(a).

[88] 8 CFR §287.3(d).

[89] *See U.S. v. Mendenhall*, 446 U.S. 544 (1980).

In *INS v. Delgado*,[90] workers challenged the legacy INS policy of conducting factory raids without having individualized suspicion that particular workers were unlawfully in the United States. The workers argued that such searches and seizures are prohibited as unreasonable under the Fourth Amendment. However, the Supreme Court decided that the workers in this case had not been "seized," even though a large number of armed legacy INS officers had entered the workplace, blocked off the exits, and forcefully questioned many of the employees. The Court found that "interrogation relating to one's identity or a request for identification by the police [or legacy INS officers] does not, by itself, constitute a Fourth Amendment seizure." But the Court did find that a seizure would have occurred if the workers had attempted to leave the factory or asserted their right not to answer questions, and the legacy INS officers had forced them to remain and/or pressed them for answers. If that had been the case, the legacy INS officers would have had to show that at the time they seized the workers, they had a reason to believe that the workers were foreign nationals unlawfully in the country. The Court established the principle that persons who confront such situations may remain silent.

> **PRACTICE TIP**
> **Being Questioned**
> **by ICE or CBP**
>
> The best advice for detained undocumented persons who are being questioned by ICE or CBP is that they give their name, ask for an attorney, and say nothing more. By giving their name, undocumented individuals make it possible for friends and family to find out that they are in ICE or CBP custody. By claiming their right to speak to an attorney, they foreclose further questioning by ICE or CBP. And by refusing to answer further questions, they make it difficult for ICE or CBP to prove that they have violated any of the immigration laws.

What Is Detentive Questioning?

An enforcement officer has moved beyond *mere questioning* when the officer *stops* a person—that is, when the officer detains the person for a short time. An officer may briefly stop an individual if he or she has a reasonable suspicion of past or present criminal activity. In the immigration context, an ICE or CBP officer has *stopped* someone when the officer has confronted a person the officer suspects is undocumented and has asked the person questions regarding alienage, while the person is not free to leave. To *stop* a person or vehicle legally, ICE or CBP must have a reasonable suspicion that the person is a foreign national illegally in the United States or that the vehicle contains such persons. This means that ICE or CBP officer must be able to point to facts that formed the basis of the suspicion. ICE and CBP officers cannot hold an individual in custody for simply refusing to answer questions.

To meet the Fourth Amendment's reasonableness standard, an agent's suspicion that a person is undocumented must not be based solely on the person's ethnic appearance. Having a foreign sounding name is not sufficient to justify a stop. But the officer may base a suspicion that a person is a foreign national unlawfully in the United States on a combination of factors, including the following:

---

[90] *INS v. Delgado*, 466 U.S. 210 (1984).

- The person's speech;

- The person's manner of dress and appearance;

- Geographic location and type of neighborhood where the person is encountered;

- The person's presence in a type of vehicle commonly used to smuggle undocumented foreign nationals;

- Prior presence of undocumented foreign nationals in the same type of employment or area; and

- Anonymous tips that undocumented foreign nationals are present.[91]

Certain reactions to mere questioning can give an officer reason to suspect that the person being questioned is undocumented; this reasonable suspicion, in turn, allows the officer to detain and hold the person for further *detentive questioning*. An agent can detain (or seize) a foreign national for failing to provide valid documents, for attempting to run away, or for attempting to hide.

It is very difficult for ICE to prove that a person is deportable if the person does not admit that he or she is undocumented. Because the government is well aware of this fact, its regulations provide that only after the initial 24-hour period has passed (and it has had a chance to build a prima facie case against the detainee) will a detainee be advised: (1) of certain key rights, including the right to counsel, and (2) that any statements the detainee makes can be used against him or her.[92] Before the first 24-hour period lapses, ICE or CBP officers handling a case are likely to try to pressure or even coerce a confession from the detained suspect.

Preparing the Motion to Suppress

Whenever evidence is introduced that the representative believes should be suppressed, a motion to suppress should be made before the tainted evidence is admitted. The attorney or BIA-accredited representative should object to statements and other evidence taken from the detained individual when ICE requests that they be introduced in removal proceedings. If an objection is not made at this point, it is waived. The individual's statements, and any information on the I-213, generally will contain inculpatory statements, because alienage and deportability often are admitted to the arresting officer, and recorded on this form. If any statements made were tainted by an unlawful arrest, a motion should be made to suppress the statements, including any evidence on the I-213.

A motion to suppress must be made in writing and be accompanied by a detailed affidavit from the respondent that explains the reasons why ICE or CBP officer's conduct when gathering the contested evidence was illegal. By itself, an affidavit is not sufficient evidence to establish a prima facie showing that the evidence was obtained unlawfully; the claim must be supported by testimony.[93] However, once the

---

[91] *United States v. Brignoni-Ponce,* 422 U.S. 873 (1975).

[92] 8 CFR §287.3.

[93] *Matter of Barcenas*, 19 I&N Dec. 609 (BIA 1988); *Matter of Burgos*, 15 I&N Dec. 278 (BIA 1975).

respondent makes out a prima facie case that ICE or CBP acted illegally, the burden shifts and ICE must show that its officer's conduct was lawful.

The affidavit must be detailed and specific, and should set forth a prima facie case of the illegality of ICE actions.[94] The motion also must list the articles and statements sought to be suppressed. If other motions also are needed (*i.e.*, a motion for a subpoena for the production of documents or witnesses), they should be filed at the same time as the motion to suppress.

Since it is preferable that a suppression hearing be held separate from the main deportation hearing (to ensure that illegally obtained evidence does not taint the deportation proceedings), the respondent's counsel should ask the presiding IJ for such a separate hearing. However, there is no right to a separate suppression hearing.[95] If the judge refuses to allow a separate hearing, the affidavit and testimony in support of the motion to suppress will not be used to determine the respondent's deportability if the judge grants the motion. If the judge goes ahead with the suppression hearing, the representative should state on the record that any testimony in support of the motion to suppress is not a concession of alienage or deportability for the case in chief.

Once the respondent's affidavit has established a prima facie case that ICE or CBP officers acted unlawfully, the burden shifts to ICE to establish that they acted lawfully. The officers will be called to testify. They should be questioned as to their reasons for conducting the search or questioning.

  – Hilaria and Monica, in the case discussed earlier in this chapter, filed motions to suppress the evidence against them obtained by ICE through ICE's arrest and questioning of them (The motion to suppress appears as Appendix 10). After hearing from both Hilaria and the ICE agents, the IJ found that ICE had stopped and questioned certain passengers based on their Hispanic appearance, rather than on an acceptable combination of factors. The IJ found that this was fundamentally unfair and required suppression of the evidence obtained through the detention and questioning.

The Right to Remain Silent

The Fifth Amendment grants all persons the right not to be compelled to incriminate themselves. This means that they cannot be compelled to testify if doing so could lead to proof that they engaged in illegal activity. Thus, even though a removal proceeding is not a criminal proceeding, respondents may assert their Fifth Amendment right not to testify against themselves.

This protection extends, however, only to incriminating facts (*i.e.*, those that provide information that could lead to proof that the suspect engaged in illegal activity).

---

[94] *Matter of Gonzalez*, 16 I&N Dec. 44 (BIA 1976); *Matter of Ramirez-Sanchez*, 17 I&N Dec. 503 (BIA 1980).

[95] *Matter of Benitez*, 19 I&N Dec. 173 (BIA 1984).

The Fifth Amendment may be asserted in removal proceedings to avoid self-incrimination of the following crimes:[96]

- Alien crewman overstay;[97]
- 18 or over, not carrying documentation;[98]
- Failing to comply with change of address within 10 days under INA §265(a);[99]
- Failure to disclose role as document preparer;[100]
- Entry without inspection;[101]
- Previously deported and reentered;[102]
- False statements/fraudulent documents;[103]
- False documents;[104]
- False statement;[105] and
- False claim to USC.[106]

This Fifth Amendment right can be invoked at any time—*e.g.*, during interrogation or at a deportation or removal hearing. Since persons who enter the country without inspection or without a proper visa may be subject to criminal penalties, suspects held for civil immigration violations can assert the right to remain silent. By asserting this right and refusing to answer incriminating questions, they force ICE to find independent evidence to establish their alienage and removability. If ICE does not have proof that a detained person is undocumented and removable, it must release the person.

The immigration court may draw negative inferences from a refusal to testify.[107] However, where ICE offers no other evidence except the respondent's silence, it is insufficient to meet ICE's burden of showing removability by clear, unequivocal, and convincing evidence.[108]

---

[96] For all of the crimes listed, *see also* I. Kurzban, *Kurzban's Immigration Law Sourcebook*, 11th Ed. (AILA 2008), at 202.

[97] INA §252(c).

[98] INA §264(e).

[99] INA §266(b).

[100] INA §274C(e).

[101] INA §275.

[102] INA §276.

[103] 18 USC §1546.

[104] 18 USC §1028(b).

[105] 18 USC §1001.

[106] 18 USC §§911, 1015.

[107] *Bilokumsky v. Tod*, 263 U.S. 149 (1923).

[108] *Matter of Guevara*, 20 I&N Dec. 238 (BIA 1991).

Conclusion

As can be seen from this chapter, the advocate has a wide range of strategies for challenging a charge of removability against his or her client. These strategies range from checking to see whether the individual might be a USC (and therefore not subject to removal), to challenging the NTA, to moving to suppress evidence wrongfully obtained by ICE or CBP. Such strategies require careful thought and preparation by the advocate, but can have immensely important results for the individual in removal proceedings.

CHAPTER FIVE
ADJUSTMENT OF STATUS

Some foreign nationals in removal proceedings may obtain or re-obtain lawful permanent residence (LPR) status by asserting the defense of adjustment of status in removal proceedings.[1] Adjustment of status is a defense to removal that may be asserted in immigration court initially, or as a renewed application when the applicant is placed in removal proceedings following the denial of an application for adjustment of status filed with USCIS.

Various Modes of Adjustment

Eligibility for adjustment may be under Immigration and Nationality Act (INA)[2] §245, on the basis of an approved family visa petition, Violence Against Women and Department of Justice Reauthorization Act of 2005 (VAWA)[3] self-petition, applicants for special immigrant juvenile status, and T and U nonimmigrants seeking to adjust status. Eligibility for adjustment also may be under INA §209, for refugees and asylees, or under special legislation, such as the Cuban Adjustment Act of 1966 (CAA),[4] the Haitian Refugee Immigration Fairness Act (HRIFA),[5] and Nicaraguan Adjustment and Central American Relief Act (NACARA) §202.[6] VAWA 2005, signed into law on January 5, 2006, contains provisions that allow for certain abused spouses and children to apply for adjustment of status under HRIFA and NACARA even if certain deadlines were missed and even if the abuser did not apply him- or herself. It also contains a provision allowing an abused spouse of a Cuban to apply for adjustment of status under the CAA up to two years after the death of, or divorce from, the Cuban abuser if the abused spouse can show a connection between the termination of the marriage and being battered or subject to extreme cruelty by the Cuban spouse.

This chapter discusses the various statutory provisions that allow adjustment of status as a defense to removal and the available procedures for adjusting status in removal proceedings. While it is beyond the scope of this manual, adjustment also may

---

[1] 8 CFR §§245.2(a)(1), 1245.2(a)(1).

[2] Immigration and Nationality Act of 1952 (INA), Pub. L. No. 82-414, 66 Stat. 163 (codified as amended at 8 USC §§1101 *et seq.*).

[3] Violence Against Women and Department of Justice Reauthorization Act of 2005 (VAWA 2005), Pub. L. No. 109-162, 119 Stat. 2960 (2006).

[4] Cuban Adjustment Act of 1966 (Cuban Adjustment Act), Pub. L. No. 89-732, 80 Stat. 1161.

[5] Haitian Refugee Immigration Fairness Act of 1998 (HRIFA), Pub. L. No. 105-277, div. A, §101(h), tit. IX (secs. 901–04), 112 Stat. 2681, 2681-538 to 2681-542.

[6] Nicaraguan Adjustment and Central American Relief Act (NACARA), Pub. L. No. 105-100, tit. II, 111 Stat. 2160, 2193–201 (1997).

be on the basis of an approved employment visa petition. Interestingly, the Board of Immigration Appeals (BIA) limited the ability of certain individuals with employment visa petitions under INA §204(j) to adjust in proceedings.[7] The BIA's reasoning, however, was rejected by several circuit courts.[8] For a discussion of this decision and strategies in light of it, see the American Immigration Law Foundation's practice advisory entitled "I-140 Portability for Employment-Based Adjustment Applicants in Removal Proceedings: Strategies for Challenging *Matter of Perez-Vargas*."[9]

Readjustment of Status

In certain circumstances, even if an individual already has LPR status, he or she may request readjustment of status in removal proceedings as a form of relief from removal.[10]

For example, an LPR placed in removal proceedings on account of a criminal conviction that renders him or her deportable can apply to readjust status as a form of relief in removal proceedings in order to cure the ground of deportability if the following conditions are met:

- The conviction does not also trigger a ground of inadmissibility for purposes of adjustment. Convictions that also might not trigger inadmissibility grounds are, for example, certain firearms, domestic violence, and aggravated felony offenses. If the conviction does trigger inadmissibility, a waiver is available.

- The LPR is otherwise admissible and eligible for adjustment of status.

- An immediate means of re-adjustment is available. This means that the individual must qualify as an immediate relative or else qualify in some other way to adjust right away under some other mode of adjustment (*e.g.*, the CAA[11]). An LPR cannot apply to re-adjust status based on a family or employer petition that was previously used to adjust status or gain admission to the United States as an immigrant.[12] Instead, a new petition must be filed.

Arriving Aliens and Adjustment in Proceedings

Until 2006, an *arriving alien* in removal proceedings that were initiated upon his or her arrival to the United States was not eligible by regulation for adjustment of status before the Immigration Judge (IJ). To review, an *arriving alien* generally means an applicant for admission arriving at a port-of-entry.[13] LPRs returning from a

---

[7] *Matter of Perez-Vargas*, 23 I&N Dec. 829 (BIA 2005).

[8] *See Sung v. Keisler*, 505 F.3d 372 (5th Cir. 2007); *Matovski v. Gonzales*, 492 F.3d 722 (6th Cir. 2007); *Perez-Vargas v. Gonzales*, 478 F.3d 191 (4th Cir. 2007).

[9] "I-140 Portability for Employment-Based Adjustment Applicants in Removal Proceedings: Strategies for Challenging *Matter of Perez-Vargas*," (updated Jan. 9, 2008), *available at http://www.ailf.org/lac/lac_pa_topics.shtml*.

[10] *Matter of Rainford*, 20 I&N Dec. 598 (BIA 1992); *Matter of Mendez*, 21 I&N Dec. 296 (BIA 1996).

[11] Cuban Adjustment Act, *supra* note 4.

[12] *Matter of Villarreal-Zuniga*, 23 I&N Dec. 886 (BIA 2006).

[13] 8 CFR §1.1(q).

trip abroad, though generally not deemed to be applicants for admission, can be labeled arriving aliens if they are deemed to fall into one of the listed exceptions at INA §101(a)(13)(C). However, in May 2006, the regulations preventing adjustment, 8 CFR §245.1(c)(8) and 8 CFR §1245.1(c)(8), were repealed and replaced with an interim rule by the Department of Homeland Security (DHS) and the Executive Office for Immigration Review (EOIR).[14]

The repeal of the prior regulations came after and in response to a growing split in the circuit courts. Indeed, prior to the May 2006 repeal, four circuits already had held that certain arriving aliens could adjust status before the IJ.[15] Specifically, these four courts held that the regulations prohibiting adjustment of arriving aliens were invalid and that paroled aliens could adjust in immigration court under INA §245(a). In contrast, the U.S. Courts of Appeals for the Fifth and the Eighth Circuits upheld the same regulations.[16]

The new interim rule that permits U.S. Citizenship and Immigration Services (USCIS) to adjudicate adjustment applications for arriving aliens in removal proceedings who are parolees. IJs do not have jurisdiction over such applications by parolees, but do have discretion to grant a continuance, administratively close or otherwise adjourn a case while USCIS adjudicates such applications. For persons with final orders of removal, USCIS should be able to consider the adjustment of status application, although many USCIS offices do not agree to hear such applications because of the outstanding removal order.[17] Under the interim rule, IJs do have jurisdiction over adjustment applications filed by an arriving alien in proceedings who entered the United States on an advance parole and whose application for adjustment of status was pending before he or she left the United States. A final rule has not yet been published.[18]

Arriving aliens paroled into the United States who qualify to adjust under the CAA (discussed in detail below) also can adjust status before the IJ pursuant to the BIA's decision in *Matter of Artigas*.[19]

---

[14] 71 Fed. Reg. 27585 (2006); USCIS Memorandum, M. Aytes, "Eligibility of Arriving Aliens in Removal Proceedings to Apply for Adjustment of Status and Jurisdiction to Adjudicate Applications for Adjustment of Stats," Jan. 12, 2007, *published on* AILA InfoNet at Doc. No. 07030661 (*posted* Mar. 6, 2007).

[15] *See Scheerer v. U.S. Atty. General*, 445 F.3d 1311 (11th Cir. 2006); *Succar v. Ashcroft*, 294 F.3d 8 (1st Cir. 2005); *Zheng v. Gonzales*; 422 F.3d 98 (3d Cir. 2005); *Bona v. Gonzales*, 425 F.3d 663 (9th Cir. 2005).

[16] *Momin v. Gonzales*, 447 F.3d 447 (5th Cir. 2006); *Mouelle v. Gonzales*, 416 F.3d 923 (8th Cir. 2005) (decisions now vacated and remanded in light of repeal).

[17] *See Matter of C–H–*, 9 I&N Dec. 265 (Regional Commissioner 1961).

[18] For an excellent discussion of these recent changes and strategies in light of these changes, see "'Arriving Aliens' and Adjustment of Status: What is the Impact of the Government's Interim Rule of May 12, 2006?," American Immigration Law Foundation (updated Nov. 5, 2008); "USCIS Adjustment of Status of 'Arriving Aliens' with an Unexecuted Final Order of Removal" (updated Nov. 6, 2008); and "Adjustment of Status of 'Arriving Aliens' Under the Interim Regulations: Challenging the BIA's Denial of a Motion to Reopen, Remand, or Continue a Case," (updated Nov. 5, 2008), *available at www.ailf.org/lac/lac_pa_topics.shtml*.

[19] *Matter of Artigas*, 23 I&N Dec. 99 (BIA 2001).

Termination to Proceed with Adjustment Before USCIS

In some situations, while a respondent might be eligible to adjust before the court it might be preferable to proceed with adjustment of status before USCIS. In other situations, a respondent is only eligible to adjust before USCIS.

If termination for adjustment before USCIS is preferred or necessary in order for a respondent to adjust, a request for termination to proceed with adjustment before USCIS should be made to the IJ. However, like a request for administrative closure, the U.S. Immigration and Customs Enforcement (ICE) trial attorney must consent to termination in order for the judge to grant such a request. If the trial attorney does not agree to termination, the IJ has no authority to grant the request. It is therefore necessary to have conferred with the ICE attorney and determine what objections, if any, he or she might have to a termination to proceed with adjustment before USCIS. Note that under the interim rule discussed in the above section, parolees who are in proceedings as arriving aliens do not need to have their cases terminated in order to proceed with adjustment before USCIS.

ICE issued a memorandum indicating that it will exercise its prosecutorial discretion to join in or file a motion to terminate proceedings without prejudice in certain cases where adjustment of status applications currently pending before the IJ are deemed by ICE to be approvable by USCIS in order to allow ICE to focus on "priority" cases. However, the memorandum sets out that ICE will not move or agree to termination where an asylum application also is pending. The memorandum also states that, in the absence of "unique or special circumstances," ICE will not join in a motion to terminate or move to terminate in cases involving threats to national security, human rights violators, criminal convictions, or cases requiring an INA §212(h) or §212(i) waiver.[20] If the termination is granted, the trial attorney will forward the file to USCIS, which in turn schedules an adjustment interview.

The respondent should evaluate carefully whether to proceed with a hearing before the IJ or to seek or agree to termination. The following factors should be considered, and generally argue in favor of termination:

- The evidentiary requirements are less stringent before USCIS;
- There is no formal, potentially intimidating cross-examination of the respondent by the ICE trial attorney and the IJ;
- USCIS adjudications officers are less likely to notice and raise detailed, legal objections;
- Some USCIS offices schedule adjustment interviews more quickly than IJs schedule merits hearings;
- The respondent's attorney can play a more informal role in the USCIS interview; and

---

[20] *See* ICE Memorandum, W. Howard, "Exercising Prosecutorial Discretion to Dismiss Adjustment Cases" (Oct. 6, 2005), *published on* AILA InfoNet at Doc. No. 05101360 (*posted* Oct. 13, 2005).

- IJs do not like to hear adjustment cases that they believe USCIS should be adjudicating.

On the other hand, there are several reasons why the respondent might prefer that the case proceed in front of the IJ:

- USCIS may be taking too long to schedule interviews;

- There may be pressing age-out issues or other timing concerns;

- The IJ is known to be sympathetic to cases involving the respondent's particular means of adjustment;

- There may be potentially problematic questions of law that the respondent would prefer the IJ to resolve;

- There are issues involving discretion that the respondent may prefer were handled by the court; and

- The respondent's attorney plays a more formal and participatory role in presenting the case and is therefore better able to formally control the proceedings.

Family-Based Adjustment of Status

Overview of Eligibility Requirements

Pursuant to INA §§245(a) and (c), beneficiaries of an approved relative petition (Form I-130) may be eligible to adjust status in the United States while in removal proceedings, if all of the following conditions are satisfied:

- They were inspected and admitted or paroled into the United States;

- A visa is immediately available;

- They never worked unauthorized in the United States (unless they are an immediate relative);

- They always maintained lawful nonimmigrant or parole status (unless they are an immediate relative);

- They are not a crew member in the D visa category, a foreign national admitted in transit without a visa, an exchange visitor admitted in the J visa category, or a foreign national admitted in the S visa category;

- They are not a nonimmigrant admitted without a visa under the visa waiver program (unless they are an immediate relative);

- They are not in removal proceedings commenced upon their arrival (this includes foreign nationals in former exclusion proceedings and those in expedited removal proceedings); and

- They are not inadmissible; unless eligible for a waiver.

In addition to the requirements stated above, the adjustment applicant must not be barred from relief by the provisions of INA §240B(d) (which states that overstaying voluntary departure bars adjustment for 10 years) nor by INA §240(c)(7) (where an in absentia order of removal bars an individual from adjustment for 10 years).

Obtaining Benefits Under §245(i)

INA §245(i) permits certain classes of foreign nationals to adjust status in the United States even though they might be disqualified under INA §§245(a) and (c), set forth above. INA §245(i) helps individuals who either:

- Were not inspected or paroled into the United States;
- Were inspected, but are not immediate relatives, and have overstayed or failed to maintain continuous lawful status since entry;
- Are not immediate relatives and have worked without authorization;
- Were admitted as crew members;
- Were admitted in S nonimmigrant status;
- Are not immediate relatives and have been admitted under the visa waiver program; or
- Have been admitted in transit without a visa.

In order to adjust status in proceedings under INA §245(i), the following conditions must be met:

- A visa must be immediately available;
- The respondent is not inadmissible under INA §212 or a waiver is available;
- The respondent has paid a $1,000 penalty fee (unless exempt); and
- The respondent must be the beneficiary of an I-130, I-360, or labor certification filed on or before January 14, 1998; or if the I-130, I-360, or labor certification was filed after January 14, 1998, but on or before April 30, 2001, then the beneficiary must have been physically present in United States on December 21, 2000.

The following individuals may qualify for INA §245(i) relief without having to pay the $1,000 penalty fee: (1) children under age 17; and (2) Family Unity recipients or applicants. Family Unity is a special temporary status for spouses and unmarried children of persons who gained their permanent residency through one of the legalization programs. The applicant must have had the relationship of spouse or child with the legalized foreign national as of May 5, 1988, have entered the United States before May 5, 1988, resided in the United States on that date, have applied for benefits under the Family Unity program and is not an LPR.[21]

USCIS has adopted an *alien-based* interpretation of INA §245(i). Under this interpretation, the beneficiary of an I-130, I-360, or labor certification properly filed before April 30, 2001, is *grandfathered* and eligible to adjust status even though he or she may be adjusting based on a different petition. The petition or labor certification must have been *approvable when filed*, which means that it was submitted with the proper fee, signature and other substantive requirements, and must have been merito-

---

[21] INA §245(i)(1).

rious in fact and nonfrivolous.[22] If the petition is considered approvable when filed, then the beneficiary is grandfathered even if the petition is unadjudicated or later denied, withdrawn or revoked.[23]

Beneficiaries under INA §245(i) include spouses and children who are accompanying or following to join the principal foreign national. The derivative beneficiary does not have to adjust with the principal to be considered a grandfathered foreign national. Additionally, *after-acquired* spouses and children—*i.e.,* children born after the petition is filed, or spouses of principal beneficiaries whose marriage did not take place until after the petition is filed—are allowed to adjust under INA §245(i) as long as they acquire their status as the spouse or child before the principal adjusts. The grandfathering provision also includes derivative beneficiaries who age out before the principal beneficiary adjusts, and who therefore require a separate I-130 petition to be filed.[24]

Procedure

The respondent bears the burden of establishing that he or she is eligible for adjustment of status and merits a favorable exercise of discretion.[25] In order to assert the adjustment of status defense, the respondent must first make a threshold showing that he or she is prima facie eligible for the relief. In family-based adjustment cases, this is made by meeting two basic requirements: (1) the respondent must be the beneficiary of an approved I-130 petition; and (2) a visa must be presently available at the time of pleading the defense. Once the IJ is satisfied that the respondent is prima facie eligible for the relief, he or she should agree to schedule a full hearing on the merits.

The respondent will make a prima facie showing by presenting copies of the following documents to the IJ and the ICE trial attorney: (1) the I-797 Notice of Action (the I-130 approval notice); (2) the I-130 petition with any supporting documentation; (3) the Form G-325A Biographic Data; and (4) proof of the respondent's relative-petitioner's status and relationship to the respondent.

In cases where the respondents are making an application for relief before the IJ for the first time, they will make a prima facie showing that a visa is presently available by indicating to the court either that they are an immediate relative or, if not, that their preference category priority date is current. In the latter circumstance it is pref-

---

[22] 8 CFR §§245.10 (a), 1245.10 (a); *see also Matter of Jara Riero*, 24 I&N Dec. 267 (BIA 2007) (applicant under INA §245(i) must prove that marriage was meritorious at its inception).

[23] 8 CFR §§245.10(i), 1245.10(i).

[24] *See* INS Memorandum, R. Bach, "Accepting Applications for Adjustment of Status Under Section 245(i) of the Immigration and Nationality Act" (June 10, 1999), *published on* AILA InfoNet at Doc. No. 99061940 (*posted* June 19, 1999). *See also* USCIS Memorandum, W. Yates, "Clarification of Certain Eligibility Requirements Pertaining to an Application to Adjust Status Under Section 245(i) of the Immigration and Nationality Act" (Mar. 9, 2005), *published on* AILA InfoNet at Doc. No. 05031468 (*posted* Mar. 14, 2005).

[25] 8 CFR §§1240.8(d), 1240.11(e).

erable to tender to the IJ and the ICE attorney a copy of the latest visa bulletin with the relevant date highlighted.

When to Assert the Defense

The defense can be asserted at any point in removal proceedings. Typically it is made at the first master calendar hearing when pleadings initially are taken. The respondent makes an oral allegation of eligibility, at which point the IJ will demand that proof of prima facie eligibility be submitted. If the respondent wishes the case to proceed more quickly, it is best to be prepared to serve the court and ICE with the prima facie proof at the first master calendar hearing appearance. If not, the IJ may set the case for another master calendar hearing.

There are times when adjustment of status does not become available until proceedings have commenced on another form of relief (*e.g.,* asylum). In those circumstances, once the relief is available, the respondent will make an oral or written motion that this new defense be interposed and be made part of the pleadings. The IJ will then schedule a hearing on the application.

Before pleading to the allegations and charges and requesting adjustment of status relief, the Notice to Appear (NTA) should be reviewed carefully, as the respondent's classification on the NTA may determine whether he or she is eligible to adjust status before the IJ.

Motions to Continue

Motions to continue are effective tools in adjustment of status cases, though their usefulness has been somewhat diminished since the passage of the Illegal Immigration Reform and Immigrant Responsibility Act of 1996 (IIRAIRA).[26] In many cases, a motion to continue is the only way a respondent may gain time so that the adjustment of status defense may ripen. For example, if adjustment of status is the only form of relief that might be asserted at the master calendar hearing, but the I-130 petition has not been approved, or the priority date on a preference petition is not yet current, the respondent will want to move to continue or adjourn the case until such time as the relief might become available.

Obtaining a continuance in cases where the I-130 petition has been filed but not yet approved can be difficult, especially where the wait for visa availability is potentially long. In cases involving immediate relatives, where a visa is immediately available, the respondent will likely fare much better. Case law provides that in situations where the I-130 petition and adjustment of status application have been filed, the IJ generally should not deny a continuance solely because the I-130 petition has not been approved.[27]

---

[26] Illegal Immigration Reform and Immigrant Responsibility Act of 1996 (IIRAIRA), Pub. L. No. 104-208, div. C, 110 Stat. 3009, 3009-546 to 3009-724.

[27] *Matter of Garcia*, 16 I&N Dec. 653 (BIA 1978).

Although *Matter of Garcia*[28] deals with a motion to reopen deportation proceedings to apply for adjustment of status based on marriage to a U.S. citizen (USC), the BIA held that an IJ should exercise discretion to grant a motion to reopen or a motion to continue pending the final adjudication of a form I-130 petition "where a prima facie approvable visa petition and adjustment application have been submitted in the course of a deportation hearing or upon a motion to reopen." To wit, a motion to reopen or a motion for a continuance, based upon the simultaneous filing of an adjustment of status application and a form I-130, generally should be granted unless the applicant is *clearly ineligible* to be a beneficiary for the underlying petition.

The BIA revisited this issue in *Matter of Arthur*.[29] *Matter of Arthur* also dealt with a motion to reopen deportation proceedings to apply for adjustment of status based on marriage to a citizen of the United States. The BIA held that a motion to reopen to apply for adjustment of status based on an unadjudicated visa petition by the USC spouse should not be considered where the marriage was entered into during deportation or exclusion proceedings, and where the applicant had not lived outside the United States for two years after the date of the marriage. In coming to this determination, the BIA noted that Congress had amended the INA after *Matter of Garcia*[30] to add §§204(g) and 245(e), which preclude:

> "an applicant from adjusting his status based on a marriage that was entered into after the commencement of proceedings to determine his right to enter or remain in the United States and barred the approval of a visa petition to accord immediate relative or preference status based on such marriage until after the beneficiary of the petition had resided outside the United States for a 2-year period following the marriage."

The BIA also noted, however, that Congress later amended the INA again to provide an exception to the two-year foreign residence requirement and the bar to adjustment of status, if the applicant could establish by clear and convincing evidence that the marriage was entered into in good faith and was not entered into to evade the immigration law. Nevertheless, the BIA determined that this exception essentially created the presumption that marriages entered into after the commencement of deportation or exclusion proceedings were fraudulent. This presumption could only be overcome by clear and convincing evidence.

The BIA determined that *Matter of Garcia's* presumption that the marriage (on which a simultaneously filed adjustment of status and unadjudicated visa petition are based) was entered into in good faith was inconsistent with the presumption by Congress that marriages entered into after commencement of proceedings are fraudulent.

Consequently, the BIA modified its decision in *Matter of Garcia* to hold that it would decline to grant motions to reopen to apply for adjustment of status where the applicant seeks to obtain an immigrant visa based on a marriage entered into after the

---

[28] *Id.*

[29] *Matter of Arthur*, 20 I&N Dec. 475 (BIA 1992).

[30] *Garcia*, *supra* note 27.

commencement of deportation or exclusion proceedings and where the applicant has not resided outside the United States for at least two years after the date of the marriage. The BIA later reaffirmed this decision in *Matter of H–A–*.[31]

The BIA revisited the issue again, however, in *Matter of Velarde*.[32] Velarde filed a motion to reopen based on an unadjudicated visa petition by a spouse who was a USC. The Immigration and Naturalization Service (legacy INS) opposed the motion to reopen, claiming that *Matter of Arthur*[33] and *Matter of H–A–*[34] precluded its consideration of the motion. The BIA, however, granted the motion to reopen, and further held that properly filed motions to reopen may be granted if the following factors are present:

- The motion is timely filed;

- The motion is not numerically barred by the immigration regulations;

- The motion is not barred by *Matter of Shaar*,[35] or on any other procedural grounds;

- The motion presents clear and convincing evidence indicating a strong likelihood that the respondent's marriage is bona fide; and

- Legacy INS either does not oppose the motion or bases its opposition solely on *Matter of Arthur*.

This holding modified the decisions in *Matter of Arthur*[36] and *Matter of H–A–*[37] to allow for the granting of a motion to reopen to apply for adjustment of status, pending approval of the visa petition, as long as the applicant meets the five requirements listed above.

By requiring that the motion not be barred by *Matter of Shaar*,[38] the BIA emphasized the statutory prohibition against applying for certain forms of relief (*e.g.*, adjustment of status) when the applicant failed to depart the United States within the time period authorized under voluntary departure. Therefore, the BIA in *Matter of Velarde*[39] realized that if the foreign national was ineligible to apply for adjustment of status because of failure to voluntarily depart the United States within the authorized period, then the BIA should not consider a motion to reopen to file such an application for adjustment of status. (For a more in depth discussion of *Matter of Shaar*,[40] *see* chapter 10).

---

[31] *Matter of H–A–*, 22 I&N Dec. 728 (BIA 1999).

[32] *Matter of Velarde*, 23 I&N Dec. 253 (BIA 2002).

[33] *Arthur, supra* note 29.

[34] *H–A–, supra* note 31.

[35] *Matter of Shaar*, 21 I&N Dec. 541 (BIA 1996).

[36] *Arthur, supra* note 29.

[37] *H–A–, supra* note 31.

[38] *Shaar, supra* note 35.

[39] *Velarde, supra* note 32.

[40] *Shaar, supra* note 35.

If *Matter of Velarde*[41] authorizes the BIA and an IJ to exercise their discretion to grant a motion to reopen removal proceedings to apply for adjustment of status based on an unadjudicated visa petition filed by a USC spouse, then implicit in this holding is the authority for an IJ to grant a motion to continue a hearing when the motion to continue is based on an unadjudicated visa petition filed by a USC spouse or other immediate relative, where it appears the petition is approvable and the respondent would be eligible for adjustment based on the petition.[42] In cases where an unapproved visa petition is based on a marriage entered into after removal proceedings were commenced, the court might decline to grant a motion to continue. The advocate should argue by analogy, however, that *Matter of Velarde*[43] permits such a continuance.

In the Miami district, IJs routinely apply the U.S. Court of Appeals for the Eleventh Circuit's decision in *Bull v. INS*[44] to allow for a continuance in cases where a marriage to a USC occurred after proceedings commenced and an I-130 has been filed and is pending, or even has yet to be filed, if the petition appears approvable and the respondent appears eligible for adjustment. In cases where the marriage took place in proceedings and the respondent has an approved I-130 petition, the court should grant a continuance. While these guidelines have general applicability, the outcome of a motion request depends on each individual IJ.

Obtaining a continuance in preference cases where the I-130 petition has been approved but the priority date is not yet current will depend on the following factors:

- The length of time it will take for the priority date to become current;
- The equities of the case;
- The hardships involved;
- The availability of other relief and redundancy of administrative effort;
- The strength of the ICE attorney's objection; and
- The willingness of the IJ to keep the case on his or her docket.

Submitting Proof of Prima Facie Eligibility and Filing the Application

After pleadings have been filed, the IJ will ask for proof that the respondent is *prima facie* eligible for adjustment of status. The respondent will then have to file the application for adjustment of status. At the master calendar hearing, the IJ will ask if the application has been filed. If the application to adjust status already has been filed with USCIS, the IJ and the ICE trial attorney should be given a copy, with all supporting documentation attached, as well a copy of the USCIS fee receipt. If the case was filed under the provisions of INA §245(i), a copy of the supplemental form, Form I-485A, with a copy of the $1,000 USCIS fee receipt, should be served on the

---

[41] *Velarde, supra* note 32.

[42] *See also Bull v. INS*, 790 F.2d 869 (11th Cir. 1986).

[43] *Velarde, supra* note 32.

[44] *Bull v. INS, supra* note 42.

court and the ICE attorney as well. If none of those documents is readily available to the respondent, a continuance should be requested so that a submission can be made.

If the adjustment application has yet to be filed, the IJ will set a date for the application to be filed with the court. Before that date, the individual should comply with the new EOIR security procedures by sending a copy of the application, with the appropriate fee, to USCIS in Texas. Specifically, pursuant to the EOIR regulatory changes in 2005, which mandated certain security checks before the grant of any relief from removal,[45] the courts now require that an applicant for adjustment of status and other forms of relief mail a copy of the application for relief with the application and biometrics fees to a designated service center address in Mesquite, TX. After a receipt is produced, the applicant then is scheduled for a biometrics appointment at an application support center (ASC).[46]

On or before the due date set by the court, the individual should submit the original application with all required attachments to the IJ with the receipt showing that a copy was filed and the proper fee was paid to USCIS in Texas. A copy of the application also should be served on ICE district counsel. To comply with these security procedures, individuals also must appear for their scheduled biometrics appointment at an ASC. The applicant should receive and retain proof of compliance at the ASC. The EOIR regulations allow for dismissal of cases where applicants are deemed to have failed to timely comply with the new security procedures.

The original photographs required with the adjustment application should be submitted to the ICE trial attorney with copies for the IJ. Depending on local court practice, the IJ may require that the medical examination results be submitted with the application, or permit submission later at the hearing on the merits of the application.

Applications for waivers of inadmissibility should be filed with the adjustment application unless otherwise instructed by the IJ.[47]

The Merits Hearing

The IJ will schedule a hearing on the merits of the adjustment application for cases that are not terminated to proceed before USCIS. The procedural and evidentiary aspects of an adjustment of status hearing before an IJ are no different from those that characterize an asylum or cancellation of removal case. The respondent bears the burden of proving by a preponderance of the evidence that he or she is eligible to adjust status and, where applicable, is eligible for a waiver of inadmissibility.[48]

---

[45] *See* 70 Fed. Reg. 4743 (Jan. 31, 2005).

[46] The instructions distributed by the courts are *published on* AILA InfoNet at Doc. No. 05040472 (*posted* April 4, 2005), and appear here as Appendix 5.

[47] 8 CFR §1240.11(a)(2).

[48] 8 CFR §1240.8(d).

Adjustment of status may be denied by the IJ as a matter of discretion. Ordinarily, however, the IJ will grant the adjustment unless there are adverse factors.[49] Some of the factors to be considered for the exercise of discretion include:

- Family ties in the United States;

- Hardship of traveling abroad to process visa;

- Length of residence in the United States;

- Good moral character during the period preceding application for adjustment of status;

- Prior immigration violations; and

- Preconceived intent to immigrate at the time of entering as a nonimmigrant

At the conclusion of the hearing, the IJ will either grant or deny the adjustment application. If a grant is issued and ICE waives appeal, the file will be sent to USCIS for processing of the alien registration card (I-551). In some districts, the respondent's passport may be stamped as temporary evidence of permanent residence status.

Removal of Conditional Residence

Overview

The Immigration Marriage Fraud Amendments of 1986[50] created the conditional permanent resident status for certain spouses and children. This conditional resident status is imposed on individuals obtaining permanent resident status on or after November 10, 1986, if that status is based on a marriage that occurred within two years of entering the United States as an LPR or adjusting to permanent resident status within the United States. Conditional status also is imposed on the LPR's son and daughter, if they obtained an immigrant visa based on the parent's marriage to a USC or LPR.

At the end of the two-year period, the couple must file a joint petition to have the condition removed. The conditional resident also may file an application to waive the joint petition requirement if he or she can show either that:

- The marriage was entered into good faith but the spouse has died;

- The marriage was enter in good faith but the marriage has been terminated by divorce or annulment;

- The marriage was entered in good faith but the conditional resident has been battered or subjected to extreme cruelty by the citizen spouse; or

- Termination of permanent residency and deportation would result in extreme hardship.[51]

---

[49] *Matter of Arai*, 13 I&N Dec. 494 (BIA 1970).

[50] Immigration Marriage Fraud Amendments Act of 1986, Pub. L. No. 99-639, 100 Stat. 3537. The statutory provision is found at INA §216. The regulatory provisions are found at 8 CFR §§216.1 through 216.5, and 1216.1 through 1216.5.

[51] 8 CFR §§216.4(a), 1216.4(a).

If USCIS grants the petition and removes the conditional status, the conditional resident spouse is accorded full LPR status. If USCIS terminates the conditional status during the two-year period or denies the couple's joint petition to remove the condition, the conditional resident loses lawful immigration status and becomes subject to removal.[52]

Failure to Comply with Procedural Requirements

USCIS will terminate conditional residence and initiate proceedings when the foreign national fails to comply with procedural requirements. These will include:

- Failure to submit a joint petition to remove the condition at the end of the two-year period;

- Failure to file the application for waiver of joint petition;

- Failure by either spouse to appear for an interview on a joint petition; or

- Failure by the conditional resident to appear for an interview in a waiver application.[53]

While ICE retains the burden of establishing deportability, the foreign national bears the burden in the removal hearing to prove that he or she complied with the joint petition requirements. The foreign national will have to show, for example, that he or she did file timely, or has good cause for filing late and is prepared to file at the present time. ICE may join in a motion to continue proceedings pending the filing of a late waiver or joint petition. Likewise, the respondent bears the burden of proving that he or she is eligible for a waiver, that a separate ground for obtaining a waiver has become available, or that some other form of discretionary relief is available.

Where a joint petition was filed but the petition was subsequently withdrawn and the status was terminated, the BIA has stated that the joint petition was not properly filed. The burden of proving otherwise in removal proceedings would therefore fall on the respondent. Likewise, the respondent would bear the burden of showing that he or she complied with the interview requirements. If the respondent receives notice of termination for failure to appear at the scheduled interview, he or she may move USCIS to reconsider its decision to terminate status.

Denial of Joint Petition or Waiver Application

USCIS also will terminate conditional residence and initiate removal proceedings when it denies the joint petition or waiver application.[54] There are two situations where USCIS will deny a timely-filed joint petition: (1) when the qualifying marriage has been annulled or terminated, other than through the death of a spouse; and (2) when it makes a finding that a fee or other compensation was given for the marriage, or that the marriage was entered in bad faith.[55] USCIS will deny a waiver ap-

---

[52] 8 CFR §§216.4(d), 1216.4(d).

[53] 8 CFR §§216.4(a)(6), 1216.4(a)(6); 216.4(b)(3), 1216.4(b)(3).

[54] 8 CFR §§216.4(d)(2), 1216.4(d)(2); 216.5(f), 1216.5(f).

[55] 8 CFR §§216.4(c), 1216.4(c).

plication when it finds that the marriage was entered into in bad faith, the foreign national has not demonstrated extreme hardship, there was no battery or extreme cruelty, or that the foreign national does not merit the granting of the relief.[56]

A foreign national may seek review of the termination of conditional residency in a removal proceeding.[57] ICE has the burden of proof to establish, by a preponderance of the evidence, that the conditional residence was properly terminated.[58] The respondent then bears the burden of proving eligibility for the joint petition or waiver. The respondent must establish all the requirements of either the joint petition or one of the three waivers, and should be prepared to submit evidence of good faith marriage.

Immigration Court Jurisdiction

IJs lack original jurisdiction to rule on the merits of joint petitions to remove conditional status or on applications for a waiver of the joint petition requirement.[59] They only can conduct a de novo review of petitions and waiver applications that have been previously considered and denied by USCIS.[60] Note, however, that while the regulations specify that there is no administrative appeal available from USCIS's denial of a joint petition or waiver application, a respondent may ask USCIS to certify the case to the Administrative Appeals Office.[61] Alternatively, the respondent may file a motion to reopen a case by alleging new facts, or a motion to reconsider the denial by providing valid reasons.[62]

The conditional resident must first file the joint petition or waiver application with USCIS. If the respondent does not petition or apply for a waiver before USCIS, he or she may not make that request before the IJ in the first instance. Similarly, a respondent whose timely-filed waiver application is denied by USCIS, but who is eligible for another waiver on different grounds, may not seek consideration of the second waiver application in removal proceedings, but must submit it first to USCIS. Conditional residents will be placed in removal proceedings in three situations:

- The marriage has terminated during the two-year conditional residency period;

- The conditional resident has failed to file a timely joint petition or waiver at the end of the two-year period; or

- The joint petition or waiver application was filed but was denied by the USCIS.

---

[56] 8 CFR §§216.5, 1216.5.

[57] 8 CFR §§216.3, 1216.3.

[58] *Id.*

[59] 8 CFR §§216.4(a)(3), 1216.4(a)(3); 216.5(c), 1216.5(c).

[60] 8 CFR §§216.4(d)(2), 1216.4(d)(2); 216.5(f), 1216.5(f).

[61] 8 CFR §§103.4(a)(4), (5).

[62] 8 CFR §103.5.

NACARA §202 and HRIFA

Introduction

Two nationality-specific forms of relief provide for adjustment of status for persons in removal proceedings: NACARA[63] §202 and HRIFA.[64] The application period for both of these programs expired on March 31, 2000, though derivatives continue to be eligible to apply under HRIFA, and VAWA 2005[65] provisions made both forms of relief available to a new set of foreign nationals.[66]

NACARA §202

NACARA §202 allows eligible Nicaraguans and Cubans to adjust status to permanent residence. They must have been continuously present in the United States since, on, or before December 1, 1995, and otherwise admissible. A number of grounds of inadmissibility are expressly waived. A foreign national may be considered to have failed to maintain continuous physical presence if he or she was absent from the United States for a period exceeding 180 days in the aggregate between December 1, 1995, and the date of filing for adjustment of status.

In addition, certain family members of NACARA beneficiaries are eligible for adjustment of status under NACARA §202. In order to benefit as a dependent, the applicant must be a Nicaraguan or Cuban national (not necessarily the same nationality as the principal) and be either the spouse, child (unmarried and under 21), or son or daughter (unmarried and 21 or older) of a NACARA principal. The relationship must exist at the time of the principal's adjustment. The dependents must:

- Be physically present in the United States at the time the application is filed;
- Be admissible, notwithstanding grounds of inadmissibility expressly waived for the principal; and
- In the case of a son or daughter, establish presence on or before December 1, 1995, and continuous presence from that date until at least the date the application for adjustment is filed.

The regulations provide that applicants must demonstrate commencement of physical presence no later than December 1, 1995, and continuity of presence. The commencement may be established by one of the following:

- An asylum application;
- An order to show cause;
- A notice commencing exclusion proceedings;

---

[63] NACARA, *supra* note 6. The regulations pertaining to §202 of NACARA are found at 8 CFR §§245.13 and 1245.13.

[64] HRIFA, *supra* note 5. The regulations pertaining to HRIFA are found at 8 CFR §§245.15 and 1245.15.

[65] VAWA 2005, *supra* note 3.

[66] Provisions relating to these forms of relief can be found at NACARA §815 and VAWA 2005 §824.

- An application for adjustment of status;

- An application for employment authorization;

- Service or employment reflected in records maintained by the commissioner for Social Security;

- An application for any benefit under the INA; and

- Any other form of proof as provided by the attorney general through regulation. Expressly authorized are state and local official records bearing a seal of authority, as well as hospital and school records.

Continuous physical presence may be established by the submission of at least one document indicating presence for each 90-day period. This is not a requirement but a guideline, and adjudicators have the discretion of requiring additional documents. Applicants may have been outside the country for periods that do not exceed 180 days in the aggregate. The regulations set forth a list of possible documents for proving continuity of physical presence. Such documents may include, but are not limited to:

- School records;

- Rental receipts;

- Utility bill receipts and other dated receipts;

- Personal checks bearing a dated bank cancellation;

- Employment records;

- Credit card statements showing transactions;

- Certified copies of records maintained by organizations such as banks and schools;

- Evidence of physical presence of family members such as spouses or parents; and

- Correspondence or interaction with USCIS that may be contained in their records.

In general, applicants must have submitted the adjustment application prior to April 1, 2000, and otherwise be eligible to immigrate into the United States. However, VAWA 2005 §815 allows abused spouses and children eligible for status under NACARA §202 to apply even if their abuser did not apply, and even though the April 1, 2000, deadline has long since passed.

The following grounds of inadmissibility do no apply: public charge, lack of labor certification, illegal entry, lack of a required visa, and unlawful presence. If the applicant is inadmissible under other grounds, he or she will not be granted adjustment unless a waiver is available and is granted.

Where an applicant for adjustment of status is in deportation, exclusion, or removal proceedings before an IJ, or where the applicant has a motion to reopen or motion to reconsider filed with the IJ on or before May 21, 1998, the jurisdiction to adjudicate the application lies exclusively with the IJ.[67] In situations where the IJ must consider the motion to reopen or motion to reconsider and where the foreign national

---

[67] 8 CFR §§245.13(d)(1), 1245.13(d)(1).

submits an application for adjustment of status under §202 of NACARA, then the IJ shall reopen the proceedings to consider the application unless the applicant is clearly ineligible for adjustment of status under §202.

The IJ has authority to close administratively deportation, exclusion, or removal proceedings to permit the foreign national to file an application for adjustment of status with USCIS.[68] ICE must concur in the foreign national's request for administrative closure of the case.[69]

Where an applicant for adjustment of status is in deportation, exclusion, or removal proceedings and has an appeal pending before the BIA or where the foreign national filed a motion to reopen or a motion to reconsider with the BIA on or before May 21, 1998, the BIA either will remand the case to the IJ or reopen the case and remand it to the IJ to adjudicate the application, unless the foreign national clearly is ineligible for relief under §202 of NACARA.[70] The BIA, upon request by the foreign national and with the concurrence of ICE, also may close the proceedings administratively to permit the foreign national to file with USCIS an application for adjustment of status under §202 of NACARA.[71]

The USCIS Texas Service Center (TSC) has jurisdiction over all NACARA §202 adjustment of status applications not under the jurisdiction of the EOIR immigration court or BIA.[72] The interviews for the adjustment of status applications, however, will be conducted by the local USCIS district offices.[73] In these situations, the TSC may permit the local USCIS office to adjudicate the application.[74] If USCIS denies an application for adjustment of status under §202 of NACARA, then the foreign national may renew the application before the immigration court in proceedings.[75]

Foreign nationals present in the United States who have been excluded, deported, removed, or have an outstanding order to voluntarily depart, may still be eligible to adjust under NACARA §202. Separate motions to reopen, reconsider, or vacate are not necessary.[76] If USCIS grants the application for adjustment, the order is rescinded automatically.[77] Alternatively, if USCIS denies the application, the order will be effective and enforceable.

---

[68] 8 CFR §§245.13(d)(3), 1245.13(d)(3).

[69] 8 CFR §§245.13(d)(3)(i), 1245.13(d)(3)(i).

[70] 8 CFR §§245.13(d)(2), 1245.13(d)(2).

[71] 8 CFR §§245.13(d)(3)(i), 1245.13(d)(3)(i).

[72] 8 CFR §§245.13(h), 1245.13(h).

[73] 8 CFR §245.13(i)(1).

[74] Id.

[75] 8 CFR §§245.13(m), 1245.13(n).

[76] 8 CFR §§245.13(d)(4)(i), 1245.13(d)(4)(i).

[77] 8 CFR §§245.13(l), 1245.13(l).

The Legal Immigration and Family Equity (LIFE) Act[78] and LIFE Act Amendments of 2000[79] amended NACARA §202(a) adjustment for certain Nicaraguans and Cubans to provide that:

- INA §241(a)(5)—reinstatement of prior removal order and ineligibility for any relief under the INA—does not apply.

- USCIS may waive INA §212(a)(9)(A)—ground of inadmissibility for Certain Aliens Previously Removed—and 212(a)(9)(C)—ground of inadmissibility for Aliens Unlawfully Present After Previous Immigration Violations.

- Notwithstanding any time and number limits imposed by law (other than those premised on conviction of aggravated felony), Nicaraguans and Cubans who become eligible for adjustment under NACARA as a result of these amendments may file one motion to reopen. The scope of the motion is limited to eligibility for NACARA adjustment; all such motions must be filed within 180 days of enactment, or June 19, 2001.

In cases where the dependent or applicant is outside of the United States, USCIS provided by regulation for the possibility of advance parole (Form I-131). USCIS has delayed the adjudication of these applications, causing problems and administrative delays.

Haitian Refugee Immigration Fairness Act (HRIFA)

The Haitian Refugee Immigration Fairness Act (HRIFA) provides for adjustment of status for certain Haitian nationals and their dependents. In order to qualify, the principal must have entered the United States on or before December 31, 1995, be continuously present since that date, and be physically present at the time of filing. A foreign national may be considered to have failed to maintain physical presence if he or she has been absent from the United States for periods, in the aggregate, exceeding 180 days between December 31, 1995, and the date of adjustment. Although the application deadline for principals expired on March 31, 2000, the application period for dependents remains open indefinitely. VAWA 2005[80] extended the availability of adjustment under HRIFA to those who can demonstrate that, during the registration period for principals, they qualified as spouses and children of foreign national abusers who were eligible, but never applied, for HRIFA as principals.

Under HRIFA, the principal applicant must satisfy one of the following:

- Applied for asylum before December 31, 1995;

- Was admitted or paroled on or before December 31, 1995;

---

[78] Legal Immigration and Family Equity Act (LIFE Act), Pub. L. No. 106-553, §1(a)(2) (appx. B, H.R. 5548, §§1101–04), 114 Stat. 2762, 2762A-142 to 2762A-149 (2000).

[79] LIFE Act Amendments of 2000, Pub. L. No. 106-554, appx. D, div. B, §§1501–06, 114 Stat. 2763, 2763A-324 to 2763A-328.

[80] VAWA 2005, *supra* note 3.

- Was a child at the time of arrival and, on December 31, 1995, arrived without parents, became orphaned subsequent to arrival, or was abandoned prior to April 1, 1998, and has remained abandoned;

The following grounds of inadmissibility do not apply: public charge, lack of labor certification, illegal entry, lack of a required visa, and unlawful presence.

To qualify as a dependent son or daughter, the applicant must:

- Be a national of Haiti;

- Have the necessary relationship to a qualified principal applicant at the time of the principal's adjustment of status and at the time of the dependent's adjustment of status, unless they qualify under the VAWA 2005 provision discussed above;

- Be physically present on or before December 31, 1995;

- Be continuously physical present since December 31, 1995 (except for absences totaling 180 days or less);

- Be present in the United States at the time of filing (which need not be before April 1, 2000); and

- Be admissible (except for the grounds that are waived).

To qualify as a dependent spouse or child, the applicant must:

- Be a national of Haiti;

- Have the necessary relationship to a qualified principal applicant at the time of the principal's adjustment of status and at the time of the dependent's adjustment of status, unless they qualify under the VAWA 2005 provision summarized above;

- In the case of a child, be under 21 years of age and unmarried;

- Be present in the United States at the time of filing (which need not be before April 1, 2000); and

- Be admissible (except for the grounds that are waived).

Commencement of presence on or before December 31, 1995, may be established by the submission of proof of one of the following:

- Admission to the United States as an immigrant or nonimmigrant;

- Parole into the United States;

- Placement into exclusion or deportation proceedings;

- Application for any benefit under the Act;

- Documentation issued by local, state or federal authorities demonstrating presence; or

- School records.

Proof of continuous physical presence may include such documents as:

- School record;

- Rental receipts;

- Utility bill receipts and other dated receipts;

- Personal checks bearing a dated bank cancellation;

- Employment records;

- Credit card statements showing transactions;

- Certified copies of records maintained by organizations such as banks and schools;

- Evidence of physical presence of family members such as spouses and parents; and

- Correspondence or interaction with USCIS that may be contained in their records similar to that required under NACARA §202.

The USCIS Nebraska Service Center (NSC) has jurisdiction over all applications for adjustment of status under HRIFA, unless the immigration court or the BIA has jurisdiction over a case.[81] The NSC director may refer an applicant for adjustment under HRIFA to a local USCIS office for an interview, in which case the local USCIS office may take jurisdiction over the case.[82] Essentially, this means that the NSC will maintain jurisdiction over an application for adjustment of status under HRIFA where it intends to approve or deny the application without interview. The local USCIS office will take jurisdiction over the case when the applicant must personally be interviewed.[83]

If a foreign national is in deportation, exclusion, or removal proceedings before either the immigration court or the BIA, or has filed on or before May 12, 1999, a motion to reopen or motion to reconsider with either the immigration court or the BIA, then the foreign national must apply for adjustment of status under HRIFA to either the immigration court or the BIA, whichever is handling the case.[84]

If a foreign national is in deportation, exclusion, or removal proceedings, or filed a motion to reopen or motion to reconsider such proceedings on or before May 12, 1999, then the foreign national can request administrative closure of such proceedings or request that the immigration court or the BIA indefinitely continue the motion so that the foreign national may apply with USCIS for adjustment of status under HRIFA.[85] ICE must concur in the request for administrative closure for the Immigration Court or the BIA to grant the request.[86] Once the case is closed administratively, USCIS has sole jurisdiction over the application for adjustment of status under HRIFA.[87] If USCIS denies an application for adjustment of status under HRIFA, then

---

[81] 8 CFR §§245.15(g)(1), 1245.15(g)(1).

[82] *Id.*

[83] 8 CFR §§245.15(o)(1)–(3).

[84] 8 CFR §§245.15(g)(2), 1245.15(g)(2).

[85] 8 CFR §§245.15(p)(4), 1245.15(p)(4).

[86] *Id.*

[87] 8 CFR §§245.15(g)(2), (p)(4)(ii), 1245.15(g)(2), (p)(4)(ii).

the foreign national may renew the application before the immigration court in proceedings.[88]

If the foreign national has a final order of deportation, exclusion, or removal, then jurisdiction over applications for adjustment of status under HRIFA lies solely with USCIS. In cases where the individual is unless they are impacted by the LIFE Act (discussed below), however, one motion to reopen may be filed.[89]

The LIFE Act and LIFE Act Amendments of 2000 modify HRIFA and its enforcement in the following ways:

- INA §241(a)(5)—reinstatement of prior removal order and ineligibility for any relief under the INA] does not apply.

- INA §212(a)(9)(A) and (C) may be waived.

- Notwithstanding any time and number limits imposed by law (other than those premised on conviction of aggravated felony), Haitians who become eligible for adjustment under HRIFA as a result of these amendments may file one motion to reopen. The scope of the motions is limited to eligibility for HRIFA adjustment, and all such motions must be filed within 180 days of enactment, or June 19, 2001.

Registry[90]

Registry is a method by which foreign nationals who have resided continuously in the United States since January 1, 1972, can gain lawful permanent residence through the creation of a record of admission. The foreign national may apply directly with the USCIS or to the IJ if in removal proceedings. Registry applications that are approved confer lawful permanent residence upon the applicant as of the date the application is granted.

Eligibility Requirements

To qualify for registry, the foreign national must meet the following requirements:

- Have entered the United States prior to January 1, 1972;
- Have maintained residence in the United States since such entry;
- Be a person of good moral character;
- Not be ineligible to citizenship pursuant to INA §101(a)(19) or deportable as a terrorist under INA §237(a)(4)(B); and
- Not be inadmissible under grounds described below.

---

[88] 8 CFR §§245.15(r), 1245.15(r).

[89] 8 CFR §§245.15(g)(3), 1245.15(g)(3).

[90] INA §249.

Residence

The burden of proof to establish an entry prior to January 1, 1972, is on the person seeking registry.[91] The entry date can be established through various forms of documentary and testimonial evidence, such as passports, Form I-94 (arrival-departure record) travel documents, receipts, and affidavits from the applicant and other witnesses.

The person seeking registry must establish that he or she has continuously resided in the United States since January 1, 1972. Although such residence must be continuous, the law does not require actual physical presence in the United States during the entire period. Temporary absences, without abandonment of residence in the United States, will not preclude establishment of the required residence.

When evaluating whether a departure by the applicant may have interrupted his or her continuous residence in the United States, consider the following factors:

- Maintenance of an apartment or home in the United States;

- Establishment of a residence outside the United States during the trip abroad;

- Personal property left in the United States (*e.g.,* car, furniture, clothing);

- Return to school or a job in the United States;

- Maintenance of a bank account in the United States or any other financial interests;

- Close family ties in the United States;

- Representations of intent to remain in the United States temporarily either at a U.S. consulate abroad or upon re-entry to the United States;

- Current driver's license issued by the state in which he or she resides;

- Income tax returns filed for past years;

- Ownership of real property in the United States;

- Number of trips outside the United States;

- Length of time outside the United States for each trip; and

- The purpose of each trip.

Neither the statute nor the cases establish a specific number of absences from the United States or a specific length of absence that precludes establishing continuous residence. In *Matter of Harrison*,[92] for example, continuous residence was not broken where the absence was for three years and five months, and was due to the foreign national's service in the Canadian military during World War II. In *Matter of Lettman*,[93] however, continuous residence was broken by a series of absences, the longest of which was not more than five months during which the applicant was a Jamaican contract worker who received renewals of his nonimmigrant status on the basis that

---

[91] 8 CFR §§1240.8(d), 1240.11(e).

[92] *Matter of Harrison,* 13 I&N Dec. 540 (Dist. Dir. 1970).

[93] *Matter of Lettman,* 11 I&N Dec. 878 (Reg. Comm'r 1966).

he had no intention of abandoning his foreign residence. In some cases, a registry applicant may prove continuous residence in the United States since entry, notwithstanding numerous brief departures from the United States. For example, in *Matter of Qutin*,[94] a merchant seaman established continuous residence in spite of 53 absences during the course of five years. The main consideration in each of these cases was not the duration or frequency of the absences, but rather the ties that the foreign national maintained to the United States during each absence, and the ties maintained to the country of origin. Obviously, the more ties in the United States and the fewer in the country of origin, the better.

Good Moral Character

Applicants must demonstrate that they are persons of good moral character (GMC). There is no fixed period for which the applicant must demonstrate good moral character, but generally he or she should be of good moral character at the time of the application and for a reasonable period of time preceding the application.[95] The burden of proof is on the registry applicant to establish GMC. In the immigration context, good moral character is a loosely-defined term based generally on adherence to the moral standards of the average person. Certain classes of persons are precluded by law from establishing good moral character, as set forth in INA §101(f). In addition to these statutory preclusions, other matters may be taken into consideration, such as neglect of family responsibilities or illegal activities where no prosecution took place. While occasional lapses may not bar a finding of GMC, the more serious any prior misconduct is, the longer the intervening period of good behavior must be before the applicant can meet his or her burden of establishing GMC.

Not Ineligible to Citizenship

An applicant for registry would be *ineligible to citizenship* if he or she had ever requested an exemption or discharge from training or service in the armed forces of the United States on the grounds that he or she was a foreign national.[96] Also, foreign nationals who deserted the United States armed forces or left the United States for the purpose of evading the draft while the United States was at war, and who were convicted of such offense by a court martial or court of competent jurisdiction, are ineligible for registry.[97] Between 1918 and 1971, the Selective Service laws allowed foreign nationals to claim an exemption from military service. However, the consequence of such a claim was also permanent disbarment from citizenship.

Grounds of Inadmissibility

Most of the grounds of inadmissibility are waived. The only grounds that apply are those related to "criminals, procurers and other immoral persons, subversives,

---

[94] *Matter of Qutin*, 14 I&N Dec. 6 (BIA 1972).

[95] *Matter of Sanchez-Linn*, 20 I&N Dec. 362 (BIA 1991).

[96] INA §315(a).

[97] INA §314.

violators of the narcotics laws or smugglers of aliens[.]"[98] The following grounds of inadmissibility (among others) do not apply to registry applicants: medical grounds; public charge; stowaway; and fraud provisions.

Exercise of Discretion

Registry is a discretionary remedy. The exercise of discretion requires a weighing of all the positive and negative factors in an applicant's case. Some of the positive factors that USCIS or the IJ may consider in determining whether a favorable exercise of discretion is warranted include:

- Family ties in the United States;
- Hardship that would result if permanent residence in denied;
- Employment history;
- Property or business ties;
- Value and service to the community;
- Payment of income taxes; and
- Other evidence of good character.

If there are substantial negative factors in a case, USCIS or the IJ might deny the application in the exercise of discretion. Some negative considerations may involve the presence of significant violations of U.S. immigration laws or criminal laws and other evidence of bad character.

The Application Process

The respondent files for registry by submitting:

- Form I-485 (Application for Adjustment of Status);
- Form G-325A (Biographic Information);
- Two photographs;
- Affidavits (preferably from USCs) establishing GMC;
- Documentary evidence supporting the foreign national's continuous residence in the United States; and
- The required fee.

Since the health-related and public charge grounds of inadmissibility do not apply, no medical exam, affidavit of support, or employer's letter is required.

The regulations provide that the "documentary evidence may include any records of official or personal transactions or recordings of events occurring during the period of claimed residence," and that "affidavits of credible witnesses may also be accepted."[99] Although affidavits stating that the applicant resided in the United States

---

[98] INA §249.

[99] 8 CFR §249.2(a) and 8 CFR §1249.2(a).

during the time in question are acceptable, it is unlikely that affidavits alone would be sufficient to establish residence.

Persons who were not the head of the household in which they lived may have difficulty documenting their presence because rental receipts, bank accounts, etc., may not have been in their names. This may be especially true for married women who have not worked outside the home, or for children who lived in their parents' home. The regulations provide, however, that "[p]ersons unemployed and unable to furnish evidence in their own names may furnish evidence in the names of parents or other persons with whom they have been living, if affidavits of the parents or other persons are submitted attesting to the residence."[100]

Proving continuous residence does not require documenting every week of the person's life since 1972. But evidence should be submitted to show a pattern that will logically lead to the conclusion that the applicant has resided continuously in the United States for the period of time alleged.

Adjustment of Status for Certain Foreign Nationals from Vietnam, Cambodia, and Laos

On December 26, 2002, a final rule was issued implementing §586 of the Foreign Operations Appropriations Act of 2001 (FOAA), signed into law by President Bill Clinton on November 6, 2000.[101] FOAA §586 provides for the adjustment of status of 5,000 natives or citizens from Vietnam, Cambodia, and Laos who are in the United States. In the Consolidated Appropriations Act of 2005,[102] Congress amended the law to eliminate both the 5,000 adjustment quota and the three-year application deadline that originally applied to these cases.

To be eligible to adjust under §586 of the FOAA, an applicant must have been physically present in the United States before and on October 1, 1997. An individual also must have been inspected and paroled into the United States before that date from a refugee camp in East Asia, a displaced persons camp run by the United Nations in Thailand, or from Vietnam under the Orderly Departure Program (ODP). The ODP program was an initiative of the U.N. High Commissioner of Refugees started in 1979 to provide a safe, legal alternative to dangerous departures by boat or over land from Vietnam to the United States.

The final rule sets forth the eligibility standards for adjustment under FOAA §586, guidance on the submission of evidence, and the application and adjudication procedures. The regulations implementing FOAA §586 are found at 8 CFR §§245.21 and §1245.21.

Certain grounds of inadmissibility do not apply to applicants for adjustment under §586 of the FOAA. These grounds of inadmissibility include:

- INA §212(a)(4)—relating to public charge;

---

[100] 8 CFR §249.2(a) and 8 CFR §1249.2(a).

[101] Pub. L. No. 106-429, 114 Stat. 1900.

[102] Pub. L. No. 108-447, 118 Stat. 2809.

- INA §212(a)(5)—relating to labor certification requirements and certifications for foreign health care workers;

- INA §212(a)(7)(A)—relating to visa and travel documents; and

- INA §212(a)(9)—relating to prior removals and unlawful presence.

Moreover, FOAA §586 allows USCIS to waive certain other grounds of inadmissibility, including grounds relating to:

- Health;

- Failure to attend removal proceedings;

- Misrepresentation;

- Document fraud violations;

- Citizenship ineligibilities;

- Guardians of helpless foreign nationals; and

- Unlawful voting.

The waiver is intended to prevent extreme hardship to the applicant or the applicant's qualifying spouse, parent, son or daughter. The applicant may apply for any other waiver under INA §212 to which the applicant is eligible but the applicant must demonstrate extreme hardship to a qualifying family member specified in that provision.

In order to prove the citizenship, physical presence, residency, and status requirements listed above, an applicant must furnish copies of:

- A birth certificate or other evidence of birth;

- Documentation showing presence in the United States before and on October 1, 1997;

- Arrival-departure record (I-94) or other evidence that the applicant was paroled into the United States before October 1, 1997, from one of the three programs (if the applicant no longer has this document, he or she may submit an affidavit discussing the loss of the document, and USCIS will attempt to verify the appropriate admission into the United States by consulting its files);

- Documentation showing proof of presence in the United States on the date of filing the application; and

- In cases where government-issued documentation (preferred as the strongest proof) is not available, school records, affidavits, and other forms of proof will be accepted and adjudicated on a case-by-case basis.

Each applicant must submit a complete application. The application to adjust status should have the following:

- Form I-485 (Application to Register Permanent Residence or Adjust Status) with appropriate filing fee or request for fee waiver;

- Fingerprinting fee if the applicant is 14 to 79 years of age;

- Evidence of eligibility (as noted above: birth certificates or other proof of birth, etc.);

- Form G-325A (Biographic Information Sheet if the applicant is 14 to 79 years of age) in quadruplicate;

- Form I-693 (Medical Examination of Aliens Seeking Adjustment of Status with Vaccination Supplement), which must be submitted in an envelope sealed by the physician;

- a complete form I-601 enclosed with the appropriate fee, if a waiver of a ground of inadmissibility is necessary; and

- Form G-28 (Notice of Appearance as Attorney or Representative) (if appropriate).

Individuals who are in removal proceedings may not receive lawful permanent residence under this law from the BIA or the IJ. Instead, they must obtain the consent of the ICE trial attorney, move jointly to close the proceedings administratively, and have USCIS adjudicate the application.[103] Applicants who are ineligible due to various grounds of inadmissibility—*e.g.*, criminal convictions, fraud, immigration violations, citizenship ineligibility, or illegal voting—will not receive a number in the adjudication queue until their waiver has been approved. While the prior removal and unlawful presence grounds do not apply to applicants, a departure followed by a denial of the application may amount to a self-deportation.

Both humanitarian and public interest parolees who otherwise fit the criteria may adjust status under the final rule. This is a significant eligibility expansion as the draft rule covered only public interest parolees.

Though applicants will not be barred due to public charge, they must supply answers to questions regarding use of public benefits. Question "h" under Part 2 on the adjustment of status application (Form I-485) should be answered "INDOCHINESE PAROLEE P.L.106-429." Applications should be filed with the NSC.

Of extreme importance to the applicants and the immigration practitioners who assist them is the fact that a foreign national's lawful permanent residence will be recorded as beginning on the date he or she was paroled into the United States. Since this had to have occurred prior to October of 1997, all successful adjustment applicants will immediately qualify for the five years of lawful permanent residence necessary for naturalization.

The final rule provides that foreign nationals with final orders of deportation, exclusion, or removal must apply for adjustment of status directly with USCIS.[104] Therefore, they need not file a motion to reopen or reconsider proceedings.

An application for adjustment of status does not automatically stay the execution of a final order of deportation, exclusion, or removal. Therefore, a foreign national eligible for adjustment of status under this provision should request from ICE a stay

---

[103] 8 CFR §§245.21(c), 1245.21(c).

[104] 8 CFR §245.21(d).

of execution of the final order of deportation, exclusion, or removal during the pendency of the application.

In the situation of a person with a final order, if USCIS grants the application for adjustment of status under this provision, then the foreign national's proceedings are considered automatically reopened; the final order is considered vacated, and the reopened proceedings are considered terminated.[105]

Cuban Adjustment Act of 1966 (CAA)[106]

The CAA permits citizens or nationals of Cuba to adjust their status if they have been physically present in the United States for at least one year after admission or parole and are admissible as immigrants. Individuals who have status in, resided in, or even are citizens of another country than Cuba still may adjust under the CAA, so long as they can prove that they remain a citizen or native of Cuba. For example, it is not uncommon to see individuals born in Cuba, who later became citizens of Spain, come to the United States and adjust under the CAA as Cuban natives.

Importantly, the CAA also permits spouses and children of Cubans to adjust status under the act, even if they are not citizens or nationals of Cuba. Adjustment of non-Cuban spouses and children under the CAA is discussed in more detail below.

The CAA is a very generous form of relief, allowing for the adjustment of individuals who arrive under almost any circumstance or status, so long as they have been inspected and admitted or paroled. For example, Cubans who originally entered on K visas have been permitted to adjust under the CAA after one year of physical presence, even if they did not marry within 90 days of entry as required by the K visa. Cubans who enter in V visa status also have adjusted under the CAA after accruing one year of physical presence in the United States. Likewise, those who entered under the Visa Waiver Program also have been permitted to adjust under the CAA.

The public charge ground of inadmissibility does not apply to applicants under the CAA. Also, Cuban nationals or citizens—as well as their spouse and children—who arrive in the United States at other than a designated port-of-entry also are eligible to adjust status as long as they receive parole.[107] Moreover, even those who are placed in removal proceedings and charged as *arriving aliens* without valid visa or entry documents may apply to adjust status to permanent residence under the CAA before an IJ.[108]

---

[105] 8 CFR §§245.21(d)(4), 1245.21(d)(4).

[106] Cuban Adjustment Act, *supra* note 4.

[107] *See* INS Memorandum, D. Meissner, "Eligibility for Permanent Residence Under the Cuban Adjustment Act Despite Having Arrived at a Place Other Than a Port-of-Entry," (April 19, 1999), *reprinted in* 76 *Interpreter Releases* 684–90 (May 3, 1999).

[108] *Matter of Artigas*, 23 I&N Dec. 99 (BIA 2001).

An applicant for adjustment of status under the CAA is not required to have an immigrant visa immediately available for him or her, unlike other applicants for adjustment of status.

Spouses and Children of Cubans

As stated above, the CAA permits spouses and children of Cubans to adjust status under the CAA even if they are not citizens or nationals of Cuba. However, in general, in order for the spouse or child of a Cuban citizen or national to be eligible for adjustment of status under the CAA, both the qualifying relationship with the principal applicant must continue to exist and the spouse and/or child must reside with the principal applicant in the United States until the spouse or child adjusts their status in the United States.

Fortunately, VAWA 2000[109] created an exception to this residence requirement for dependent spouses or children who have suffered domestic violence at the hands of the principal applicant. Further, new VAWA 2005 provisions allow the spouse of an abusive Cuban to apply for adjustment of status up to two years after the death of, or divorce from, the spouse, so long as the abused spouse can show a connection between the termination of the marriage and being battered or subject to extreme cruelty by the Cuban spouse.[110] In all cases, the spouse or child must file his or her own separate applications for adjustment of status under the CAA, and he or she must be eligible to receive an immigrant visa and be admissible as an immigrant. While spouses or children also must establish that they themselves have been admitted or paroled and have accumulated one year of physical presence, they can apply for adjustment even if the Cuban citizen or native has not applied to adjust. Moreover, spouses who adjust under the CAA are not subject to conditional residency—they get full residency immediately.

How to Apply

Each applicant in proceedings must file Form I-485 with the immigration court after complying with the new EOIR security procedures. The applicant must submit a birth certificate or other record of birth (with a translation to English), as well as two photographs. If the applicant is between the ages of 14 and 79, then he or she must submit a completed Form G-325A (Biographic Information). The applicant also must submit evidence of his or her admission or parole into the United States, such as the Form I-94 Arrival/Departure card, and evidence of physical presence in the United States for at least one year. He or she must undergo and submit the results of a medical examination (which might include vaccinations). Additionally, the applicant must submit a clearance from the local police in the United States for any area he or she has lived for six months or more since his or her 14th birthday.

---

[109] Violence Against Women Act of 2000 (VAWA 2000), Pub. L. No. 106-386, div. B, 114 Stat 1464, 1491–539.

[110] VAWA 2005, *supra* note 3.

CHAPTER SIX
WAIVERS OF INADMISSIBILITY AND DEPORTABILITY IN REMOVAL PROCEEDINGS

This chapter addresses how waivers may be used to overcome inadmissibility and deportability in removal proceedings. It begins with a discussion of the waivers of inadmissibility grounds, under the Immigration and Nationality Act (INA)[1] §212.

Inadmissibility grounds may arise in several ways during a removal proceeding. First, the respondent may be in removal proceedings based on an inadmissibility ground. Second, he or she may be in removal proceedings based on the deportability ground under INA §237(a)(1)(A)—*i.e.*, having been inadmissible at the time of entry or adjustment of status on a ground of inadmissibility existing at that time. Third, if a respondent who is found removable is eligible for an immigrant visa, he or she may seek relief from removal in the form of adjustment of status to permanent residence. This requires the respondent to establish that he or she is admissible. If the respondent is found inadmissible in any of these circumstances, he or she may apply for any of the waivers of inadmissibility for which he or she is eligible.

Note that the respondent may apply for a waiver of inadmissibility in removal proceedings only to overcome removability based on inadmissibility or to establish admissibility for purposes of adjustment of status. Unlike other forms of relief from removal, waivers of inadmissibility standing alone cannot be asserted as affirmative applications for relief from removal.[2]

This chapter first focuses on six specific waivers of inadmissibility. These waivers are:

- INA §212(g) waiver for certain health-related grounds;
- INA §212(h) waiver for criminal conduct;
- INA §212(i) waiver for fraud or misrepresentation;
- INA §212(a)(9)(B)(v) waiver for unlawful presence;
- INA §212(d)(3) waiver for nonimmigrants; and
- INA §209(c) waiver for asylees and refugees.

Next, the chapter examines a waiver-like provision: permission to reenter the United States after a formal deportation or removal order. Under this provision, a per-

---

[1] Immigration and Nationality Act of 1952 (INA), Pub. L. No. 82-414, 66 Stat. 163 (codified as amended at 8 USC §§1101 *et seq.*).

[2] *Matter of Balao*, 20 I&N Dec. 440 (BIA 1992); *but see Yeung v. INS*, 76 F.3d 337 (11th Cir. 1995) (finding INA §212(h) waiver available as a stand alone application for relief for a person who never left the United States).

son ordered deported or removed from the United States (and, therefore, inadmissible for a certain period of time) may request permission to return to the United States before the period of inadmissibility ends.

Finally, the chapter looks at two waivers of deportation grounds: (1) the INA §237(a)(1)(H) waiver for material misrepresentations, and (2) the INA §237(a)(2)(E) waiver of the domestic violence deportation ground. Like the inadmissibility waivers described above, these waivers provide only a defense to a ground of deportability, and do not in themselves provide an affirmative basis for regularization of immigration status.

All of these applications—waivers of inadmissibility; permission to reapply for admission after deportation or removal; and waivers of deportability—may be adjudicated by the immigration judge (IJ).[3]

Before looking at the waivers mentioned above, two important components of a waiver application must be examined:

- The government's exercise of discretion; and
- The concept of extreme hardship.

The Exercise of Discretion

Waivers and permission to reapply for admission are granted at the government's discretion. This means that, even if the applicant meets all of the statutory requirements for the waiver, the government (either the Department of Homeland Security (DHS) or the IJ) may deny the waiver if it believes that the person does not merit it. The exercise of discretion requires a weighing of all of the positive and negative factors in the applicant's case. Because of the important role of discretion in waiver applications, a favorable showing of discretionary factors should be seen as another element in the waiver application.

The Board of Immigration Appeals (BIA) has listed the sorts of discretionary factors that should be considered in determining whether a favorable exercise of discretion is warranted in a particular case.

Favorable factors include:

- Family ties within the United States;
- Residence of long duration in the United States, particularly when starting at a young age;
- Hardship that would result if permanent residence is denied;
- Service in the U.S. armed forces;
- Employment history;

---

[3] *See* 8 CFR §1240.1(a)(ii) [setting out IJ's authority to hear applications under INA §§212(a)(9)(B)(v), 212(g), 212(h), 212(i), 237(a)(1)(H), 237(a)(3)(C)(ii), and 245, inter alia]; 8 CFR §§1240.11(a)(2) (authorizing IJ to hear applications for waivers of inadmissibility grounds in connection with applications for adjustment of status); §§212.2(h) and 1212.2(h) (authorizing renewal of application for consent to reapply for admission after deportation or removal before IJ after denial by DHS).

- Property or business ties;
- Value and service to the community;
- Genuine rehabilitation;
- Payment of taxes; and
- Other evidence of good character.[4]

Negative factors include:

- The nature and underlying circumstances of the grounds of inadmissibility or deportability;
- The presence of additional significant violations of U.S. immigration laws;
- Any criminal record (and its nature, recency, and seriousness); and
- Any other evidence of bad character or undesirability as a lawful permanent resident (LPR).

In general, the more serious the reason for the waiver application, the more positive factors must be shown to convince DHS or the IJ to exercise discretion favorably.[5]

Extreme Hardship

Definition

Extreme hardship is a statutory requirement for several of the inadmissibility waivers, including the INA §212(h) waiver of certain criminal inadmissibility grounds, the INA §212(i) fraud and misrepresentation waiver, and the INA §212(a)(9)(B)(v) waiver of the unlawful presence inadmissibility ground. It may arise in any waiver application, however, because, as seen in the preceding subsection, hardship caused by denial of permanent residence to an applicant can be a favorable discretionary factor. For these reasons, it is important to examine what is meant by the term *extreme hardship* and consider ways to document it.

The BIA has stated that *extreme hardship* does not have a fixed definition. Instead, the elements to establish extreme hardship depend on the facts and circumstances of each case.[6] In general, *extreme hardship* means something more than the ordinary hardship one would suffer in being separated from a spouse, children, and other loved ones, or from a country and life style one had become accustomed to.[7]

---

[4] *Matter of Mendez*, 21 I&N Dec. 296 (BIA 1996) (in deciding waiver applications under INA §212(h), the BIA will consider the factors it has set forth in *Matter of Marin*, 16 I&N Dec. 581 (BIA 1978)). *See also Matter of C–V–T–*, 22 I&N Dec. 7 (BIA 1998) (applying the *Matter of Marin* factors to discretionary decisions of applications for relief under cancellation of removal part A).

[5] *Matter of Mendez*, *supra* note 4.

[6] *Matter of Cervantes*, 22 I&N Dec. 560 (BIA 1999).

[7] *Id.*; *See also Matter of Pilch*, 21 I&N Dec. 627 (BIA 1996); *Matter of L–O–G–*, 21 I&N Dec. 413 (BIA 1996); *Matter of O–J–O–*, 21 I&N Dec. 381 (BIA 1996); *Matter of Anderson*, 16 I&N Dec. 596 (BIA 1978).

Successful applicants generally must demonstrate something out of the ordinary, such as a specific medical hardship, loss of special educational opportunities, or inability to provide for oneself and one's family in the home country.

The BIA has enumerated the following hardship factors:

- The age of the applicant, both at entry and at the time of application for relief;

- The age of the qualifying relatives;

- The applicant's length of residence in the United States over the statutory minimum;

- The applicant's family ties, both in the United States and abroad;

- The health of the applicant and qualifying relatives;

- The applicant's financial status and occupation;

- The applicant's ties to the community;

- The economic and political conditions in the home country;

- Any disruption of educational opportunities;

- Any adverse psychological impact of deportation;

- Linguistic or cultural factors that make securing employment in the home country difficult;

- Additional factors relevant to conditions in the home country;

- The applicant's involvement and position in the local community; and

- The applicant's immigration history.[8]

Advocates should not feel limited to the above list of factors, however, but should include all factors that are relevant to the particular case. For example, former BIA board member Lory Rosenberg has given a useful list of factors that might establish extreme hardship to children, as well as the types of evidence that might be presented to demonstrate that hardship. These include:

- A professional evaluation of the children's language capabilities;

- Individual medical and psychological reports by expert witnesses indicating the potential impact of relocation to a foreign country on the children's development and ability to flourish;

- Authoritative documentation indicating the similarities and differences between the school systems in the United States and the foreign country;

- Recognized sociological studies reflecting the ability of U.S. citizen (USC) children to adapt to different cultures and countries; economic studies indicat-

---

[8] *See INS v. Wang*, 450 U.S. 139 (1981); *see also Matter of Kao and Lin*, 23 I&N Dec. 45 (BIA 2001); *Matter of Cervantes*, 22 I&N Dec. 560 (BIA 1999); *Matter of O–J–O–*, 21 I&N Dec. 381 (BIA 1996); *Matter of Pilch*, 21 I&N Dec. 627 (BIA 1996); *Matter of L–O–G–*, 21 I&N Dec. 413 (BIA 1996); *Matter of Anderson*, 16 I&N Dec. 596 (BIA 1978).

ing the likely employment prospects for the respondent and the resulting effect on the children's standard of living;

- Reports regarding the anticipated ease or difficulty of later adjustment to social and educational standards in the United States, should the children wish to return when they reach college age; and

- Any information concerning the children's ability to maintain contacts with their aunts, uncles, grandparents, friends, teachers, or other influential figures in the United States.[9]

The BIA also has stated, however, that the following factors, taken alone, should not be considered to determine extreme hardship:

- Birth of USC children,[10]

- Significant reduction in standard of living,[11] and

- Lower quality medical or educational facilities in the native country.[12]

Difficulty in re-adjusting to life in the native country, taken alone, also is insufficient to establish extreme hardship. Where the applicant has "strongly embraced and deeply immersed himself in the social and cultural life of the United States," however, the emotional and psychological impact of readjustment must be considered in assessing hardship.[13]

When analyzing a claim of extreme hardship, U.S. Citizenship and Immigration Services (USCIS), U.S. Immigration and Customs Enforcement (ICE), and the IJ must consider all of the hardship factors cumulatively. Thus, even though a particular factor might not in itself rise to the level of extreme hardship, two or more hardship factors, taken together, might rise to that level.[14] For this reason, it is very important to document all the hardship factors in a client's case.

For Violence Against Women Act (VAWA) of 1994[15] cases, the Immigration and Naturalization Service (legacy INS) and the Executive Office for Immigration Review (EOIR) have set out special factors to be considered when determining whether extreme hardship exists. These factors reflect the special issues involved in a domestic abuse situation. Legacy INS guidance was issued in the form of a memorandum[16] concerning

---

[9] *Matter of Monreal*, 23 I&N Dec. 56 (BIA 2001) (Rosenberg, board member, concurring and dissenting).

[10] *Matter of Pilch, supra* note 7; *Matter of L–O–G–, supra* note 8.

[11] *Matter of L–O–G–, supra* note 8.

[12] *Matter of Corea*, 19 I&N Dec. 130 (BIA 1984); *Matter of Pilch, supra* note 7; *Matter of Kim*, 15 I&N Dec. 88 (BIA 1974).

[13] *Matter of O–J–O–, supra* note 8.

[14] *Matter of Pilch, supra* note 7; *Matter of L–O–G–, supra* note 8; *Matter of Ige*, 20 I&N Dec. 880 (BIA 1994); *Matter of O–J–O–, supra* note 8.

[15] Violence Against Women Act of 1994, Pub. L. No. 103-322, tit. IV, 108 Stat. 1796, 1902–55.

[16] INS Memorandum, P. Virtue, "Extreme Hardship and Documentary Requirements Involving Battered Spouses and Children," at 4 (October 16, 1998), *reprinted in* 76 *Interpreter Releases* 162 (Jan. 25, 1999).

VAWA self-petitions, which, until the VAWA amendments in 2000,[17] required a showing of extreme hardship. EOIR's guidance was issued in the form of regulations, setting out factors to be considered in assessing extreme hardship for purposes of VAWA cancellation and suspension applications.[18]

The hardship factors identified by legacy INS and EOIR for consideration in VAWA cases are:

- The nature and extent of the physical or psychological consequences of abuse;

- The impact of loss of access to the United States courts and criminal justice system, including, but not limited to, criminal investigations; the ability to obtain and enforce orders of protection; and prosecution of court orders regarding child support, maintenance, child custody, and visitation;

- The likelihood that the batterer's family, friends, or others acting on behalf of the batterer in the home country would physically or psychologically harm the applicant or the applicant's child(ren);

- The applicant's needs and/or the needs of the applicant's child(ren) for social, medical, mental health or other supportive services for victims of domestic violence that are unavailable or not reasonably accessible in the home country;

- The existence of laws and social practices in the home country that punish the applicant or the applicant's child(ren) because they have been victims of domestic violence or have taken steps to leave an abusive household; and

- The abuser's ability to travel to the home country and the ability and willingness of authorities in the home country to protect the applicant and/or the applicant's child(ren) from future abuse.[19]

The legacy INS memorandum[20] also indicated some additional hardship factors to be considered in VAWA applications. These are: linguistic or cultural factors that make securing employment in the home country difficult; additional factors relevant to conditions in the home country; and any other economic factors in the United States or abroad.

Experts note that child custody disputes and protection orders are compelling hardship factors. A grant of custody is meaningless if the parent is deported; the abusive parent would then be free to reopen the custody decision without challenge.[21] A protection order is of little use abroad if the abuser travels back and forth to the victim's homeland. Experts also relate that the effect on children of domestic violence in the household has been considered a significant hardship factor.

---

[17] Violence Against Women Act of 2000, Pub. L. No. 106-386, div. B, 114 Stat 1464, 1491–539.

[18] 8 CFR §§1240.20(c) (VAWA cancellation), 1240.58(c) (VAWA suspension).

[19] 8 CFR §1240.58(c).

[20] Virtue memo, *supra* note 16.

[21] G. Pendleton & A. Block, "Applications for Immigration Status under the Violence Against Women Act," *Immigration and Nationality Law Handbook* 436, 457 (AILA 2001–2002).

Documenting Extreme Hardship

The following list gives examples of ways to document extreme hardship. Each case must be analyzed individually to determine what hardship factors exist in the case and the best way of documenting those hardship factors.

- Thorough, well-drafted declarations, statements, or letters from the applicant, his or her qualifying relatives, and other persons—*e.g.*, church officials; employers; neighbors; teachers; counselors; and other community members—who can attest to the hardship that will result from denial of permanent residence to the applicant.

- Evidence of any problems in the applicant or family member's physical, mental, and emotional health, including the treating physician's or other health care professional's diagnosis, the current or anticipated treatment, and an indication of whether treatment would be available in the applicant's home country. Evidence on these points should include copies of medical records and a letter or report from the treating physician or other health care professional. The availability of treatment in the home country may be demonstrated by statements from physicians, other medical personnel, or other knowledgeable persons who are familiar with the country's medical care conditions and by reports from the U.S. Department of State (DOS), the United Nations (UN), and non-governmental organizations (NGOs) concerning the country's economic and development status.

- Titles, deeds, or other evidence of the applicant's or qualifying relative's ownership of real or personal property in the United States.

- Evidence of the applicant's or qualifying relative's family ties in the United States and comparative lack of family ties abroad. This can be done through attaching a list of the family members in the United States, together with birth or marriage certificates or, where those documents are not available, secondary evidence such as baptismal records or affidavits. It is also crucial to show the closeness of the family relationship. These must be accompanied by a translation into English if they are in a foreign language. This can be done by submitting statements describing how frequently the family members see each other, whether they rely on each other and for what, and other indications of the closeness of the relationship. Finally, if the applicant's relatives are USCs or LPRs, evidence of the citizenship or LPR status must be presented. This may be done by submitting a copy of the relative's birth certificate showing birth in the United States or birth abroad to a USC parent, a naturalization certificate, a certificate of citizenship, a passport, or other evidence of naturalization by admission of a child of a USC to the United States as an LPR while under the age of 18. If the relative is an LPR or other "qualified alien," that status may be shown by USCIS documents verifying the status. If those documents are unavailable, secondary evidence may be submitted. In addition, if the applicant cannot obtain these documents, the applicant may ask USCIS to assist by searching its files for evidence of a qualifying relative's status. On copies of permanent resident cards and naturalization certificates, draw a line in red diagonally across the document and write in above the diagonal red line "For USCIS use only."

- Evidence of children's educational level and achievements and the quality of the education they would receive in the applicant's country. Include copies of the children's report cards, letters from teachers describing the children's progress and the anticipated effect of departure on that progress, and statements from persons familiar with the educational system in the applicant's home country. The types of evidence suggested by board member Lory Rosenberg in *Matter of Monreal*[22] particularly are helpful.

- If the applicant or his or her qualifying relatives do not speak the language of the applicant's home country, present evidence on that point. This can be done through statements from the applicant or the applicant's parent or qualifying relatives.

- If the applicant's home country is less developed than the United States, give evidence of the unequal development. This can be done from reports from DOS, the UN, and NGOs, and by newspaper articles concerning the country's development, both economic and otherwise.

- Evidence of any current dangerous or difficult conditions in the applicant's home country, such as ongoing civil unrest or war, drought, or famine. Newspaper and magazine articles, as well as reports from DOS, the United Nations, and NGOs, are useful for this purpose.

Always remember that it is the cumulative effect of the evidence that matters.

As can be seen, some of the hardship factors examined in a waiver application involve conditions, including laws and law enforcement practices, in the applicant's home country. It is often difficult to obtain information on specific laws and conditions in other countries. It is helpful to review country reports from DOS, Human Rights Watch, Amnesty International, and the U.N. High Commissioner for Refugees. Affidavits from expert and lay witnesses who have knowledge of the home country, including family members, women's groups, and lawyers in the home country, can be effective. Major newspapers such as *The New York Times* and *The Washington Post* are also good sources of information. There are excellent websites accessing foreign law, as well as political and social conditions, including *www.findlaw.com* and *www.asylumlaw.org*. Advocates also can contact the Library of Congress's Law Division, at (202) 707-5065 (fax: (202) 707-1820) and request certified copies of foreign laws.

---

[22] *Matter of Monreal, supra* note 9.

Waivers of Inadmissibility Grounds in Removal Proceedings

INA §212(g) Waivers for Health-Related Inadmissibility Grounds

Waivers for Communicable Disease of Public Health Significance

INA §212(g)(1) provides a waiver for persons who are inadmissible because of having a communicable disease of public health significance. There are both general and VAWA-specific waivers. Under the general waiver, the government may waive this inadmissibility ground in its discretion for an individual who is the parent, spouse, or unmarried son or daughter of a USC, LPR, or immigrant visa recipient.[23] In contrast, the VAWA waiver requires only that the visa applicant qualify as a VAWA self-petitioner.[24] There is no statutory requirement of any qualifying relative for the VAWA waiver.

There are special requirements for waivers of the communicable disease inadmissibility ground if the disease in question is HIV infection. Even if an immigrant who is HIV-positive meets the requirements for the INA §212(g)(1) general waiver or VAWA waiver, certain discretionary factors still must be considered. In general, current USCIS policy requires that the applicant establish the following in order to obtain the waiver:

- The danger to the public health of the United States created by her or his admission is minimal;

- The possibility of the spread of the infection created by her or his admission to the United States is minimal; and

- There will be no cost incurred by any government agency of the United States because of the applicant's admission, without the prior consent of that agency.[25]

Examples that the government considers sufficient to meet these criteria include evidence that:

- The applicant has arranged for medical treatment in the United States;

- The applicant is aware of the nature and severity of his or her medical condition;

- The applicant is willing to attend educational seminars and counseling sessions;

- The applicant understands the ways the disease is transmitted; and

---

[23] INA §§212(g)(1)(A), (B).

[24] INA §212(g)(1)(C).

[25] INS Memorandum, T. Aleinikoff, "Immigrant Waivers for Aliens Found Excluded under §212(a)(1)(A)(i) of the Immigration and Nationality Act due to HIV Infection," September 6, 1995, at 5, *reprinted in* 72 *Interpreter Releases* 1347 (Oct. 2, 1995), *published on* AILA InfoNet at Doc. No. 95092690 (*posted* Sept. 26, 1995).

- A government agency has agreed to provide medical treatment to the applicant.[26]

Waivers for Physical or Mental Disorders with Associated Harmful Behavior

The government may waive the inadmissibility ground of having a physical or mental disorder with associated harmful behavior, upon such conditions as the government may set.[27]

Waivers of the Vaccination Requirement

There are three waivers available for persons deemed inadmissible because they cannot present proof of vaccinations. The vaccination requirement may be waived if:

- The immigrant is vaccinated against a disease for which he or she failed to present documentation of previous vaccination;[28]

- A civil surgeon or panel physician certifies that the vaccination would not be medically appropriate;[29] or

- The vaccination would be contrary to the foreign national's religious or moral beliefs.[30]

Under the first waiver, if the applicant presents documentation showing that all immunizations have been obtained, he or she is no longer inadmissible.

For the second waiver, a vaccination is considered to be *not medically appropriate* in the following circumstances:

- The vaccine is not age appropriate, because it is not recommended for the applicant's age group;

- There is a contraindication against the vaccine (*e.g.*, pregnancy; allergy; or hypersensitivity to the vaccine);

- The person has taken the initial vaccine, but is unable to complete the entire series within a reasonable period of time (*e.g.*, the recommended series of hepatitis vaccines may take as long as six months to complete); and

- The medical examination is not being performed during the flu season (this will only apply to the influenza vaccine, as it generally is given only during the fall season).[31]

---

[26] *Id.* An excellent resource on HIV-infection and immigration is the National Immigration Law Project's HIV manual, *available at www.nationalimmigrationproject.org.*

[27] INA §212(g)(3).

[28] INA §212(g)(2)(A).

[29] INA §212(g)(2)(B).

[30] INA §212(g)(2)(C).

[31] INS Memorandum, P. Virtue, "New Vaccination Requirements," at 3 (April 10, 1997), *reprinted in* 74 *Interpreter Releases* 660 (April 21, 1997).

The government treats the first two of these waiver grounds (for subsequent vaccination or medical certificate) as blanket waivers.[32] In these cases, no waiver application form is required, and the applicant does not have to pay an application fee.[33] The prospective immigrant's vaccination history, or a finding that a vaccination is not medically appropriate, is noted by the civil surgeon on the foreign national's medical examination report (Form I-693).[34]

Under the third waiver of the vaccination inadmissibility ground, the vaccination requirement may be waived if the vaccination would be contrary to the prospective immigrant's moral or religious beliefs.[35] In these cases, there is no *blanket* waiver, and USCIS must adjudicate each waiver request on a case-by-case basis.[36] This means that the applicant must file the standard waiver form (Form I-601) and pay the corresponding fee.

To qualify for a moral/religious waiver under INA §212(g)(2)(C), the applicant must show that:

- He or she is opposed to vaccinations in any form;
- The objection is based on religious belief or moral convictions (whether or not as a member of a recognized religion); and
- The religious belief or moral conviction (whether or not as part of a "mainstream" religion) is sincere.[37]

When the waiver application is for a child, the child's parent must satisfy these three requirements.[38] The applicant does not have to be an active member of any particular denomination to qualify for the waiver.[39] This means, for example, that if an individual is a vegetarian for moral reasons, and those reasons preclude him or her from receiving the vaccinations, he or she should be eligible for the waiver.

INA §212(h) Waivers for Criminal Inadmissibility Grounds

What Criminal Inadmissibility Grounds Does INA §212(h) Waive?

INA §212(h) provides three separate waivers of criminal grounds for immigrants. Each of those waivers will waive the following criminal inadmissibility grounds:

---

[32] *Id.* at 2; *see also*, "PL-104-208 Update Number 23: 212(a)(1)(A) (ii) Vaccination Requirements; Technical Instructions and Procedural Guidance," 97 State 071637 (April 17, 1997), *published on* AILA InfoNet at Doc. No. 97041791 (*posted* April 17, 1997).

[33] Virtue April 21, 1997, memo on vaccinations, *supra* note 31.

[34] *Id.*

[35] INA §212(g)(2)(C).

[36] *Id.*

[37] INS Memorandum, P. Virtue, "Vaccination Requirements under Section 212(a)(1)(A)(ii) of the Act" (Sept. 29, 1997), *reprinted at* 74 *Interpreter Releases* 1687 (Nov. 3, 1997), *published on* AILA InfoNet at Doc. No. 97101090 (*posted* Oct. 10, 1997).

[38] *Id.*

[39] *Id.*

- Crimes of moral turpitude;
- Multiple criminal convictions;
- Prostitution and commercialized vice;
- Immunity from prosecution for serious criminal misconduct; and
- A single offense of simple possession of 30 grams or less of marijuana.

These waivers do not waive substance abuse offenses—other than a single offense of simple possession of 30 grams or less of marijuana—nor do they waive trafficking in controlled substances or persons, money laundering, or engaging in particularly severe violations of religious freedom.

What Are the Eligibility Requirements for §212(h) Waivers?

Under the three INA §212(h) waivers, the criminal inadmissibility grounds listed above may be waived for:

- Persons who are inadmissible only under the prostitution or commercialized vice grounds of inadmissibility, or because of activities occurring more than fifteen years ago, if the person's admission would not be contrary to the welfare or security of the United States and if the person has been rehabilitated.[40]

- Persons who are the spouse, parent, son, or daughter of a USC or LPR, if it is established to the government's satisfaction that refusing admission to the foreign national would result in extreme hardship to the USC or LPR relative.[41]

- Persons who have qualified as VAWA self-petitioners. Note that there are no further statutory requirements for VAWA self-petitioners.[42]

The following additional requirements apply to each of the INA §212(h) waivers:

- The government must have consented to the person's applying or reapplying for a visa, admission to the United States, or adjustment of status.

- The person cannot have been convicted of or admitted committing murder, torture, or an attempt or conspiracy to commit those crimes.

- LPRs are ineligible for the INA §212(h) waivers if (1) they have been convicted of an aggravated felony; or (2) they have not resided lawfully and continuously in the United States for seven years prior to the initiation of removal proceedings.[43]

---

[40] INA §212(h)(1)(A).

[41] INA §212(h)(1)(B).

[42] INA §212(h)(1)(C).

[43] *But see Martinez v. Mukasey*, 519 F.3d 532 (5th Cir. 2008), holding that LPRs who had entered the United States is a status other than LPR and then adjusted to LPR status could apply for a §212(h) waiver even if the individual was convicted of an aggravated felony.

Remember that INA §212(h) waivers are granted in the government's discretion. Thus, in addition to the requirements set forth above, the applicant must present evidence showing that the positive factors in his or her case outweigh the negative factors.[44]

– Eva was admitted to the United States as an F-1 student. After her admission, she was convicted of two offenses: shoplifting and simple possession of 20 grams of marijuana. ICE has served Eva with a Notice to Appear (NTA), charging her with being removable under INA §237(a)(2)(A)(i) (conviction of one crime involving moral turpitude) and INA §237(a)(2)(B) (conviction of a controlled substance offense). Eva is married to John, an LPR who suffers from a progressive muscular disease. John has filed an I-130 relative visa petition for Eva, which USCIS recently approved.

Based on these facts, it appears that Eva is eligible to apply for adjustment of status as a form of relief from removal. Because her convictions make her inadmissible, she will have to file an application for a waiver of the criminal inadmissibility grounds under INA §212(h), together with her application for adjustment of status. The INA §212(h) waiver will waive both of Eva's offenses, if she can meet the other requirements of the waiver. To meet those requirements, Eva must provide evidence of her marriage to John and that it would cause John (not Eva herself) extreme hardship if Eva were not granted an immigrant visa. She also should present evidence of positive discretionary factors, to convince the IJ to exercise discretion favorably.

In 2003, the attorney general (AG) issued a new regulation concerning INA §212(h). The regulation, found at 8 CFR §212.7(d) and 8 CFR §1212.7(d), became effective on January 27, 2003. Under it, the government generally will not exercise discretion favorably in considering an application for an INA §212(h) waiver where the case involves violent or dangerous crimes, except in extraordinary circumstances or where the applicant demonstrates that denial of the visa would result in exceptional and extremely unusual hardship.

Note that the INA §212(h) waiver will not cure ineligibility for immigration benefits based on lack of good moral character. Thus, even if the applicant is granted a §212(h) waiver, he or she will not be eligible for any relief from removal that requires proof of good moral character. Such forms of relief include suspension of deportation, cancellation of removal for non-LPRs, registry, and post-proceeding voluntary departure.

INA §212(i) Waivers for Fraud or Misrepresentation

Inadmissibility because of general fraud or misrepresentation under INA §212(a)(6)(A)(i) may be waived under INA §212(i). There is both a general and a VAWA-specific waiver under this provision. Practitioners should note that §212(i) will not waive the inadmissibility ground of having made a false claim to U.S. citizenship, although there is an exception to that ground of inadmissibility for persons

---

[44] *Matter of Mendez*, 21 I&N Dec. 296 (BIA 1996).

whose parents are or were USCs, who resided permanently in the United States prior to age 16, and who reasonably believed themselves to be USCs.[45]

To qualify for the general waiver, the applicant must establish that his or her USC or LPR spouse or parent would suffer extreme hardship if permanent residence is denied.[46] Due to changes brought on by the Illegal Immigration Reform and Immigrant Responsibility Act of 1996 (IIRAIRA),[47] the waiver no longer is available based on a showing of extreme hardship to the applicant's USC or LPR child.

In contrast, VAWA self-petitioners are eligible for an INA §212(i) waiver if they demonstrate extreme hardship to themselves or to their USC, LPR, or *qualified alien* parent or child.[48] The term *qualified alien* includes:

- LPRs;
- Asylees;
- Refugees;
- Persons paroled into the country for at least one year;
- Foreign nationals granted withholding of deportation or removal;
- Foreign nationals granted conditional entry under INA §203(a)(7) as it existed prior to April 1, 1980; and
- Cuban and Haitian entrants.[49]

The term also includes abused foreign nationals or the parents of abused children, if they have an approved VAWA self-petition or application for VAWA cancellation of removal or if they have a pending petition for one of those types of relief that sets forth a prima facie case of eligibility.[50]

As with other waivers, the INA §212(i) waiver is granted or denied in the government's discretion. As part of the discretionary determination, DHS or the IJ may consider the nature of the applicant's fraud or misrepresentation.[51]

INA §212(a)(9)(B)(v) Waiver for Unlawful Presence

The government may waive the INA §212(a)(9)(B) unlawful presence inadmissibility ground if refusing permanent residence would result in extreme hardship to a USC or LPR spouse or parent.[52] The waiver is not available based on extreme hardship to a USC or LPR child. In addition, the unlawful presence ground of inadmissi-

---

[45] INA §212(a)(6)(C)(ii)(II).

[46] INA §212(i).

[47] Illegal Immigration Reform and Immigrant Responsibility Act of 1996 (IIRAIRA), Pub. L. No. 104-208, div. C, 110 Stat. 3009, 3009-546 to 3009-724.

[48] INA §212(i).

[49] 8 USC §1641(b).

[50] 8 USC §1641(c).

[51] *Matter of Cervantes*, *supra* note 8; *Matter of Tijam*, 22 I&N Dec. 408 (BIA 1998).

[52] INA §212(a)(9)(B)(v).

bility does not apply to VAWA self-petitioners who entered the United States before April 1, 1997, nor does it apply to VAWA self-petitioners who entered after that date but can show a substantial connection between the violation of the self-petitioner's nonimmigrant visa and the abuse he or she suffered.[53]

The VAWA Waiver for the "Permanent Bar"

There is a special VAWA waiver for individuals who are inadmissible under INA §212(a)(9)(C) because of having reentered the United States unlawfully after having been removed, or after having acquired more than one year of unlawful presence. This waiver is available if the VAWA self-petitioner establishes a connection between the abuse the self-petitioner suffered and the self-petitioner's:

- Removal;
- Departure from the United States;
- Reentry or reentries into the United States; or
- Attempted reentry into the United States.

The VAWA self-petitioner also must show that he or she merits a favorable exercise of discretion.

The INA §212(d)(3) Nonimmigrant Waiver

The government may waive all inadmissibility grounds for nonimmigrants, with the exception of the drug trafficking and national security grounds.[54] Like the immigrant waivers discussed above, the INA §212(d)(3) waiver is granted in the exercise of discretion. The exercise of discretion involves a balancing of the negative and positive factors in the applicant's case. Thus, the applicant should present as many positive factors as possible to overcome the negative effect of the inadmissibility ground. Positive factors, in the context of the nonimmigrant waiver, can include the following:

- The purpose of the visit, particularly if there is some compelling need (*i.e.*, urgent medical treatment; or a visit to a sick or dying relative);
- The applicant's rehabilitation and remorse; and
- Any hardship that would result from a denial of the visa.

Waivers for Refugees and Asylees

Under INA §209(c), persons admitted as refugees or granted asylum may apply for adjustment of status one year after admission or grant of asylum. This section of the law allows waiver of any ground of inadmissibility except for drug trafficking and security-related grounds. All other grounds are waivable for humanitarian purposes, to assure family unity, or when it is otherwise in the public interest. A refugee or asylee who has not yet adjusted status to LPR and who becomes removable may apply for adjustment of status in removal proceedings.[55] However, such a refugee

---

[53] INA §212(a)(9)(B)(iv).

[54] INA §212(d)(3).

[55] *Matter of H–N–*, 22 I&N Dec. 1039 (BIA 1999).

first must apply for adjustment before USCIS, even if the refugee is placed in removal proceedings before applying for adjustment, and then can renew the application before the IJ.[56]

Where a refugee is inadmissible because of having committed a violent or dangerous crime, the refugee will be granted the INA §209(c) waiver only in extraordinary circumstances such as those involving security or foreign policy considerations, or cases in which the refugee clearly demonstrates that denial of adjustment would result in exceptional and extremely unusual hardship. Depending on the gravity of the refugee's underlying criminal offense, even a showing of exceptional and extremely unusual hardship might not be sufficient.[57]

The INA §209(c) waiver is applied for by filing Form I-602 (Application by Refugee for Waiver of Grounds of Excludability), in conjunction with the application for Adjustment of Status.

Waivers Under Special Forms of Relief

Over the years, Congress has created a number of special forms of relief for special groups of people, and these special forms of relief frequently include special provisions exempting individuals from, or waiving certain of, the inadmissibility grounds. Congress continues to create similar programs. We have noted special waivers for VAWA self-petitioners above. Other groups of individuals eligible for special waivers include, among others:

- Minors under the Special Immigrant Juvenile status;[58]

- Victims of human trafficking applying for the T nonimmigrant visa or to adjust to permanent residence;[59]

- Victims of severe crime applying for the U nonimmigrant visa or to adjust to permanent residence;[60]

- Applicants for temporary protected status;[61]

- Applicants for adjustment of status under §202 of the Nicaraguan Adjustment and Central American Relief Act;[62] and

- Applicants for adjustment under the Cuban Adjustment Act of 1966.[63]

Thus, if your client is applying for a special form of relief, check for special inadmissibility waivers connected with the relief. The information set out earlier in this

---

[56] *Id.*

[57] *Matter of Jean*, 23 I&N Dec. 373 (A.G. 2002).

[58] INA §245(h).

[59] INA §245(l).

[60] INA §245(m).

[61] INA §244(c)(2).

[62] Nicaraguan Adjustment and Central American Relief Act (NACARA), Pub. L. No. 105-100, tit. II, 111 Stat. 2160, 2193–201 (1997).

[63] Cuban Adjustment Act of 1966, Pub. L. No. 89-732, 80 Stat. 1161.

chapter about the importance of discretionary factors and the importance of documenting the application applies to waivers under special forms of relief, as well.

Strategy and Procedure for Waivers of Inadmissibility Grounds in Removal Proceedings

The INA §§212(h), 212(i), 212(g), and 212 (a)(9)(v) waivers are made on Form I-601 and should be supported by documentary and photographic evidence. They are filed as follows:

- If applying for adjustment of status, file with USCIS;
- If applying for consular processing, file with the consulate, which will forward the application to the appropriate USCIS overseas office for a decision; and
- If in removal proceedings, file with the immigration court

Where the application is made before the immigration court as a defense to removal, the waiver is granted as if it had been requested prior to the applicant's entry to the United States.

The waiver application consists of the application form itself, together with the filing fee or a request for a fee waiver. In addition, the applicant should attach documentation to establish the statutory requirements and documentation to convince the adjudicator that a favorable exercise of discretion is warranted. The application should be paginated consecutively. For applications filed with the immigration court as part of an application for relief from removal, advocates also must check the local immigration court rules for any special content or format requirements.

The I-601 application should contain the following items:

- Form I-601;
- Check or money order for the fee or request for fee waiver;
- An index to the application;
- Evidence to establish statutory requirements.
- For the INA §§212(h), 212(i) and 212(a)(9)(B) waivers, evidence of extreme hardship to the qualifying relative, as discussed in the section of this chapter dealing with extreme hardship. For INA §212(h) applications where the criminal offense involved was a dangerous or violent one, the evidence must meet the higher exceptional and extremely unusual standard;
- For the INA §§212(h), 212(i), and 212(a)(9)(B) waivers, evidence of the relationship to the qualifying relative and the closeness of the relationship. This evidence must include birth certificates and marriage certificates to establish the relationship, as well as evidence of the qualifying relatives' USC or LPR status;
- Documents to support a favorable exercise of discretion by the trier of fact, as discussed earlier in this chapter in the section on the exercise of discretion. The more serious the crime necessitating the INA §212(h) waiver, the more positive

factors will be required in order to balance out the negative factors and support the AG's favorable exercise of discretion; and

- Although optional, it is a nice touch to submit color photographs (or copies) of the applicant with his or her family.

Form I-212 Consent to Reapply for Admission

Eligibility and Strategy

Persons who have departed or been removed from the United States subsequent to a deportation or removal order are inadmissible for a specified number of years.[64] This ground of inadmissibility does not apply to persons who received a final order but who have not subsequently left the United States. Rather, those persons may be able to adjust their status before the IJ if they are successful in reopening their proceedings.[65]

To ameliorate the harshness of the inadmissibility ground for prior deportation or removal orders, the government is permitted to waive inadmissibility by granting not a waiver, but a *consent to reapply* (Form I-212) for admission.[66]

In adjudicating an I-212, the government will not require extreme hardship to any specific family member. Rather, it will consider the following factors:

- The applicant's moral character;
- The need for the applicant's services in the United States;
- Whether the applicant was ignorant of the fact that he or she was deported;
- The length of time the applicant had been in the United States;
- The reason the applicant was originally deported;
- Hardships resulting from the deportation;
- Recency of the deportation or removal order;
- Evidence of reformation and rehabilitation;
- The applicant's family responsibilities and ties in the United States; and
- The existence of an approved immigrant visa petition for the applicant.[67]

Permission to reapply is granted in the exercise of discretion, so the government will balance the positive and negative factors in the applicant's case. The following negative factors also will be considered:

- Repeated and significant immigration violations; and

---

[64] INA §212(a)(9)(A).

[65] INS Memorandum, L. Crocetti, "INS Advises on Processing INA §245(i) Adjustment Applications" (May 1, 1997), *reprinted at* 74 *Interpreter Releases* 791–94, 792 (May 12, 1997).

[66] INA §212(a)(9)(A)(iii).

[67] *Matter of Tin*, 14 I&N Dec. 371 (Reg'l. Commr. 1971); *Matter of Lee*, 17 I&N Dec. 275 (BIA 1978).

- The fact that the applicant is inadmissible based on other grounds for which there is no waiver.[68]

If the applicant already has reentered the United States, he or she may still request the government's consent to reenter on Form I-212.[69] If granted, the consent is deemed to date back to before the reentry.[70] However, this area of the law is currently in flux, with the BIA, various circuit courts and USCIS weighing in with various interpretations of when a foreign national who unlawfully reentered after removal can file an I-212 in conjunction with an application for adjustment of status.[71] Note that other circuit courts have held that the filing of an adjustment of status application with a waiver does not protect someone from reinstatement of removal under INA §241(a)(5).[72] VAWA 2005[73] provisions also contain new guidance on the I-212.

In response to the issues raised by the U.S. Court of Appeals for the Ninth Circuit's decision in *Perez-Gonzalez v. Ashcroft*[74] (which held that a foreign national who illegally reentered after removal could file for adjustment of status in conjunction with an I-212 application before the prior removal order was reinstated), USCIS issued a memorandum on I-212 applications.[75] The memorandum instructs its adjudicators to deny an I-212 filed by an applicant inadmissible under INA §212(a)(9) where 10 years have not passed since the date of the applicant's last departure from the United States. The memorandum also instructs adjudicators to deny an I-212 from an applicant even if 10 years have passed if ICE has instituted reinstatement of removal proceedings. If 10 years have passed and ICE has not yet instituted reinstatement proceedings, the memorandum instructs USCIS to refer the case to ICE to make a decision on reinstatement. If ICE declines to reinstate the order, USCIS then can adjudicate the waiver.

As mentioned above, VAWA 2005 also contains a section specifically dealing with I-212 waivers, which the recent USCIS memorandum did not address. Specifically, VAWA 2005 §813(b) encourages DHS to use its authority to grant these waivers in conjunction with an adjustment of status application in VAWA, U visa, and T visa cases. The U visa regulations, which were published in September 2007, stated that persons who are under a final removal order may file a petition for U nonimmi-

---

[68] *Matter of Tin, supra* note 67.

[69] 8 CFR §212.2(e).

[70] 8 CFR §212.2(i); *Matter of Ducret*, 15 I&N Dec. 620 (BIA 1976).

[71] *See, e.g., Matter of Torres-Garcia*, 23 I&N Dec. 866 (BIA 2006); *Perez-Gonzalez v. Ashcroft*, 379 F.3d 783 (9th Cir. 2004); *see also Duran-Gonzales v. DHS*, 508 F.3d 1227 (9th Cir. 2007).

[72] *See, e.g., Delgado v. Mukasey*, 516 F.3d 65 (2d Cir. 2008); *Lino v. Gonzales*, 467 F.3d 1077 (7th Cir. 2006).

[73] Violence Against Women and Department of Justice Reauthorization Act of 2005 (VAWA 2005), Pub. L. No. 109-162, 119 Stat. 2960 (2006).

[74] *Perez-Gonzalez v. Ashcroft, supra* note 71.

[75] *See* USCIS Memorandum, W. Aytes, "Effect of *Perez-Gonzalez v. Ashcroft* on adjudication of Form I-212 applications filed by aliens who are subject to reinstated removal orders under INA §241(a)(5), (March 31, 2006), *published on* AILA InfoNet at Doc. No. 06080967 (*posted* Aug. 9, 2006).

grant status with USCIS. If the application is granted, the order of removal is automatically cancelled if it was a removal order issued by DHS and not a court (*i.e.,* an expedited removal order); it is not necessary to file a motion to reopen. If the application is granted and the person is under a final order of removal issued by the immigration court or the BIA, it is necessary to file a motion to reopen.[76]

Procedure

The application for consent to reapply is made on Form I-212 (Application for Permission to Reapply for Admission Into the United States After Deportation or Removal). A person seeking permanent residence through adjustment of status must file the application with the USCIS office having jurisdiction over the place where the applicant resides.[77] If the person is applying for adjustment before the IJ, the I-212 must be referred to the IJ.[78] A person applying for permanent residence at a U.S. consulate must file the application with the USCIS office having jurisdiction over the place where the deportation or removal proceedings were held.[79]

An exception to this requirement of filing with USCIS occurs where the applicant must file both an I-212 request for permission to reapply and an I-601 application for an INA §212(g), (h), or (i) waiver. In that case, the I-212 must be filed at the U.S. consulate having jurisdiction over the applicant's place of residence.[80] Persons who will apply for permanent residence through a consulate may file Form I-212 with the USCIS regional service center prior to leaving for the visa appointment.[81]

The applicant should attach the filing fee and the following supporting documents to Form I-212:

- Immigrant visa approval notice;
- Proof of USC or LPR family members in the United States;
- A copy of the final deportation or removal order;
- Proof of current and prior employment;
- Proof of filing federal and state taxes;
- Medical records or doctor's statement indicating health-related problems;
- Results of FBI fingerprint check indicating criminal record;
- Affidavits from the applicant, the applicant's family members, and any other person who can vouch for the foreign national's good moral character and hardship that would be suffered if the application is denied; and

---

[76] 8 CFR §214.14(c)(1)(ii).

[77] 8 CFR §212.2(e).

[78] *Id.*

[79] 8 CFR §212.2(d). *See also,* "P.L. 104-208 Update No. 36: 212(a)(9)(A)–(C), 212(a)(6)(A) and (B)," 98 State 060539 (Apr. 4, 1998), *published on* AILA InfoNet at Doc. No. 98040490 (*posted* Apr. 4, 1998).

[80] *Id.*

[81] S. Ignatius & E. Stickney, *Immigration Law and the Family*, (West 2008), §12.75.

- Any other evidence of positive equities in the case.

A denial of an I-212 application is appealable to the USCIS associate commissioner for examinations,[82] unless filed in conjunction with an adjustment application in removal proceedings, in which case the denial is appealable to the BIA.[83]

Waivers of Deportation Grounds in Removal Proceedings

INA §237(a)(1)(H) Deportability Waiver for Fraud or Misrepresentation

The first ground of deportability amounts to a form of delayed inadmissibility, because it makes deportable "[a]ny alien who at the time of entry or adjustment of status was within one or more of the classes of aliens inadmissible by the law existing at such time."[84] Under this ground, having been inspected and admitted does not protect a person from being deported because of a ground of inadmissibility existing when the person entered or adjusted status. A respondent charged with deportability under this ground, however, may apply for any of the waivers of inadmissibility for which he or she might be eligible.

The INA provides a special waiver (under INA §237(a)(1)(H)) for a respondent charged with being removable on the basis of having been inadmissible at the time of entry or adjustment because of fraud or a willful misrepresentation of material fact under INA §212(a)(6)(C)(i). Although a respondent charged with this ground of deportability could apply for the waiver of fraud and misrepresentation under INA §212(i), the INA §237(a)(1)(H) waiver provides broader protection. Moreover, the BIA has held that the INA §237(a)(1)(H) waiver can waive a misrepresentation at the time of admission whether the misrepresentation was innocent or not.[85] The requirements for this waiver are that the respondent:

- Is the spouse, parent, son, or daughter of a USC or LPR; and

- Is in possession of an immigrant visa or equivalent documents, and otherwise is inadmissible to the United States, except for the requirements of having a labor certification and having a valid passport and immigrant visa.

Thus, comparing the INA §237(a)(1)(H) waiver with the INA §212(i) waiver, the INA §237(a)(1)(H) waiver is less onerous than the INA §212(i) waiver on at least three points:

- First, the INA §212(i) waiver is available only to persons who are the spouse, son, or daughter of a USC or LPR, while the INA §237(a)(1)(H) is available to persons who are the spouse, son or daughter, or parent of a USC or LPR.

- Second, the INA §212(i) waiver requires that the qualifying USC or LPR relative would be caused extreme hardship if the waiver were not granted, while the INA §237(a)(1)(H) waiver does not require any showing of hardship.

---

[82] 8 CFR §103.1(f)(3)(iii)(E).

[83] 8 CFR §1003.1(b).

[84] INA §237(a)(1)(A).

[85] *Matter of Guang Li Fu*, 23 I&N Dec. 985 (BIA 2006).

- Third, the INA §237(a)(1)(H) waiver waives not only the fraud or misrepresentation, but any inadmissibility directly resulting from that fraud or misrepresentation.

  - Laura immigrated to the United States as the unmarried daughter of an LPR. USCIS later learns that Laura was married when she obtained her residency status. Laura may be placed in proceedings and charged with being deportable because she was inadmissible at the time of her entry to the United States.

Laura may apply for the waiver under INA §237(a)(1)(H), and, if granted, that waiver would take effect as of the time of Laura's admission. Laura must establish that she meets all the statutory requirements for the waiver and also must convince the IJ to exercise discretion favorably.

Persons who were inadmissible at the time of entry also may apply for this waiver if they are VAWA self-petitioners, even if such an applicant does not have a qualifying relative.[86]

Waiver of Deportability Ground of Crimes of Domestic Violence, Stalking, or Violation of a Protection Order

A person who has been convicted at any time after entry of a crime of domestic violence, stalking, child abuse, child neglect, or child abandonment is deportable.[87] In addition, a person who at any time after entry is enjoined under a protection order issued by a court is deportable.[88] Under INA §237(a)(7), however, the government may waive INA §237(a)(2)(E)(i) (with respect to domestic violence and stalking crimes) and INA §237(a)(2)(E)(ii) (with respect to violations of protective orders) for certain persons. The requirements for this waiver are the following:

- The applicant has been battered or subjected to extreme cruelty;
- The applicant is not the primary perpetrator of violence in the relationship; and
- Either:

  - the applicant was acting in self-defense;

  - the applicant violated a protective order intended to protect him- or herself; or

  - the crime in question did not result in serious bodily injury and there was a connection between the crime and the person's having been battered or subjected to extreme cruelty.

VAWA 2005 clarified that this waiver also can be used in VAWA cancellation or suspension cases to waive a failure to meet the good moral character requirements, or to waive criminal ineligibility grounds.[89] In adjudicating a waiver application under

---

[86] INA §237(a)(1)(H)(ii).

[87] INA §237(a)(2)(E)(i).

[88] INA §237(a)(2)(E)(ii).

[89] VAWA 2005, *supra* note 73.

this provision, the government is not limited to the criminal record and must consider any credible evidence relevant to the application.

As with all the other waivers discussed in this chapter, the waiver of the domestic violence deportation ground is granted in the exercise of the government's discretion. Because of this, the applicant must present evidence of favorable discretionary factors and evidence to overcome negative discretionary factors, in addition to evidence to establish each of the statutory eligibility requirements for the waiver.

Conclusion

Waivers are one way in which a respondent in removal proceedings may overcome being found removable on certain inadmissibility or deportation grounds. Advocates must be careful to document the client's application fully in order to establish the statutory requirements and to convince the IJ to exercise discretion in the client's favor.

CHAPTER SEVEN
INA §212(c) AND CANCELLATION OF REMOVAL FOR LAWFUL PERMANENT RESIDENTS

Lawful permanent residents (LPRs), particularly long-time LPRs with prior convictions, have suffered some of the harshest consequences as a result of changes in the immigration laws over the last several years.

Despite these harsh provisions, there are several forms of relief from removal for which LPRs with criminal antecedents may qualify. For example, they may qualify for Cancellation of Removal Part A, readjustment of status with or without a waiver, or termination of proceedings for the purpose of naturalization. In addition, while Congress eliminated the broad waiver for LPRs under former Immigration and Nationality Act (INA)[1] §212(c) in 1996[2] and replaced it with cancellation of removal part A, §212(c) relief still is available to certain lawful residents who pled guilty in reliance on the availability of §212(c) relief, thanks to the U.S. Supreme Court's decision in *INS v. St. Cyr*.[3]

This chapter discusses Cancellation of Removal Part A and INA §212(c) relief.

Cancellation for LPRs—Cancellation of Removal Part A

Under INA §240A(a), an LPR is eligible for the relief of cancellation if he or she:

- Has been an LPR for at least five years;
- Has resided in the United States continuously for seven years after having been admitted in any status;
- Has not been convicted of an aggravated felony; and
- Merits a favorable exercise of discretion.

On a positive note, unlike suspension and cancellation for non-LPRs, neither a showing of hardship nor a U.S. citizen (USC) or LPR qualifying relative is necessary to qualify for this type of relief. Moreover, no numerical limit applies to the total number of cancellation of removal applications granted to LPRs each year.

Unfortunately, however, the eligibility requirements for Cancellation Part A exclude many LPRs from qualifying for this form of relief from removal. Ineligible

---

[1] Immigration and Nationality Act of 1952 (INA), Pub. L. No. 82-414, 66 Stat. 163 (codified as amended at 8 USC §§1101 *et seq.*).

[2] Illegal Immigration Reform and Immigrant Responsibility Act of 1996, Pub. L. No. 104-208, div. C, 110 Stat. 3009, 3009-546 to 3009-724.

[3] *INS v. St. Cyr*, 533 U.S. 289 (2001).

LPRs include those with aggravated felony convictions and those excluded by the "stop time" rule, discussed below.

LPR for Five Years

The INA defines "lawfully admitted for permanent residence" as having been lawfully accorded the privilege of residing permanently in the United States as an immigrant in accordance with immigration laws, such status not having changed.[4]

Permanent residence begins on the date of adjustment or admission pursuant to an immigrant visa. Time spent as a conditional resident counts toward the five years of permanent residence. In contrast to continuous residence (discussed below), the accrual of time as a permanent resident does not stop with the commission of certain crimes or with the service of a Notice to Appear (NTA).[5] However, in *Matter of Koloamatangi*,[6] the Board of Immigration Appeals (BIA) held that individuals who had acquired their permanent resident status through fraud or misrepresentation have never been lawfully admitted for permanent residence, and, thus, are ineligible to apply for cancellation of removal for LPRs.

For asylees and refugees, a strong argument can be made that special statutory rollback provisions should apply toward meeting the five-year residence requirement for Cancellation Part A. Under those provisions, refugees who adjust status are regarded as having obtained residence status as of the date of their arrival into the United States.[7] Asylees who adjust status are deemed to have become permanent residents as of the date one year before the approval of their adjustment application.[8]

Seven Years Continuous Residence After Lawful Admission

The required seven years of continuous residence in the United States can take place after the foreign national is admitted in any status.[9] It can continue to accrue even if the foreign national falls out of status.[10] Continuity of residence, however, will end when the foreign national is served with an NTA, or when the foreign national has committed an offense that renders him or her inadmissible under INA §212(a)(2) (criminal inadmissibility grounds) or deportable under INA §237(a)(2) (crime involving moral turpitude (CMT), multiple CMTs, aggravated felonies, and high speed flight) or INA §237(a)(4) (security grounds), whichever is earliest. This is known as the *stop time* rule. For most criminal grounds, the commission of the act will precede the service of the NTA. In *Matter of Jurado*,[11] the BIA held that an individual need not be actually

---

[4] INA §101(a)(20).

[5] *Matter of Perez*, 22 I&N Dec. 689 (BIA 1999).

[6] *Matter of Koloamatangi*, 23 I&N Dec. 548 (BIA 2003).

[7] INA §209(a)(2).

[8] INA §209(b); *but see Matter of C–V–T–*, 22 I&N Dec. 7 (BIA 1998) (length of lawful permanent residence of refugee measured from date of adjustment of status).

[9] *See Matter of Blancas-Lara*, 23 I&N Dec. 458 (BIA 2002).

[10] *Id.*

[11] *Matter of Jurado*, 24 I&N Dec. 29 (BIA 2006).

charged and found inadmissible or deportable on a criminal ground in order for criminal conduct to stop a period of continuous residence. For many LPRs, this *stop time* provision will prove the greatest barrier to eligibility for cancellation of removal.

Fortunately, commission or conviction of a CMT will not cut off accrual of continuous residence if it falls within either of the INA §212(a)(2)(A)(ii) exceptions. Under these exceptions, neither an offense committed while the individual is under 18, nor a petty offense makes the person inadmissible on the basis of conviction or commission of a CMT and, therefore, does not cut off the accrual of continuous residence. However, these two exceptions allow continuous residence to continue to accrue through just one qualifying crime, a rule that the BIA has clarified in two decisions.

In the first of these decisions, *Matter of Deanda-Romo*,[12] the BIA held that a person who has committed one offense that qualifies for an exception, and then commits further offenses, remains eligible for the petty offense exception for the first crime until the commission of the second offense. Thus, the respondent accrued the required seven years of continuous residence because his first crime, which qualified as a petty offense, did not render him inadmissible, and he had accrued the required seven years before committing the second offense.

In the second decision, *Matter of Garcia-Hernandez*,[13] the BIA interpreted the phrase "only one crime" for purposes of the INA §212(a)(2)(A)(ii) exceptions as "only one such crime." Thus, a second offense that is not a CMT will not render the individual ineligible for the exception and continuous residence will continue to accrue.

The accrual of continuous residence also does not stop if the respondent committed an offense that made him deportable, but the offense was not *referred to* in INA §212(a)(2).[14] Thus, the BIA held that a firearms offense did not stop the accrual of continuous presence because the offense was *referred to* in INA §212(a)(2).[15] Note, however, that a firearms offense could render a person inadmissible if it is also a CMT.[16] Therefore, a respondent who is deportable for an aggravated felony,[17] a firearms offense,[18] a crime of domestic violence, stalking, or crime against children,[19] or a violation of a protection order[20] does not have a stop-time problem if the offense

---

[12] *Matter of Deanda-Romo*, 23 I&N Dec. 597 (BIA 2003).

[13] *Matter of Garcia-Hernandez*, 23 I&N Dec. 590 (BIA 2003).

[14] INA §240A(d)(1).

[15] *Matter of Campos-Torres*, 22 I&N Dec. 1289 (BIA 2000).

[16] *Compare Matter of S*, 8 I&N Dec. 344 (BIA 1959) (possession of a firearm with intent to use it is a crime involving moral turpitude (CMT)) *with Matter of Granados,* 16 I&N Dec. 726 (BIA 1979) (possession of a firearm is not a CMT).

[17] INA §237(a)(2)(iii).

[18] INA §237(a)(2)(C).

[19] INA §237(a)(2)(E)(i).

[20] INA §237(a)(2)(E)(ii).

also is not covered in the grounds of inadmissibility. It is important to analyze whether the offense is a crime covered in the grounds of inadmissibility, since many offenses also may be CMTs for which no exception applies.

In the context of cancellation of removal, the BIA has interpreted the date of *commission* of an offense to be the date the offense actually was committed, and not the later date of conviction.[21] Thus, under BIA precedent, the "stop time" rule kicks in and stops the accrual of continuous residence (and also continuous physical presence for non-LPR cancellation) on the day the triggering offense actually is committed.

Some have argued that there is nothing in the statute to stop a new period of continuous residence from accruing after the act is committed, or after an NTA is issued.[22] The BIA has held, in the context of non-LPR cancellation of removal (which shares the same "stop time" provision with LPR cancellation), that a new period of continuous presence can begin after a departure and a subsequent return, even if that return is without inspection or admission and even though under the *stop time* rule the service of an NTA had stopped accumulation of the prior period of presence before the departure and subsequent reentry.[23] Advocates can argue that for LPR cancellation, the continuous presence need not immediately precede the application. This is different from non-LPR cancellation of removal, which requires that the noncitizen prove continuous presence *immediately preceding* the application.[24]

Since the cancellation statute requires continuous residence, the rules that apply here should be distinguished from those regarding continuous physical presence, which is needed for such forms of relief as cancellation of removal for non-LPRs. Note that residence is defined at INA §101(a)(33) as a place of general abode—*i.e.*, the principal, actual dwelling place, without regard to intent. With continuous residence, the statute does not expressly state that absences from the United States will stop the accumulation of continuous residence. However, in the naturalization context, a period of continuous residence is presumed to be broken when a foreign national has been absent from the United States for a period of six months to one year, unless the applicant can establish otherwise. Absences of one year or more will establish conclusively a break in continuous residence.

The concept of continuous residence also should be distinguished from that of abandonment of LPR status. An LPR can be deemed to have abandoned his or her permanent resident status if it is determined that the LPR intended to abandon his or her status when traveling abroad, regardless of the length of the departure. If LPR status is found to have been abandoned, the LPR could face rescission proceedings.

---

[21] *Matter of Perez*, 22 I&N Dec. 689 (BIA 1999).

[22] *But see Matter of Mendoza-Sandino*, 22 I&N Dec. 1236 (BIA 2000) (in context of suspension of deportation, stop-time rule prevented accrual of continuous presence after order to show cause issued).

[23] *Matter of Cisneros-Gonzalez*, 23 I&N Dec. 668 (BIA 2004); *see also Okeke v. Gonzales*, 407 F.3d 585 (3d Cir. 2005) (citing *Cisneros* with approval and finding that petitioner began to accrue a new period of continuous presence upon his legal reentry after departure, even though the commission of an offense pre-departure likely would have stopped the accrual of time under any prior period of presence).

[24] *See* INA §240A(b)(1)(A) (emphasis added).

Bars to Cancellation Eligibility

Certain categories of persons are ineligible for cancellation. These include:

- Crewmen who entered after June 30, 1964;

- J visa holders subject to the foreign residence requirement;

- Persecutors of others;

- LPRs convicted of an aggravated felony; and

- Persons previously granted cancellation or suspension.

Because of the expansive definition of what constitutes an aggravated felony and the even more expansive definition of what U.S. Immigration and Customs Enforcement (ICE) believes constitutes an aggravated felony, the most common bar likely to be an issue in this section is the aggravated felony bar. Indeed, the reality is that the drastic expansion of the definition of aggravated felony under the Illegal Immigration Reform and Immigrant Responsibility Act of 1996 (IIRAIRA)[25] means that many LPRs will be ineligible for cancellation.

Since removal cannot be canceled for an LPR who has been convicted of an aggravated felony, it is important to understand the definition of that term (as set forth in INA §101(a)(43)), and to challenge ICE's designation of a crime as an aggravated felony in removal proceedings whenever possible. This is discussed in more detail in chapter 2.

The term *aggravated felony* first was added to the statute in 1988, and was limited at the time to murder, drug trafficking, and illicit trafficking in firearms. The definition was expanded by Congress several times thereafter, including many additions made by IIRAIRA.

As discussed in more detail in chapter 2, the expanded definition of aggravated felony now encompasses more than 20 categories of offenses, including:

- A crime of violence that has a sentence of imprisonment of one year or more, regardless of the time actually served;

- A theft offense (including shoplifting) with a sentence of imprisonment of one year or more, regardless of the time served;

- A smuggling offense (though there is an exception for a first offense for aiding one's spouse, parent or child);

- Money laundering of more than $10,000;

- An offense involving fraud or deceit in which the loss or attempted loss to the victim or victims exceeds $10,000;

- A gambling or racketeering offense with a sentence of one year or more;

- Tax evasion where revenue lost to the government is in excess of $10,000;

---

[25] IIRAIRA, *supra* note 2.

- A passport fraud offense with a sentence of 12 months imprisonment or more; and

- Bribery, counterfeiting, forgery or trafficking in vehicles with a sentence of imprisonment of one year or more.

Two other changes made by IIRAIRA in 1996 have a critical impact on what offense will be defined as an aggravated felony. The term *conviction* is defined at INA §101(a)(48)(A) as:

a formal judgment of guilt of the foreign national entered by a court or, if adjudication off guilt has been withheld, where (i) a judge or a jury has found the foreign national guilty or the foreign national has entered a plea of guilty or *nolo contendere* or has admitted sufficient facts to warrant a finding of guilt, and (ii) the judge has ordered some form of punishment, penalty, or restraint on the foreign national's liberty to be imposed.

With the new definition of *conviction* (discussed in more detail in chapter 2), criminal court dispositions that would not have been considered convictions under the prior definition now are considered convictions for purposes of immigration law. Therefore, if the offense meets the expanded definition of *aggravated felony*, then a conviction for such an offense will constitute a bar to eligibility for cancellation.

The phrase *term of imprisonment* is defined at INA §101(a)(48)(B) as:

the period of incarceration or confinement ordered by a court of law regardless of any suspension of the imposition or execution of that imprisonment or sentence in whole or in part.

Because of these new definitions imposed by IIRAIRA in 1996, even a conviction where the punishment imposed is a one-year suspended sentence may result in an offense being classified as an aggravated felony offense for which a sentence of one year is required.

The 1996 law also provided that the new definition of aggravated felony applies retroactively to convictions on, after, or before the date of its enactment on September 30, 1996. While retroactive application is being challenged in some federal circuit courts, the attorney general (AG), the BIA, and most immigration courts accept the retroactive application of the aggravated felony definition.

It also can be important to consider post-conviction relief to ameliorate the consequences of a conviction. Immigration judges (IJs) are very aware that many LPRs will have no shot at immigration relief unless they are able to get some sort of post-conviction relief in criminal court. Some judges allow continuances for respondents to file and process motions to reduce a criminal sentence nunc pro tunc, so that a respondent might become eligible for cancellation. For example, an otherwise eligible LPR who might be considered an aggravated felon because he had received a sentence of one year incarceration for a crime of violence or theft might return to criminal court with a motion and reduce the sentence to 364 days, and, thus, not be considered an aggravated felon.[26]

Discretionary Factors

Even if an applicant is eligible statutorily for cancellation of removal, he or she still must convince the IJ that he or she deserves a grant of cancellation in an exercise of the judge's discretion. The BIA has held that an IJ must balance the adverse facts showing the foreign national's undesirability as an LPR with the social and other considerations presented to determine whether the granting of relief appears to be in the best interest of the country.[27]

As mentioned above, unlike several other forms of relief from removal, hardship is not a requirement for Cancellation Part A. Furthermore, the applicant need not have a qualifying USC or LPR relative in order to be eligible. Nonetheless, both of these factors are important to the consideration of discretion.

In *Matter of C–V–T*,[28] an IJ denied cancellation of removal to an LPR on discretionary grounds. The LPR had been convicted of a cocaine possession offense (that did not meet the definition of aggravated felony) and had served 90 days in jail for the offense. The district attorney who prosecuted the case submitted a letter recommending that the Immigration and Naturalization Service (legacy INS) allow the applicant to remain in the United States. The BIA reversed the IJ's decision, stating that the numerous favorable factors in the LPR's case outweighed the negative factors. According to the BIA, the factors to consider all cases were the following:

Positive factors to consider:

- Family ties in the United States;
- Employment history;
- Service in the U.S. armed forces;
- Hardship to family in the United States and to the LPR if deported;
- Value and service to the community;
- Rehabilitation; and
- Other evidence of good moral character.

Adverse factors to consider:

- Nature and circumstances of the ground of removal;
- Additional violations of the immigration laws;
- Nature, recency and seriousness of the criminal record; and
- Other evidence of bad moral character.

---

[26] *See Matter of Cota-Vargas*, 23 I&N Dec. 849 (BIA 2005) (a reduced sentence is recognized for immigration purposes regardless of the reasons for the reduction).

[27] *Matter of C–V–T–*, 22 I&N Dec. 7 (BIA 1998); *see also Matter of Marin*, 16 I&N Dec. 581 (BIA 1978) (discretionary factors utilized in applications for §212(c) relief).

[28] *Matter of C–V–T–*, *supra* note 27.

It is helpful to examine the particular facts in *Matter of C–V–T*[29] in more detail. The respondent was a citizen of Vietnam who had entered the United States as a refugee in 1983, after having served in the military forces of South Vietnam. He spoke and read English, and had held a job as a mechanic for many years in the United States. He also had a brother here. The respondent fled Vietnam after being imprisoned by the Communist regime for his military support of South Vietnam. His cocaine possession offense resulted from a delivery incident where the respondent acted as a middleman for a friend. The district attorney who prosecuted the case stated that the respondent's conduct in the incident was perhaps the most amateur incident of drug delivery he had ever encountered, and recommended that the respondent not be deported. There were no other offenses in the respondent's record. The respondent had been a volunteer in a city clean-up program. Once the respondent was arrested, he cooperated with the police by disclosing the name of the drug supplier. The respondent served the 90-day sentence given for his offense and was in legacy INS custody at the time of his hearing. The BIA found him eligible for cancellation based on these equities, and found that although it was difficult to assess his rehabilitation while he was still incarcerated, the respondent had no records of infractions while in jail, his criminal record was that of an amateur, and he had expressed remorse for his crime, promising never to break the law again if forgiven.

Although many clients may not have facts as sympathetic as those in *Matter of C–V–T–*,[30] it is important to focus on the factors that the IJ must balance. For example, a client who faces severe hardship if deported because of a mental illness or medical condition that cannot be treated in the home country, or a client who faces extreme poverty or human rights abuses in the home country may be able to outweigh a long criminal record. Representatives should include evidence of conditions in the home country to show hardship to the client if deported.

Where and How to File

Jurisdiction over an application for cancellation of removal lies solely with the immigration court. To apply for cancellation of removal, the LPR must file an original Executive Office for Immigration Review (EOIR) Form 42A with the immigration court after complying with the new EOIR security procedures by sending a copy of the application, along with the application fee and the biometrics fee to the designated USCIS address. In addition to EOIR Form 42A, the applicant must file a G-325A biographic information form, and submit documentary evidence to establish the required elements of relief and demonstrate favorable discretionary factors.

INA §212(c) Relief

Relief Under §212(c)

Because one of the ineligibility grounds for Cancellation of Removal Part A is conviction of an aggravated felony, many long-term LPRs will not be eligible for that

---

[29] *Id.*

[30] *Id.*

form of relief. Persons who pled to, or at least agreed to, a plea agreement for an aggravated felony offense prior to April 24, 1996, however, still may be eligible for relief under former INA §212(c). Also, there is no *stop time* rule in §212(c) relief, permitting LPRs who do not qualify for cancellation of removal because of the stop time rule potentially to qualify for §212(c) relief if they agreed to a plea agreement before April 1, 1997. Persons in new or pending proceedings who meet the eligibility requirements still may apply for §212(c) relief. Persons who already have had a final decision in their deportation or removal proceedings, however, must have filed a motion to reopen by April 26, 2005, in order to be eligible for §212(c) relief.

Background

Prior to 1996, §212(c) waivers were available for certain LPRs who had been residing permanently in the United States for at least seven years. This relief waived most convictions—even those classified as aggravated felonies—unless the LPR had served a term of imprisonment of five years or more. On April 24, 1996, the Anti-Terrorism and Effective Death Penalty Act (AEDPA)[31] was signed into law. AEDPA removed INA §212(c) eligibility from any noncitizen deportable for having committed an aggravated felony, controlled substance violation, firearms offense, miscellaneous crime, or multiple criminal convictions. On September 30, 1996, IIRAIRA repealed INA §212(c) altogether, replacing it with LPR cancellation of removal under INA §240A(a).

AEDPA did not specify whether it barred the AG from acting on applications filed before the date of the statute's enactment. In *Matter of Soriano*,[32] the BIA held that INA §212(c) still was available if the application was filed before that date. It referred the case to the AG, however, for her review. On February 21, 1997, the AG instructed EOIR to reopen cases upon petition by a noncitizen who had conceded deportability before the effective date of AEDPA in reliance on the availability of §212(c) relief. Questions remained, however, regarding the scope of §212(c) relief in other contexts, and litigation throughout the federal circuits ensued.

On January 22, 2001, EOIR issued a final rule that restored §212(c) eligibility for most individuals who were in proceedings prior to April 24, 1996. Then, on June 25, 2001, the U.S. Supreme Court breathed new life into INA §212(c), ruling in *INS v. St. Cyr*[33] that §212(c) relief remained available to respondents who had pled guilty to a criminal offense prior to AEDPA's passage in reliance on the availability of §212(c) relief, but who were not placed into proceedings until after the law went into effect.

In *INS v. St. Cyr*, the Supreme Court held that the restrictions on §212(c) relief imposed by AEDPA, and the subsequent elimination of the §212(c) waiver by the passage of IIRAIRA,[34] cannot be applied retroactively to an LPR who pled guilty before the effective dates of those acts. In so ruling, the Court stated that §212(c) re-

---

[31] Antiterrorism and Effective Death Penalty Act of 1996, Pub. L. No. 104-132, 110 Stat. 1214.

[32] *Matter of Soriano*, 21 I&N Dec. 516 (BIA 1996).

[33] *INS v. St. Cyr*, 533 U.S. 289 (2001).

[34] IIRAIRA, *supra* note 2.

lief remains available for foreign nationals "whose convictions were obtained through plea agreements and who, notwithstanding those convictions, would have been eligible for §212(c) relief at the time of their plea under the law then in effect."

In *INS v. St. Cyr*, St. Cyr had pled guilty before April 24, 1996, to an offense that made him deportable, but that would have been waivable under the §212(c) provisions then in effect. He subsequently was placed in removal proceedings after April 1, 1997, when §212(c) had been completely eliminated with the passage of IIRAIRA. Under the Court's ruling, St. Cyr was eligible to seek a §212(c) waiver in removal proceedings because at the time of his plea agreement he would have been eligible for this relief.

What remains of INA §212(c) relief is a matter of some ongoing litigation and governmental interpretation. Section 212(c) waivers were available for certain LPRs who had been residing permanently in the United States for at least seven years. This waiver was used to waive most convictions—even those classified as aggravated felonies—unless the LPR had served a term of imprisonment of five years or more. Applicants who had filed a §212(c) application prior to the effective date of AEDPA, or were in proceedings prior to that date, were encouraged to continue seeking relief and appeal any denial. The same also was true for persons with an aggravated felony conviction entered prior to that date.

As a result, noncitizens who pled guilty or nolo contendere to a crime or crimes prior to April 24, 1996 (the date of enactment of AEDPA), and who would have been eligible for §212(c) relief under the law as it had existed prior to AEDPA but were not placed into proceedings until after the law's effective date, now are eligible for §212(c) relief under the majority's decision in *U.S. v. St. Cyr*.

On September 28, 2004, the Department of Justice (DOJ) issued a final rule implementing the Supreme Court's decision. The rule took effect on October 28, 2004, and is codified at 8 CFR §§212.3, 1003.44, and 1212.3. The next section of this chapter will set out the requirements for §212(c) relief under the 2004 regulations.

Eligibility Under Former INA §212(c)

Pursuant to the final rule, to qualify for INA §212(c) relief, all applicants must meet the following criteria:

- He or she is now an LPR or was an LPR prior to receiving a final order of deportation or removal;

- He or she had seven consecutive years of lawful unrelinquished domicile in the United States prior to the date of the final administrative order of deportation or removal, or, if the person does not have a final order, by the time that he or she applies for §212(c) relief;

- If he or she is charged under the deportability grounds, there is a comparable ground of inadmissibility or exclusion;

- He or she pled guilty or nolo contendere to a deportable offense through a plea agreement made before April 1, 1997; and

- He or she was otherwise eligible to apply for §212(c) at the time the plea was made.

Beyond the above requirements, the final rule then impacts on eligible LPRs in different ways because an LPR is only eligible to apply for the version of §212(c) in effect on the day of the plea agreement. Specifically, because §212(c) eligibility requirements pertaining to convictions of aggravated felonies were modified twice between 1990 and 1996, the result is three different versions of the provision during that time period. Which version applies in a particular individual's case depends on the date that the applicant pled guilty, as follows:

- Plea agreements before November 29, 1990 (the date of the first amendment): §212(c) as it existed prior to the 1990 amendment applies.

  Under 8 CFR §1212(f)(4)(ii), LPRs who pled guilty to an aggravated felony offense before November 29, 1990 are eligible for a §212(c) waiver without regard to how much time s/he may have served for the offense. This rule implements the decision in the U.S. Court of Appeals for the Ninth Circuit decision *Toia v Fasano*,[35] which held that the 1990 amendment to the INA eliminating §212(c) relief for LPRs with aggravated felony convictions who served a sentence of at least five years does not apply retroactively to persons who entered guilty pleas prior to the November 29, 1990, enactment date.

- Plea agreements on or after November 29, 1990, and before April 24, 1996 (AEDPA enactment date): §212(c) as it existed between 1990 and AEDPA applies.

  The applicant must have served a term of less than five years imprisonment if the conviction is an aggravated felony.[36] Note, however, that the regulations do not address at what point the time in prison should be measured. A number of district courts have found that LPRs who had not served five years in prison at the time of their immigration court hearing are eligible to apply for §212(c) relief,[37] but the U.S. Court of Appeals for the First Circuit, in *Gomes v. Ashcroft*,[38] found that the relevant date is when the BIA makes a decision on appeal.[39]

- Plea agreements after April 24, 1996, but before April 1, 1997 (IIRAIRA effective date): §212(c) as modified by AEDPA applies.

  As a result, the following individuals are not eligible: LPRs convicted of an aggravated felony, controlled substance offense, certain firearms offenses, espionage or treason, or two or more CMTs committed within five years after entry and for which the sentence is one year or longer. Moreover, because the IIRAIRA expanded definition of aggravated felony is retroactive, a foreign na-

---

[35] *Toia v Fasano*, 334 F.3d 917 (9th Cir. 2003).

[36] 8 CFR §1212.3(f)(4)(i).

[37] *See, e.g., De Cardenas v. Reno,* 278 F. Supp. 2d 284 (D. Conn. 2003); *Hartman v. Elwood,* 255 F. Supp. 2d 510 (E.D.P.A. 2003).

[38] *Gomes v. Ashcroft,* 311 F.3d 43 (1st Cir. 2002).

[39] *See also Buitrago-Cuesta v. INS,* 7 F.3d 291 (2d Cir. 1993).

tional with a post–April 24, 1996, conviction for an offense that was not an aggravated felony at the time of the conviction still will be barred from §212(c) relief.

Finally, for persons who were in deportation proceedings commenced before April 24, 1996, the DOJ's January 21, 2001, rule—called the *Soriano*[40] *rule*—allowed §212(c) eligibility for LPRs in deportation proceedings before April 24, 1996, regardless of whether the conviction was obtained through plea agreement or after trial. The new rule retains this (at 8 CFR §1212.3(g)), but the deadline for filing motions to reopen deportation proceedings under this provision was July 23, 2001, and the new rule did not extend that deadline.

Comparable Ground of Inadmissibility
or Exclusion for Those Charged with Deportability

Section 212(c) relief was written as a waiver of inadmissibility or exclusion grounds. It was extended to serve as a form of relief from removal for persons subject to deportation grounds, however, as long as there was a *comparable ground* of exclusion or inadmissibility under (INA §212(a)) to the deportation ground with which the applicant is charged. Thus, an applicant charged with deportability had to be able to show the immigration court that there was such a comparable inadmissibility or exclusion ground, though the BIA had made it clear that there did not have to be exact parity between grounds. For example, where the ground of deportability was that of conviction of an aggravated felony (for which there is no directly corresponding inadmissibility ground), the BIA looked to the specific category of aggravated felony at issue to see if there was a comparable ground for that category of offense. Drug offenses were found to have a corresponding ground.[41] The most notable category of non-aggravated felony offenses, which was found not to have a comparable ground, was firearms offenses.[42]

Unfortunately, however, the BIA has issued two decisions that explicitly signal that this *comparable ground* requirement, first developed in §212(c) case law and then codified in the regulations is to be applied more stringently and literally than it was, perhaps, in the past. Specifically, in *Matter of Blake*,[43] the BIA, acknowledging that its prior decisions suggested a more *relaxed approach* to comparable grounds for aggravated felonies in the past, found that the new regulations *clarified* that a more stringent approach must be taken. Applying this new approach, the BIA held that the specific aggravated felony of which the respondent had been charged—sexual abuse of a minor—had no statutory inadmissibility ground counterpart, and that, therefore, the respondent was not eligible for §212(c) relief. While the BIA recognized the "significant overlap between offenses categorized as sexual abuse of a minor and those considered crimes of moral turpitude," the BIA declined to find that the CMT ground

---

[40] *Matter of Soriano, supra* note 32.

[41] *Matter of Meza*, 20 I&N Dec. 257 (BIA 1991).

[42] *Matter of Esposito*, 21 I&N Dec. 1 (BIA 1995).

[43] *Matter of Blake*, 23 I&N Dec. 722 (BIA 2005).

of inadmissibility could serve as a corresponding ground, stating that "the test for compatibility is not met merely by showing that some or many of the offenses included in the charged category could also be crimes involving moral turpitude." Instead, according to the BIA, "whether a ground of deportation or removal has a statutory counterpart … turns on whether Congress has employed similar language to describe substantially equivalent categories of offenses."[44] In *Matter of Brieva*,[45] the BIA held that the specific aggravated felony of which the respondent was convicted was a crime of violence (here, unauthorized use of a motor vehicle), and that a crime of violence also had no corresponding inadmissibility ground counterpart, dismissing the very significant overlap between crimes of violence and CMTs. Most circuit courts have upheld *Matter of Blake*.[46] The only circuit that has refused to follow *Matter of Blake* is the U.S. Court of Appeals for the Second Circuit.[47]

The BIA has held that there is an exception to the requirement of a corresponding inadmissibility ground discussed in the preceding paragraph. This exception occurs where a former LPR seeks to waive inadmissibility through §212(c) in connection with a new application for adjustment of status, rather than applying for §212(c) alone as a form of relief from removal. In this situation, the BIA has held that §212(c) may be used to waive inadmissibility even if the individual was deportable for a ground that has no inadmissibility counterpart.[48] Any new adjustment of status application will require a new I-130 or I-140 to be filed and approved. A beneficiary may not take advantage of a previously-granted visa petition on which he or she already adjusted status.[49]

Motions to Reopen to Apply for INA §212(c) Relief

Under the 2004 rule implementing *St. Cyr*,[50] former LPRs who are subject to an administratively final order of deportation, exclusion or removal had until April 26, 2005, to file the motion to reopen.[51] This deadline applies only to motions to reopen and does not affect eligibility to apply for relief in any new or pending cases.

The Application for INA §212(c) Relief

To apply for §212(c) relief, the LPR must file an original I-191 with the immigration court after complying with the new EOIR security procedures by sending a copy of the application along with the application fee and the biometrics fee to the designated USCIS

---

[44] *Id.*

[45] *Matter of Brieva*, 23 I&N Dec. 766 (BIA 2005).

[46] *Matter of Blake, supra* note 43. *See, e.g., Abebe v. Mukasey*, No. 05-76201, U.S. App. LEXIS 23859 (9th Cir. Nov. 20, 2008); *Vue v. Gonzales*, 496 F.3d 858 (8th Cir. 2007); *Vo v. AG*, 482 F.3d 363 (5th Cir. 2007); *Caroleo v. Gonzales*, 476 F.3d 158 (3d Cir. 2007); *Valere v. Gonzales*, 473 F.3d 757 (7th Cir. 2007); *Kim v. Gonzales*, 468 F.3d 58 (1st Cir. 2006).

[47] *See Blake v. Carbone*, 489 F.3d 88 (2nd Cir. 2007).

[48] *Matter of Azurin*, 23 I&N Dec. 695 (BIA 2005).

[49] 8 CFR §204.2(h)(2); *Matter of Villarreal-Zuniga*, 23 I&N Dec. 886 (BIA 2006).

[50] INS v. St. Cyr, *supra* note 33.

[51] 8 CFR §1003.44.

address. In addition, Form I-191 should be accompanied by supporting documents to establish the statutory eligibility requirements and favorable discretionary factors. Since relief under INA §212(c) is discretionary, the same guidelines discussed above for documenting favorable factors for LPR cancellation of removal should be followed in establishing eligibility for discretionary relief under INA §212(c).[52]

Persons Not Covered in the §212(c) Regulations

Two big categories of LPRs with pre–April 1, 1997, convictions get no benefit from the new regulations. First, the new rules do not provide for §212(c) eligibility for those LPRs convicted as a result of a trial. Citing several post–*St. Cyr* federal courts of appeals decisions rejecting an extension of the *St. Cyr* ruling to include LPRs convicted after trial, the comments to the rules describe such LPRs as not having the kind of reliance interests that the Supreme Court focused on in *St. Cyr*. In addition, the regulations offer no redress for those persons who would have qualified for §212(c) relief but already have been deported; the regulations preclude §212(c) eligibility for foreign nationals abroad as a result of deportation or removal. Specifically, the regulations provide that individuals are ineligible for a §212(c) waiver if they departed the United States and currently are outside the country, returned illegally to the United States after having been issued a final order of deportation or removal, or are present in the United States without having been admitted or paroled.[53]

Looking Ahead

Expect ongoing court challenges to the regulatory restrictions on §212(c) eligibility. The U.S. Courts of Appeals for the Third and Tenth Circuits have held that LPRs convicted after trial prior to April 1, 1997, may apply for §212(c) relief.[54] The Second Circuit decision has indicated that some LPRs with pre-AEDPA post-trial convictions may be eligible for a §212(c) waiver.[55] Other circuit decisions have rejected the argument that LPRs with post-trial convictions are eligible for §212(c) relief.[56] However, not all arguments supporting §212(c) eligibility for such LPRs have been raised in these cases, and this should be considered an area where case law is developing.

---

[52] *See Matter of Marin*, 16 I&N Dec. 581 (BIA 1978) (discussing discretionary factors relevant in §212(c) application).

[53] 8 CFR §1003.44; *but cf. William v. Gonzales*, 49 F.3d 329 (4th Cir. 2007) (holding that the post-departure bar on motions to reopen contained in 8 CFR §1003.2(d) is invalid, on the grounds that it conflicts with the clear statutory language of INA §240(c)(7)(A), permitting motions to reopen without specifying that the applicant must be within the United States when filing such motions).

[54] *See Hem v.Mauerer*, 458 F.3d 1185 (10th Cir. 2006); *Atkinson v. AG*, 479 F.3d 222 (3d Cir. 2007); *Ponnapula v. Ashcroft*, 373 F.3d 480 (3d Cir. 2004).

[55] *See Walcott v. Chertoff*, 517 F.3d 149 (2d Cir. 2008); *Restrepo v. McElroy*, 369 F.3d 627 (2d Cir. 2004).

[56] *See, e.g., Thom v. Ashcroft*, 369 F.3d 158 (2d Cir. 2004), *cert. denied*, 126 S. Ct. 40 (2005); *Chambers v. Reno*, 307 F.3d 284 (4th Cir. 2002); *Armendariz-Montoya v. Sonchik*, 291 F.3d 1116 (9th Cir. 2002), *Hernandez-Castillo v. Moore*, 436 F.3d 516 (5th Cir. 2006).

Proposed Repapering Rule

On November 30, 2000, legacy INS proposed a rule explaining the circumstances and procedure for terminating deportation proceedings and initiating removal proceedings. This procedure is called *repapering*, and would allow LPRs to qualify for cancellation of removal where they were formerly eligible for relief under §212(c) before statutory changes in 1996 disqualified them. This procedure also would allow non-LPRs to qualify for Cancellation of Removal Part B, where they would have been eligible for seven– or 10-year suspension but for the *stop time* rule created by IIRAIRA. Qualified applicants must submit a written request to the appropriate U.S. Immigration and Customs Enforcement (ICE) district counsel, who has the discretion to grant or deny it. To qualify for repapering, an applicant must be in deportation proceedings, not have received a final administrative deportation order, and establish prima facie eligibility for cancellation. If the request is granted, ICE then would move the IJ or BIA to terminate deportation proceedings. Upon termination, ICE then would initiate removal proceedings by serving the foreign national with an NTA.

The rule is not in effect yet. The comment period ended on January 29, 2001. Obviously, the relevance of this rule is diminished by the continuing availability of §212(c) relief for certain noncitizens with convictions predating April 1, 1997. Nonetheless, there may be some situations where an LPR in deportation proceedings would not be eligible for §212(c) relief, but would be eligible for LPR cancellation if placed into removal proceedings. This might occur, for example, where the conviction was for a deportable crime that did not have a parallel ground of exclusion, and that did not constitute an aggravated felony (*i.e.*, certain firearms convictions).

CHAPTER EIGHT
CANCELLATION AND SUSPENSION FOR
NON–PERMANENT RESIDENT FOREIGN NATIONALS

This chapter covers a form of relief available under the pre–Illegal Immigration Reform and Immigrant Responsibility Act of 1996 (IIRAIRA)[1] immigration laws—*suspension of deportation*. It also covers the post-IIRAIRA form of relief that replaced suspension of deportation—*cancellation of removal*. Moreover, the chapter covers a variation of cancellation of removal for abused immigrant women, as well as *special rule* cancellation of removal and suspension of deportation for certain nationals of El Salvador, Guatemala, and certain former Soviet-bloc countries under the Nicaraguan Adjustment and Central American Relief Act (NACARA).[2]

Former Suspension of Deportation

Overview

Before the enactment of IIRAIRA in 1996, persons in what was then called *deportation* proceedings could apply for a remedy called *suspension of deportation* under §244(a) of the Immigration and Nationality Act (INA).[3] Under the former INA §244(a), the Executive Office for Immigration Review (EOIR) could exercise discretion to grant suspension of deportation to a person who proved that he or she had seven years of continuous physical presence in the United States, good moral character during all of that time, and that deportation would cause extreme hardship to the applicant or the applicant's U.S. citizen (USC) or lawful permanent resident (LPR) spouse, parent, or child. If EOIR granted suspension of deportation, the person would become an LPR as of the date of the EOIR order.

IIRAIRA Changes

With the passage of IIRAIRA, Congress changed the former *deportation* proceedings into *removal* proceedings. In addition, IIRAIRA deleted suspension of deportation, except in certain circumstances, and replaced it with cancellation of removal under INA §240A. The passage of IIRAIRA also ushered in the following changes:

---

[1] Illegal Immigration Reform and Immigrant Responsibility Act of 1996 (IIRAIRA), Pub. L. No. 104-208, div. C, 110 Stat. 3009, 3009-546 to 3009-724.

[2] Nicaraguan Adjustment and Central American Relief Act (NACARA), Pub. L. No. 105-100, tit. II, 111 Stat. 2160, 2193–201 (1997).

[3] Immigration and Nationality Act of 1952 (INA), Pub. L. No. 82-414, 66 Stat. 163 (codified as amended at 8 USC §§1101 *et seq.*).

- Increased the continuous physical presence requirement from seven years to 10 years, which also then increased the length of time required to demonstrate good moral character;

- heightened the hardship standard from *extreme hardship* to *exceptional and extremely unusual hardship*;

- eliminated the ability to prove hardship to the applicant, and restricted the demonstration of hardship to the applicant's USC or LPR spouse, parent or child;

- established a numerical cap that limits cancellation of removal grants to only 4,000 per year; and

- most significantly, IIRAIRA established the *stop time* rule that stopped the accrual of *physical presence* in the United States at the moment removal proceedings are initiated against the person (upon issuance of the Notice to Appear (NTA)). The stop time rule also ends the accrual of physical presence upon the commission of a criminal offense that renders the person inadmissible to the United States.

In *Matter of N–J–B–,*[4] the Board of Immigration Appeals (BIA) held that the *stop time* rule applied retroactively to individuals placed in deportation proceedings even before IIRAIRA went into effect on April 1, 1997. The ruling sent shock waves throughout the Salvadoran and Guatemalan immigrant communities. Many Salvadorans and Guatemalans had been caught and put into deportation proceedings shortly after arriving in the United States. These same Salvadorans and Guatemalans subsequently had become plaintiffs in a class action lawsuit against the Immigration and Naturalization Service (legacy INS) called *American Baptist Churches (ABC) v. Thornburgh,*[5] which allowed all class members to have new asylum interviews. However, due to the passage of time and the signing of peace agreements in both El Salvador and Guatemala, the vast majority of plaintiffs intended to pursue claims for suspension of deportation rather than political asylum. The retroactive application of the stop time rule under IIRAIRA would have barred tens of thousands of class members from pursuing their suspension claims. Fortunately, Congress subsequently enacted legislation—NACARA—that allowed Salvadorans and Guatemalans who arrived in the United States by a certain date to apply for suspension or cancellation without the stop time rule.

Current Standard and Procedure for Suspension Applicants

Even though the suspension statute was repealed by IIRAIRA effective April 1, 1997, this relief remains available to respondents in deportation proceedings initiated prior to April 1, 1997. Not only must the foreign national meet the statutory eligibility requirements, he or she also must demonstrate that suspension is merited as a matter of discretion. Suspension is available to undocumented as well as documented

---

[4] *Matter of N–J–B–,* 21 I&N Dec. 812 (BIA 1997).

[5] *American Baptist Churches (ABC) v. Thornburgh,* 760 F. Supp. 796 (1991).

foreign nationals. If the foreign national establishes statutory eligibility, and if the immigration judge (IJ) exercises his or her discretion favorably, the ground of deportability is waived and the applicant becomes eligible for LPR status.

Eligibility

Where the applicant for suspension is deportable for relatively minor offenses (*e.g.*, entry without inspection), deportation may be suspended at the discretion of the IJ. To qualify for suspension of deportation under former INA §244(a)(1), the applicant must establish the following:

- He or she has seven years of continuous physical presence in the United States;

- He or she has been of good moral character during those seven years; and

- Deportation would result in extreme hardship either to the applicant or to certain relatives lawfully residing in the United States.

Exchange visitors, crew persons, and persons who have engaged in Nazi-sponsored persecution of others are statutorily barred from relief through suspension of deportation.

For foreign nationals deportable for more serious offenses (*e.g.*, narcotics or other crimes), the suspension requirements are stricter. The continuous physical presence requirement is increased to 10 years "immediately following the commission of an act ... constituting a ground for deportability ...." Furthermore, the hardship proved must be "exceptional and extremely unusual."

Continuous Physical Presence

The statute requires applicants to have been "physically present in the United States for a continuous period of not less than seven years immediately preceding the date of [the] application." Individuals who are deportable because of criminal convictions, failure to register, falsification of documents, having a final civil document fraud order, or security or related grounds must establish 10 years of continuous physical presence *following* the commission of the act or assumption of the status that rendered the foreign national deportable under these provisions. The fact that the 10-year period must follow the act for which the foreign national is being deported severely limits the availability of suspension to foreign nationals deportable for these offenses.

The continuous physical presence requirement does not apply to foreign nationals who, while in the United States, enlisted in or were inducted into the U.S. armed forces, served for at least 24 months in an active-duty status, and, if separated from such service, were separated under honorable conditions.

The suspension statute allows foreign nationals to continue to maintain *continuous physical presence* despite brief departures from the United States. An applicant is not to be considered to have failed to maintain continuous physical presence "if the absence from the United States was brief, casual, and innocent and did not meaningfully interrupt the continuous physical presence." This standard is modeled after that enun-

ciated by the U.S. Supreme Court, where the return of an LPR following a brief departure from the United States does not constitute an entry.

Two provisions of IIRAIRA may place a further severe restriction on suspension
applicants seeking to meet the *continuous physical presence* requirement. INA
§240A(d)(1) provides that for purposes of the *cancellation of removal* defense to removal, an individual's period of continuous physical presence is deemed to end when
the foreign national is served an NTA for removal proceedings under INA §239(a).
On its face, this provision applies only to cancellation of removal in *removal* proceedings, and IIRAIRA's general rule is that the new removal provisions apply only
to cases initiated on or after April 1, 1997. However, IIRAIRA §309(c)(5) provides,
in a paragraph titled "Transitional Rule with Regard to Suspension of Deportation,"
that INA §240A(d) "shall apply to notices to appear issued before, on, or after the
date of the enactment of this Act."

In a divided decision, a majority of the BIA construed this provision to apply not
only to NTAs for removal proceedings, but also to orders to show cause (OSCs) for
deportation proceedings.[6] The BIA further ruled that the service of an OSC on a suspension applicant occurring prior to IIRAIRA's enactment nonetheless terminated his
or her accrual of time toward the required period of continuous physical presence.

Partly in response to litigation, the BIA's decision subsequently was vacated by
the attorney general (AG), who has not yet issued a new decision in the case. In light
of the AG's action, interim instructions have been issued directing U.S. Immigration
and Customs Enforcement (ICE) trial attorneys to join in motions to reopen deportation proceedings for respondents who were placed in proceedings prior to April 1,
1997, who had less than seven years' continuous physical presence at the time they
were served with an OSC, and who do not appear clearly ineligible for cancellation.
This last eligibility requirement is very important. Cancellation of removal for non-
LPRs requires a qualifying relative, whereas suspension of deportation did not.

Proposed Rule on Repapering

On November 30, 2000, legacy INS proposed a rule explaining the circumstances
and procedure for terminating deportation proceedings and initiating removal proceedings. This procedure is called *repapering*, and would allow foreign nationals to qualify
for cancellation of removal where they formerly were eligible for suspension of deportation before statutory changes in 1996 disqualified them. Qualified applicants must
submit a written request to the appropriate ICE district counsel who has the discretion
to grant or deny it. If granted, ICE then would move the IJ or BIA to terminate deportation proceedings. Upon termination, ICE then would initiate removal proceedings by
serving the foreign national with an NTA.

Non-LPRs who were disqualified from suspension of deportation by retroactive application of the stop time rule (service of the OSC occurring before they had acquired
seven years of physical presence), but who would qualify for cancellation under
§240A(b), may make such a request. These persons now must have at least 10 years of

---

[6] *See Matter of N–J–B–, supra* note 4.

continuous presence and would not be affected by the stop time rule if the OSC is withdrawn and they are served with an NTA. They must be in deportation proceedings, not have received a final administrative deportation order, and establish prima facie eligibility for cancellation (note necessity for qualifying USC or LPR relative).

The rule is not in effect yet. The comment period ended on January 29, 2001. In lieu of regulations, there is a legacy INS memorandum that states the policy on when to re-paper.[7]

Good Moral Character

INA 101(f) precludes the IJ from finding that an applicant has good moral character if he or she either currently is, or during the period for which good moral character is required was, one of the following:

- A habitual drunkard;
- One who was convicted of, or who admitted the elements of, a crime that would make him or her inadmissible (whether or not the person is found to be inadmissible), except for:
  - (a) convictions described in INA §212(a)(2)(e) (government representatives who asserted immunity to avoid prosecution in the United States); and
  - (b) controlled substance convictions in which the only offense is a single case of simple possession of 30 grams or less of marijuana;
- One who engaged in foreign national smuggling as described in INA §212(a)(6)(E) (whether or not found to be inadmissible);
- A practicing polygamist;
- One whose income is derived principally from illegal gambling activities;
- One who has been convicted of two or more gambling offenses committed during the period for which good moral character is required;
- One who has given false testimony for the purpose of obtaining any benefits under the INA;
- One who, during the period for which good moral character is required has been confined, as a result of conviction, to a penal institution for an aggregate period of 180 days or more, regardless of whether the offense or offenses for which he or she has been confined were committed within or outside the required period; or
- One who, at any time, has been convicted of an aggravated felony (on or after November 29, 1990).

In addition, the IJ has broad discretion to find that the applicant does not possess the requisite good moral character, even in cases where there is no statutory preclu-

---

[7] INS Memorandum, B. Cooper, "Administrative Closure of EOIR Proceedings for Non-Lawful Permanent Resident Aliens Eligible for Repapering" (Dec. 7, 1999), *published on* AILA InfoNet at Doc. No. 99122371 (*posted* Dec. 23, 1999).

sion. For example, IJs have denied suspension applications for lack of good moral character where the applicant was convicted of crimes many years ago and where the applicant concealed prior marriages or bigamy. The seven-year period of good moral character is measured backward from the final IJ or BIA decision.

Extreme Hardship

Of the three elements that must be present for a foreign national to be eligible for suspension, the one that usually is the most difficult to establish is that the foreign national, or his or her relatives residing lawfully in the United States, would experience extreme hardship should the foreign national be deported. Because only limited review of the foreign national's case is available on appeal, it is crucial that his or her representative establish a record during deportation proceedings that documents the foreign national's contention that hardship would follow if the foreign national were deported. The IJ examines the following factors in determining whether deportation would result in extreme hardship:

- The foreign national's family ties and community ties in the United States;
- His or her social adjustment;
- The physical/mental medical problems the foreign national might have;
- The foreign national's length of time in the United States;
- His or her age;
- The language(s) he or she speaks; and
- The economic hardship the foreign national might experience if deported.

Economic hardship alone generally is not enough to meet the eligibility test, but severe economic detriment may constitute extreme hardship. If the IJ does not consider economic hardship factors, this constitutes an abuse of discretion. Although the statute allows an applicant to establish extreme hardship based solely on hardship to him- or herself, the BIA rarely has found extreme hardship in the absence of hardship to a qualifying relative.

If the applicant has a minor child who is a USC and who would be forced either to remain behind or be uprooted and moved to a strange place, this in itself does not constitute hardship extreme enough to merit suspension of deportation. However, evidence of the adverse effects of uprooting a USC child from this country, especially if he or she has entered school, is very important to establishing extreme hardship. A psychologist's report evaluating the effects of such a disruption, for example, could be very effective evidence to support an application for suspension. Chapter 6, pertaining to waivers of grounds of inadmissibility and deportability as relief from removal, discusses extreme hardship further.

The BIA issued a decision defining *extreme hardship* in the suspension of deportation context.[8] Mr. Kao and Ms. Lin were a married couple from Taiwan who lived in the United States for more than 17 years. They had five children, all of whom were

---

[8] *Matter of Kao and Lin*, 23 I&N Dec. 45 (BIA 2001).

citizens of the United States, and were expecting a sixth child. The children spoke limited Chinese, and the parents testified that they could not afford the tuition for an English school in Taiwan. The respondents owned a house in Texas and would lose money if they had to sell it.

The BIA identified the following factors to consider in determining whether the respondents' deportation would cause extreme hardship:

- The age of the respondents, both at entry and at the time of application for relief;
- The respondents' family ties in the United States and abroad;
- The length of residence in the United States over the minimum seven-year requirement;
- The respondents' own health, as well as that of their USC or LPR children;
- The political and economic conditions in the home country;
- The financial impact of departure from the United States;
- The possibility of other means of adjusting status in the United States;
- The respondents' involvement and position in the local community; and
- The respondents' immigration history.

Using these factors, the BIA found that Mr. Kao and Ms. Lin had not established hardship to themselves. They had, however, established that their deportation would cause extreme hardship to qualifying relatives, namely their USC children. The BIA placed special emphasis on the children's lack of fluency in Chinese and their integration into the United States. In particular, the BIA believed that uprooting the oldest daughter (who was 15) and forcing her to survive in a Chinese-only environment would be a significant disruption in her education and her social development.

Discretion

An IJ grants suspension as a matter of discretion, and, therefore, he or she could deny relief even where the applicant has met the statutory requirements discussed above. Suspension has been denied in the IJ's discretion where the applicant received public assistance, became a public charge, or had a preconceived intent at the time of entry. The standard for review of the IJ's exercise of discretion is whether the decision was "arbitrary, capricious, an abuse of discretion, or otherwise not in accordance with law." Chapter 6, pertaining to waivers of inadmissibility and deportability as a form of relief from removal, also discusses discretion.

Cancellation of Removal for Non-LPRs

Introduction

Cancellation of removal is a form of discretionary relief from removal that is available only in removal proceedings initiated on or after April 1, 1997. This relief is not available to individuals in deportation or exclusion proceedings, unless ICE brings new charges against them to institute removal proceedings. There are four forms of cancellation of removal relief:

- Cancellation for LPRs (addressed in chapter 7);
- Cancellation for non-LPRs;
- Cancellation for a battered spouse or child; and
- Cancellation pursuant to NACARA §203.

Eligibility

Cancellation of removal for non-LPRs under INA §240A(b)(1) is analogous to suspension of deportation relief in deportation proceedings. To be eligible for this relief, individuals must establish that:

- They have been physically present in the United States for a continuous period of not less than 10 years immediately preceding their application for relief;
- They have had good moral character during the 10-year period prior to the entry of final administrative decision in the case;
- They have not been convicted of an offense that would make them inadmissible or deportable; and
- Their removal would result in *exceptional and extremely unusual hardship* to the foreign national's USC or LPR spouse, parent or child.

In *Matter of Ortega-Cabrera,*[9] the BIA held that the 10 years needed for good moral character is calculated backward from the date on which the application finally is resolved by the IJ or BIA. The 10 years of physical presence is calculated differently, as described below. Further, the BIA clarified that the requirement in the regulations that an applicant for non-LPR cancellation demonstrate statutory eligibility prior to the service of an NTA,[10] applies only to the physical presence requirement, and not to other requirements—*e.g.*, good moral character; qualifying relatives; and exceptional and extremely unusual hardship—that can continue to be considered and developed up to the time the application finally is decided.[11]

Continuous Residence or Physical Presence

As discussed below, all four forms of cancellation require that the foreign national establish that he or she either continuously resided or physically was present in the United States continuously for a specified period of time. These requirements do not apply to a foreign national who, while in the United States, enlisted in or was inducted into the U.S. armed forces, served at least 24 months in an active-duty status, and, if separated from such service, separated under honorable conditions.[12] Special rules govern the determination of continuous residence or physical presence for pur-

---

[9] *Matter of Ortega-Cabrera*, 23 I&N Dec. 793 (BIA 2005).

[10] 8 CFR §1003.23(b)(3).

[11] *Matter of Bautista-Gomez*, 23 I&N Dec. 893 (BIA 2006).

[12] INA §240A(d)(3).

poses of eligibility for cancellation. The period is deemed to end when the foreign national is served an NTA initiating removal proceedings, or when the foreign national has committed an offense making the foreign national inadmissible or deportable because of a criminal conviction.[13] In other words, the foreign national generally must have accumulated the required period of continuous residence or physical presence prior to the initiation of removal proceedings, and prior to commission of a deportable offense.

Commission or conviction of a crime involving moral turpitude (CMT), however, will not cut off accrual of continuous residence or physical presence if it falls within one of the INA §212(a)(2)(A)(ii) exceptions. Under these exceptions, certain offenses committed while the individual is under 18, or petty offenses, do not make the person inadmissible on the basis of a conviction or commission of a CMT and, therefore, do not cut off the accrual of continuous residence or presence. These two exceptions allow time to continue to accrue through the commission of one qualifying crime, and up until a second qualifying crime is committed.[14]

A period of continuous physical presence is cut off by a departure for a single period of more than 90 days or by periods of 180 days in the aggregate.[15] There is an exception to this rule for certain Violence Against Women and Department of Justice Reauthorization Act of 2005 (VAWA 2005)[16] cancellation applicants, discussed below. The BIA, in *Matter of Romalez*,[17] held that continuous physical presence also is deemed to end at the time a foreign national is compelled to depart the United States under the threat of the institution of deportation or removal proceedings. Romalez was a Mexican citizen who lived in the United States since 1984. On two separate occasions, the U.S. Border Patrol arrested Romalez and threatened to commence formal proceedings against him unless he voluntarily returned to Mexico. Each time, Romalez returned to Mexico only to come back to the United States unlawfully after one or two days. Legacy INS instituted removal proceedings against Romalez and charged him as being inadmissible for a previous entry without being admitted or paroled.

The BIA conducted a statutory analysis of INA §240A(b) by comparing it with former INA §244(a) (suspension of deportation). In doing so, the BIA found that INA §240A(d) is not the *exclusive* rule for *all departures*, but rather for *certain breaks* in physical presence. In other words, §240A(d) does not support just any departure of 90 days or less. The BIA determined that this language implied that there are "*breaks* other than those which exceed 90– or 180-day statutory limits[.]" The BIA also determined that, in addition to enforced voluntary departure, the purpose of removal or deportation is to terminate *residence* in the United States. It therefore followed that

---

[13] INA §240A(d).

[14] *Matter of Deanda-Romo*, 23 I&N Dec. 597 (BIA 2003); *Matter of Garcia-Hernandez*, 23 I&N Dec. 590 (BIA 2003).

[15] INA §240A(d)(2).

[16] Violence Against Women and Department of Justice Reauthorization Act of 2005, Pub. L. No. 109-162, 119 Stat. 2960 (2006).

[17] *Matter of Romalez*, 23 I&N Dec. 423 (BIA 2002).

physical presence could not be preserved after an enforced departure. Finally, the BIA held that it was contrary to the overall objectives of IIRAIRA to allow a foreign national to continue to accrue time for purposes of obtaining relief after the foreign national departs under a formal order of deportation or removal or under the threat of such an order.

However, a few caveats have emerged since *Matter of Romalez*.[18] In *Morales-Morales v. Ashcroft*,[19] the court held that a foreign national who repeatedly had been taken to the border by U.S. Border Patrol, then entered Mexico voluntarily, did not have a break in her *continuous physical presence* in the United States.

Morales was a Mexican citizen who lived in the United States since June 1985. She was married to an LPR and had four USC children. In March 1999, she left the United States for the first time to visit her sick mother in Mexico. When she attempted to return to the United States, she was stopped informally by U.S. Border Patrol, and returned to Mexico. This process was repeated three times in the next six days. Morales never appeared before an IJ, and no removal proceedings were initiated. On her fifth attempt to enter illegally, Morales was arrested and removal proceedings were initiated upon her release.

The U.S. Court of Appeals for the Seventh Circuit concluded that the facts did not demonstrate that Morales "voluntarily departed under threat of proceeding." The court believed that returning Morales to the border did not constitute a threat of removal proceedings. Thus, unlike Romalez, she was not subject to the break in continuous physical presence.

In *Matter of Avilez-Nava*,[20] the BIA held that continuous physical presence also can continue to accrue where, for example, a foreign national departs under no such threat, is then denied admission by an immigration official without any such threat, and subsequently reenters without inspection before triggering the time bars.

Moreover, the BIA has held that a new period of continuous presence can begin after a departure and a subsequent return, even if that return is without inspection or admission and even though under the *stop time* rule the service of an NTA had stopped accumulation of the prior period of presence before the departure and subsequent reentry.[21]

Exceptional and Extremely Unusual Hardship

The hardship requirement for cancellation is more restrictive than that for suspension of deportation in deportation proceedings. Instead of *extreme hardship*, the foreign national must establish *exceptional and extremely unusual* hardship. Moreover,

---

[18] *Id.*

[19] *Morales-Morales v. Ashcroft*, 384 F.3d 418 (7th Cir. 2004).

[20] *Matter of Avilez-Nava*, 23 I&N Dec. 799 (BIA 2005).

[21] *Matter of Cisneros-Gonzalez*, 23 I&N Dec. 668 (BIA 2004); *see also Okeke v. Gonzales*, 407 F.3d 585 (3rd Cir. 2005) (*citing Cisneros* with approval and finding that petitioner began to accrue a new period of continuous presence upon his legal reentry after departure, even though the commission of an offense pre-departure likely would have stopped the accrual of time under any prior period of presence).

this standard may not be satisfied by showing hardship to the foreign national, but rather the applicant must establish that the hardship will be suffered by a USC or LPR spouse, parent or child.

In *Matter of Monreal*,[22] the BIA discussed what constituted *exceptional and extremely unusual hardship* in the context of cancellation of removal for non-LPRs. In that case, the applicant was a 34-year-old citizen of Mexico who had entered the United States when he was 14. His wife, who was not a citizen or resident of the United States, had returned to Mexico with the couple's youngest child. The couple's other two children, 12 and 8 years old, lived with Mr. Monreal. All three children were USCs. Mr. Monreal had worked continuously since 1991 and was the sole support of his family. His parents and seven of his siblings were LPRs, and he had one brother living in Mexico.

The BIA stated that, by replacing the old relief of suspension of deportation with cancellation of removal, Congress narrowed the class of foreign nationals who could qualify for relief. It was obvious, said the BIA, that the hardship standard for cancellation of removal is a higher one than that required for suspension of deportation. The BIA concluded that Congress intended cancellation of removal to be available only in compelling and truly exceptional cases, involving harm substantially beyond that which ordinarily would be expected to result from the foreign national's deportation.

The BIA listed various factors to consider in determining whether exceptional and extremely unusual hardship had been demonstrated. Many of those factors are the same ones considered in determining extreme hardship for purposes of suspension of deportation, but they must be weighed according to the higher standard required for cancellation. In particular, hardship to the respondent cannot be considered in an application for cancellation.

The factors identified by the BIA to determine exceptional and extremely unusual hardship include the ages, health, and circumstances of qualifying LPR and USC relatives. For example, said the BIA, an applicant who has elderly parents in this country, parents who are dependent solely on the applicant for support, might well have a strong case. Another strong applicant might have a qualifying child with very serious health issues, or compelling special needs in school. A lower standard of living or adverse country conditions in the country of return are factors to consider, but generally will be insufficient in themselves to support a finding of exceptional and extremely unusual hardship. As with extreme hardship, all hardship factors should be considered in the aggregate when assessing exceptional and extremely unusual hardship. The BIA emphasized that, although guidance as to the term's meaning can be provided, each case must be assessed and decided on its own facts.

Applying these factors, the BIA found that Mr. Monreal had not established that his removal would cause exceptional and extremely unusual hardship to a qualifying relative. The BIA commented, however, that had this been an application for suspension, Mr. Monreal might well have been found eligible for the relief.

---

[22] *Matter of Monreal*, 23 I&N Dec. 56 (BIA 2001).

During 2002, the BIA twice more revisited the issue of demonstrating *exceptional and extremely unusual* hardship for cancellation purposes.

First, in *Matter of Andazola*,[23] the BIA held that a 30-year-old unmarried mother from Mexico did not establish eligibility for cancellation of removal because she failed to demonstrate that her removal would cause exceptional and extremely unusual hardship to her USC children who were ages 6 and 11. In fact, the BIA compared *Andazola* to *Monreal*[24] by noting that the facts presented in *Andazola* were "common" and the "hardships that the Respondent has outlined are simply not substantially different from those that would normally be expected upon removal to a less developed country."

The BIA found that because Andazola still lived with the father of her children, who sometimes provided support to the family and who had only temporary permission to be in the United States, the father would be able to help support her and the children if she were to return to Mexico.

Although Ms. Andazola had lived in the United States since August of 1985, the BIA determined that she was still young and able to work and that she would be able to use the job skills that she developed in the United States to help her establish herself back in Mexico. Moreover, the BIA found it "significant" that Andazola had a great deal of assets in the United States, which also could help establish her in Mexico. The BIA viewed negatively the fact that even though all of her siblings lived in the United States, none of them had lawful status.

Although Andazola argued that her children would have diminished educational opportunities in Mexico, the BIA determined that there was no showing that her children would be completely deprived of education in Mexico. Moreover, the BIA noted that "a finding that diminished educational opportunities result in 'exceptional and extremely unusual hardship'" would mean that cancellation of removal would be granted in virtually all cases involving Respondents from developing countries who have young USC or LPR children. This view is not consistent with congressional intent."

In *Matter of Recinas*,[25] the BIA stated that cancellation of removal cases before IJs and the BIA "must be examined under the standards set forth in *Matter of Monreal*[26] and *Matter of Andazola*"[27] because they are the "seminal" cases on the meaning of "exceptional and extremely unusual hardship."

Ariadna Recinas was a 39-year-old citizen of Mexico and the single mother of six children, four of whom were USCs ages 12, 11, 8, and 5 years. The two non-USC children, ages 15 and 16, were co-respondents in the case. The three respondents had lived in the United States since 1988. Recinas also had two LPR parents and five

---

[23] *Matter of Andazola*, 23 I&N Dec. 319 (BIA 2002).

[24] *Id.*

[25] *Matter of Recinas,* 23 I&N Dec. 467 (BIA 2002).

[26] *Matter of Monreal*, *supra* note 22.

[27] *Matter of Andazola*, *supra* note 23.

USC siblings living in the United States. She had no immediate relatives living in Mexico.

Recinas' mother cared for her children while Recinas managed her own vehicle inspection business. Recinas lived near her mother, who had a close relationship with the children. The father of Recinas' children was not involved in their lives and was in immigration proceedings at the same time Recinas was in proceedings.

In reviewing all the factors in this case, the BIA determined that this case was different from *Monreal*[28] and *Andazola*[29] in the degree of hardship that would be suffered by the qualifying family members. In particular, the BIA relied on seven factors to find that Recinas demonstrated that exceptional and extremely unusual hardship would occur to her four USC children. First, the BIA noted that Recinas and her family had lived in the United States since 1988, and that her children did not know any other life. Moreover, the children did not speak Spanish well, nor could they read and write it. The BIA also noted that the four USC children were entirely dependent on the single-mother respondent for support because the father was not involved in their lives. So the single mother in Mexico not only would have to find employment, but also support their emotional needs, which would be very difficult on her own without help. The BIA also pointed to the fact that Recinas' LPR mother took care of Recinas' children while Recinas formed a business and that this was a stable environment for the kids. By contrast, in Mexico, without family support, Recinas would have difficulty finding work and creating a supportive environment for kids. The USC children also would suffer significant hardship from the mother's loss of economic stake in the United States, coupled with the difficulty she would have in establishing any comparable economic stability in Mexico (Here the BIA emphasized the fact that she is a single mother of six children *and* had no family in Mexico). Finally, the BIA noted that Recinas' prospects for immigration through her USC siblings or LPR parents were unrealistic, due to the backlog in the visa availability preference system for Mexico. There were no other apparent methods to adjust status.

Separately, after granting Recinas cancellation of removal, the BIA remanded the case back to the IJ for the other two minor respondents, with the order to hold their cases in abeyance until Recinas received lawful permanent residence. This way, the two children would be able to apply for cancellation of removal based on their relationship to their LPR mother.

Grounds of Ineligibility

Apart from the requirements listed in INA §240A(b)(1), under INA §240A(c), non-LPRs are ineligible for this relief if any of the following applies in their case:

- They entered the United States as a crewman subsequent to June 30, 1964;

- They were admitted as an *exchange alien* or acquired such status in order to receive graduate medical education or training;

---

[28] *Matter of Monreal, supra* note 22.

[29] *Matter of Andazola, supra* note 23.

- They were admitted or acquired *exchange alien* status for other purposes, but were subject to the two-year foreign residence requirement and failed to fulfill that requirement or (have it waived);

- They are inadmissible or deportable under the security and related grounds;

- They ordered, incited, assisted, or otherwise participated in the persecution of others; or

- They previously were granted cancellation of removal, suspension of deportation, or a §212(c) waiver.

The 4,000 Annual Cap

Under INA §240A(e)(1), the immigration court or the BIA can cancel the removal and adjust the status of no more than 4,000 people during the fiscal year. The date that the order granting cancellation of removal and adjustment of status becomes final is the date the foreign national is recorded as having received lawful permanent residence in the United States as long as the foreign national is within the 4,000 annual cap. Where the 4,000 annual cap has been reached, however, the immigration court or the BIA will reserve decision on an application for cancellation of removal until a number becomes available in the next fiscal year, or unless they can deny the applications based on statutory grounds other than hardship.[30]

Cancellation of Removal for Abused Immigrant Women and Children

Background

Immigrants often are trapped in abusive relationships due to a fear of deportation and separation from children. Congress recognized the impact of domestic violence on immigrants and in 1994 passed the Violence Against Women Act (VAWA),[31] then re-authorized and modified it in 2000 (VAWA 2000) and 2005.[32] It affords two forms of relief for battered immigrants abused by their USC or LPR spouses or parents:

- They may "self-petition" for LPR status without the cooperation of the abusive spouse or parent; and

- They may request cancellation of removal as a defense to removal to the immigration court. This chapter will only discuss VAWA cancellation of removal.

Requirements

INA §240A(b)(2) provides that the applicant for VAWA cancellation of removal must:

---

[30] 8 CFR §240.21(c).

[31] Violence Against Women Act of 1994, Pub. L. No. 103-322, §§40701–03, 108 Stat. 1796, 1953–55.

[32] Violence Against Women Act of 2000, Pub. L. No. 106-386, div. B, 114 Stat 1464, 1491–539; VAWA 2005, *supra* note 16.

- Have been battered or suffered extreme cruelty by a spouse or parent who is or was a USC or LPR, or is the parent of a child in common with the USC or LPR abuser, and the child has suffered abuse;

- Have been present physically in the United States for three years before applying;

- Be a person of good moral character during the period of physical presence;

- Not have been convicted of an aggravated felony;

- Not be inadmissible or deportable due to certain criminal, security, or marriage fraud violations; and

- Demonstrate that removal would result in extreme hardship to the applicant, or the applicant's child, or in the case of an applicant child, to the applicant's parent.

The following persons are eligible to apply for VAWA cancellation and suspension:

- Abused spouses of USCs and LPRs;

- Abused sons and daughters of USCs and LPRs;

- Non-abused parents of abused children of USCs or LPRs, even if not married to the abuser; and

- Abused *intended spouses* of USCs or LPRs. The term *intended spouse* means a foreign national who believed that he or she married a USC or LPR and went through a marriage ceremony, but whose marriage is not legitimate solely because of the USC's or LPR's bigamy.

Marital Relationship

VAWA cancellation does not require that the applicant be married currently to the abuser or demonstrate a good faith marriage. However, it would be wise to document a good faith marriage, since a finding of having entered into a fraudulent marriage would make the applicant ineligible.

The parent who has an abused child in common with the USC or LPR abuser is not required to have been married to the abuser. More than one IJ has granted cancellation to an unmarried woman, abused by a USC with whom she had a child in common. In one case, the child never was beaten, but the IJ found that the child suffered extreme cruelty by viewing the mother's beatings. Although the abuse was not directed to the child, the woman was granted VAWA cancellation as the parent of an abused child. In another case, the child again was not beaten, but he was being raised in an abusive home by his USC father, a former policeman who had impregnated his mother when she was just 15, and was being denied almost all access to his mother, who did not live in the home. According to an affidavit from a social worker, the child, who was 4 at the time of the grant, already was showing signs of abuse, including delayed emotional development and inappropriate aggressiveness.

Children

In the case of a mother who is applying for cancellation of removal because her child has been abused, the child must meet the definition of *child* under immigration law—unmarried and under 21 years of age. However, when the parent is the abuser, the statute only requires that the abused applicant be the son or daughter of the abuser, and does not require that the applicant conform to the definition of child. The statute states that the applicant must be abused by *a spouse or parent* not that the applicant be a child.

Unfortunately, children cannot gain status through their parent's VAWA cancellation. VAWA 2000, however, directs the AG to grant parole to the children of VAWA cancellation recipients and, if the recipient is a child, to the parent, until the relative can obtain immigrant status. Even when the parent is applying as the parent of the abused child, the child will not be included in the parent's cancellation application. The abused child must apply separately. The court may consolidate the cases or the parent may ask the judge for a continuance to allow her to file a self-petition with USCIS that would include the child. Once the self-petition is approved by USCIS, the judge then may consider both applications. If the batterer is a USC, the judge may adjust the status of both mother and child. Another option is that once the mother gains LPR status, she could file a family-based petition for the child.

Battery or Extreme Cruelty

In order to qualify for cancellation of removal, the domestic abuse must rise to the level of *battery or extreme cruelty*. Domestic abuse covers a broad area of activity, including physical, sexual, and psychological attacks, as well as economic coercion.

While there is little case law defining battery or extreme cruelty in VAWA cancellation of removal cases, the regulations defining the terms for VAWA self-petitioners should serve as a guideline.[33] Under the regulations' definition of battery or extreme cruelty, the phrase includes, but is not limited to, "being the victim of any act or threatened act of violence, including any forceful detention, which results or threatens to result in physical or mental injury. Psychological or sexual abuse or exploitation, including rape, molestation, incest (if the victim is a minor), or forced prostitution shall be considered acts of violence."

Extreme cruelty also includes:

- Social isolation of the victim;
- Accusation of infidelity;
- Incessantly calling, writing, or contacting;
- Interrogating friends and family members;
- Stalking;
- Making threats;
- Economic abuse (*e.g.*, not allowing the victim to get a job or controlling all money in the family); and
- Degrading the victim.

---

[33] *See* 8 Code of Federal Regulations (CFR) §204.2(c)(1)(vi).

Other abusive acts that may not initially appear violent but are part of an overall pattern of violence also are included in the definition. Violence against another person or thing may be considered abuse if it can be established that the act was deliberately made to perpetrate extreme cruelty.

In 1996, legacy INS stated that the definition of *battery or extreme cruelty* in the regulations is flexible and should also be applied to claims of extreme mental cruelty as well as to claims of physical abuse. The preamble to the regulations states that the definition is flexible and sufficiently broad to encompass all types of domestic battery and extreme cruelty.[34]

In *Hernandez v. Ashcroft*, the Ninth Circuit has applied a holistic interpretation to the requirement of extreme cruelty within the context of domestic violence.[35] The court first established that extreme cruelty is not discretionary, and, thus, is not subject to review by the judiciary. Extreme cruelty is a question of fact, determined to the application of legal standards, similar to the question of whether a person is a habitual drunkard. Battery is interpreted as the existence of physical abuse in a domestic violence case, whereas extreme cruelty is an objective inquiry into an individual's experience of psychological cruelty. "Extreme cruelty simply provides a way to evaluate whether an individual has suffered psychological abuse that constitutes domestic violence."[36]

The Ninth Circuit concluded that extreme cruelty describes the non-physical manifestations of domestic violence. The court relied on testimony given by expert witnesses that define domestic violence as a cycle of violence perpetrated in a pattern of behavior used by the abuser to maintain control over the victim. Within this context, non-physical actions constitute domestic violence when they are intertwined with the threat of harm in order to maintain the abuser's control over the victim through fear and dominance. In *Hernandez*, the husband's non-physical actions–calling his wife; promising to change; and begging her to come back—rose to the level of domestic violence because:

- The victim was emotionally vulnerable;

- There was a strong emotional bond necessitated by violence; and

- There was an underlying threat that failure to meet the abuser's requests would bring violence.[37]

Three-year Continuous Physical Presence

The applicant for VAWA cancellation of removal has to show three years of continuous presence in the United States immediately preceding the date of the application. Amendments enacted in the Battered Immigrant Women Protection Act of

---

[34] *See* 61 Fed. Reg. 13065 (March 26, 1996).

[35] *Hernandez v. Ashcroft*, 345 F.3d 824 (9th Cir. 2004).

[36] *Id.*

[37] *Id.*

2000^{38} significantly eased the provisions regarding physical presence. First, the amendments exempted VAWA cancellation applicants from INA §240A(d)(1), which provided that issuance of an NTA—the charging document in a removal case—stops continuous physical presence from accruing, and exempted VAWA suspension applicants from a similar provision, under which issuance of an OSC tolled the accumulation of continuous presence. Second, the amendments provide that a foreign national is not considered to have failed to maintain continuous physical presence because of absence if the foreign national demonstrates a connection between the absence and the abuse. No absence or portion of an absence connected to the abuse counts toward the 90– or 180-day limits.

No Residence with Abuser

The applicant is not required to have resided with the abuser.

Where Abuse Took Place

The abuse or extreme cruelty need not have taken place in the United States.

Good Moral Character

While it generally is stated that an applicant for VAWA cancellation of removal must show that he or she has been a person of good moral character for three years preceding the date of the application, the reasoning set out in *Matter of Ortega-Cabrera*[39] (discussed above) gives strong support to the idea that this three-year period actually should be counted backwards from the date in which the application is finally resolved by the IJ or the BIA. Still, the IJ, as a matter of discretion, may inquire into good moral character beyond the statutory period. Also, VAWA self-petitioning regulations allow U.S. Citizenship and Immigration Services (USCIS) to deny a self-petition if the applicant has not been a person of good moral character in the past.[40]

Good moral character, as defined in the INA, applies to VAWA cancellation of removal cases. Therefore, consult INA §101(f) to determine if the person is unable to satisfy the requirement.

When determining good moral character, extenuating circumstances may be considered. For example, in *Matter of M–*,[41] the BIA ruled that a person who admitted to, but was not convicted of, having engaged in prostitution under duress was not excludable because she was reduced to a state of mind that prevented her from exercising free will through the use of wrongful and oppressive threats. The preamble to the VAWA regulations also states that if a person is not convicted and was subjected to abuse by being

---

[38] Battered Immigrant Women Protection Act of 2000, Pub. L. No. 106-386, §§1501–13, 114 Stat. 1464, 1518–37.

[39] *Matter or Ortega-Cabrera*, 23 I&N Dec. 793 (BIA 2005).

[40] 8 CFR §204.2(c)(1)(vii).

[41] *Matter of M–*, 7 I&N Dec. 51 (BIA 1956).

forced into prostitution or forced to engage in other excludable behavior, she would not be precluded from being found to be a person of good moral character.[42]

Amendments passed in 2000 slightly eased the application of §101(f) for VAWA self-petitioners and applicants for cancellation. Under those amendments, an act or conviction that does not bar the AG from granting relief under INA §240A(b)(2)(A)(iv)—inadmissibility under INA §§212(a)(2) or (3); or deportability under INA §§237(a)(1)(G), (a)(2), (a)(3), or (a)(4))—does not bar a finding of good moral character if the government finds that the act or conviction was connected to the abuse and that a waiver otherwise is warranted.

A memorandum issued by USCIS provides some insight into determining whether an act or conviction contained in §101(f) is waivable under §§212(h)(1), 212(i)(1), 237(a)(7), and 237(a)(1) of the Battered Immigrant Women Protection Act.[43] Waivable offenses include:

- Engaging in prostitution;
- Knowingly encouraging, inducing, assisting, abetting or aiding another foreign national to enter the United States in violation of the law;
- Having been removed previously from the United States;
- One drug conviction for simple possession of marijuana of 30 grams or less;
- Having been convicted for two or more offences; and
- Giving false testimony.

The offenses are waivable if the foreign national can show that she would not have committed the crime but for the batter or extreme cruelty. The evidence submitted must demonstrate:

- Circumstances surrounding the offence, including the relationship the abuser had to the offense, and the abuser's role in it; and
- The causal relationship between the offence and the battery or extreme cruelty.

The offense did not have to occur during the marriage. In addition, the adjudicator must consider the full history of the case, including the need to escape.[44]

In the context of suspension or cancellation under VAWA, prior arrests or convictions may make it more difficult to establish good moral character, because the same waivers available to adjustment applicants are not available to VAWA suspension or cancellation applicants. VAWA 2000[45] did, however, create a limited waiver under INA §237(a)(7) for certain domestic violence victims deportable for having a conviction of domestic violence, stalking, or violation of a protective order who could show that they were not the primary perpetrators of violence, and that there was some rela-

---

[42] 61 Fed. Reg. 13066 (March 26, 1996).

[43] Battered Immigrant Women Protection Act, *supra* note 38.

[44] USCIS Memorandum, W. Yates, "Determinations of Good Moral Character in VAWA-Based Self-Petitions" (Jan. 19, 2005), *published on* AILA InfoNet at Doc. No. 05012561 (*posted* Jan. 25, 2005).

[45] VAWA 2000, *supra* note 32.

tionship between their conviction and their having been abused. Thus, VAWA applicants in proceedings with certain convictions may still be eligible to establish good moral character if they are eligible for a waiver under INA §237(a)(7). VAWA 2005,[46] signed into law on January 6, 2005, clarified that this waiver is available to abused spouses and children in cancellation of removal and adjustment of status cases and that it can be used to overcome good moral character issues.

Inadmissible or Deportable

An applicant is not eligible for VAWA cancellation if he or she is inadmissible or deportable under certain statutory sections. These include the following:

- INA §212(a)(2)—conviction of certain crimes;
- INA §212(a)(3)—security and related grounds;
- INA §237(a)(1)(G)—marriage fraud;
- INA §237(a)(2)—criminal offenses, including:
  - CMTs
  - multiple criminal convictions
  - aggravated felony
  - high speed flight
  - controlled substances violation
  - firearm offenses
  - miscellaneous crimes
  - domestic violence
  - stalking
  - crimes against children
- INA §237(a)(3)—failure to register and document fraud; and
- INA §237(a)(4)—security and related grounds

As mentioned above, the Battered Immigrant Women Protection Act created new waivers found at INA §237(a)(7) for:

- convictions of domestic violence and stalking under INA §237(a)(2)(E)(i); and
- crimes and violations of domestic violence protection orders under INA §237(a)(2)(E)(ii).

The waiver also applies to foreign nationals who have been battered or subjected to extreme cruelty, and who were not the primary perpetrator of violence in the relationship, if

- the foreign national was acting in self-defense;

---

[46] VAWA 2005, *supra* note 16.

- the foreign national violated a protection order intended to protect the foreign national; or

- the crime in question did not result in serious bodily injury, and there was a connection between the crime and the abuse.

This waiver extends to ineligibility for cancellation for abused foreign nationals, based upon INA §§237(a)(2)(E) and (ii). VAWA 2005 clarified that this waiver could in fact be used in VAWA cancellation cases.

Extreme Hardship

The applicant for cancellation of removal must show that he or she would suffer extreme hardship if deported. The hardship can be to the applicant or applicant's child, or if a child applicant, to his or her parent.

EOIR has issued regulations on factors to be considered in assessing extreme hardship in cancellation of removal cases for battered spouses and children. The regulations were part of the interim rule on NACARA,[47] issued by legacy INS and EOIR, effective June 21, 1999. These are the same hardship factors considered by USCIS when adjudicating cases under VAWA, and include the following:

- Nature and extent of the physical or psychological consequences of abuse;

- Impact of loss of access to the U.S. courts and criminal justice system. This includes, but is not limited to:

  - the ability to obtain and enforce orders of protection,

  - criminal investigations, and

  - prosecution or court orders regarding child support, maintenance, child custody, and visitations

- Likelihood that the abuser's family, friends, or others acting on behalf of the abuser in the home country would physically or psychologically harm the applicant or the applicant's child(ren);

- Applicant's needs and/or needs of the applicant's child(ren) for social, medical, mental health, or other supportive services unavailable or not reasonably accessible in the home country;

- Existence of laws and social practices in the home country that punish the applicant or the applicant's child(ren) because they have been victims of domestic violence or have taken steps to leave an abusive household; and

- Abuser's ability to travel to the home country and the ability and willingness of authorities in the home country to protect the applicant and/or the applicant's children from future abuse.

Other extreme hardship factors enumerated by the BIA under traditional suspension of deportation cases also may be applicable to VAWA cancellation cases. These include the applicant's:

---

[47] NACARA, *supra* note 2.

- Age;
- Length of time in the United States;
- Family ties in the United States;
- Health;
- Financial status and/or occupation;
- Ties to the community;
- Home country economic and political conditions;
- Likelihood of encountering disruption of educational opportunities; and
- Likelihood of suffering adverse psychological impact due to deportation.

The following cases set forth these factors in greater detail: *INS v. Wang*,[48] *Matter of Anderson*,[49] *Matter of Pilch*,[50] and *Matter of O–J–O*.[51] *Matter of O–J–O* is particularly important for VAWA cancellation cases because it illustrates other equities for extreme hardship when the applicant has weak family ties in the United States.[52]

Legacy INS memoranda provide insight into the agency's interpretation of extreme hardship. Although IJs are not required to follow these directives, they can be used to guide the advocate in presenting evidence of extreme hardship to the court. For example, an October 16, 1998, memorandum provides that the approach in determining extreme hardship should be flexible, stating that "reviewers of these cases should take an open and flexible approach to the issue of extreme hardship, keeping in mind that the fact that a particular scenario has not previously appeared in the 'extreme hardship' case law by no means suggests that it cannot now amount to 'extreme hardship'...."[53]

In addition, a 1996 legacy INS memorandum states that extreme hardship "is not a definable term of fixed and inflexible content or meaning; it necessarily depends upon the facts and circumstance peculiar to each case."[54]

Evidence

Under INA §240A(b)(2)(D), *any credible evidence* relevant to the application is acceptable, and the applicant does not have to demonstrate the unavailability of sec-

---

[48] *INS v. Wang*, 450 U.S. 139 (1981).

[49] *Matter of Anderson*, 16 I&N Dec. 596 (BIA 1978).

[50] *Matter of Pilch*, 21 I&N Dec. 627 (BIA 1996).

[51] *Matter of O–J–O*, 21 I&N Dec. 381 (BIA 1996).

[52] *Id.*

[53] *See* INS Memorandum, P. Virtue, "Extreme Hardship and Documentary Requirements Involving Battered Spouses and Children" (Oct. 16, 1998), *reprinted in* 76 *Interpreter Releases* 162 (Jan. 25, 1999).

[54] *See* INS Memorandum, T. Aleinikoff, "Implementation of Crime Bill Self-Petitioning for Abused or Battered Spouses or Children of U.S. Citizens or Lawful Permanent Residents," (Apr. 16, 1996), *reprinted in* 73 *Interpreter Releases* 737 (May 24, 1996).

ondary evidence. This applies to every element of the claim. Evidence of the abuse can include the following:

- Affidavit of the applicant;
- Civil protection orders;
- Medical records of the abuse;
- Photographs of the injury;
- Shelter record;
- Psychological reports;
- Domestic violence counselor's report;
- Police reports; and
- Affidavits of neighbors or family members who know of abuse.

Intake Interview

The intake interview lays the foundation for obtaining the above information and proving the case. It is important to consider the following when interviewing an abused woman:

- Be aware that you are dealing with a woman who has suffered profound violence and be sensitive to the ways that different cultures deal with such issues;
- If you are doing a general intake interview and are not aware of the applicant's situation, do not overlook a general question that may enable the person to qualify for relief under VAWA;
- Set aside enough time to interview the client. Domestic violence cases take more time due to the fact that the story usually is not divulged at one time, and there is a need to establish a rapport;
- Before you interview, familiarize yourself with country conditions so that you are aware of the treatment of women in her country of nationality;
- Be aware of the domestic violence syndrome of power and control and the cycle of violence: tension building, explosion, and then the honeymoon phase; and
- Frame particular questions. Rather than asking "Did you suffer domestic violence?" ask "Were you hit, punched, pushed, allowed to work, allowed to have friends, insulted, mistreated in front of friends, family, children?"

A battered immigrant's affidavit is similar to an asylum affidavit. It should be detailed, specific, and in the client's own words. VAWA experts say that developing a partnership with a domestic violence counselor, who can help in gathering information and evidence, is really essential to representing a VAWA client.

Self-Petitions

In a VAWA cancellation case, a VAWA self-petition approved by USCIS proves both battery or extreme cruelty and extreme hardship. Therefore, encourage the filing of a self-petition. If USCIS approves the petition, it can be presented to the court as evidence that the Department of Homeland Security (DHS) acknowledges that the person has demonstrated the elements of abuse and extreme hardship. The remaining elements to prove in court are three years continuous presence, three years of good moral character, and eligibility.

Laws of Other Countries

As can be seen from the types of hardship factors examined in adjudicating a VAWA cancellation case, some of those factors involve conditions—including laws and law enforcement practices—in the applicant's home country. It often is difficult to obtain information on specific laws and conditions in other countries. It is helpful to review country reports from the U.S. Department of State, Human Rights Watch, Amnesty International, and the U.N. High Commissioner for Refugees. Affidavits from experts who have knowledge of the home country—including family members, women's groups, and lawyers in the home country—also can be effective. There are excellent websites accessing foreign law and political and social conditions. You also may contact the Library of Congress's Law Division, at (202) 707-5065 (fax: (202) 707-1820), and ask to have certified copies of foreign laws sent to you.

VAWA Cancellation Cap

Under INA §240A(e)(1), Congress limited the number of cancellation applicants who may adjust status to lawful permanent residence each year to 4,000. However, Congress exempted VAWA suspension applicants—those who received an OSC charging document before April 1, 1997—from the 4,000 person cap when it passed NACARA.

NACARA §203

Introduction

The regulatory requirements for NACARA §203 are located at 8 CFR §§240.60 through 240.70. There are two ways in which a person may apply for relief under NACARA. Persons not in removal or deportation proceedings who have an asylum application pending with the USCIS asylum office, may submit an application for NACARA relief with the asylum office. Persons in removal or deportation proceedings may submit a NACARA application with EOIR. This section will focus on applying for NACARA relief as a defense against deportation/removal.

In response to the immigrant community's outcry over the unfairness of the retroactive application of IIRAIRA's stop time rule, Congress passed NACARA and it was signed into law in November 1997. NACARA §203 permits all the *ABC* class members,[55] along with other Salvadoran, Guatemalan, and Eastern European asylum-seekers, to proceed under the former pre-IIRAIRA suspension of deportation rules. Therefore, persons in deportation proceedings before April 1, 1997, would obtain NACARA benefits through suspension of deportation claims. Persons in removal

---

[55] *ABC v. Thornburgh, supra* note 5.

proceedings commenced on or after April 1, 1997, would obtain NACARA benefits through *special rule* cancellation of removal. NACARA also exempted NACARA beneficiaries from the annual limit now placed on the number of suspension of deportation and cancellation of removal requests that may be granted.

Beneficiaries of NACARA

Eligibility to Apply

Guatemalans. A Guatemalan who is in either of the two categories described below, and who has not been convicted of an aggravated felony, is eligible for NACARA benefits:

Category 1:

- Entered the United States on or before October 1, 1990;

- Registered for *ABC* benefits on or before December 31, 1991; and

- Has not been apprehended at time of entry after December 19, 1990.

Category 2:

- Filed an application for asylum on or before April 1, 1990.

Salvadorans. A Salvadoran who is in either of the two categories described below, and who has not been convicted of an aggravated felony, is eligible for NACARA benefits:

Category 1:

- Entered the United States on or before September 19, 1990;

- Registered for *ABC* benefits on or before October 31, 1991 (by direct registration or by applying for Temporary Protected Status); and

- Has not been apprehended at time of entry after December 19, 1990.

Category 2:

- Filed an application for asylum on or before April 1, 1990.

Nationals of Former Soviet Bloc Countries. An individual from a former Soviet bloc country who has not been convicted of an aggravated felony is eligible to apply for benefits under NACARA if he or she meets the following criteria:

- Entered the United States on or before December 31, 1990;

- Filed an application for asylum on or before December 31, 1991; and

- At the time of filing was a national of one of the following:
  - Soviet Union
  - Russia
  - any republic of the former Soviet Union
  - Latvia
  - Estonia

- Lithuania

- Poland

- Czechoslovakia

- Romania

- Hungary

- Bulgaria

- Albania

- East Germany

- Yugoslavia

- Any state of the former Yugoslavia

Dependent Spouses and Children

The spouse or child of a member of one of the three groups described above who has not been convicted of an aggravated felony also is eligible to apply for NACARA benefits. The principal spouse or parent must first be granted suspension or *special rule* cancellation of removal in order for the dependent to be eligible for NACARA. The family relationship must exist at the time the principal spouse or parent is granted the benefit.

Unmarried Sons and Daughters

The unmarried son or daughter (21 years of age or older) of a principal NACARA beneficiary who has not been convicted of an aggravated felony is eligible to apply for benefits under NACARA if the following criteria are met:

- The principal must have been granted suspension of deportation or cancellation of removal;

- If the son or daughter is 21 years of age or older at the time the parent is granted the benefit, the son or daughter must have entered the United States on or before October 1, 1990; and

- The relationship to the parent must exist at the time the parent is granted NACARA relief.

Other Requirements

In addition to being in a category of people who are eligible to apply for NACARA, as described above, applicants must demonstrate seven years of continuous presence, good moral character and extreme hardship to the applicant or the applicant's USC or LPR spouse, parent or child. These requirements are discussed in more detail below.

Jurisdiction of NACARA Application

Asylum Office

Although this section will focus only on NACARA applications in immigration court, a NACARA eligible person with an asylum application pending at the asylum office may file the NACARA application with that office. In some cases, a person in removal proceedings may want to move to close the proceedings in order to pursue the NACARA application at the asylum office, if possible. If it appears that an asylum officer might be more sympathetic to the NACARA application than the IJ, a motion to administratively close may be a wise strategy. Also, if there are dependents who are not in proceedings, it may be a good idea to try to close the principal's case administratively because, otherwise, the dependents will need to be placed in proceedings to have their application adjudicated.

In addition, *ABC* class members with asylum applications pending at the asylum office are entitled to a *de novo* asylum hearing at the asylum office. Even if a NACARA applicant has a strong case, he or she may not want to forfeit the possibility of obtaining asylum. Status as an asylee generally is more advantageous than status as an LPR through NACARA. Asylees may bring their spouses and children to the United States without the dependents needing to prove anything other than family relationship. Asylees also have access to public benefits unavailable to certain LPRs. Thus, it is important to understand when the asylum office has jurisdiction over a case.

In most cases, where the asylum application still is pending with the asylum office, the person will not be in removal proceedings, but it is important to investigate—particularly with Salvadorans and Guatemalans—whether an asylum application is pending with the asylum office.

Guatemalans. A Guatemalan who meets each of the following criteria is eligible for a de novo asylum adjudication under the *ABC* settlement agreement:

- First entered the United States on or before October 1, 1990;
- Registered for *ABC* benefits on or before December 31, 1991;
- Applied for asylum on or before January 3, 1995;
- Has not been served a final asylum officer decision on the *ABC* claim; and
- Has not been apprehended at the time of entry after December 19, 1990.

Salvadorans. A Salvadoran who meets each of the following criteria is eligible for a de novo asylum adjudication under the *ABC* settlement agreement:

- First entered the United States on or before September 19, 1990;
- Registered for *ABC* benefits on or before October 31, 1991;
- Applied for asylum on or before January 31, 1996 (with an administrative grace period to February 16, 1996);
- Has not been served a final asylum officer decision on the *ABC* claim; and
- Has not been apprehended at time of entry after December 19, 1990.

Dependents

The asylum office also has jurisdiction over NACARA applications of a spouse, child, or unmarried son or daughter eligible to apply under NACARA where the spouse or parent either has a NACARA application pending or approved with the asylum office. However, since such dependents are not *ABC* class members, an IJ is not *required* to close removal proceedings administratively in order to permit the dependent to file his or her NACARA application with the asylum office. If the dependent provides evidence that the spouse or parent has applied for NACARA with the asylum office and the spouse or parent appears to be eligible for NACARA benefits, the IJ *may* close the case administratively. The dependent then may submit his or her NACARA application to the asylum office.

Even if the IJ is willing to close the case administratively, the IJ may not do so without the consent of ICE district counsel. Thus, it is best to consult with ICE district counsel in advance of the hearing to see if ICE will join in the motion to administratively close the case.

Executive Office for Immigration Review

Except as explained above, once a person has been placed in removal or deportation proceedings, the immigration court has exclusive jurisdiction over the NACARA application. The immigration court may take over jurisdiction of a NACARA case from the asylum office where the asylum office has referred it after determining that the applicant is not eligible, does not merit relief, or is only eligible for the *10-year* NACARA.

Requirements for NACARA Suspension of Deportation or Cancellation of Removal

To qualify for NACARA suspension of deportation, the applicant must be in deportation proceedings—*i.e.*, an OSC was issued prior to April 1, 1997—and be deportable. To qualify for NACARA special rule cancellation of removal, the applicant must be in removal proceedings—*i.e.*, an NTA issued on or after April 1, 1997—and be inadmissible or deportable. All applicants must merit a favorable exercise of discretion, in addition to proving the following:

- Continuous physical presence in the United States for seven years before the application for suspension of deportation or cancellation of removal is filed;

- Good moral character during the seven year period; and

- Removal would cause extreme hardship to the applicant or the applicant's USC or LPR spouse, parent, or child.

Continuous Physical Presence

Seven Years. Generally, NACARA applicants must demonstrate seven years of continuous physical presence immediately prior to filing the NACARA application. However, if the applicant is inadmissible or deportable under certain grounds of inadmissibility or deportability (usually for criminal conduct), the applicant must establish 10 years of physical presence. In a September 6, 2007, memorandum, USCIS took the position that grounds of deportation only apply to person who were admitted, and grounds of inadmissibility only apply to those persons who are in the United States without having been admitted.[56] For applicants applying for suspension of deportation, this includes individuals found deportable under the following sections of the INA:

- §241(a)(2)—crimes;
- §241(a)(3)—failure to register and falsification of documents; or
- §241(a)(4)—security grounds as they existed prior to IIRAIRA.

For applicants applying for special rule cancellation of removal, this includes individuals found inadmissible or deportable under the following sections of the INA:

- §212(a)(2)—crimes,
- §237(a)(2)—crimes other than aggravated felonies; or
- §237(a)(3)—failure to register and falsification of documents.

Departures. If the applicant is applying for suspension of deportation, the applicant must establish that any absence from the United States during the seven years (or 10 years, if the higher standard applies) prior to filing the application was *brief, casual, and innocent* and did not interrupt meaningfully the applicant's period of presence in the United States. Absences from the United States for 90 days or less, or in the aggregate of 180 days or less, are considered brief. Absences beyond the 90– or 180- day bright-line test will be considered on a case-by-case basis.

Departures pursuant to an order of deportation or voluntary departure are not considered casual, nor are any departures that reveal a lack of commitment to living in the United States. Advance parole does not necessarily interrupt meaningfully continuous physical presence. However, applicants in deportation proceedings will lose the right to pursue suspension of deportation upon being paroled into the United States. Instead, such applicants will be placed into removal proceedings, where they can apply for cancellation of removal.

If the applicant is applying for cancellation of removal, *any* absence from the United States for more than 90 continuous days, or 180 days in the aggregate will be considered to break continuous presence. There are no exceptions.

Good Moral Character

A NACARA applicant must demonstrate that he or she has been a person of good moral character for the required period of physical presence in the United States. A child under 14 years of age is presumed to be a person of good moral character and is not required to submit documentation establishing good moral character.

An applicant cannot establish good moral character if he or she falls into one of the categories listed in INA §101(f). These categories include:

---

[56] USCIS Memorandum, J. Langois, "Revision to the NACARA Lesson Plan and Change to NACARA Quality Assurance Review Categories" (Sept. 6, 2007), *published on* AILA InfoNet at Doc. No. 07092562 (*posted* Sept. 25, 2007).

- Habitual drunkard;
- Drug offenses (except for a single offense of simple possession of marijuana);
- CMTs;
- Multiple crimes;
- Prostitute;
- Practicing polygamist;
- Alien smuggler;
- One whose income is derived principally from illegal gambling activities;
- One who has been convicted of two or more gambling offenses;
- One who has given false testimony for the purpose of obtaining any benefits under the INA;
- One who has been confined to a penal institution as a result of a conviction for an aggregate of 180 days or more during the good moral character period; and
- One who has been convicted of an aggravated felony on or after *November 29, 1990*.

The fact that an applicant is not within any of the above categories does not compel a finding that the applicant is a person of good moral character. The good moral character inquiry may extend beyond the statutory period and to other factors not listed in INA §101(f). However, any relevant negative factors must be weighed along with all positive factors. Negative factors not included in INA §101(f) include failing to file income taxes, falsifying tax returns, and neglecting family responsibilities. Positive factors include involvement in the community, volunteer work, and participation in church activities.

Extreme Hardship

The list of factors relevant to the evaluation of extreme hardship to the applicant or the applicant's USC or LPR spouse, parent or child is codified in 8 CFR §1240.58. However, there is no requirement that an applicant establish each of the factors, nor is the list in the regulation exclusive. Factors may be considered in the aggregate. The IJ must evaluate each application on a case-by-case basis.

The factors listed in 8 CFR §1240.58 include:

- Age of the applicant and age at time of entry;
- Applicant's children (how many, along with information on age, immigration status, and ability to speak native language);
- Health conditions of the applicant and the applicant's child, spouse or parent;
- Employment opportunities in the native country;
- Length of presence in the United States;
- Family members legally residing in the United States;
- Financial impact of departure from the United States;

- Irreparable harm as a result of disruption of educational opportunities;
- Psychological impact of return to native country;
- Political and economic conditions in the country of return;
- Ties to the country to which the applicant would be returned;
- Ties to the United States;
- Immigration history in the United States; and
- Absence of other means to adjust status in the United States.

Presumption of Extreme Hardship for Certain NACARA Beneficiaries

The AG has concluded that sufficient evidence exists to support an evidentiary presumption of extreme hardship for *ABC* class members who are eligible to apply for relief under NACARA. This conclusion is based on a determination that the *ABC* class members share certain characteristics that give rise to a strong likelihood that an *ABC* class member or qualified relative would suffer extreme hardship if deported or removed.

The presumption means that an IJ must find that an *ABC* class member who completes the NACARA application has established extreme hardship, unless a preponderance of the evidence establishes that neither the applicant nor a qualified family member would suffer extreme hardship if the class member is removed.

However, the presumption of extreme hardship is rebuttable. The IJ still must review the applicant's responses to questions on the NACARA application and evaluate the applicant's particular circumstances to determine whether a preponderance of the evidence establishes extreme hardship.

The presumption operates as an evidentiary tool that shifts the focus of inquiry of the IJ to whether there is sufficient evidence to *disprove* extreme hardship. *ABC* class members must submit a completed NACARA application that includes answers to questions relating to extreme hardship. If evidence in the record shows no evidence of factors associated with extreme hardship, the presumption may be overcome. In addition, if the evidence in the record significantly undermines the assumptions on which the presumption is based, the presumption may be overcome. For example, an individual who has great wealth and invested it in his or her home country may be able to return to that country without experiencing hardship.

The presumption of extreme hardship applies to all Salvadoran and Guatemalan principals, whether they actually applied for *ABC* benefits or not. The presumption does not apply to their dependents applying for relief under NACARA, nor does it apply to nationals of the former Soviet Bloc. However, evidence that a NACARA applicant's spouse or parent has obtained NACARA relief may assist in proving extreme hardship.

Statutory Bars to NACARA

Bars Relating to Immigration Violations

Before pursuing a NACARA application in immigration court, it is important to go through all of the statutory grounds of eligibility. Although both suspension of deportation and cancellation of removal under NACARA result in the same benefit—LPR status—different statutory bars apply in certain cases.

NACARA Suspension of Deportation. A person in deportation proceedings may not apply for relief under NACARA if the person:

- Was convicted of an aggravated felony under INA §101(a)(43);
- Participated in Nazi persecution or genocide;
- Entered the United States as a crewman after June 30, 1964; or
- Entered the United States as an exchange visitor.

In addition, violation of certain grounds of pre-IIRAIRA deportability will bar a person from applying for the *seven-year* suspension of deportation under NACARA. Such persons still may be able to apply for NACARA, but must prove 10 years of continuous physical presence since the commission of the disqualifying conduct, good moral character during those 10 years, and that deportation would cause exceptional and extremely unusual hardship. Grounds of deportation only apply to persons who were admitted, whereas grounds of inadmissibility will apply to those persons who are in the United States without having been admitted.[57] The grounds of deportability that will bar application for the seven-year NACARA are:

- CMT within five years of entry with a sentence of one year or longer;
- Two or more convictions for CMTs;
- Controlled substance violation, other than a single offense of possession of 30 grams or less of marijuana;
- Drug abuser or addict;
- Firearms offense;
- Conviction for attempt to commit espionage, treason or sabotage;
- Failure to register and falsification of documents; and
- Security and related ground (except Nazi persecutors).

Cancellation of Removal. A person in removal proceedings may not apply for NACARA cancellation of removal if he or she:

- Participated in the persecution of another based on race, nationality, religion, political opinion, social group,
- Entered the United States as a crewman after June 30, 1964, or
- Entered the United States as an exchange visitor.

---

[57] Langois memo, *supra* note 56.

Just as with NACARA suspension of deportation, certain grounds of deportability (post-IIRAIRA) will bar a person from applying for seven-year cancellation of removal under NACARA. In addition, certain grounds of inadmissibility will bar application for the seven-year NACARA, as well. Such persons also still may be able to apply for NACARA under the higher burden of ten years of continuous physical presence, plus exceptional and extremely unusual hardship. Grounds of inadmissibility only apply to those persons who are in the United States without having been admitted, whereas the grounds of deportability apply to those who have been admitted.[58] The grounds of inadmissibility and deportability that will bar application for the seven-year cancellation of removal under NACARA are:

- CMT within five years of entry with a sentence of one year or longer;
- Two or more convictions for CMTs;
- Two or more convictions with an aggregate sentence of five years;
- Controlled substance violation, other than a single offense of possession of 30 grams or less of marijuana;
- Drug abuser or addict;
- Firearms offense;
- Conviction for attempt to commit espionage, treason or sabotage;
- Failure to register and falsification of documents;
- Conviction for high speed flight from an immigration checkpoint;
- Crimes of domestic violence;
- Violation of protective orders;
- False representation of U.S. citizenship;
- Prostitution and commercialized vice;
- Criminals who have asserted immunity; and
- Membership in a totalitarian party.

Bars Relating to Failure to Comply with Immigration Proceedings

Before deciding whether to apply for relief under NACARA, the immigration history of the person must be analyzed. A person's failure to appear at a prior hearing or for deportation could bar him or her from applying for NACARA benefits. The bars to discretionary relief for persons pursuing suspension of deportation generally are more lenient than the bars imposed for persons pursuing cancellation of removal.

SUSPENSION OF DEPORTATION: FIVE-YEAR BARS

Failure to appear at deportation proceedings. A person is barred from applying for NACARA relief for five years after the date of the final order of deportation if the person failed to appear at his or her deportation proceeding. However, this bar only

---

[58] *Id.*

applies if the person was given oral notice in a language that the person understands of the time and place of the proceedings and the consequences of failing to appear at the deportation proceeding. An individual may get around only the five-year bar if exceptional circumstances existed for the failure to appear.

Failure to voluntarily depart. A person is barred from applying for NACARA suspension of deportation for five years if the person remained in the United States after the date granted to depart the United States voluntarily. The five years begins to run on the scheduled date of departure, unless the person can prove that *exceptional circumstances* prevented the departure. The five-year bar will apply only if the person was given notice of the consequences of the failure to depart in a language that the person understood.

Failure to appear under deportation order. A person is barred from applying for NACARA suspension of deportation for five years if the person failed to appear for his or her deportation. The five years begins to run on the date he or she was required to appear, unless the person can prove that *exceptional circumstances* prevented his or her appearance. The five-year bar will apply only if the person was given oral and written notice, in a language that the person understood, of the consequences of the failure to appear.

Failure to appear for asylum hearing. A person is barred from applying for NACARA suspension of deportation for five years if the person failed to appear for his or her asylum hearing. The five years begins to run on the date he or she was scheduled to appear, unless the person can prove that *exceptional circumstances* prevented his or her appearance. The five-year bar will apply only if the person was given written notice, in English and Spanish, of the hearing date, and oral notice of the same in a language the applicant understood.

CANCELLATION OF REMOVAL: TEN-YEAR BARS

Failure to appear at removal hearing. A person is barred from applying for NACARA cancellation of removal for 10 years if the person failed to appear for his or her removal hearing. The 10 years begins to run on the date of the final order of removal if the order was issued in absentia. The ten-year bar will only apply if the person was given oral notice, in a language that the person understood, of the time and place of the hearing and the consequences of the failure to appear.

Failure to voluntarily depart. A person is barred from applying for NACARA cancellation of removal for 10 years if the person failed to leave by the voluntary departure date given. The 10 years begins to run on the final date given to depart. The ten-year bar will only apply if the voluntary departure order informed the person of the consequences of the failure to depart.

Process for Applying in Removal Proceedings

Application

To apply for NACARA, a person must file a completed Form I-881 with the immigration court, along with the accompanying fee and supporting evidence. In addition, each applicant over 14 years of age must pay a biometrics fee. The applicant also may apply simultaneously with USCIS for employment authorization.

Unmarried Sons and Daughters

A dependent of a NACARA principal who is 21 years of age or older at the time his or her parent is granted NACARA must overcome the additional eligibility hurdle of proving that he or she entered the United States on or before October 1, 1990. Thus, for persons who did not enter the United States until after that date and are nearing age 21, it will be important to try to expedite adjudication of the parent's case. If the parent's case is pending with the USCIS asylum office, a request for expedited interview should be sent there. If the parent's case is pending with the immigration court, a motion to expedite should be filed with the court to preserve the dependent's right to pursue relief under NACARA.

Motions to Reopen

In general, an individual who received a final order of deportation or removal must have filed at least a skeletal (without a completed Form I-881) motion to reopen by September 11, 1998, to be eligible to pursue a NACARA claim. If a skeletal motion to reopen was filed, the completed Form I-881 must have been filed by November 18, 1999 in order to preserve the right to pursue a NACARA application. Upon an order by an IJ to reopen the case, the applicant must pay the required fee for the NACARA application.

The government allowed certain individuals to file motions to reopen beyond the September 11, 1998, deadline. Such individuals had to demonstrate that they were prima facie eligible for NACARA as of September 11, 1998 and that their failure to file on time was inadvertent. In such cases, DHS district counsel would join the motion to reopen. Such cases should have been filed by November 18, 1999. Some district counsels still will join in late-filed motions to reopen for NACARA-eligible individuals. The advocate should document the humanitarian equities as well as statutory eligibility of the applicant before filing such a proposed joint motion to district counsel.

The Ninth Circuit held that the statutory time bar on the motion to reopen deportation or removal proceedings is a statute of limitations subject to equitable tolling.[59] In *Albillo-DeLeon v. Gonzales,* the court held that equitable tolling was appropriate for the respondent because he was deceived and prejudiced by a person purporting to be his legal advocate.

The U.S. Court of Appeals for the Fifth Circuit held that it lacked jurisdiction to review a failure to reopen NACARA case due to untimely filing.[60] The court stated that a "failure to meet the … deadline constituted a failure to exhaust his administrative remedies," which deprived the court of jurisdiction. In addition, the statute states that an IJ may reopen any case. This instruction is not reviewable by courts because it

---

[59] *Albillo-DeLeon v. Gonzales*, 410 F.3d 1090 (9th Cir. 2005).
[60] *Enriquez-Alvarado v. Ashcroft,* 371 F.3d 246, 248 (5th Cir. 2004).

does not provide a meaningful standard against which to judge the IJ's decision. Every circuit court has agreed that they lack jurisdiction to review motion to reopen claims.[61]

Burden of Proof

The burden of proof is on the NACARA applicant. For NACARA applicants who are eligible for the presumption of extreme hardship, the extreme hardship element is considered established as soon as the applicant submits a completed application. The IJ then must evaluate whether other evidence overcomes the presumption.

A NACARA applicant should submit evidence to corroborate his or her testimony regarding physical presence, good moral character, and extreme hardship. Credible testimony alone may, in some instances, be sufficient to win a NACARA case. However, for most cases, documentary evidence and witnesses will be necessary. Where such evidence is not available, the applicant should submit a reasonable explanation as to why certain documentary evidence cannot be produced.

Types of Evidence

Physical Presence. An applicant need not document everyday in the United States for the prior seven years. However, the applicant should provide documentation for every three to four months in the United States for the prior seven years. If the applicant departed the United States during the prior seven years, the applicant should submit documentation to prove that such departure did not disrupt physical presence.

Evidence that should be submitted to prove presence includes:

- Bankbooks;
- Leases/deeds;
- Receipts;
- Letters;
- Birth, church, or school records;
- Employment records;
- USCIS, ICE, and CBP records;
- Tax records; and
- Witness affidavits.

Good Moral Character. Absence of an arrest or conviction record based on the FBI security check is strong evidence that the applicant has good moral character. However, documentary evidence should be submitted including affidavits from witnesses, preferably USCs.

Extreme Hardship. NACARA applicants eligible for the presumption of hardship are not initially required to submit documentary evidence to prove hardship. If

---

[61] *See Marekegn Asfaw Tamenut v. Mukasey,* 521 F.3d 1000 (8th Cir. 2008) (other circuit cases cited therein).

ICE presents evidence that overcomes the presumption, then the applicant must present evidence of hardship to counter ICE's evidence.

Applicants who are not eligible for the presumption of hardship should present documentary evidence. This evidence includes:

- School records of applicant and/or applicant's children;
- Medical records;
- Records of ties to the community;
- Country conditions information; and
- Affidavits from witnesses.

Reinstatement of Removal Does Not Bar NACARA Application

The Legal Immigration and Family Equity (LIFE) Act[62] and LIFE Act Amendments of 2000[63] made the following changes to NACARA §203 suspension and cancellation for certain Central Americans:

INA §241(a)(5) (reinstatement of prior removal orders and ineligibility for relief under the INA) does not bar Salvadorans and Guatemalans from eligibility, and notwithstanding any time and number limits imposed by law (other than those premised on conviction of aggravated felony), Salvadorans and Guatemalans eligible for NACARA 203 suspension or cancellation who have become eligible for suspension or cancellation as a result of these amendments may file one motion to reopen; the scope is limited to eligibility for cancellation or suspension.[64]

Deadline for Applications

One of the great benefits of NACARA §203 is that, other than the motion to reopen deadlines, there is no deadline for filing a NACARA application. Thus, persons in the United States who currently are not qualified for NACARA, either because they do not have seven years of physical presence in the United States or for some other reason, may become eligible and apply at any time in the future.

---

[62] Legal Immigration and Family Equity Act, Pub. L. No. 106-553, §1(a)(2) (appx. B, H.R. 5548, §§1101–04), 114 Stat. 2762, 2762A-142 to 2762A-149 (2000).

[63] LIFE Act Amendments of 2000, Pub. L. No. 106-554, appx. D, div. B, §§1501–06, 114 Stat. 2763, 2763A-324 to 2763A-328.

[64] *See* 8 CFR §241.8(d). On July 17, 2001, the Executive Office for Immigration Review issued an interim rule that set October 16, 2001, as the deadline for filing these motions to reopen.

CHAPTER NINE
ASYLUM, WITHHOLDING OF REMOVAL, AND PROTECTION UNDER THE CONVENTION AGAINST TORTURE

Three important defenses to removal are asylum, withholding of removal, and protection under the Convention Against Torture and Other Cruel, Inhuman or Degrading Treatment or Punishment (CAT).[1] Both asylum and withholding of removal are premised on a fear of persecution on account of one of five factors:

- Race;
- Religion;
- Nationality;
- Membership in a particular social group; or
- Political opinion.

Protection under CAT is premised on fear of torture by the government or with the government's acquiescence, and does not require a showing that the feared torture is on account of one of the five protected grounds. Part One of this chapter will cover asylum and withholding of removal, including changes introduced by the REAL ID Act of 2005 (REAL ID).[2] Part Two will cover protection under CAT.

Part One: Asylum and Withholding of Removal

Asylum vs. Withholding

Withholding is country-specific, meaning that the applicant still can be removed to a country other than the one in which *persecution* is claimed. Asylum is universal, and the client cannot be removed to any country while in valid asylee status.

Withholding of removal cannot be converted into any kind of permanent residence. Asylum, on the other hand, may be converted to lawful permanent resident (LPR) status once the asylee has had asylum status for one year.

Withholding is available just to the applicant—it does not cover any spouses or children of the applicant. On the other hand, asylum applicants can include their spouse and unmarried children less than 21 years of age in their asylum applications. They are known as *derivatives* on the principal's asylum application. These included

---

[1] Convention Against Torture and Other Cruel, Inhuman or Degrading Treatment or Punishment (CAT), Dec. 10, 1984, 1465 U.N.T.S. 85 (entered into force June 26, 1987). For a practical guide on CAT and other asylum relief, see *AILA's Asylum Primer*, 5th Ed. (AILA 2007), *www.ailapubs.org*.

[2] REAL ID Act of 2005 (REAL ID), Pub. L. No. 109-13, div. B, 119 Stat. 231, 302–23.

derivatives also are granted asylum when the principal applicant is granted asylum. Previously, when an included child turned 21 years of age while the application was pending, he or she *aged out* and lost derivative status, although he or she still could submit an asylum application on his or her own. However, the Child Status Protection Act (CSPA) of 2002[3] amended the definition of *child* under the Immigration and Nationality Act (INA)[4] to provide that derivative children on an asylum application would not lose their derivative status if they turn 21 years of age *after* the asylum application is filed but *before* it is adjudicated (*i.e.*, the child must be under 21 years of age on the date that the parent, who is the principal asylum applicant, filed the asylum application). The child need not have been included on the asylum application at the time of filing as long as he or she is included on it at the time of adjudication. The date U.S. Citizenship and Immigration Services (USCIS) *receives* the asylum application is the filing date.

Withholding requires a showing of a *clear probability of persecution*, while asylum-seekers need show only past persecution or a *well-founded fear* of future persecution. Asylum, however, is discretionary while withholding is mandatory if a clear probability of persecution is established. Clear probability is solely an objective test: the foreign national has to show a greater than 50 percent likelihood of persecution. On the other hand, well-founded fear has both subjective and objective components. The objective component is satisfied if there is as little as a 10 percent chance of persecution.

Asylum applications may be filed in one of two ways. Affirmative applications are made before the USCIS asylum office. If the application is denied, the asylum office will refer the applicant to the office of the Immigration Judge (IJ) for a removal hearing. Alternatively, if the person did not apply affirmatively, he or she still may request asylum in removal proceedings.

The Illegal Immigration Reform and Immigrant Responsibility Act of 1996 (IIRAIRA)[5] mandated that the asylum application be filed within one year of the foreign national's arrival in the United States. Moreover, no application will be entertained by a foreign national who has previously applied for asylum and been denied. The interim regulations make it clear that these prohibitions apply to asylum only, and do not preclude an application for withholding of removal. Exceptions to the one-year deadline exist for foreign nationals who meet the well-founded fear standard by virtue of changed circumstances in their country of nationality or last residence after their arrival in the United States and those who can show that extraordinary circumstances occasioned the delay in filing.

---

[3] Child Status Protection Act of 2002 (CSPA), Pub. L. No. 107-208, 116 Stat. 927 (2002). For an in-depth discussion and advice on handling CSPA cases, see *AILA's Focus on the Child Status Protection Act* (AILA 2008), *www.ailapubs.org*.

[4] Immigration and Nationality Act of 1952 (INA), Pub. L. No. 82-414, 66 Stat. 163 (codified as amended at 8 USC §§1101 *et seq.*).

[5] Illegal Immigration Reform and Immigrant Responsibility Act of 1996 (IIRAIRA), Pub. L. No. 104-208, div. C, 110 Stat. 3009, 3009-546 to 3009-724.

In December 2000, final regulations were published providing more guidance on the one-year deadline.[6] Perhaps most helpful for asylum-seekers, the final regulations provide for a more liberal interpretation of exceptions to the one-year filing deadline for asylum claims.[7] While the filing deadline still may be waived only if the applicant can show either changed circumstances that affect his or her eligibility for asylum or extraordinary circumstances relating to the delay in filing, the final regulations try to ensure that asylum-seekers with legitimate claims will not be denied the opportunity to apply for asylum. The regulations attempt this in four ways:

- First, the regulations provide that an asylum officer or IJ *must* question an asylum applicant before rejecting an application as untimely filed. The applicant will have the opportunity to present any information bearing on whether he or she fits within either exception to the one-year deadline. Also, the IJ then can determine whether the applicant is eligible for withholding of removal or CAT relief, to which the one-year deadline does not apply.

- Second, the regulations provide for additional factors that the decision-maker may consider, such as the death or serious illness of the applicant's lawyer or immediate family member, ineffective assistance of counsel, and maintaining valid immigrant or nonimmigrant status, including Temporary Protected Status (TPS).[8] The government believed there were sound policy reasons to permit persons who were in valid immigrant or nonimmigrant status, or who were given parole, to apply for asylum within a reasonable period after termination of parole or immigration status. The final regulations define a *reasonable period* to be a relatively short period.[9]

- Third, the regulations state that the list of circumstances that may constitute changed or extraordinary circumstances is not all-inclusive, and that other situations may fit within the exceptions. For *changed circumstances* the applicant must show that those changes affect the applicant's eligibility for asylum.[10] For *extraordinary circumstances*, the asylum-seeker must show that the circumstances directly relate to the applicant's failure to file within the one-year deadline.[11]

- Fourth, for applications filed with USCIS, in cases where the one-year deadline otherwise is not met, if the applicant can prove *by clear and convincing evidence* that the application was *mailed* within the one-year period, the mailing date shall be considered the filing date.[12]

---

[6] 65 Fed. Reg. 76121 (Dec. 6, 2000).

[7] 8 CFR §208.4.

[8] 8 CFR §208.4(a)(5).

[9] *Id.*

[10] 8 CFR §208.4(a)(4).

[11] 8 CFR §208.4(a)(5).

[12] 8 CFR §208.4(a)(2)(B)(ii).

In *Matter of Y–C–*,[13] the Board of Immigration Appeals (BIA) relied on the regulations—in particular 8 CFR §208.4(a)(5)—to determine whether an unaccompanied minor who failed to file his asylum application within one year of arrival in the United States was precluded from applying for asylum thereafter. The BIA noted that not only did the regulations define *extraordinary circumstances* that could delay filing of the asylum application, they also specifically included as an example of *extraordinary circumstances* an applicant for asylum who is an unaccompanied minor during the one-year period. Nevertheless, the BIA concluded that the precisely on point example found in the regulations did not require it to find that extraordinary circumstances existed in this particular case. Instead, the BIA stated that it must conduct individualized determinations in each case to determine whether extraordinary circumstances exist to pardon a failure to file within one year. Specifically, it held that the applicant for asylum who failed to file the application within one year of arrival must demonstrate that an extraordinary circumstance existed, that the circumstance directly related to the applicant's failure to file the application within the one-year period, and that the delay in filing was reasonable under the circumstances.

In *Matter of Y–C–*,[14] the BIA determined that the respondent demonstrated all of the above because he was a minor during the entire one-year period, he was detained by the Immigration and Naturalization Service (legacy INS) during the entire period, and he did not intentionally create, through his own action or inaction, these circumstances relating directly to his failure to meet the filing deadline. Accordingly, the BIA determined that extraordinary circumstances excused his failure to file within one year.

Standards of Proof, Evidentiary Considerations, and the REAL ID Act of 2005[15]

Respondents in proceedings always have the burden of proving eligibility for any relief sought. Asylum and withholding applicants must establish eligibility by a preponderance of the evidence. Of particular importance is the nexus between the persecution feared and one of the five statutory grounds stated above. Asylum applicants must prove by a preponderance of the evidence that they have suffered past persecution, or that there is at least a 10 percent likelihood that they will be persecuted in the future on account of one of the five protected grounds. Withholding applicants must prove by a preponderance of the evidence that it is more likely than not that they will be persecuted in the future on account of one of the five protected grounds. As discussed below, REAL ID has made it potentially more difficult to meet these burdens of proof.

Persecution is not defined by statute, but instead by case law. It is considered an extreme concept and does not include every type of conduct society regards as offensive. The harm or suffering need not be physical (though it can be), and may include other violations of human rights, including psychological torture, the imposition of

---

[13] *Matter of Y–C–*, 23 I&N Dec. 286 (BIA 2002).

[14] *Id.*

[15] REAL ID, *supra* note 2.

severe economic disadvantage, or the deprivations of liberty, food, housing, employment, and other essentials.

Apart from establishing a *well-founded fear* of future persecution, an asylum applicant may also establish eligibility for asylum by showing past persecution. In other words, an applicant is eligible for asylum if he or she has suffered past persecution on account of a protected ground *or* has a well-founded fear of future persecution. The final regulations issued in December 2000 provide further clarification regarding past persecution.

Where an applicant makes a showing of past persecution, he or she is presumed to have a well-founded fear of future persecution "unless a preponderance of the evidence establishes that since the time the persecution occurred conditions in the applicant's country of nationality ... have changed to such an extent that the applicant no longer has a well-founded fear of being persecuted if he were to return."[16] Thus, if an asylum-seeker demonstrates past persecution, this creates a presumption that the applicant has a well-founded fear of future persecution. The burden then shifts to U.S. Immigration and Customs Enforcement (ICE) to demonstrate by a preponderance of the evidence that there has been a change in circumstances.

The final regulations provide that, in past persecution cases, ICE may prevail if it can establish, by a preponderance of the evidence (more than 50 percent), that a *fundamental change in circumstances* has occurred, such that the applicant no longer has a well-founded fear. The fundamental change can be in country conditions or even in changes in the applicant's personal circumstances.[17] The rules do go on to provide that an applicant may be granted asylum where the applicant can demonstrate that he or she would suffer other serious harm if removed to that country.[18] The rules place the burden on the applicant to show that any fear of persecution unrelated to past persecution is well-founded, or, in withholding cases, that the applicant would suffer a threat to life or freedom.[19]

Even if it is shown that future persecution is unlikely, an applicant still may be granted asylum in a favorable exercise of discretion if the past punishment he or she suffered was of such an unconscionable nature that the applicant should not be repatriated in any case.[20] In exercising discretion, the IJ should consider the totality of the circumstances. Favorable factors include such humanitarian considerations as the applicant's age, health, and family ties in the United States; negative factors may be found in the foreign national's actions in fleeing to the United States. In contrast, withholding cannot be granted if future persecution is unlikely.

Perhaps the most troublesome provision in the final regulations relates to internal flight alternatives. The final rules provide that in past-persecution cases, ICE can

---

[16] 8 CFR §208.13(b)(1)(i).

[17] 8 CFR §208.4(a)(4).

[18] 8 CFR §108.13(b)(1)(iii).

[19] 8 CFR §§208.13(a), 1208.16(b).

[20] 8 CFR §208.13(b)(1)(ii); *Matter of Chen,* 20 I&N Dec. 16 (BIA 1989).

overcome the presumption of well-founded fear if it can show that the asylum-seeker could avoid persecution by relocating to another part of the country.[21] Similarly, in claims based on a well-founded fear of future persecution, an asylum-seeker is deemed not to have a well-founded fear of persecution if the applicant could avoid persecution by relocating internally, and if, under all the circumstances, it would be reasonable to expect him or her to do so.[22] Where the persecutor is a non-state actor, the asylum-seeker has the burden of showing it would not be possible to relocate.[23]

In preparing and presenting an asylum or withholding claim, great care should be taken to make the asylum and/or withholding application both internally consistent and consistent with testimony, to provide supporting documentation whenever available, and to explain its absence if it is not available. While case law previously has indicated the importance of such factors, the recent passage of REAL ID has made such considerations even more critical in presenting a successful claim.

The REAL ID Act of 2005

REAL ID[24] was enacted on May 11, 2005. Its asylum and withholding provisions cover applications filed on or after that date. On the positive side, it eliminated the 10,000 persons per year quota on asylee adjustments and the 1,000 persons per year quota on coercive population control asylum claims. Other changes are less generous to asylum and withholding applicants, and it remains unclear how strictly they will be implemented. REAL ID includes new, troublesome provisions regarding motivation of the persecutor and credibility standards.

Regarding a persecutor's motivation, REAL ID requires that the applicant, "must establish that race, religion, nationality, membership in a particular social group, or political opinion was or will be at least one central reason for persecuting the applicant."[25] This seems to be a higher standard than previously imposed by much of the relevant case law, which only required a showing that the persecution be "at least in part" on account of a protected ground. The BIA clarified this standard in *Matter of J–B–N– & S–M–*[26] stating that "an applicant does not bear the unreasonable burden of establishing the exact motivation of a persecutor where different reasons for actions are possible."

Regarding corroboration, REAL ID states, "Where the trier of fact determines that the applicant should provide evidence that corroborates otherwise credible testimony, such evidence must be provided unless the applicant does not have the evidence and cannot reasonably obtain the evidence."[27]

---

[21] 8 CFR §208.13(b)(1)(i)(B).

[22] 8 CFR §208.13(b)(2)(ii).

[23] 8 CFR §208.13(b)(3)(ii).

[24] REAL ID, *supra* note 2.

[25] REAL ID §101(a)(3)(B)(i), codified at INA §208(b)(1)(B)(i).

[26] *Matter of J–B–N– & S–M–*, 24 I&N Dec. 208 (BIA 2007).

[27] REAL ID §101(a)(3)B)(ii), codified at INA §208(b)(1)(B)(ii).

Regarding credibility determinations, REAL ID specifies that the standard to be applied is a *totality of the circumstances*, where the adjudicator may look to demeanor, candor, responsiveness, plausibility, consistency or any other relevant factor. Consistency is to be examined as between any written and oral statements, whether made under oath or not, and considering the circumstances under which the statements were made. The internal consistency of a statement, and its consistency with other evidence of record, shall be considered. Inaccuracies and falsehoods in such statements will be weighed in such a credibility determination. Significantly, even an inconsistency, inaccuracy, or falsehood that does not go to the heart of the applicant's claim can be considered in making a credibility determination.[28] Previously, incidental or minor inconsistencies that did not go to the heart of the application would not destroy an otherwise strong asylum or withholding claim. Now, it remains to be seen how even such minor inconsistencies will affect such claims. The BIA, in *Matter of J–Y–C–*,[29] interpreted this provision of REAL ID to uphold a negative credibility determination by an IJ despite the fact that the inconsistencies did not go to the heart of the claim.

On the issue of applicant's testimony and burden of proof, REAL ID states that testimony may be sufficient without corroboration, "but only if the applicant satisfies the trier of fact that the applicant's testimony is credible, is persuasive, and refers to specific facts sufficient to demonstrate that the applicant is a refugee."[30]

REAL ID also altered judicial review provisions. See chapter 8 for a summary of these changes.[31]

Elements of Persecution

Economic Refugee

Economic reasons alone usually cannot form the basis for asylum. A claim will be denied where the exclusive motive for coming to the United States is to improve one's economic lot or to obtain better employment. However, an applicant may establish a claim where the government has deliberately imposed a substantial economic disadvantage and this disadvantage was imposed on account of one of the five statutory grounds.[32]

Persecution by Groups That the Government Cannot Control

Persecution can be imposed either by the government or by a group that the government is unwilling or unable to control.[33] Cases decided under the Refugee Act of

---

[28] *See* INA §208(b)(1)(B)(iii).

[29] *Matter of J–Y–C–*, 24 I&N Dec. 260 (BIA 2007).

[30] REAL ID §101(a)(3)(B)(ii).

[31] *See also* AILF, "Judicial Review Provisions of the REAL ID Act," June 7, 2005, *available at* www.ailf.org/lac/lac_pa_topics.shtml.

[32] *See Matter of T–Z–*, 24 I&N Dec. 163 (BIA 2007) (discussion of when economic harm would amount to persecution).

[33] *Matter of Acosta*, 19 I&N Dec. 211 (BIA 1985).

1980[34] have been consistent in applying this principle. Accordingly, it is recognized that, for example, persecution or fear of persecution by guerrillas acting in an uncontrolled environment can support an application for political asylum.

Internal Flight Alternative

The final asylum regulations state that an asylum seeker is deemed not to have a well-founded fear of persecution if the applicant could avoid persecution by relocating internally and if, under all the circumstances, it would be reasonable to expect her or him to do so.[35] Where the persecutor is a non-state actor, the asylum seeker has the burden of showing it would not be possible to relocate.[36] Where the persecutor is a state actor, it is presumed that internal relocation would not be reasonable unless ICE establishes by a preponderance of the evidence that it would in fact be reasonable.[37]

Persecution vs. Prosecution

There is a significant difference in the applicant's home country between prosecution and the neutral application of criminal statutes, and persecution. An example of prosecution would be where a foreign national is punished for refusing to serve in the national army.[38] The general rule is that fear of prosecution does not make out a claim of asylum.

Nonetheless, punishments that are inflicted for expressions of political opinion are persecution. While it is prosecution if the asylum applicant has taken part in an act of armed rebellion and faces punishment, it can be persecution if the country does not provide for orderly democratic change.

Coercive Family-Planning Programs

In 1989, the BIA, in *Matter of Chang*,[39] determined that violations of China's coercive family planning policy did not give rise to a claim of asylum. Fundamental to this ruling was the BIA's finding that the one-child/one family program was not specifically designed to punish individuals on account of a ground that is recognized in the refugee definition, but instead was aimed at containing China's burgeoning population crisis. As such, the law complained about was not discriminatory, but was based instead on putatively legitimate public policy.

This long-standing interpretation was overturned with IIRAIRA[40] in 1996. The definition of refugee in INA §101(a)(42) now contains language to the effect that a

---

[34] Refugee Act of 1980, Pub. L. No. 96-212, 94 Stat. 102.

[35] 8 CFR §208.13(b)(3).

[36] *Compare Da Silva v. Ashcroft*, 394 F.3d 1 (1st. Cir. 2006) *with Sepulveda v. Attorney General*, 378 F.3d 1260 (11th Cir. 2005).

[37] 8 CFR §208.13(b)(3)(ii); *see also Singh v. Moschorak*, 53 F.3d 1031 (9th Cir. 1995).

[38] *See Matter of A–G–*, 19 I&N Dec. 502 (BIA 1987), *aff'd sub nom. M.A. v. INS*, 899 F.2d 304 (4th Cir. 1990) (punishment for failure to serve in the military is not persecution unless disproportionately severe punishment).

[39] *Matter of Chang*, 20 I&N Dec. 38 (BIA 1989).

[40] IIRAIRA, *supra* note 5.

person who was forced to terminate a pregnancy or undergo involuntary sterilization, or who was persecuted for having failed to comply with a coercive population control program, shall be deemed to have been persecuted on account of political opinion. Similarly, an individual shall be deemed to have a well-founded fear of persecution on account of political opinion upon showing that he or she would be made the subject of involuntary sterilization or forced abortion, or otherwise punished for failing to comply with a coercive population control program.

Former INA §207(a)(5) allowed only 1,000 such foreign nationals to be granted asylum or admitted as refugees in any given year under this provision. REAL ID eliminated the 1,000 limit on May 11, 2005.

After IIRAIRA amended the definition of *refugee* to include people with asylum claims based on opposition to coercive population control policies, the BIA issued its decision in *Matter of X–G–W–*,[41] allowing for reopening of proceedings to pursue asylum claims based on coerced population control policies. Under this policy, the BIA would grant reopening where the respondent presented persuasive evidence of persecution based on China's "one couple, one child" policy, and where the BIA previously had denied the asylum based on *Matter of Chang*.[42] The policy, in effect, resulted in an exception to the time and number limitations on motions to reopen for people with asylum claims based on coercive population control policies.

In *Matter of G–C–L–*,[43] the BIA stated that it was ceasing the policy started in *Matter of X–G–W–*[44] effective 90 days after issuance of the decision. It noted that five years had passed since issuance of the policy in *Matter of X–G–W–*, and that that was enough time for people with final orders of exclusion, deportation, or removal to take advantage of the change in the law to file a motion to reopen to apply for asylum based on coercive population control policies.

The BIA issued its decision on April 10, 2002. Therefore, the policy of granting untimely motions to reopen to apply for asylum based on coercive population control policies ended on July 9, 2002.

The BIA held in *Matter of C–Y–Z*[45] that spouses of persons who suffered forced abortions or sterilizations could make a claim for asylum as well. In *Matter of S–L–L*,[46] the BIA clarified its holding in *Matter of C–Y–Z*[47] and held that applicants who sought asylum based on the forced sterilization or abortion of a spouse must be legally married that that person under Chinese law. Also, the asylum applicant must not have encouraged or supported a spouse's abortion or sterilization.

---

[41] *Matter of X–G–W–*, 22 I&N Dec. 71 (BIA 1998).

[42] *Matter of Chang*, *supra* note 39.

[43] *Matter of G–C–L–*, 23 I&N Dec. 359 (BIA 2002).

[44] *Matter of X–G–W–*, *supra* note 41.

[45] *Matter of C–Y–Z*, 21 I&N Dec. 915 (BIA 1997).

[46] *Matter of S–L–L*, 24 I&N Dec. 1 (BIA 2006).

[47] *Matter of C–Y–Z*, *supra* note 45.

Neutrality and Imputed Political Opinion

Considerable case law has developed on the question of what constitutes political opinion where the country of putative persecution is enmeshed in civil war. The U.S. Court of Appeals for the Ninth Circuit had long held that fear of retaliation because of a reluctance to be recruited by guerrillas would give rise to an asylum claim on one of two theories:

- The reluctance to be conscripted would give rise to an inference that the applicant was politically neutral, an expression of political opinion for which the guerrillas would punish him or her; or

- The guerrillas would *impute* to the applicant an opinion of hostility to the guerrillas for which they would punish him or her. The U.S. Supreme Court has ruled, however, that such a set of facts does not necessarily make out a claim.

The theory of imputed political opinion views the situation from the perspective of the persecutor. Essentially, the doctrine asserts that, irrespective of the political opinions actually maintained by the applicant, if the persecutor views the victim as possessing a political opinion, then he or she will be deemed to possess a political opinion as a matter of law.

A clear example of the doctrine in practice is the case of *Desir v. Ilchert.*[48] In *Desir*, the applicant had been threatened by the Ton Ton Macoutes as the result of his refusal to cooperate in extortion demands. The Ton Ton Macoutes, however, treated the applicant's refusal as an act of political insubordination. The Ninth Circuit held: "We must view Desir as possessing a political opinion because his persecutors, the Ton Ton Macoutes, both attributed subversive views to Desir and treated him as a subversive."

The doctrine of imputed or attributed political opinion may arise in a number of contexts. It is most important to note that where there is little or no evidence of the applicant's political opinion, but an abundance of evidence regarding the persecutor's intent and willingness to ascribe views to the applicant, attributed or imputed political opinion is an appropriate way in which to present the applicant's claim.

On the other hand, the imputation of an opinion to an asylum applicant may not be inferred where there are other non-political explanations for the persecutor's conduct. It also would seem that if neutrality is going to be relied on as the theory upon which the asylum case is presented, that the applicant must have expressed, while in his country, a *principled position of neutrality*. It also should be shown that this position will trigger persecution in the foreign national's country, as evidenced by the experience of others who are similarly situated.

In *Matter of S–P–*,[49] the BIA determined that extra-judicial punishment was tantamount to persecution based on imputed political opinion, rather than mistreatment arising out of intelligence gathering. Distinguishing its earlier decisions, the BIA ruled that an asylum seeker is not under a burden to establish the exact motivation of

---

[48] *Desir v. Ilchert,* 840 F.2d 723 (9th Cir. 1988).

[49] *Matter of S–P–,* 21 I&N Dec. 486 (BIA 1996).

the persecutor, but only to adduce some evidence showing that persecution on one of the protected grounds is reasonable. In that case, the BIA also pointed to the criteria it would consider in determining whether serious harm had been imposed on account of an enumerated ground:

- Indications in the particular case that the abuse was directed toward modifying or punishing opinion rather than conduct (*e.g.,* statements or actions by the perpetrators or abuse out of proportion to nonpolitical ends);

- Treatment of others in the population who might be confronted by government agents in similar circumstances;

- Conformity to procedures for criminal prosecution or military law, including developing international norms regarding the law of war;

- The extent to which anti-terrorism laws are defined and applied to suppress political opinion, as well as illegal conduct; and

- The extent to which suspected political opponents are subjected to arbitrary arrest, detention, and abuse.

Conscription by the Government

Conscription by the government, or a fear thereof, does not itself give rise to a claim of persecution. If the applicant can show that punishment will be *disproportionate*, however, a claim of asylum may be sustained.[50] In addition, if the type of military action that the application is avoiding is condemned by the international community as contrary to basic rules of conduct, punishment for desertion or draft evasion could be considered persecution.[51]

Where the nation from which the applicant seeks asylum status is an egregious humanitarian law violator, an asylum applicant may be successful if he or she establishes the following:

- The military practices complained of constitute official policy of government;

- The applicant would be singled out for punishment for refusal on account of political beliefs;

- The acts that are said to be *condemned by the international community* have been so adjudged by international governmental bodies; and

- The applicant will be subject to disproportionate and severe punishment.

Legacy INS's *Basic Law Manual*[52] also states that violations of the Geneva Convention Relative to the Treatment of Civilian Persons in Time of War (Geneva Convention)[53] may provide the basis for an asylum claim. The *Basic Law Manual* does

---

[50] *Matter of R–R–*, 20 I&N Dec. 547 (BIA 1992).

[51] *UNHCR Handbook on Procedures and Criteria for Determining Refugee Status Under the 1951 Convention and the 1967 Protocol Relating to the Status of Refugees,* ¶171.

[52] *Basic Law Manual: U.S. Law and INS Refugee/Asylum Adjudications* (INS 1995).

[53] Geneva Convention Relative to the Treatment of Civilian Persons in Time of War, 12 August 1949, 6 U.S.T. 3316, T.I.A.S. No. 3365, 75 U.N.T.S. 287.

not specify how such violations are to be proved, suggesting that any probative evidence, including reports by private human rights groups, will be relevant. The Geneva Convention contains humanitarian rules prohibiting acts of war against noncombatants.

The Ninth Circuit has been far more willing to entertain asylum claims that are premised on refusal to be inducted into the army for reasons of conscience. In this respect, the Ninth Circuit has upheld such claims in the following circumstances:

- Members of the Jehovah's Witnesses who showed they would be punished as the result of their conscientious religious aversion to military service generally were granted asylum;[54] and

- Persons who showed conscientious aversion to *inhuman acts*—in this case, paid assassination—were eligible for asylum.[55]

Membership in a Particular Social Group

Membership in a particular social group now comprises one of the most vital and flexible bases for refugee status. Although the BIA originally had given this category a restricted interpretation, the particular social group basis of persecution is now the foundation for many of the most interesting cases being decided by the BIA and the courts.

In *Matter of Acosta,*[56] the BIA set forth its formulation of the particular social group rubric. According to the BIA, a particular social group either is based on an immutable characteristic (something the applicant cannot change) or one that is so fundamental to the applicant's identity or conscience that he or she ought not to be required to change it. The BIA also included certain past associations (*i.e.*, prior military service or the ownership of land) that, because they are viewed as being linked permanently to the applicant, will, under specific conditions, satisfy the particular social group criteria.

Under the foregoing definition, the family has been held to be a particular social group.[57] Homosexuals who have been targeted in the country of claimed persecution also may qualify under the particular social group category.[58] And, in *Matter of H-,*[59] the BIA determined that members of the Darood clan and of the Marehan sub-clan in Somalia are members of a particular social group, and can claim eligibility for asylum under this category. In contrast, in a recent decision, the BIA held that a group of "former noncriminal drug informants working against the Cali drug cartel" did not have the requisite social visibility to constitute a *particular social group*.[60] In so

---

[54] *Canas-Segovia v. INS*, 902 F.2d 717 (9th Cir. 1990).

[55] *Barranza-Rivera v. INS*, 913 F.2d 1443 (9th Cir. 1990).

[56] *Matter of Acosta,* 19 I&N Dec. 211 (BIA 1985).

[57] *Gebremichael v. INS*, 10 F.3d 28 (1st Cir. 1993).

[58] *Matter of Toboso-Alfonso*, 20 I&N Dec. 819 (BIA 1990).

[59] *Matter of H–*, 21 I&N Dec. 337 (BIA 1996).

[60] *Matter of C–A–*, 23 I&N Dec. 951 (BIA 2006).

holding, the BIA identified the "social visibility of the members of a claimed social group" as an important consideration in identifying the existence of a *particular social group*.[61]

Membership in a particular social group has served as the basis for the emerging gender-based persecution claims now dominating much of modern asylum law. In *Fatin v. INS*,[62] the U.S. Court of Appeals for the Third Circuit ruled that "to the extent that the petitioner in this case suggests that she would be persecuted or has a well-founded fear that she would be persecuted ... simply because she is a woman, she has satisfied the three elements that we have noted." The *Fatin* decision was followed by several adjudications before IJs in which the judges have been prone to grant asylum, under limited conditions, to women who have been subject to domestic abuse and other violations of protected human rights.

In *Fatin v. INS*,[63] the applicant had left Iran while still a teenager and with the Shah still in power. She contended that she was opposed to the practice of Islam (particularly its gender-based behavioral code) and that subjecting her to such a code would constitute persecution in the statutory sense. The Third Circuit ruled that gender was an immutable characteristic so that it would satisfy the particular social group definition. The court also determined that feminism or opposition to male dominance constitutes a political opinion for which one could be subject to persecution. On the merits of the claim, however, the court found that the applicant had not shown a well-founded fear of persecution on either of these grounds.

In *Safaie v. INS*,[64] another Iranian claim, the asylum-seeker alleged persecution arising from her opposition to the Khomeini regime and its treatment of women. The court found that the particular social group under which the applicant sought to establish her claim (Iranian women) was over broad, and that no fact finder could reasonably conclude that all Iranian women had a well-founded fear of persecution based solely on their gender. The court did conclude, however, that the particular social group definition might well be satisfied by a formulation that included "a group of women ... who refuse to conform and whose opposition is so profound that they would chose to suffer the severe consequences of noncompliance ...."

---

[61] *See also Matter of E–A–G–*, 24 I&N Dec. 591 (BIA 2008) (holding that a young Honduran male, failed to establish that he was a member of a particular social group of "persons resistant to gang membership," as the evidence failed to establish that members of Honduran society, or even gang members themselves, would perceive those opposed to gang membership as members of a social group); *Matter of S–E–G–*, 24 I&N Dec. 579 (BIA 2008) (holding that neither Salvadoran youth who have been subjected to recruitment efforts by the MS-13 gang and who have rejected or resisted membership in the gang based on their own personal, moral, and religious opposition to the gang's values and activities nor the family members of such Salvadoran youth constitute a particular social group).

[62] *Fatin v. INS*, 12 F.3d 1233 (3d Cir. 1994).

[63] *Id.*

[64] *Safaie v. INS*, 25 F.3d 636 (8th Cir. 1994).

Finally, *Fisher v. INS*[65] is itself really three cases in one. The applicant, an Iranian national, claimed that she had been stopped on the street by government officials and ordered into a car at gunpoint because a strand of her hair was visible from beneath her chador. The applicant also contended that she strongly disagreed with the Kohmeini regime's interpretation of Islamic law, particularly as it was applied in a discriminatory way as to women. Initially, the Ninth Circuit determined that the applicant had made out a claim finding that she would be exposed to persecution on account of her opposition to the way in which Islamic law is interpreted and enforced by the Kohmeini regime. In a subsequent hearing en banc, however, the circuit court reversed this result and found that the applicant had failed to establish persecution on one of the enumerated grounds.

Reading these cases together, it appears that gender alone usually has not been sufficient to establish a conventional gender-based asylum claim that is based on a discriminatory cultural or social code. However, where the asylum-seeker can show that he or she openly defied that code, and that serious harm will flow as a result, the applicant can make out a claim of persecution either based on the political opinion ground or as the member of a particular social group.

On June 13, 1996, the BIA issued a precedent decision in *Matter of Kasinga,*[66] where the BIA found that female genital mutilation (FGM) constituted persecution within the meaning of the refugee standard. The BIA concluded that the claimant had established that she had a well-founded fear of persecution on account of a statutory ground—namely, membership in a particular social group. The BIA defined the protected class as young women of the Tchamba-Kunsuntu Tribe who have not had FGM, as practiced by their tribe, and who oppose the practice.

The BIA issued two controversial opinions in FGM asylum law in September 2007. In *Matter of A–T–,*[67] the BIA held that an applicant for asylum who already suffered FGM cannot prove future persecution because the FGM that she suffered could not occur twice. The BIA rejected arguments that the continuing physical and psychological effects of FGM constitute continuing persecution in the same way that persons who have suffered forced sterilization continue to suffer harm that constitutes persecution.[68] The U.S. Court of Appeals for the Second Circuit disagreed with the BIA's reasoning that FGM could only be suffered once; the human rights reports evidenced many instances of repeated FGM performed on women.[69] The Attorney Gen-

---

[65] *Fisher v. INS,* 37 F.3d 1371 (9th Cir. 1994), *amended* 61 F.3d 1366 (9th Cir. 1995), *decided de novo, Fisher v. INS,* 79 F.3d 955 (9th Cir. 1996).

[66] *Matter of Kasinga,* 21 I&N Dec. 357 (BIA 1996).

[67] *Matter of A–T–,* 24 I&N Dec. 296 (BIA 2007),

[68] *See Matter of Y–T–L–,* 23 I&N Dec. 601 (BIA 2003) (someone who has suffered forced sterilization has a continuing fear of persecution because of the physical and psychological effects); *see also Mohammed v. Gonzales,* 400 F.3d 785 (9th Cir. 2005) (someone who has suffered FGM has a continuing fear of persecution).

[69] *See Bah v. Mukasey,* 529 F.3d 99 (2d Cir. 2008).

eral (AG) ultimately withdrew the BIA's decision in *Matter of A–T–*[70] reasoning that FGM was persecution that a woman could suffer more than once.[71]

In *Matter of A–K–,*[72] the BIA held that an asylum applicant cannot prove fear of future persecution based solely on the fear that the applicant's daughter will suffer future persecution in the home country. However, the BIA left open the possibility of humanitarian asylum—under 8 CFR §208.13(b)(1)(iii)(A)—for persons who have suffered FGM in aggravated circumstances, because a grant in such case would not require the applicant to prove likelihood of future persecution.[73]

These gender-based claims continue to develop in federal case law. In granting asylum to a Chinese applicant who fled a proposed forced marriage, the Second Circuit found that "women who have been forced into marriage and who live in a feudal community in China where forced marriage is condoned" did constitute a particular social group.[74] In articulating this social group, the Second Circuit noted that this group "shared more than a common gender."[75] The Supreme Court vacated the Second Circuit's decision in *Gao* and remanded the case to the Second Circuit for further consideration in light of *Gonzales v. Thomas*.[76]

Another growing class of gender-related claims arises in the area of household domestic violence. No circuit court or BIA decision has articulated application of the statutory standard in this setting. However, a number of IJs have written strong decisions granting asylum, under limited conditions, to women who have been subject to domestic abuse and other violations of protected human rights. One example of such adjudications has been *Matter of A– and Z–,*[77] where the IJ awarded asylum to a Jordanian woman based on the fact that her husband mistreated her by beating her in front of friends, seeking to control her activities, and isolating her. The IJ found the applicant to be a member of a particular social group, consisting of women who espouse western values and are unwilling to live their lives at the mercy of their husbands, their society, or their government.[78]

---

[70] *Id.*

[71] *Matter of A–T–,* 24 I&N Dec. 617 (A.G. 2008).

[72] *Matter of A–K–,* 24 I&N Dec. 275 (BIA 2007).

[73] *Matter of S–A–K and H–A–H–,* 24 I&N Dec. 464 (BIA 2008).

[74] *Gao v. Gonzales,* 440 F.3d 62 (2d Cir. 2006).

[75] *Id.*

[76] *Gonzales v. Thomas,* 547 U.S. 183 (2007) (vacating the Ninth Circuit's decision regarding family as a social group and directing the Ninth Circuit to remand to the agency to permit the agency to make a legal determination regarding social group).

[77] *Matter of A– and Z–,* A72 793 219 (IJ Arlington, VA. Dec. 20, 1994), *abstracted in* 70 *Interpreter Releases* 521 (April 17, 1995).

[78] *See also* Stephen M. Knight, "Seeking Asylum from Gender Persecution: Progress Amid Uncertainty," 79 *Interpreter Releases* 689 (May 13, 2002), digesting decisions concerning gender-related asylum claims.

The jurisprudence relating to asylum as it applies to domestic violence situations was threatened by the BIA holding in *Matter of R–A–*.[79] In *Matter of R–A–*, the BIA overturned an IJ's grant of asylum to a Guatemalan woman who had shown that her husband had subjected her to inhuman treatment, including kicking her violently when she declined to abort a fetus. The applicant had demonstrated that spousal abuse in Guatemala is common, and that her efforts to secure state protection were unavailing. Nonetheless, the BIA denied the claim ruling: (a) applicant was not persecuted on account of a protected ground (*i.e.,* gender); and (b) there was no evidence that the Guatemala willfully was withholding protection from a specific class in failing to provide her any security from this abuse. In December 2000, legacy INS issued proposed domestic violence asylum regulations that would reverse the government's initial position on asylum cases involving domestic violence. Just before stepping down as AG in January 2001, Janet Reno instructed the BIA to reconsider *Matter of R–A–* in light of the proposed domestic violence asylum regulations, thus overturning it. The proposed regulations still have not been finalized.

As of this writing, *Matter of R–A–* has not been resolved. Nonetheless, there have been positive signs. On September 25, 2008, AG Michael Mukasey certified *Matter of R–A–* to himself, and issued a decision ordering the BIA to reconsider it, removing the requirement that the BIA await the issuance of proposed regulations. Notwithstanding this bureaucratic holdup, a handful of gender-related asylum claims, some based on domestic violence, have been granted by the asylum office, IJs, and the BIA.[80] Advocates also may view summaries of gender-related asylum decisions on the Center for Gender and Refugee Studies website.[81] The Department of Homeland Security (DHS) itself filed a brief with AG John Ashcroft in *Matter of R–A–*, stating its support for Alvarado's claim, though it urged Ashcroft to dispose of the case without a detailed precedent-breaking decision. However, just before leaving his position as AG in January 2005, Ashcroft remanded the case back to the BIA with instructions to hold off on a decision until the final rule is published.

Until the future of the proposed rules becomes more certain, attorneys and other representatives should weigh carefully their clients' options in considering whether to bring an asylum claim based on domestic violence. For clients who are in removal proceedings and have no other options, asylum may well be a remedy worth pursuing. For clients who are not in proceedings but are facing their one-year filing deadline, it will depend on the strength of their case. They may wish to go ahead and file, recognizing that it will be an uphill battle. It is very important that clients make this

---

[79] *Matter of R–A–*, 22 I&N Dec. 906 (BIA 1999), *vacated and remanded for reconsideration* (AG 2001).

[80] *See*, Stephen M. Knight, "Seeking Asylum from Gender Persecution: Progress Amid Uncertainty," 79 *Interpreter Releases* 689 (May 13, 2002) (digesting decisions concerning gender-related asylum claims).

[81] *http://cgrs.uchastings.edu.*

decision themselves, and that their attorneys and representatives fully advise them of the risks and consequences. [82]

The Proposed Regulations

Among other things, the proposed regulations would codify the BIA's ruling in *Matter of Kasinga*[83] that a subjective intent to harm or punish, while normally present, is not required for persecution to exist. Rather, the asylum-seeker must demonstrate that:

- The harm or suffering is objectively serious; and
- It has been experienced subjectively by the applicant as serious harm.

Persecution normally relates to actions by government authorities. It also may emanate from groups or individuals the government is unable or unwilling to control. In evaluating whether the government is unable or unwilling to control the infliction of harm or suffering by a non-state actor, the proposed rules call on the IJ or asylum officer to determine whether the government has taken reasonable steps to control the infliction of harm or suffering, and whether the applicant has reasonable access to state protection. The applicant has the burden of proving that the harm or suffering was inflicted by the government or an entity it was unable or unwilling to control. Evidence can include:

- Government complicity with respect to the infliction of harm or suffering;
- Attempts by the applicant to obtain protection by government officials and the government's response to such efforts;
- Official action which is perfunctory;
- A pattern of government unresponsiveness;
- General country conditions and the denial of services;
- Government policies regarding the harm at issue; and
- Any steps the government has taken to prevent such harm or suffering.

The applicant must demonstrate that the persecution was inflicted *on account of* the applicant's race, religion, nationality, membership in a particular social group, or political opinion. The Supreme Court held in *Elias Zacarias v. INS*[84] that the applicant must present evidence that the persecutor seeks to harm the victim because of the victim's possession of a protected characteristic. This decision has raised difficult interpretive issues. The proposed rule seeks to provide guidance in this area.

In recent case law, both the BIA and the federal courts have recognized that a persecutor may have *mixed motives* and that the *on account of* requirement is met if the

---

[82] For an excellent overview of gender-based asylum claims, see the asylum chapter of CLINIC's and ILRC's manual entitled, "VAWA: Immigration Relief for Abused Immigrants." *See also* the Center for Gender and Refugee Studies website at *http://cgrs.uchastings.edu. See also* R. Germain, *AILA's Asylum Primer*, 5th Ed. (AILA 2002).

[83] *Matter of Kasinga, supra* note 66.

[84] *Elias Zacarias v. INS*, 502 U.S. 478 (1992).

persecutor acted *at least in part* because of a protected characteristic. The proposed rules would allow for the possibility of mixed motives, but require that "the applicant's protected characteristic [be] central to the persecutor's motivation to act against the applicant." REAL ID,[85] enacted on May 11, 2005, already has narrowed in a similar way the *mixed motive* doctrine, stating that an applicant, "must establish that race, religion, nationality, membership in a particular social group, or political opinion was or will be at least one central reason for persecuting the applicant."

The proposed rules also provide that an applicant may satisfy the *on account of* requirement if the persecutor acts against the victim on account of what the persecutor *perceives to be* the applicant's race, religion, nationality, membership in a particular social group, or political opinion. The rule thus would codify the doctrine of imputed political opinion and extend it to the other grounds. Many courts and the BIA already have recognized that each of the grounds can be imputed.

In *Matter of R–A–,*[86] the BIA found that the violence against the applicant was not *on account of* a particular social group because there was no evidence that the applicant's husband would harm any other member of the asserted social group. In other words, there was no evidence that the abuser would seek to harm other women living with abusive partners.

The proposed rules seek to modify the BIA's position in *Matter of R–A–*[87] by providing that "[e]vidence that the persecutor seeks to act against other individuals who share the applicant's characteristic is *relevant* and may be considered but shall not be required." Just as a slave owner was motivated to beat his own slave because of his race, but not the slave of his neighbor, a victim of domestic violence should be able to satisfy the requirement even though social limitations result in her abuser having the motivation to harm her alone in a society where wife beating is condoned.

The proposed rules also would codify the BIA's decision in *Matter of Acosta*[88] by providing that "a particular social group is composed of members who share a common, immutable characteristic, such as sex, color, kinship ties, or past experience, that a member either cannot change or that is so fundamental to the identity or conscience of the member that he or she should not be required to change it." The proposed rules are groundbreaking in that they explicitly recognize gender as the basis for membership in a particular social group.

The rules underscore, however, that a particular social group must exist independently of the persecution. For example, in domestic violence cases, a social group could not be defined as "women who have been battered."

If past experience defines a particular social group, the rules provide that the experience must be one that, *at the time it occurred*, the member either could not have changed, or should not have been required to change. For example, the rules indicate

---

[85] REAL ID, *supra* note 2.

[86] *Matter of R–A–, supra* note 79.

[87] *Id.*

[88] *Matter of Acosta*, 19 I&N Dec. 211 (BIA 1985).

that past membership in a violent gang would not qualify because the applicant could have refrained from joining. On the other hand, an applicant's marital status or involvement in an intimate relationship could be considered an immutable characteristic if evidence indicates that the victim reasonably could not be expected to leave.

The rules provide that the following factors may be considered in determining whether a particular social group exists:

- Members of the group are closely affiliated with each other;
- Members are driven by a common motive or interest;
- Voluntary associational relationship exists among members;
- The group is recognized as a societal faction or recognized segment of the population;
- Members view themselves as members of the group; or
- The society distinguishes members of the group for different treatment or status.

The first three factors are from the Ninth Circuit's decision in *Sanchez Trujillo v. INS*,[89] which held that a particular social group implied a collection of people closely affiliated with each other who were actuated by some common impulse or interest. The last three factors are from the BIA's decision in *Matter of R-A-*.[90] The BIA found no evidence that the claimed particular social group in the case—Guatemalan women intimately involved with male partners who believe women should live under male domination—was a group recognized or understood to be a societal faction, or that victims of spousal abuse viewed themselves as members of this group.

The proposed rules indicate that, while each of these factors may be considerations, they are not prerequisites. The proposed regulations also suggest that it would be relevant to consider evidence of societal attitudes towards group members. In asylum claims based on domestic violence, for example, do societal institutions—*i.e.*, the courts and police—fail to intervene because they view domestic violence as a private family matter? Do they offer fewer protections or benefits to women trapped in abusive relationships than to other victims of crimes?

Exercise of Discretion

Asylum is a discretionary remedy. Under prior law, it was considered to be a basis for discretionary denial if the applicant sought entry with false documents. Now, however, the decision-maker is obligated to take into account "the totality of the circumstances and actions of the foreign national in his flight from the country in which he fears persecution should be examined in determining whether a favorable exercise of discretion is warranted."[91] The factors that should be analyzed include the following:

---

[89] *Sanchez Trujillo v. INS*, 801 F.2d 1572 (9th Cir. 1986).

[90] *Matter of R–A–, supra* note 79.

[91] *Matter of Pula,* 19 I&N Dec. 467 (BIA 1987).

- The countries passed through en route to the United States;

- Whether, in fact, orderly refugee procedures existed that the foreign national could have taken advantage of; and

- Any attempts at seeking asylum before arriving here in the United States.

In conducting this analysis, the BIA has directed that the "danger of persecution should outweigh all but the most egregious factors."

However, in *Matter of Jean*,[92] the AG held that even if an asylum applicant technically is eligible for such relief, if the applicant committed violent or dangerous crimes, then the applicant will not be granted asylum except in extraordinary circumstances—*i.e.*, those involving national security or foreign policy considerations, or cases in which the applicant clearly demonstrates that the denial would result in exceptional and extremely unusual hardship. Moreover, the AG held that, depending on the gravity of the underlying criminal conduct, even the demonstration of exceptional and extremely unusual hardship may not be enough to merit a grant of asylum.

The respondent in *Matter of Jean*, Ms. Jean, was 45-year-old national of Haiti. In November 1994, Ms. Jean, along with her husband and five children, were admitted *conditionally* to the United States as refugees. (According to the AG, the "conditional" admission had the effect of deferring her admissibility inspection and examination by federal immigration officials). In August 1995, she pled guilty in New York state court to one count of second-degree manslaughter in connection with the earlier death of a 19-month-old child who was left in her care at her apartment. According to Ms. Jean's signed confession, the child had fallen off the couch onto the floor and began to cry. Ms. Jean hit him two or three times with her open hand on his buttocks to quiet him. This did not stop his crying so she picked him up by his armpits and shook him to make him stop crying. She then hit him several times on his head with her fist. She shook him again until he lost consciousness. Although she had realized that he was not breathing nor blinking, she merely placed him on a bed and never called 911 or sought help. The child died from bleeding and swelling inside the skull caused by blunt trauma. She was sentenced to two-to-six years of incarceration.

After she served her sentence, Ms. Jean applied for adjustment of status, pursuant to INA §209(a). In July 1999, legacy INS denied the application and commenced formal removal proceedings against her as an inadmissible foreign national convicted of a crime of moral turpitude (CMT).[93]

Ms. Jean did not dispute that she was inadmissible for having a conviction for a CMT but she applied for a waiver of the ground of inadmissibility pursuant to INA §209(c). She cited her fear of persecution in Haiti and her desire to keep her family together in the United States. She also applied for asylum, withholding of removal, and Article 3 protection under CAT.

---

[92] *Matter of Jean*, 23 I&N Dec. 373 (A.G. 2002).

[93] INA §212(a)(2)(A)(i)(I).

After the BIA considered the case twice, the AG had the BIA refer the case to him. He determined that she was unfit for a discretionary grant of relief because her "conduct involving the death of the child was sufficiently severe as to make the conferral of asylum upon her entirely inappropriate."[94]

In *Matter of A–H–,*[95] the AG denied asylum in the exercise of discretion to the exiled leader of an Algerian group associated with other groups that persecuted others and committed acts of terrorism in Algeria. The AG found that it was inconsistent for the United States to actively oppose persecution and terrorism on the one hand, and provide safe haven to those with connections to such actions on the other.

Ineligible Classes

Certain classes of foreign nationals are ineligible for withholding of removal and asylum.

Ineligible for Asylum

Under INA §208(b)(2)(A), the following persons are ineligible for asylum:

- Persons who have participated in the persecution of others;

- Persons who having been convicted of a particularly serious crime and who constitute a danger to the community of the United States (foreign nationals who have been convicted of an aggravated felony will be considered to have been convicted of a particularly serious crime);

- Persons who have committed a serious non-political crime outside the United States;

- Persons who can reasonably be regarded as a security risk to the United States;

- Persons who are inadmissible on security grounds or are removable as terrorists; and

- Persons who have been firmly resettled in a third country before coming to the United States.

Persons Inadmissible on Security Grounds or Removable as Terrorists

With respect to the instance above, where a person is ineligible to apply for asylum because he or she is inadmissible as a terrorist, INA §208(b)(2)(A)(v) sets forth the prohibition and refers specifically to the ground of inadmissibility in INA§212(a)(3)(B)(i)(II) (*i.e.,* terrorist activities).

INA §212(a)(3)(B)(i)(II), in turn, provides that a foreign national is inadmissible if the consular officer or the immigration officer knows or *has a reasonable ground to believe*, is engaged, or is likely to engage after entry, in any terrorist activity.

In addition to the prohibition against granting asylum to terrorists, the INA includes a similar provision to prevent granting withholding of removal to terrorists. INA

---

[94] *Matter of Jean, supra* note 92.

[95] *Matter of A–H–,* 23 I&N Dec. 774 (A.G. 2005).

§241(b)(3)(B)(iv) specifically restricts granting withholding where "there are *reasonable grounds to believe* that the foreign national is a danger to the security of the United States."

In *Matter of U–H–*,[96] Mr. U–H– applied for asylum and withholding of removal and argued that §412 of the Uniting and Strengthening America by Providing Appropriate Tools Required to Intercept and Obstruct Terrorism (USA PATRIOT) Act of 2001[97] set a new and higher standard for the government to determine whether a person was ineligible for asylum and withholding of removal pursuant to INA §§208(b)(2)(A)(v) and 241(b)(3)(B)(iv).

Looking at the plain language of the statute, the BIA determined that §412 did not establish a new or higher standard for determining whether an applicant for asylum and withholding of removal was ineligible for such relief. Instead, the BIA pointed out that §412 merely created another avenue for the AG to detain suspected terrorists. In other words, the *reasonable ground to believe* standard remained the same as before the enactment of the USA PATRIOT Act.

The BIA also noted, however, that the *reasonable ground to believe* standard in §§208(b)(2)(A)(v), 212(a)(3)(B)(i)(II), and 241(a)(3)(B)(iv) were all the same, and that the standard was "akin to the familiar *probable cause* standard." The BIA further stated that the *reasonable ground to believe* "may be formed if the evidence is sufficient to justify a reasonable person in the belief that the foreign national falls within the proscribed category."

In *Matter of S–K–*,[98] the BIA held that an applicant's monetary contribution over an 11-month period to the Chin National Front—identified by statute as a terrorist organization—was substantial enough to constitute material support to a terrorist organization under INA §212(a)(3)(B)(iv)(VI), thus barring the applicant from asylum and withholding relief. The BIA held that the language of INA §212(a)(3)(B) did not permit consideration of certain factors—*i.e.*, the democratic goals of the organization, or the nature of the regime it opposes—in determining whether an organization is a terrorist organization. The BIA also stated that it did not consider a foreign national's intent in making a donation, or the intended use of the donation, in determining whether the foreign national has provided material support.

After significant bad press about the *material support bar* and its effect on asylum cases and processing of refugees into the United States, DHS Secretary Chertoff made a statement on January 19, 2007, allowing for a totality of circumstances consideration to be used to consider the cases of those who provided material support under duress to *Tier III* organizations.[99] Later statements by Chertoff allowed this

---

[96] *Matter of U–H–*, 23 I&N Dec. 355 (BIA 2002).

[97] Uniting and Strengthening America by Providing Appropriate Tools Required to Intercept and Obstruct Terrorism (USA PATRIOT) Act of 2001, Pub. L. No. 107-56, 115 Stat. 272.

[98] *Matter of S–K–*, 23 I&N Dec. 936 (BIA 2006).

[99] 72 Fed. Reg. 9958 (March 6, 2007).

totality of the circumstances test to be used when considering the cases of those who provided material support under duress to *Tier I and II* organizations.

In a follow-up precedent decision, *Matter of S–K–*,[100] the BIA discussed INA §212(a)(3)(B) and the effect of the passage of the Consolidated Appropriations Act (CAA) of 2008[101] on December 26, 2007, which stated that certain groups shall not be considered to be a terrorist organization on the basis of any act or event occurring before December 26, 2007. Though the respondent in the case was deemed to have provided material support to the CNF/Chin National Army, this group was not considered a terrorist organization as a result of the CAA, so the respondent was no longer ineligible for asylum based on the material support to terrorism bar. The BIA added, however, that their decision in *Matter of S–K–*[102] still was the law with respect to the material support bar to asylum and withholding of removal. Therefore, persons who have given support to other organizations deemed *terrorist organizations*, regardless of the level of support, are inadmissible under this ground.[103]

Firm Resettlement

The regulatory provision for determining firm resettlement replaces the common law discretionary consideration laid out in *Matter of Pula*,[104] regarding whether a respondent has *found a safe haven* in another country.[105] The regulations define *firmly resettled* as situations where the foreign national has been offered permanent residence (or its equivalent) in a third country.[106] Exceptions exist where:

- The foreign national's stay in a third country is really a part of an unbroken chain of flight, and the asylum-seeker remained in the third country only so long as was necessary to arrange travel to another country; or

- The foreign national was subject to discriminatory treatment in the third country so that he or she was not given equal access to such basic rights as housing, employment, or food rations.

Safe Third Country

Foreign nationals may not apply for asylum if the AG concludes that there exists a safe third country to which the asylum-seeker may be removed under a bilateral or multilateral agreement providing for a full and fair procedure governing the determi-

---

[100] *Matter of S–K–*, 24 I&N Dec. 475 (BIA 2008).

[101] Consolidated Appropriations Act, 2008, Pub. L. No. 110-161, §6, div. J, sec. 691, 121 Stat. 1844, 2364–66.

[102] *Matter of S–K–*, 23 I&N Dec. 936 (BIA 2006).

[103] For a detailed discussion of the changes in this ground, consult Human Rights First, "Refugees at Risk Under Sweeping 'Terrorism' Bar," available with other information, including Secretary Chertoff's statements and other relevant documents, at *www.humanrightsfirst.org/asylum/asylum_refugee.asp*.

[104] *Matter of Pula*, 19 I&N Dec. 467 (BIA 1987).

[105] *Tandia v. Gonzales*, 437 F.3d 245 (2d Cir. 2006); *Andrasian v. INS*, 180 F.3d 1033 (9th Cir. 1999) (explaining that 8 CFR §1208.15 replaced the *Matter of Pula* standard).

[106] 8 CFR §1208.15.

nation of refugee status. A safe-third-country agreement between the United States and Canada came into effect on December 29, 2004. Asylum officers in the United States, therefore, will conduct a threshold screening of arriving asylum seekers at U.S.-Canada land and border ports of entry. The interviewer will determine whether the individual qualifies for an exception or will be returned to Canada to pursue his or her asylum claim there.[107]

Particularly Serious Crime in the Asylum Context

Conviction of an aggravated felony as defined in INA §101(a)(43) constitutes a per se conviction for a particularly serious crime in the asylum context. The definition of what constitutes an aggravated felony has been expanded greatly since 1996 (See chapter 2 for a more in-depth discussion of the aggravated felony definition).

Importantly, however, even if an offense is not an aggravated felony, it still may be considered a particularly serious crime for purposes of asylum, withholding, and CAT.[108] In most cases, what is a particularly serious crime requires an examination of the elements of the offense; if the elements bring the offense within the possible realm of *particularly serious crimes*, the immigration court examines underlying circumstances of the conviction.[109] Crimes against persons are much more likely to be considered particularly serious than crimes against property. Furthermore, the adjudicator will consider a variety of factors in making the determination, including:

- The nature of the conviction;
- The circumstances and underlying facts of the conviction;
- The type of sentence imposed; and, most importantly,
- Whether the type and circumstances of the crime indicate that the foreign national will be a danger of the community.[110]

Ineligible for Withholding

Under INA §241(b)(3), the following persons are ineligible for withholding of removal:

- Persons who have participated in the persecution of others;
- Persons who having been convicted of a particularly serious crime and who constitute a danger to the community;
- Persons who have committed a serious non-political crime outside the United States; and

---

[107] *For more information on this process see* M. von Sternberg, "The U.S. Canada Safe Third Country Agreement: Is It Safe for Refugees?" 24 *Immigration Law Today* 12 (March/April 2005).

[108] *Matter of N–A–M–*, 24 I&N Dec. 336 (BIA 2007); *but see Alaka v. AG*, 456 F.3d 88 (3d Cir. 2006) (holding, in the context of a particularly serious crime determination for the purposes of withholding of removal under INA §2419b)(3), that conviction must be an aggravated felony in order to constitute a particularly serious crime).

[109] *Matter of N–A–M–*, *supra* note 108.

[110] *Matter of Frentescu*, 18 I&N Dec. 244 (BIA 1982).

- Persons who can reasonably be regarded as a security risk to the United States.

Particularly Serious Crime in the Withholding Context

A foreign national who has been convicted of an aggravated felony (or felonies) for which he or she has been sentenced to an aggregate term of imprisonment of at least five years will be considered to have committed a particularly serious crime for purposes of withholding.[111] However, as with asylum, the length of sentence will not preclude the AG from determining that an offense is a particularly serious crime.[112]

In *Matter of Y–L–, A–G–, and R–S–R–,*[113] the AG had the BIA refer three cases to him where the BIA had determined that the aggravated felonies involved in each case did not amount to particularly serious crimes. All three cases involved convictions for trafficking in cocaine.

In reviewing the three cases, the AG determined that the BIA had given too much weight to the relatively short sentences of incarceration each respondent had received for their aggravated felony convictions rather than looking at the nature or category of the crime that resulted in the conviction. He then held that aggravated felonies involving unlawful trafficking in controlled substances presumptively constituted *particularly serious crimes* within the meaning of INA §241(b)(3)(B)(ii). He went on to state that this was now a rule rendering all convictions for unlawful trafficking in controlled substances *per se* particularly serious crimes. He held, however, that "only under the most extenuating circumstances that are both extraordinary and compelling would departure from this interpretation be warranted or permissible."

Refraining from setting bright-line boundaries as to when a drug-trafficking conviction would *not* constitute a particularly serious crime, the AG did, however, provide some guidelines on when extenuating circumstances might be considered extraordinary and compelling enough to find that a drug-trafficking crime is not a particularly serious crime. He stated that:

At a minimum, in order for a drug-trafficking conviction to be considered not particularly serious, an applicant for withholding of removal must demonstrate *all* of the following:

- A very small quantity of controlled substance (*e.g.,* it was *de minimis* or inconsequential);

- A very modest amount of money paid for the drugs in the offending transaction (*e.g.,* it was *de minimis* or inconsequential);

- Merely peripheral involvement by the foreign national in the criminal activity, transaction, or conspiracy;

---

[111] INA §241(b)(3)(B).

[112] *Matter of N–A–M–, supra* note 108; *but see Alaka v. AG,* 456 F.3d 88 (3d Cir. 2006) (holding that conviction must be an aggravated felony with the requisite sentence in order to constitute a particularly serious crime).

[113] *Matter of Y–L–, A–G–, and R–S–R–,* 23 I&N Dec. 270 (A.G. 2002).

- The absence of any violence or threat of violence, implicit or otherwise, associated with the offense;

- The absence of any organized crime or terrorist organization involvement, direct or indirect, in relation to the offending activity; and

- The absence of any adverse or harmful effect of the activity or transaction on juveniles.

The AG emphasized that commonplace circumstances—*e.g.*, cooperation with law enforcement authorities; limited criminal histories; downward departures at sentencing; and post-arrest (let alone post-conviction) claims of contrition or innocence—do not justify departure from the general rule that drug-trafficking convictions are to be considered particularly serious crimes.

Termination of Asylum or Withholding

A foreign national who has been granted asylum may not be deported or removed unless asylum status is terminated.[114] Similarly, a foreign national granted withholding of removal cannot be removed to the country to which removal has been ordered withheld unless the withholding order is terminated. Upon termination, ICE will commence exclusion, deportation or removal proceedings, as appropriate.[115] In reality, however, while it is certainly possible, it is relatively rare for asylum or even withholding status to be terminated.

An asylum officer can terminate asylum that was granted by USCIS if there was fraud in the application, or the foreign national was not eligible for the relief at the time it was granted.[116] In addition, for applications made on or after April 1, 1997, the asylum officer can terminate asylum if:

- The foreign national no longer has a well-founded fear of persecution owing to a fundamental change in circumstances;

- There exists a safe third country to which the asylum-seeker may be removed under a bilateral or multilateral agreement providing for a full and fair procedure governing the determination of refugee status;

- The foreign national voluntarily has availed him- or herself of the foreign national's country of nationality or last residence (if there is no nationality);

- The foreign national has acquired a new nationality and has availed him- or herself of its protection; or

- The foreign national becomes subject to a mandatory ground of disqualification.

With regard to applications filed before April 1, 1997, the asylum officer may terminate if the foreign national becomes subject to a mandatory ground of denial in

---

[114] INA §208(c).

[115] 8 CFR §1208.24(e).

[116] 8 CFR §1208.24(a).

effect at that time (*e.g.,* the foreign national is convicted of a particularly serious crime).

USCIS may terminate a grant of withholding of deportation or removal (made under its jurisdiction) if:

- It determines that the foreign national no longer meets the statutory standard for the remedy;

- There was fraud in the application or the foreign national was not eligible for the relief at the time it was granted;

- The foreign national has committed some act that constitutes a mandatory ground of denial (*e.g.,* has been convicted of a "particularly serious crime" under new INA §241(b)(3); or

- For claims filed before April 1, 1997, the foreign national has committed some act that would have been a ground of ineligibility under former INA §243(h)(2).

Credible Fear Process

Arriving aliens, or those apprehended within 100 miles of the border within 14 days of entry who present false documents or no documents, will be removed expeditiously unless they either indicate a desire to apply for asylum or express a fear of returning. Those who make such an indication will be placed in a credible fear interview.[117] An *arriving alien* determined to have a *credible fear of persecution* shall be detained for further consideration of his or her claim in a removal proceeding.[118]

A *credible fear of persecution* is defined narrowly. The foreign national must prove that there is a significant possibility that he or she could meet the refugee standard, bearing in mind his or her credibility and other facts known to the officer.[119] A determination that the foreign national does not meet the credible fear standard may be reviewed promptly by an IJ (either personally or telephonically); this review must be held expeditiously and in no case later than seven days after the initial negative determination on the credible fear standard.[120] During the pendency of this process, the foreign national will be detained. Foreign nationals who are deemed not to have a credible fear will be summarily removed.

---

[117] INA §235(b)(1)(A); 8 CFR §208.30.

[118] INA §235(b)(1)(B)(iii)(IV).

[119] INA §235(b)(1)(B)(v).

[120] INA §235(b)(1)(B)(iii)(III).

Part Two: Protection Under the Convention Against Torture (CAT)

Overview

Article 3 of CAT[121] provides broad protection to potential victims of torture. CAT prohibits one country from sending a person to another country where he or she would be in danger of torture. There are no exceptions to this protection; CAT protects a violent criminal, terrorist or torturer from removal to a country where he or she would be tortured. In addition, a person seeking protection under CAT does not have to prove that the torture would be on account of the enumerated grounds of political opinion, religion, nationality, race, or membership in a particular social group. This distinguishes CAT from current law on asylum and withholding of removal under INA §241(b)(3), law that limits eligibility for certain groups and requires that persecution be on account of one of the five enumerated grounds.

While CAT protection is broad, its benefits in the United States are narrow. The United States became a party to the CAT in 1994, and legacy INS activated an interim rule to implement CAT on March 22, 1999. The rule creates two different statuses for those who seek CAT protection. The first is essentially the same as withholding of removal under INA §241(b)(3). It is known as *Article 3 withholding* (named for the section of CAT that applies).[122] The second is *deferral of removal*—a very limited protection for those who do not qualify for withholding.[123] Under these rules, ICE may attempt to terminate *deferral of removal* at any time. The difference between withholding and deferral of removal is explained in more detail below. Neither status leads to permanent residency, and neither provides any mechanism for family members to join the protected person. Finally, neither prohibits removal to a safe third country.

Definitions

An applicant under CAT must meet the definition of torture to be eligible for protection. Torture is defined at 8 CFR §208.18 as:

- An act that inflicts severe pain or suffering, mental or physical;
- Intentional;
- With the consent, instigation, or acquiescence of a person acting in an official capacity;
- On a person or a third person who is in the custody or control of the torturer; and
- For such purposes as coercing, intimidating, or punishing the person or a third person, or obtaining a confession or information from the person or a third person.

---

[121] CAT, *supra* note 1.

[122] 8 CFR §208.16.

[123] 8 CFR §208.17.

All of these elements must be present for a person to establish eligibility for protection under CAT.

In some cases, it may be difficult to prove that a government official *acquiesced* to the torture. Acquiescence of the public official is defined in the regulation as prior awareness of the torture, plus a subsequent breach of the legal responsibility to intervene to prevent the torture—in other words, that the official knew about the torture but did not try to stop it.[124] It is helpful to document through country conditions and expert witnesses the knowledge of the public officials. These cases will be harder to prove than those in which the public official is clearly the torturer.[125]

Torture does not include acts that unintentionally cause severe pain and suffering, or acts that constitute *lawful sanctions*. The rule offers a circular definition of lawful sanctions, describing them as "legally imposed sanctions ... that do not defeat the object and purpose of the CAT to prohibit torture."[126] So as not to conflict with practices in the United States, the death penalty specifically is included as a lawful sanction.[127]

Mental torture is defined in greater detail than physical torture. To constitute torture, mental pain or suffering must be:

- Prolonged mental harm; and

- Caused by the intentional or threatened infliction of:

   – Severe pain;

   – The use or threat of serious mind-altering substances or procedures;

   – The threat of death; or

   – The threat that another person will be subject to these harms.[128]

The applicant must prove that the physical or mental harm he or she likely would suffer meets the definition of torture.

In *Matter of J–E–*,[129] the BIA considered whether a Haitian citizen in removal proceedings demonstrated that it was more likely than not he would be tortured if he were deported to Haiti. Mr. J–E–, the respondent, had a Florida state conviction for sale of cocaine. Legacy INS placed him in removal proceedings for having a conviction for a controlled substance violation, as well as for being present in the United States without admission or parole. While he was before the IJ, Mr. J–E– applied for asylum, withholding of removal, and protection under CAT.

---

[124] 8 CFR §208.18(a)(7).

[125] *See Matter of S–V–*, 22 I&N Dec. 1306 (BIA 2000); *but see Zheng v. Ashcroft*, 332 F.3d 1186 (9th Cir. 2003) (finding that it is only necessary to prove "awareness" by the government officials—*i.e.,* "willful blindness" is sufficient).

[126] 8 CFR §208.18(a)(3).

[127] *Id.*

[128] 8 CFR §208.18(a)(4).

[129] *Matter of J–E–*, 23 I&N Dec. 291 (BIA 2002).

Mr. J–E– claimed that, as a deportee with a criminal conviction, he would be subjected to torture by the Haitian authorities by being detained indefinitely in inhumane conditions in police holding cells. Moreover, he feared torture through police mistreatment. Mr. J–E– submitted evidence of the inhuman prison conditions in Haiti. The evidence showed that prison facilities were overcrowded and inadequate, and that inmates were deprived of adequate food, water, medical care, sanitation, and exercise. The evidence also indicated that many prisoners in Haiti suffered, and even died, from malnourishment. Finally, the evidence submitted demonstrated that the Haitian government indefinitely detained deportees with criminal convictions.

The IJ determined that Mr. J–E– was statutorily ineligible for asylum and withholding of removal because of his aggravated felony conviction. The IJ also denied the application for deferral of removal under CAT, finding that Mr. J–E– had failed to prove that it was more likely than not that he would be tortured by the Haitian authorities if he were returned to Haiti. Mr. J–E– appealed the denial of the CAT claim to the BIA.

In considering Mr. J–E–'s claim, the BIA noted that the definition of *torture* is intended to cover only *extreme* forms of cruel, inhuman, or degrading treatment or punishment, and should exclude "other acts of cruel, inhuman or degrading treatment or punishment." To wit, torture differs from acts other than torture in the *severity* of the pain and suffering inflicted.

Relying on the definition of torture in the regulations, the BIA considered whether the acts Mr. J–E– feared—indefinite detention; inhuman prison conditions; and police mistreatment—amounted to torture.

First, the BIA held that indefinite detention of criminal deportees by Haitian authorities does not constitute torture within the meaning of the regulations where there is no evidence that the authorities intentionally and deliberately detain deportees in order to inflict torture. The BIA came to this conclusion because it found that the Haitian government's policy of detaining deportees with criminal convictions was a law enforcement act authorized by law to prevent crime and insecurity. Therefore, as a lawful sanction, the policy of indefinite detention was not intended specifically to inflict severe physical or mental pain or suffering. The BIA also noted that there was no evidence to indicate that the policy of indefinitely detaining criminal deportees was inflicted on them for a proscribed purpose.

Second, the BIA held that substandard prison conditions in Haiti do not constitute torture within the meaning of the regulations where there is no evidence that the authorities intentionally create and maintain such conditions in order to inflict torture. Here, the BIA determined that, although the Haitian authorities detained people in facilities which they knew were substandard, there was no evidence to indicate that the Haitian government intentionally and deliberately created and maintained those substandard conditions in order to inflict torture on the inmates.

Finally, the BIA held that evidence of the occurrence in Haitian prisons of isolated instances of mistreatment that may rise to the level of torture (as defined in the CAT) is insufficient to establish that it is more likely than not that Mr. J–E– would be tortured if returned to Haiti. Although the BIA acknowledged that there was some evidence of mistreatment by Haitian authorities of indefinitely detained people, it determined that Mr. J–E– failed to submit sufficient evidence to show that these isolated instances of mistreatment were so pervasive as to establish a probability that Mr. J–E– would be subjected to torture.

At the circuit court level, only the Second, Third, and Eleventh Circuits have decided cases of Haitian applicants for deferral of removal under CAT who attempted to distinguish *Matter of J–E–*[130] based on their medical or mental health conditions. The Third and Eleventh Circuits have remanded cases where Haitian petitioners with mental or physical illnesses were denied deferral of removal under CAT by the BIA. In both of these cases, the circuit courts reasoned that the IJ and BIA could not merely rubber-stamp the holding in *Matter of J–E–*; rather, the agency was required to determine whether respondents with these physical or mental health issues could distinguish *Matter of J–E–*.[131] The Third Circuit in *Lavira*[132] also suggested that specific intent to cause severe pain and suffering could be proven through evidence of willful blindness by the Haitian government.[133] The Second Circuit upheld the agency's denial of deferral of removal under CAT because the IJ already had made a finding that the respondent presented insufficient evidence that persons with his physical condition would suffer torture in the Haitian prison.[134]

In *Matter of G–A–*,[135] the BIA considered the case of an Iranian Christian citizen of Armenian heritage, Mr. G–A–, who feared torture by the authorities in Iran on account of his religion, his heritage, his lengthy residence in the United States, and because he had a drug trafficking conviction. Mr. G–A– applied for deferral of removal under CAT.

Specifically, the BIA considered that fact that Mr. G–A– was an Armenian Christian who had lived in the United States for over 25 years, and who had a felony conviction for a controlled substance violation. The BIA noted that the evidence supported Mr. G–A–'s claim that the Iranian authorities subject Armenian Christians to harsh discrimination and abuse, and that people with narcotics violations "face particularly severe punishment." Moreover, the BIA noted that the evidence indicated that people like Mr. G–A–, who have lived for a long period of time in the United States, "are perceived to be opponents of the Iranian Government or even Pro-American spies." The BIA noted the widespread use of torture in Iran. Taking this all

---

[130] *Id.*

[131] *Jean-Pierre v. USAG*, 500 F.3d 1315 (11th Cir. 2007); *Lavira v. AG*, 478 F.3d 158 (3d Cir. 2007).

[132] *Lavira v. AG*, *supra* note 131.

[133] *See Lavira*, *supra* note 131; *but see Pierre v. AG*, 528 F.3d 180, 189-91 (3d Cir. 2008) (disagreeing with the *Lavira* court's reasoning that specific intent could be proven through evidence of willful blindness and upholding denial of Convention Against Torture relief to applicant who suffered from physical ailment and feared conditions in Haitian detention).

[134] *Pierre v. Gonzales*, 502 F.3d 109 (2d Cir. 2007).

[135] *Matter of G–A–*, 23 I&N Dec. 366 (BIA 2002).

into consideration, the BIA determined that it was more likely than not Mr. G–A–
would be subject to torture if he were forced to return to Iran.

Establishing Eligibility

Burden of Proof

The regulatory provisions for the burden of proof in CAT cases are found at 8
CFR §208.16(c)(2). The applicant has the burden of establishing eligibility for protection under CAT. He or she must prove it is *more likely than not* that he or she
would be tortured if returned to the proposed country of removal. Credible testimony
alone may sustain the burden of proof. The IJ must consider "all evidence relevant to
the possibility of future torture." This includes, but is not limited to:

- Evidence of past torture;

- Evidence on whether the person could relocate to a safe part of the country;

- Evidence of country conditions; and

- Evidence of "gross, flagrant or mass violations of human rights" in the country.

The evidentiary burden to qualify for CAT protection is substantially similar to the
burden to prove asylum or withholding of removal under current law. The new provisions contained in REAL ID[136] regarding corroboration and credibility also apply to
CAT claims.

In *Matter of J–F–F–*,[137] the BIA held that a Dominican man was not eligible for deferral of removal under CAT because he could not show that it was more likely than not
he would suffer torture. The respondent argued that upon his return to the Dominican
Republic, he might not have been able to take his psychiatric medications, which then
would cause him to become "rowdy." This, then, might lead to his subsequent arrest by
Dominican police, resulting in a likelihood of torture once in jail. The BIA held, however, that an applicant cannot string together a series of suppositions to show that it is
more likely than not that torture will result when the evidence does not show that each
step in the hypothetical chain of events is more likely than not to happen.

Article 3 Withholding or Deferral of Removal

After the IJ decides that a person is entitled to protection under the CAT, he or she
must consider whether any bars prohibit withholding of removal. If a bar applies, the
IJ must grant deferral of removal (8 CFR §208.16 governs withholding and 8 CFR
§208.17 governs deferral of removal). The mandatory bars to Article 3 withholding
are the same as the bars in current withholding law. These are contained in INA
§241(b)(3)(B), and include the following:

- Persecutors of others;

- Persons convicted of a particularly serious crime;

---

[136] REAL ID, *supra* note 2.

[137] *Matter of J–F–F–*, 23 I&N Dec. 912 (BIA 2006).

- Persons who pose a danger to the community or to the security of the United States; and

- Persons about whom there are serious reasons to believe they have committed a serious non-political crime outside the United States.

If one of the bars applies to a person otherwise eligible for CAT protection, the IJ must grant deferral of removal. Deferral is an extremely limited protection that is subject to termination. The IJ must notify the person that deferral does not confer any lawful or permanent immigration status. Furthermore, it does not mean the person will be released from custody, and the status may be terminated at any time if the IJ finds there is no longer a likelihood of torture in the person's country.[138] However, persons who are granted deferral of removal who cannot be removed to any third country cannot be detained indefinitely, and are subject to the post-final order of removal custody determination process detailed in 8 CFR §§241.13–14.

Termination of deferral is an easy process for ICE and a difficult one for the person granted deferral to defend against. ICE may file a motion to schedule a hearing on whether deferral should be terminated. There is no time or number limit on the motions ICE may file. The IJ must grant the motion if it is accompanied by "evidence that is relevant to the possibility that the foreign national would be tortured ... that was not presented at the previous hearing." The IJ will notify the person of the hearing, and the person must prove again, for a de novo review by the IJ, that he or she is more likely than not to be tortured if removed to his or her country. If deferral is terminated, the person may appeal to the BIA.[139]

Procedures

In general, the procedures to determine whether a person is eligible for CAT protection track the asylum procedures. There are provisions in the law on *reasonable fear* determinations.[140]

Persons Arriving at a Port of Entry

Persons who present false or no documents at the border, or within 100 miles of the border, within 14 days of entry are subject to expedited removal proceedings.[141] In general, the review of eligibility for relief under CAT follows the same process as the review of asylum and withholding cases. If the person indicates a fear of persecution or torture during the expedited removal process, he or she will be referred for a credible fear interview by an asylum officer (AO). If the AO finds credible fear, the person is referred for a §240 removal proceeding. If the AO finds there is no credible fear, the person may request a review by the IJ, and the IJ will review the decision de novo. If the IJ finds no credible fear, the person will be removed (per INA §235(b)(1)(B)(iii)(1)), with no further review of the decision. If the IJ determines a

---

[138] 8 CFR §208.17(b)(1).

[139] 8 CFR 208.17(d).

[140] 8 CFR §208.31.

[141] INA §235(b)(1).

credible fear exists, the IJ will place the person in §240 removal proceedings. The process is slightly different for stowaways.

Persons in Removal Proceedings

The IJ's consideration of a request for CAT protection is described above. For the most part, consideration of the new protection from torture fits into the existing process for asylum and withholding. The applicant for asylum and withholding also will be considered for CAT protection if he or she requests such consideration, or if the evidence indicates he or she may be tortured. Asylum applicants who filed on or after April 1, 1997, and are ineligible for asylum due to the one-year filing deadline now will be considered for both types of withholding. In addition, the provision at 8 CFR §208.16(e) states that asylum will be reconsidered in some cases if it was denied for discretionary reasons and the person is later granted CAT withholding. This is significant because a spouse or minor child cannot join a person who is granted only withholding.

Persons Who Apply Affirmatively for Asylum and Withholding

Applicants who are present in the United States, not in deportation or removal proceedings, and apply for asylum are interviewed first by an AO. If the AO finds the person is ineligible for asylum, the case is referred to an IJ. The AO will not reach the question of whether the applicant is eligible for withholding unless the person otherwise is eligible for asylum, but subject to the 1,000 cap in family planning cases.

Persons Ordered Removed or Those Who Had Final Orders of Removal Before March 22, 1999

This group includes persons who were ordered removed by the IJ and appealed to the BIA, or persons who have a final order from the IJ or the BIA. Such persons had 90 days from March 22, 1999, to move to reopen their cases for CAT relief, under more generous reopening provisions. In general, the motions had to comply with the regulations on reopening in 8 CFR §§1003.23 and 1003.2. However, the usual time and numerical limits regarding the motions did not apply, nor did the requirement to demonstrate that the evidence was unavailable at the previous hearing. The motion had to include evidence of a prima facie case for eligibility. A motion to reopen under these provisions was due by June 21, 1999.

Nothing in the CAT regulations prohibits a person from moving to reopen under the regular, more limited reopening procedures.

Persons Who Had CAT Cases Pending with Legacy INS on or Before March 22, 1999

If legacy INS had not yet decided the case by March 22, 1999, it was required to provide a notice to persons affected, telling them they must file a motion to reopen with the IJ or the BIA. The notice gave the person a 30-day stay of removal. The motion to reopen for the limited purpose of Article 3 withholding or deferral was not subject to the §§1003.2 and 1003.23 limitations on motions to reopen. The motion was to be granted if it was accompanied by the notice from legacy INS about this procedure, or accompanied by other proof that the person filed for CAT relief prior to March 22, 1999. The filing of the motion extended the stay of removal during the pendency of the motion.

To avoid execution of any final order of removal, a person who had a CAT case pending on March 22, 1999, was required to file the motion to reopen within 30 days of receiving the notice from legacy INS.

Persons Whose Previous Removal Order Is Reinstated and Persons Who Are Not LPR Aggravated Felons

The regulations created a *reasonable fear* process that applies to persons ordered removed under INA §238(b), which governs expedited removal of non-LPR aggravated felons, and persons whose removal is reinstated under INA §241(a)(5), which governs persons who re-entered after a removal order. It applies to the new CAT cases and to persons with CAT cases pending on March 22, 1999.[142] ICE is required to inform a person subject to §§238(b) or 241(a)(5) of his or her right to apply for withholding or deferral of removal if there is a fear of torture or persecution.

A person in one of these proceedings who indicates a fear of torture or persecution will be referred to an AO for a reasonable fear determination. The determination should be made within 10 days of the referral. The reasonable fear interview is set up much like a credible fear interview in that :

- It is a nonadversarial procedure;
- The AO must be sure the person understands the process;
- A lawyer may be present;
- An interpreter may be present if necessary; and
- The AO will issue a written record.

A reasonable fear is established if there is a reasonable possibility that a person would be tortured, or that he or she would be persecuted on account of one of the five enumerated grounds.[143]

If the AO finds there is a reasonable fear, the case is referred to the IJ for adjudication within 10 days to determine whether the person is eligible for withholding of removal. The IJ's decision can be appealed to the BIA.

If the AO finds there is no reasonable fear, the person may appeal to the IJ. If the IJ agrees with the AO, the person is removed. If the IJ believes there is reasonable fear, the person may submit a Form I-589 application, and the IJ will adjudicate the withholding of removal eligibility. At that point, the IJ's decision on whether to grant withholding or deferral of removal is appealable to the BIA. This is very similar to the current process for persons who undergo credible fear determinations.

---

[142] 8 CFR §208.31.
[143] 8 CFR §208.31.

Persons Who Are Subject to Administrative Removal per INA §235(c)

INA §235(c) governs removal procedures for persons who are inadmissible on security or related grounds. If a person in these proceedings requests Article 3 protection, ICE will "assess the applicability of Article 3" to ensure that a removal order would not violate the obligations of the United States under CAT. There is no review by an IJ, AO, or the BIA. Those who already have a §235(c) removal order may be considered for deferral under the new regime. However, they will not be able to request a review by an IJ.

Diplomatic Assurances

The CAT interim rule contains a provision that would allow the State Department to obtain assurances from the government of a country that it will not torture a person returned by the United States. The AG, the AG's deputy, or the top immigration officer then may decide to remove a person to that country. There would be no consideration of the matter by an IJ, AO, or the BIA.[144]

---

[144] 8 CFR §208.18(c).

CHAPTER TEN
VOLUNTARY DEPARTURE

Voluntary departure is a form of relief from removal that allows a respondent to leave the United States on his or her own, rather than under a removal order. U.S. Immigration and Customs Enforcement (ICE), prior to instituting removal proceedings, or the Immigration Judge (IJ), at the beginning or end of removal proceedings, may grant voluntary departure in lieu of ordering the respondent removed from the United States.

Voluntary departure carries a number of benefits. First, because it is not a removal order, leaving the United States under voluntary departure does not result in inadmissibility for 10 years under Immigration and Nationality Act (INA)[1] §212(a)(9)(A). In addition, since it is not a removal order, voluntary departure does not subject a person to reinstatement of removal, should that person subsequently enter the United States unlawfully. Finally, voluntary departure allows the individual to leave on his or her own, avoiding the stigma of deportation. Persons who most benefit from a grant of voluntary departure in lieu of removal are those who ultimately will have to travel abroad to obtain their immigrant visas because they do not qualify for adjustment of status.

On the other hand, if the respondent is granted voluntary departure and does not leave in a timely manner, there are significant negative consequences, outlined below. Because of these consequences, voluntary departure should be requested only when a respondent truly is willing to leave the United States.

The statutory requirements for voluntary departure are found at INA §240B, and the regulations are found at 8 Code of Federal Regulations (CFR) §240.25 and 8 CFR §1240.26.

Requirements

The requirements for voluntary departure vary significantly, depending on when it is granted. It may be granted by ICE prior to the institution of removal proceedings, or by the IJ at the beginning of proceedings. Alternatively, it may be granted by the IJ at the conclusion of the proceedings.

Note that voluntary departure at the beginning of removal proceedings is not available to *arriving aliens*,[2] although ICE or the IJ may allow them to withdraw their applications for admission under INA §235(a)(4). There is nothing in the statutory

---

[1] Immigration and Nationality Act of 1952 (INA), Pub. L. No. 82-414, 66 Stat. 163, (codified as amended at 8 USC §§1101 *et seq.*).

[2] INA §240B(a)(4).

section governing voluntary departure at the conclusion of proceedings, however, preventing *arriving aliens* from applying.[3] In order to apply for voluntary departure at the conclusion of removal proceedings, the respondent must have been physically present in the United States for a period of at least one year immediately preceding the application for voluntary departure.[4]

Prior to the Conclusion of Removal Proceedings

For voluntary departure granted by ICE prior to institution of removal proceedings or by the IJ at the commencement of proceedings, the individual must be able to pay his or her own way out of the country. The individual also must not be deportable as an aggravated felon under INA §237(a)(2)(A)(iii), or under the terrorist deportation grounds at INA §237(a)(4)(B). In addition, for a grant of voluntary departure by the IJ at the commencement of proceedings, the respondent must concede removability, make no other requests for relief from removal, and waive appeal of all issues. Moreover, voluntary departure is a discretionary form of relief, so that the respondent also must present evidence of favorable discretionary factors, and try to minimize or explain negative discretionary factors.[5]

ICE and the IJ may grant a maximum of 120 days voluntary departure, if granted prior to completion of proceedings. The respondent may be required to post a departure bond, but this is not mandatory.

Once ICE issues the voluntary departure grant, the respondent must present his or her passport or other travel documentation to ICE for inspection, copying, and verification of validity. The requirements for presentation of travel documents for voluntary departure granted by the IJ prior to completion of removal proceedings are stringent. In this situation, if the respondent does not have the required travel documents, voluntary departure is granted subject to the condition that the respondent must secure the documents and present them to the ICE within 60 days. ICE may extend that period. If the documentation is not secured and presented within the 60-day period (or within any authorized extension), the voluntary departure order vacates automatically, and the alternate order of removal takes effect.[6]

At the Conclusion of Removal Proceedings

The requirements for voluntary departure granted by an IJ at the conclusion of removal proceedings are more onerous than the requirements for voluntary departure granted prior to the completion of proceedings. In order to obtain post-hearing voluntary departure, applicants must establish each of the following:

- The applicant has been physically present in the United States for a period of at least one year prior to the initiation of removal proceedings;

---

[3] *See* INA §240B(b).

[4] INA §240B(b)(1).

[5] *Matter of Arguelles*, 22 I&N Dec. 811 (BIA 1999).

[6] 8 CFR §1240.26(b)(3).

- The applicant has been a person of good moral character for at least five years prior to their application for voluntary departure;

- The applicant is not deportable as an aggravated felon or terrorist; and

- The applicant has established by clear and convincing evidence that he or she has the means to depart the United States and intends to do so.[7]

Voluntary departure at the conclusion of removal proceedings may be granted for no more than 60 days. The statute requires the respondent to post a voluntary departure bond to ensure that he or she complies with the grant of voluntary departure. If this voluntary departure bond is not posted with ICE within five business days of the IJ's order granting voluntary departure, the voluntary departure order is vacated automatically, and the alternate order of deportation takes effect on the following day.[8]

– Jaime has been in the United States for 12 years, after crossing the border without inspection. He is in removal proceedings based on inadmissibility. The IJ finds that he is removable, and Jaime applies for relief from removal in the form of Cancellation of Removal Part B. In the alternative, in the event that the IJ denies his application for cancellation, he applies for voluntary departure.

Had Jaime not been in the United States for a year or more, he would have been eligible only for pre-hearing voluntary departure, and a decision to contest removability and apply for relief from removal in the form of cancellation would have meant foregoing the opportunity to apply for voluntary departure.

**Negative Consequences for Failure to Timely Depart
Under a Grant of Voluntary Departure**

Under current law, there are three negative consequences for failing to depart by the designated voluntary departure date:

- First, the IJ is required by regulation to issue an alternate order of removal, so that, if the respondent does not leave by the designated date, the voluntary departure order automatically converts to a removal order, thus raising the inadmissibility ground of INA §212(a)(9)(A).

- Second, the statute provides that a person who fails to depart by the designated date shall be subject to a civil penalty of not more than $1,000 and not more than $5,000.

- Third, under INA §240B(d), a person who fails voluntarily to depart timely is ineligible for a period of 10 years for several types of relief:
  – voluntary departure;
  – cancellation of removal;

---

[7] INA §240B(b).
[8] 8 CFR §1240.26(c)(3).

- adjustment of status;
- registry; and
- change of nonimmigrant status.

There is no requirement that the 10 years be spent outside the United States. The order permitting the foreign national to depart voluntarily must inform the foreign national of these penalties. These penalties apply regardless of whether the voluntary departure is granted by ICE or the IJ.

- Tsip was placed in removal proceedings. At the end of the proceedings, in September 1, 2002, the IJ granted voluntary departure until November 1, 2002. Tsip has not left, and is now married to a U.S. citizen (USC). Is Tsip eligible to adjust status on the basis of an approved I-130 relative visa petition?

Tsip's advocate should first check to see whether the required notices were provided to Tsip and the proper procedures were followed. If not, it may be possible to argue that it is unfair to impose the penalties upon him.

If Tsip was given the proper notices and proper procedures were followed, however, he probably is not eligible for adjustment at this time. Because Tsip was granted voluntary departure under the law currently in effect, he is ineligible for the listed forms of relief, including adjustment of status, for 10 years. Tsip's failure to comply with the voluntary departure order does not bar him from obtaining a visa through consular processing, but, since the

> **PRACTICE TIP**
> **Voluntary Departure and Post–Sept. 11 Detainees**:
> Some advocates report that clients detained after Sept. 11, 2001 have been granted voluntary departure, but that FBI security checks take so long that the voluntary departure period has expired before they are able to leave the United States. Some ICE offices have assured advocates that the detainees' files are marked showing they left under voluntary departure. Advocates should attempt to document the reasons for overstaying voluntary departure and to obtain something in writing from ICE confirming that the client left under voluntary departure.

voluntary departure order converted to an order of removal when Tsip did not leave, he will not be able to obtain a visa until his INA §212(a)(9)(A) inadmissibility period has expired (10 years after his departure or removal), unless an immigration officer grants him advance permission to reapply before that period ends.

Paradoxically, if Tsip had not requested voluntary departure and instead had been ordered removed from the United States, he would not have incurred the statutory bar to adjustment of status caused by failure to comply with voluntary departure, and might have been able to reopen his removal proceedings in order to apply for adjustment of status.

The current penalties for failing to comply with an order of voluntary departure became effective on April 1, 1997. Note that the Violence Against Women and Department of Justice Reauthorization Act of 2005 (VAWA)[9] provisions include an ex-

[9] Violence Against Women and Department of Justice Reauthorization Act of 2005, Pub. L. No. 109-162, 119 Stat. 2960 (2006).

ception to some of these penalties for VAWA self-petitioners, VAWA cancellation applicants, and VAWA suspension applicants who can demonstrate that battery or extreme cruelty was at least one central reason for their failure to depart in accordance with a voluntary departure order. Specifically, if such applicants can demonstrate the required connection between the battery/cruelty and the failure to depart, they will not be subject to the civil penalty, nor will they be barred from relief under INA §§240A or 245.[10]

There were two precursors to the current voluntary departure statute. Prior to the effective date of the Immigration Act of 1990 (IMMACT90),[11] which was June 23, 1992, the only penalty for failure to depart by the designated date was the conversion of the voluntary departure order into an order of deportation.

Effective June 23, 1992, under IMMACT90 §545,[12] an individual who was given certain required warnings with a grant of voluntary departure and thereafter failed to depart (for reasons other than because of exceptional circumstances), was ineligible for five years after the scheduled date of departure for relief for several forms of relief, including adjustment of status, registry, change of nonimmigrant status, and voluntary departure. There was no requirement that the time have been spent outside the United States. These penalties under the law in existence between June 23, 1992, and April 1, 1997, applied only if the IJ provided to the respondent written notice (in English and Spanish) and oral notice (either in the respondent's native language or in another language that the respondent understood) of the consequences of overstaying.

– Margarita was placed in deportation proceedings in August 1993, and was granted voluntary departure until October 30, 1993. She has never left. She now is married to a USC, who filed an I-130 relative visa petition for her. U.S. Citizenship and Immigration Services (USCIS) approved the petition. Is Margarita barred from adjustment of status because of her failure to comply with the voluntary departure order?

Probably not. Her voluntary departure order was granted under the law as it existed between June 23, 1992, and April 1, 1997. First, her representative should check the immigration court record to be sure that she was given the required warnings. Even if she was and the penalties were triggered, they only lasted for five years after her scheduled departure—*i.e.*, until October 29, 1998. She no longer is subject to those penalties. It does not matter that she has not left the United States. However, Margarita may adjust status only before the IJ, and must file a motion to reopen requesting that relief. Because the statutory period for filing the motion to reopen has expired, her case may be reopened only if ICE joins in the motion, or if the IJ reopens the case on his or her own motion.

---

[10] *See* INA §240B(d)(2).

[11] Immigration Act of 1990 (IMMACT90), Pub. L. No. 101-649, 104 Stat. 4978.

[12] Codified as INA §242B(e)(2).

Arguments to Avoid the Consequences of a Failure to Depart

As suggested in the examples above, if a foreign national fails to depart by the required date and, thus, possibly triggers the consequences, it is certainly worthwhile to investigate whether there is any argument that the voluntary departure order was in some way invalid. For example, after reviewing the record, it may be possible to argue that the order was invalid because required pre-order or post-order procedures were not followed, or that the foreign national was ineligible for voluntary departure in the first place.[13]

Appeals While the Voluntary Departure Clock Is Ticking

What if the respondent files a timely appeal to the Board of Immigration Appeals (BIA) from the decision of the IJ, and the voluntary departure period expires while the appeal is pending?

Generally, if a voluntary departure period expires while a nonfrivolous appeal is pending, the BIA will reinstate voluntary departure for the same period of time granted by the IJ.[14] Where the BIA finds that the appeal was frivolous, however, it has declined to reinstate voluntary departure.[15]

Persons seeking review in federal court after the BIA's decision also have a difficult decision, because voluntary departure, even if reinstated by the BIA, will expire before most federal cases can be decided. While some federal courts may reinstate a voluntary departure period when issuing their decisions, others will not.[16]

The Effect of a Motion to Reopen Upon a Grant of Voluntary Departure

The U.S. Supreme Court recently decided the effect of filing a motion to reopen on a request for voluntary departure.[17] The Court saw the tension between the voluntary departure provision at INA §240B, and the motion to reopen provision at INA §240(c)(7). Individuals can file a motion to reopen within 90 days of a final removal order, yet individuals who have been granted voluntary departure must depart within 30 or 60 days or risk being ineligible for several forms of relief. Many noncitizens could get a grant of voluntary departure, and during the 60 days following the voluntary departure grant, could become eligible for relief (e.g., adjustment of status based on marriage to a USC). In *Dada v. Mukasey*, the Supreme Court decided to protect an individual's right to file a motion to reopen in that situation. The Supreme Court

---

[13] For suggestions of ways to argue that the consequences of a failure to depart should not apply, *see* the American Immigration Law Foundation's (AILF) practice advisory entitled "Failure to Depart After a Grant of Voluntary Departure: The Consequences and Arguments to Avoid Them" (Feb. 21, 2006), *available at www.ailf.org/lac/lac_pa_topics.shtml.*

[14] *Matter of A-M-*, 23 I&N Dec. 737 (BIA 2005).

[15] *See Matter of Patel*, 19 I&N Dec. 394 (BIA 1986).

[16] For excellent information and tips on preserving the voluntary departure period before a federal circuit court, see AILF's practice advisory entitled "Protecting Voluntary Departure During Court of Appeals Review" (Oct. 25, 2005), *available at www.ailf.org/lac/lac_pa_topics.shtml.*

[17] *Dada v. Mukasey*, 128 S. Ct. 2307 (2008).

stated that a noncitizen must be permitted an opportunity to withdraw a request for voluntary departure, provided that the request is made before the expiration of the departure period. This allowed individuals to file motions to reopen after a voluntary departure grant. If the motion to reopen is granted, the individual is not barred from seeking the underlying relief due to overstaying the voluntary departure period.

Prior to the Supreme Court's holding in *Dada*,[18] the BIA and several circuit courts had considered this tension between the motion to reopen statute and the voluntary departure statute. In *Matter of Shaar*,[19] the respondent filed a motion to reopen during the pendency of the voluntary departure period, seeking the relief of suspension of deportation. Though the motion was filed prior to the expiration of the voluntary departure period, it still was pending at the end of the period. The respondent then failed to depart by the voluntary departure date. The BIA held that "Neither the filing of a motion to reopen to apply for suspension of deportation during the pendency of a period of voluntary departure, nor the Immigration Judge's failure to adjudicate the motion to reopen prior to the expiration of the alien's voluntary departure period constitutes an 'exceptional circumstance' that excused the failure to comply with the voluntary departure order." The BIA found, therefore, that the penalties for failing to comply with a grant of voluntary departure made the respondent ineligible for any of the barred forms of relief, including suspension of deportation.

Although *Matter of Shaar*[20] was decided prior to the April 1, 1997, effective date of INA §242B(d), the BIA continued to apply it. In *Matter of Velarde*,[21] the BIA held that a motion to reopen based on an approved I-130 relative visa petition may be granted by the IJ or BIA to allow the respondent to apply for adjustment of status, as long as certain conditions are met. One of those conditions was that adjustment of status was not precluded under *Matter of Shaar*[22] by the statutory bar caused by failure to comply with a voluntary departure order.

Prior to the Supreme Court's ruling in *Dada*,[23] four circuits had limited significantly the applicability of *Shaar*.[24] The U.S. Court of Appeals for the Ninth Circuit, in *Azarte v. Ashcroft*,[25] was the first circuit to limit *Shaar*'s applicability in post April 1, 1997, cases by concluding that the voluntary departure period was tolled while a motion to reopen was pending if a foreign national had filed a motion for a stay of removal or stay of voluntary departure. In *Barroso v. Gonzales*,[26] a decision issued a few months after *Azarte*,[27] the Ninth Circuit went further and held that the voluntary

[18] *Id.*

[19] *Matter of Shaar*, 21 I&N Dec. 541 (BIA 1996).

[20] *Id.*

[21] *Matter of Velarde*, 23 I&N Dec. 253 (BIA 2002).

[22] *Matter of Shaar, supra* note 19.

[23] *Dada v. Mukasey, supra* note 17.

[24] *Matter of Shaar, supra* note 19.

[25] *Azarte v. Ashcroft*, 394 F.3d 1278 (9th Cir. 2005).

[26] *Barroso v. Gonzales*, 429 F.3d 1195 (9th Cir. 2005).

[27] *Azarte v. Ashcroft, supra* note 25.

departure period was tolled automatically in post–April 1, 1997, cases when a motion to reconsider or a motion to reopen was timely filed. Furthermore, the U.S. Courts of Appeals for the Third, Eighth, and Eleventh Circuits also held that the voluntary departure period would be tolled in post April 1, 1997, cases when timely motions to reopen were filed.[28] The Third Circuit, in *Barrios v. Attorney General*,[29] limited the application of *Matter of Shaar* in deportation cases. However, the U.S. Court of Appeals for the Fifth Circuit, in *Banda-Ortiz v. Gonzales*,[30] the U.S. Court of Appeals for the Fourth Circuit, in *Dekoladenu v. Gonzales*,[31] and the U.S. Court of Appeals for the First Circuit, in *Chedad v. Gonzales*,[32] explicitly rejected the holdings of the Third, Eighth, Ninth, and Eleventh Circuits on this issue, concluding that the filing of a motion to reopen does not automatically toll a period of voluntary departure.

Advocates should carefully consider the merits of the underlying motion to reopen before seeking to withdraw a request for voluntary departure. The Supreme Court in *Dada*[33] decided that the petitioner could not seek a motion to reopen and, if that did not work out, take advantage of the benefits of voluntary departure. If an individual wishes to seek a motion to reopen, he must withdraw his request for voluntary departure before the expiration of the departure period. The Supreme Court did not specifically state whether the filing of a motion to reopen would be construed as an automatic termination of the voluntary departure grant. However, prior to the Supreme Court's decision in *Dada*,[34] the Department of Homeland Security issued a proposed regulation construing the filing of a motion to reopen during the voluntary departure period as an automatic termination of the voluntary departure grant.[35] Moreover, since most motions to reopen are not decided prior to the expiration of the voluntary departure period, advocates should file affirmatively a motion to withdraw a request for voluntary departure if they are also seeking a motion to reopen.[36]

The Application for Voluntary Departure

There is no application form for requesting voluntary departure. When requesting voluntary departure from the IJ at the commencement or the end of removal proceedings, however, it is a good idea to draft a document entitled "Motion for Voluntary Departure," with an index of supporting documents, for presentation to the IJ.

---

[28] *Kanivets v. Gonzales*, 424 F.3d 330 (3d Cir. 2005), *Sidikhouya v. Gonzalez*, 407 F.3d 950 (8th Cir. 2005), *Ugokwe v. U.S. Atty. Gen.*, 453 F.3d 1325 (11th Cir. 2006).

[29] *Barrios v. Attorney General*, 399 F.3d 272 (3rd Cir. 2005).

[30] *Banda- Ortiz v. Gonzales*, 445 F.3d 387 (5th Cir. 2006).

[31] *Dekoladenu v. Gonzales*, 459 F.3d 500 (4th Cir. 2006).

[32] *Chedad v. Gonzales*, 497 F.3d 57 (1st Cir. 2007).

[33] *Dada v. Mukasey, supra* note 17.

[34] *Id.*

[35] *See* 72 Fed. Reg. 67674 (Nov. 30, 2007).

[36] For an excellent discussion of the Supreme Court's decision in *Dada* and how to proceed on cases involving the interplay between voluntary departure and motions to reopen, see AILF's practice advisory entitled "*Dada v. Mukasey* Q&A Preliminary Analysis and Approaches to Consider," (June 17, 2008), *available at www.ailf.org/lac/lac_pa_topics.shtml.*

Establishing Compliance with Voluntary Departure

When a person granted voluntary departure leaves the United States, he or she should keep the airline tickets or other evidence of transportation out of the country, including the travel document with any notations or stamps indicating that they left the United States and entered into another country. In addition, the person should go to the United States consulate in his or her home country as soon as possible after leaving the United States to request confirmation of departure from the United States.

Conclusion

Prior to the Immigration Reform and Immigrant Responsibility Act of 1996,[37] respondents in deportation proceedings routinely requested voluntary departure as a last choice alternative to deportation. As can be seen from the negative consequences of failing to timely depart (described above), however, requesting voluntary departure no longer is a routine or light decision. Only where the respondent is truly willing to leave the United States should voluntary departure be requested, and advocates must explain carefully to respondents who choose to request voluntary departure the negative consequences of failure to depart.

---

[37] Illegal Immigration Reform and Immigrant Responsibility Act of 1996, Pub. L. No. 104-208, div. C, 110 Stat. 3009, 3009-546 to 3009-724.

CHAPTER ELEVEN
NATURALIZATION AS A DEFENSE TO REMOVAL

When a lawful permanent resident (LPR) is served with a notice to appear (NTA), the advocate immediately should consider all potential forms of relief from removal, including naturalization. Surprisingly, an LPR still may be eligible for naturalization even if he or she is removable under the deportability grounds. For example, an LPR convicted of two crimes of moral turpitude (CMT) in 1997 may be removable under the deportability grounds and served with an NTA, but still may be eligible to become a U.S. citizen (USC) because he or she meets all the basic requirements for naturalization. Similarly, an LPR convicted of an aggravated felony in 1989 is removable under Immigration and Nationality Act (INA)[1] §237, but also may still be eligible to naturalize. Thus, naturalization can be a defense to removal.

Prima Facie Eligibility for Naturalization

If an LPR who has been served with an NTA appears to be prima facie eligible for naturalization by meeting the basic requirements set out in INA §§312–337, it may be possible to terminate the LPR's case for naturalization by filing an N-400 application with U.S. Citizenship and Immigration Services (USCIS). To establish a prima facie case for naturalization, a person must demonstrate that he or she:

- Is at least 18 years of age;

- Is an LPR;

- Has resided continuously within the United States for five years;

- Has resided continuously in the United States since the date of application;

- Has been present physically for half of the last five years;

- Has been a person of good moral character for the relevant time period; and

- Adheres to the principles of the U.S. Constitution.

As discussed later in this chapter, because of a new Board of Immigration Appeals (BIA) case—*Matter of Acosta Hidalgo*[2]—the immigration court will not be able to terminate the case for naturalization without a communication of prima facie eligibility for naturalization from the Department of Homeland Security (DHS). Circuit courts that have considered the issue have deferred to the BIA in its decision in *Matter of Acosta Hidalgo*.[3] One circuit court has decided that only DHS can give the re-

---

[1] Immigration and Nationality Act of 1952 (INA), Pub. L. No. 82-414, 66 Stat. 163, (codified as amended at 8 USC §§1101 *et seq.*).

[2] *Matter of Acosta Hidalgo*, 24 I&N Dec. 103 (BIA 2007).

[3] *Id. See also, e.g., Hernandez de Anderson v. Gonzales,* 497 F.3d 927 (9th Cir. 2007); *Sadowski v. Mukasey,* No. 07-1020-ag, 2008 WL 731245 (2d Cir. Mar 18, 2008) (unpublished).

quired communication of prima facie eligibility for naturalization; this court decided that a federal court cannot make this determination.[4] However, it may a good idea to file the N-400 application immediately, especially if the advocate plans to challenge the BIA's ruling in *Matter of Acosta Hidalgo*.

Bars to Establishing Good Moral Character

The good moral character requirement is the most common obstacle to persons in removal proceedings attempting to naturalize. Good moral character is absent if the person fits into any of the categories listed in INA §101(f). More specifically, *if, during the statutory period* (either three or five years before the filing of the N-400, and up until the time of taking the oath of allegiance) the applicant falls into any of the following categories, he or she is unable to establish good moral character and, thus, will be unable to establish prima facie eligibility for naturalization:

- Habitual drunkard;
- Engaged in prostitution;
- Engaged in any other commercial vice, regardless of relation to prostitution;
- Involved in smuggling people into the United States;
- A practicing polygamist;
- Convicted of, or admits to, committing certain acts of moral turpitude;
- Convicted of, or admits to, violating laws relating to controlled substances (except for simple possession of marijuana less than 30 grams);
- Drug trafficking;
- Convicted of two or more offenses for which the aggregate sentence is five years or more;
- Income derived principally from illegal gambling;
- Convicted of two or more gambling offenses;
- Gave false testimony for purposes of obtaining an immigration benefit;
- Been incarcerated for 180 days or more as a result of a conviction; and
- Convicted of an aggravated felony *at any time (but see below)*.

Aggravated Felony Convictions

With the passage of the Illegal Immigration Reform and Immigrant Responsibility Act of 1996 (IIRAIRA)[5] and the subsequent expansion of the list of what constitutes an aggravated felony under the INA, increasing numbers of people have been charged by DHS as aggravated felons and placed in removal proceedings. Since INA §101(f) bars a person from demonstrating good moral character for an aggravated felony

---

[4] *Saba-Bakare v. Chertoff*, 507 F.3d 337 (5th Cir. 2007).

[5] Illegal Immigration Reform and Immigrant Responsibility Act of 1996, Pub. L. No. 104-208, div. C, 110 Stat. 3009, 3009-546 to 3009-724.

conviction *at any time*, such convictions often eliminate naturalization as a defense to removal. However, it is important to note that the aggravated felony language in INA §101(f) was substituted for the former *crime of murder* by the Immigration Act of 1990 (IMMACT90).[6] The amendment became effective as of the date of the enactment of IMMACT90—November 29, 1990. Thus, convictions (other than murder) occurring *before* November 29, 1990, should not be considered aggravated felonies for the purpose of good moral character. As a result, while an LPR with a post–November 29, 1990, aggravated felony conviction is barred statutorily from establishing good moral character and, thus, ineligible for naturalization, it still is possible for an LPR with only a pre–November 29, 1990, aggravated felony conviction (other than murder) to establish good moral character for purposes of naturalization.

Nevertheless, it remains important to remember that if an individual with only a pre–November 29, 1990, aggravated felony conviction has not yet been issued an NTA, it is extremely risky for that individual to apply for naturalization since an aggravated felony conviction at any time is a ground of deportation under INA §237. Filing an application under these circumstances likely will result in an immigration officer discovering the conviction and making the LPR deportable. Also likely is the issuance of an NTA by USCIS, U.S. Customs and Border Protection (CBP), or U.S. Immigration and Customs Enforcement (ICE). However, if an NTA already has been issued, the individual no longer has anything to lose and, as discussed below, may file for naturalization.

Naturalization as a Defense to Removal

Procedure

If an LPR is not per se barred from establishing good moral character and appears otherwise eligible to naturalize, the applicant must file an N-400 application with the USCIS service center having jurisdiction over the applicant's place of residence. The N-400 must be accompanied by the filing fee, fingerprinting fee, and proof of lawful permanent residency. An advantage of filing the application before the NTA is filed with the immigration court is that the practitioner then will be able to ask whichever component of DHS issued the NTA—USCIS, CBP or ICE—to exercise prosecutorial discretion before power shifts to the immigration judge (IJ).

If DHS refuses to exercise prosecutorial discretion in an LPR's favor, advocates should think carefully before spending money to file an N-400 after the NTA has been filed with the immigration court. In *Matter of Acosta Hidalgo*,[7] the BIA took away the power of the immigration court to terminate proceedings for naturalization without a communication of prima facie eligibility from DHS. The filing of the N-400 after an NTA has been issued may be a waste of money if it appears unlikely that DHS will communicate that the LPR is prima facie eligible. However, if the advocate plans to challenge the BIA's decision in *Matter of Acosta Hidalgo*,[8] it is im-

---

[6] Immigration Act of 1990, Pub. L. No. 101-649, 104 Stat. 4978.

[7] *Matter of Acosta Hidalgo*, *supra* note 2.

[8] *Id.*

portant to file the N-400 and move to terminate for naturalization, so that the issues are preserved on appeal.

Of course, in many instances, the practitioner will find that a naturalization application is already on file. In fact, the application itself often is what triggered the issuance of the NTA in the first place. This occurs because, while many LPRs are eligible to naturalize and, in fact, do apply, they still are subject to the grounds of deportability for prior criminal offenses. Thus, applying for naturalization is likely to trigger the deportability ground and result in the naturalization applicant being placed into removal proceedings.

If the USCIS naturalization unit determines that an applicant may be deportable, the operating instructions require that the examiner forward the case to the ICE investigations unit to determine whether to issue an NTA. If an NTA is issued, and the applicant is placed into removal proceedings, USCIS is barred from further considering the application for naturalization.[9] ICE thus has the discretion to allow the naturalization application to proceed or to commence removal proceedings and stay naturalization. If ICE chooses to commence removal proceedings and files the NTA with the immigration court, jurisdiction transfers to the IJ, who must agree to terminate proceedings in order for the naturalization application to be considered again by USCIS. Such termination cannot happen without a communication from DHS that the respondent is prima facie eligible to naturalize.[10] Thus, while the IJ does not have the power to approve an application for naturalization, he or she can terminate removal proceedings to allow USCIS to consider or reconsider such an application.

Prosecutorial Discretion

Where the USCIS naturalization unit finds a naturalization applicant to be deportable and the ICE district office issues an NTA, the advocate should determine immediately whether the applicant is, in fact, eligible to naturalize. If this is the case, and the NTA has not been filed yet with the immigration court, it may be possible to persuade ICE to exercise its *prosecutorial discretion* not to initiate removal proceedings, and to cancel the NTA to allow the applicant to proceed with his or her application for naturalization.

Prosecutorial discretion is the authority of an agency charged with enforcing a law to decide whether to do so. The decision whether to initiate removal proceedings is always an individual determination. There is no *bright line* test, and it is important to develop the facts in advocating for its exercise. Some of the factors ICE will consider in deciding whether to exercise *prosecutorial discretion* include:

- Immigration status;
- Length of residence;
- Criminal history;
- Humanitarian concerns;

---

[9] INA §318.

[10] *See Matter of Acosta Hidalgo, supra* note 2.

- Immigration history;
- Likelihood of removal;
- Likelihood of ICE achieving its enforcement goals by other means;
- Eligibility for relief;
- Effect on future admissibility;
- Cooperation with law enforcement;
- U.S. military service;
- Community involvement; and
- ICE resources.[11]

Where an applicant with convictions that make him or her deportable is eligible to naturalize and can demonstrate good moral character, this would seem like an ideal occasion for ICE to exercise prosecutorial discretion. If the applicant has a criminal record, ICE should look at the circumstances surrounding any convictions and whether the applicant can demonstrate rehabilitation. ICE may be interested in hearing from the applicant's arresting officer or parole officer. ICE is far less likely, however, to exercise prosecutorial discretion with repeat offenders or aggravated felons than in situations where the offender committed a single, isolated offense a long time ago, and has demonstrated rehabilitation.

Termination of Proceedings Under 8 CFR §1239.2(f)

Even when ICE refuses to exercise prosecutorial discretion and places the naturalization applicant into removal proceedings, or when the respondent first applies for naturalization after being placed in proceedings, the respondent still may be eligible for administrative naturalization if proceedings are terminated by the IJ.

Once the NTA is filed with the court, jurisdiction shifts from ICE to the immigration court. The regulations grant the IJ authority to terminate removal proceedings to allow an applicant to proceed to a final hearing on a pending naturalization application.[12] However, this authority was curtailed severely by the BIA's precedent decision in *Matter of Acosta Hidalgo*,[13] which held that an IJ cannot terminate for naturalization under this regulation without a communication from DHS that the respondent is prima facie eligible for naturalization. The regulation at 8 Code of Federal Regulations (CFR) §1239.2(f) provides that:

> "An immigration judge may terminate removal proceedings to permit the respondent to proceed to a final hearing on a pending application or petition for naturalization, when the respondent has established a prima facie eligibility for naturalization and the matter involves exceptionally appealing or humanitarian factors; in every other case, the deportation hearing shall be completed as promptly as possi-

---

[11] *See* INS Memorandum, D. Meissner, "Exercising Prosecutorial Discretion" (Nov. 17, 2000), *published on* AILA InfoNet at Doc. No. 00112702 (*posted* Nov. 27, 2000).

[12] *See* 8 CFR §1239.2(f).

[13] *Matter of Acosta Hidalgo, supra* note 2.

ble notwithstanding the pendency of an application for naturalization during any state of the proceedings."

Thus, to obtain termination on this basis, the respondent must demonstrate three things:

(1) He or she has an application for naturalization pending before USCIS.

> In order to demonstrate that the respondent has a pending application before USCIS, the practitioner should submit a copy of the application to the court, a copy of the receipt notice, and any evidence that the application is still pending. If USCIS issues a quick denial of the application—and it often does under INA §318 when the applicant is placed in removal proceedings—the practitioner should submit evidence that this decision was appealed timely to USCIS using Form N-336 (discussed below) and that the appeal still is pending.

(2) He or she *is* prima facie eligible for naturalization and has an affirmative communication from DHS attesting to such eligibility.

> In order to establish prima facie eligibility for naturalization, the practitioner should submit evidence to DHS showing that the respondent meets the basic eligibility requirements discussed above, set out at INA §312–337. For example, if the respondent has any criminal convictions, the advocate should submit evidence establishing that such convictions do not bar him or her from establishing good moral character. To illustrate, if the respondent has a pre-1990 aggravated felony conviction, the practitioner should submit a certified copy of the record of conviction showing that the date of conviction was before November 29, 1990.

(3) He case involves exceptionally appealing or humanitarian factors.

> In order to establish the existence of exceptionally appealing or humanitarian factors, the advocate should submit all evidence of any good works by the respondent, or particular hardships the respondent and/or his or her family have faced or are currently facing. For example, if the respondent is a pillar of the community, affidavits from employers, associates, and community leaders should be submitted to the court. If the respondent has a USC child with a medical condition requiring specialized care, letters from treating physicians discussing the condition and the need for specialized care should be submitted to the court. Evidence showing that such care either is not available in the respondent's home country, or is prohibitively expensive, also should be submitted when available, along with evidence that the respondent actively is involved in the care of his or her USC child. If the respondent has no other relief available, this also should be presented as a humanitarian factor in favor of termination.

If the IJ is satisfied that these three requirements are met, and there is an affirmative communication of prima facie eligibility from DHS, the IJ simply decides to terminate the respondent's removal proceedings under 8 CFR §1239.2(f). While there is no guarantee that the IJ will terminate proceedings, many practitioners have had success in getting such terminations by establishing that an application for naturalization is pending, clearly establishing prima facie eligibility, and submitting a plethora of evidence establishing exceptionally appealing or humanitarian factors. If the proceedings are terminated by the IJ, the applicant proceeds with the naturalization process before USCIS.

Termination can be an especially important form of relief for those who were convicted of an aggravated felony prior to November 29, 1990. Remember, conviction of an aggravated felony is only a *permanent* bar to establishing good moral character if the conviction occurred on or after November 29, 1990. The only exception to this rule is a conviction for murder, which is a permanent bar to establishing good moral character regardless of the date of conviction. Thus, a person who was convicted of attempted murder on November 28, 1990, has been convicted of an aggravated felony for many purposes, but not for the purpose of the permanent bar to good moral character. As a result, while such a person may be ineligible for many types of relief before the IJ, he or she still may be prima facie eligible for naturalization and, therefore, still may be able to get his or her proceedings terminated under 8 CFR §1239.2(f).

This form of relief also can be critical for those who find themselves deportable on non–aggravated felony grounds but barred from relief like cancellation of removal because of the *stop time* rule, or from INA §212(c) relief because their ground of removability under INA §237 does not have a corresponding ground of inadmissibility.[14] Even if an applicant is eligible for some kind of other relief before the IJ (*e.g.*, INA §212(c) or cancellation of removal), if he or she also is eligible to naturalize, in many circumstances it also would be advisable to seek termination to proceed on a pending application for naturalization. If it is granted, it saves LPRs the stress and aggravation of proceeding on applications for discretionary forms of relief, which may be denied, and also puts LPRs on a faster path to citizenship.[15]

After Termination of Proceedings

After an IJ terminates proceedings under 8 CFR §1239.2(f), the naturalization applicant is sent back to USCIS to complete the naturalization process. If USCIS denies the applicant's naturalization application even after proceedings are terminated, the applicant may file a request for administrative review, within 30 days of the USCIS denial, on Form N-336. Administrative review is basically a second bite at the apple before an USCIS examiner of equal or higher rank than the original hearing officer. It also is a prerequisite to seeking review in federal court. If the administrative review also is denied, the applicant then may seek review of the USCIS denial in district court.[16] The petition for review must be filed in district court in the district in which the applicant resides within 120 days of the USCIS denial of administrative review. The review is de novo, meaning that the court must make its own findings of fact and

---

[14] *See* INA §240A(d)(1); *Matter of Blake*, 23 I&N Dec. 722 (BIA 2005).

[15] For advocates who wish to challenge the BIA's decision in *Matter of Acosta Hidalgo*, see AILF's practice advisory, "Terminating Removal Proceedings to Pursue Naturalization Before DHS: Strategies for Challenging *Matter of Acosta Hidalgo*" (March 18, 2008), *available at www.ailf.org/lac/lac_pa_topics.shtml.*

[16] INA §310(c).

conclusions of law, and must conduct a hearing on the application at the request of the petitioner.

Final Finding of Deportability Bars Naturalization

Once there is a final finding of deportability, however, an applicant cannot be naturalized. It also has been held that a naturalization applicant is not allowed to attack collaterally a final order of deportability in judicial naturalization proceedings before the district court.[17]

---

[17] *See In re Terzich,* 153 F. Supp. 651 (W.D.Pa. 1957).

CHAPTER TWELVE
ADMINISTRATIVE REVIEW OF REMOVAL ORDERS

Overview

There are three major forms of administrative review of adverse decisions of the immigration court in removal proceedings. These are:

- Appeals to the Board of Immigration Appeals (BIA);
- Motions to reopen; and
- Motions to reconsider.

In addition, advocates may ask the BIA to reopen or reconsider its own decisions through a motion to reopen or reconsider.

If administrative review is unsuccessful, the parties may be able to seek review in federal court. In part because of BIA streamlining procedures (discussed below), the number of cases being appealed up through to the federal courts has increased tremendously in spite of various restrictions placed on judicial review by the Anti Terrorism and Effective Death Penalty Act of 1996,[1] the Illegal Immigration Reform and Immigrant Responsibility Act of 1996,[2] and, most recently, the REAL ID Act of 2005.[3]

This chapter discusses administrative review of immigration court decisions through appeals to the BIA. It also focuses on review of both immigration court and BIA decisions through motions to reopen and motions to reconsider. Judicial review in federal courts is the subject of chapter 13.

Appeals to the BIA

The decision of the immigration judge (IJ) may be appealed by either party to the BIA. Form EOIR 26 (Notice of Appeal to the BIA), together with the filing fee or a request for fee waiver, must be filed directly with the BIA in Falls Church, VA, no later than 30 calendar days after the judge's decision.[4] If an individual is going to be represented on appeal, his or her representative also should file form EOIR-27 (Notice of Entry of Appearance before the BIA).[5] There is an automatic stay of removal during the appeal to the BIA.[6]

---

[1] Antiterrorism and Effective Death Penalty Act of 1996, Pub. L. No. 104-132, 110 Stat. 1214.

[2] Illegal Immigration Reform and Immigrant Responsibility Act of 1996, Pub. L. No. 104-208, div. C, 110 Stat. 3009, 3009-546 to 3009-724.

[3] REAL ID Act of 2005, Pub. L. No. 109-13, div. B, 119 Stat. 231, 302–23.

[4] 8 CFR §1003.3; *Matter of Liadov*, 23 I&N Dec. 990 (BIA 2006).

[5] These forms are available online at *www.usdoj.gov/eoir*.

[6] 8 CFR §1003.6(a).

It is customary for the appellant to indicate on the notice of appeal that he or she will be filing a separate brief. Following the BIA's receipt of the record from the immigration court and preparation of a written transcript, the BIA sets a schedule for filing briefs in support of the appeal and reply briefs by U.S. Immigration and Customs Enforcement (ICE). The appellant's brief normally is due 21 days after provision of the transcript of the hearing, but the BIA may extend this time for good cause.[7] The appellee's brief normally is due 21 days after the appellant's brief is filed. For cases involving individuals in custody, the parties are provided 21 days to file simultaneous briefs, unless a shorter period is specified. For detained cases, parties are allowed only one extension of the briefing deadline.

An appeal to the BIA may be dismissed summarily if the appellant fails to identify the reasons for the appeal in the notice of appeal, or if the respondent indicates that he or she will file a brief, but does not.[8] The appellant must specifically identify the findings of fact, the conclusions of law, or both, being challenged. If a question of law is presented, supporting authority must be cited. If the dispute is over the findings of fact, the specific facts contested must be identified. Where the appeal concerns discretionary relief, the appellant must state whether the alleged error relates to statutory grounds of eligibility, or to the exercise of discretion, and must identify the specific factual and legal findings being challenged.[9]

Because of these requirements, it is crucial that notices of appeal to the BIA contain specific reasons for the appeal, and that a brief be filed in accordance with the briefing schedule if it was indicated that a brief would be filed. In the notice of appeal, the advocate should include all possible bases for the appeal, but also should include as the last basis the following sentence: "Such other errors of fact or law or abuse of discretion as may become apparent after a review of the record." Regarding brief due dates, it is customary for the BIA to grant each side one 21-day extension to file their respective briefs if either party so requests in a written motion properly filed before the brief due date.

> **PRACTICE TIP:**
> **The *BIA Practice Manual***
>
> The *BIA Practice Manual* is available on the Executive Office for Immigration Review (EOIR) website at *www.usdoj.gov/eoir*. For a bound copy that you can keep at your fingertips, see AILA's Online Bookstore at *www.ailapubs.org/eoirmanual.html*. This manual provides concise information about practice before the BIA and contains a number of helpful forms.

In addition to the summary dismissal described above, the regulations allow for affirmance of certain USCIS and IJ decisions without an opinion.[10] These *affirmance*

---

[7] 8 CFR §1003.3(c)(1).

[8] 8 CFR §1003.1(d)(2). *But see Esponda v. United States A.G.*, 453 F.3d 1319 (11th Cir. 2006) (holding that the BIA abused its discretion in dismissing an appeal based solely on an alien's failure to submit a brief that the alien indicated would be filed without considering whether or not the notice of appeal adequately identified the reasons for the appeal).

[9] 8 CFR §1003.3(b).

[10] 8 CFR §1003.1(e)(4).

without opinion (AWO) regulations came into effect in 2002 and are troubling. The regulations state that affirmance without an opinion may be done by a single BIA Member, if the BIA member determines that the result reached in the U.S. Citizenship and Immigration Services' (USCIS) or IJ's decision was correct, that any errors in the decision were harmless or nonmaterial, and that either:

- The issue on appeal is controlled squarely by existing BIA or federal court precedent and does not involve the application of precedent to a novel fact situation; or

- The factual and legal questions raised on appeal are so insubstantial that a three-member review is not warranted.

Such an order must not include further explanation or reasoning. Because of this provision, it also is essential that advocates demonstrate, preferably in the notice of appeal and certainly in the written brief to the BIA, that the individual's case does not meet the requirements for affirmance without an opinion.[11]

Motions to Reopen and Motions to Reconsider

Purpose

A motion to reopen is a request to the agency or court that has or last had jurisdiction over the case to rethink a decision because of new information that was not available previously. In immigration practice, it frequently is used to apply for relief that an individual did not qualify earlier for, or to raise new *equities* (*e.g.*, marriage to a USC or a child born in the United States). If a motion to reopen is granted by the BIA, the BIA customarily remands the case to the immigration court for presentation of evidence on the relief being requested. If the motion to reopen is granted by the IJ, the IJ will reopen the proceedings for presentation of evidence on the requested relief.

The purpose of a motion to reconsider is to correct an error of law or re-examine the facts. If a motion to reconsider is granted, the decision-maker, who might be the IJ or BIA, will either affirm (*i.e.*, maintain), modify, or reverse the original decision.

Time and Number Limits

There are both time limits and number limits for motions to reopen and motions to reconsider in removal proceedings. An individual may file one motion to reconsider a decision that he or she is removable, and one motion to reopen his or her removal proceedings.[12] Motions to reconsider orders of removal must be filed within 30 days

---

[11] While all circuit courts have held that the AWO procedures are constitutional, there remain ways to challenge the application of AWO procedures in certain cases. For a detailed discussion of some arguments that remain, see the American Immigration Law Foundation's (AILF) Practice Advisory entitled "Affirmance Without Opinion: What Federal Court Challenges Remain?" (April 27, 2005), *available at www.ailf.org/lac/lac_pa_topics.shtml.*

[12] Immigration and Nationality Act of 1952 (INA), Pub. L. No. 82-414, 66 Stat. 163, (codified as amended at 8 USC §§1101 *et seq.*), §§240(c)(6) and (7).

of the order. Motions to reopen removal proceedings must be filed within 90 days of the final administrative order of removal.[13]

There are several exceptions, however, to these time and numerical requirements for motions to reopen. Some of these exceptions are:

- The time and numerical limitations do not apply to motions to reopen requesting reopening to apply or reapply for asylum, withholding of removal, or relief under the Convention Against Torture and Other Cruel, Inhuman or Degrading Treatment or Punishment[14] based on new evidence of changed circumstances in the applicant's country;[15]

- Where the removal order was entered in absentia, a motion to reopen may be filed within 180 days of the in absentia order, if the applicant demonstrates that the failure to appear was due to exceptional circumstances. A motion to reopen an in absentia removal order may be filed at any time if the individual demonstrates that he did not receive proper notice, or if the individual was detained in federal, or state custody and could not attend;[16]

- The time and numerical limitations do not apply to motions agreed upon by all parties and filed jointly;[17]

- Both the IJ and the BIA may reopen cases sua sponte (*i.e.*, on their own initiative);[18]

- Certain ICE motions to reopen are not be subject to the time and number limits;[19]

- Motions filed before Sept. 30, 1996, do not count against the number limit;

- The time and numerical limitations also do not apply to abused immigrants seeking VAWA[20] cancellation or suspension, provided that they are physically in the United States at the time of filing; and

- Other exceptions may be created by special statutes, case law, directives, or other special legal circumstances.

If a joint motion is necessary in order to get around a time and/or number limitation, a request should be submitted in writing, with copies of all supporting documents, to the ICE district counsel's office that handled the case. A 2001 Immigration

---

[13] *Id.*

[14] Convention Against Torture and Other Cruel, Inhuman or Degrading Treatment or Punishment, Dec. 10, 1984, 1465 U.N.T.S. 85 (entered into force June 26, 1987).

[15] 8 CFR §1003.23(b)(4)(i), 1003.2(c)(3)(ii).

[16] INA §240(b)(5)(C); 8 CFR §§1003.2(c)(3)(i),1003.23(b)(4)(ii), 1003.23(b)(4)(iii)(A). (See Section IV below).

[17] 8 CFR §1003.2(c)(3)(iii), 8 CFR §1000.23(b)(4)(iv).

[18] 8 CFR §§1003.2(a), 1003.23(b).

[19] 8 CFR §1003.2(c)(2), (3).

[20] Violence Against Women and Department of Justice Reauthorization Act of 2005 (VAWA), Pub. L. No. 109-162, 119 Stat. 2960 (2006), modifying INA §240(c)(7)(C)(iv).

and Naturalization Service (legacy INS) memorandum discusses when district counsel should consider joining in a motion to reopen for purposes of adjustment of status. It states, "[t]he INS may join in a motion to reopen (or motion to the BIA to remand) for consideration of adjustment of status pursuant to INA §245 if such adjustment of status was not available to the respondent at the former hearing, the alien is statutorily eligible for adjustment of status, and the respondent merits favorable exercise of discretion."[21]

The regulations state that once a person has departed the United States, he or she may not file a motion to reopen.[22] However, the U.S. Court of Appeals for the Fourth Circuit decided that this regulation did not comport with the statutory language and permitted a motion to reopen to be filed once the individual had been deported.[23] Other courts have allowed motions to reopen filed outside of the United States in certain circumstances.[24]

Content, Format, and Filing Requirements for Motions to Reopen and Motions to Reconsider

A motion to reopen must state the new facts to be provided in the reopened proceeding, and must be supported by affidavits or other documentary evidence.[25] The new evidence must be material and not available, and could not have been discovered or presented at the earlier hearing.[26] If the motion to reopen is for the purposes of giving the respondent an opportunity to apply for any form of discretionary relief, the application for relief must be attached to the motion to reopen,[27] but the fee for the application for relief need not be paid unless the motion to reopen is granted.

A motion to reconsider must state the errors of fact or law that require reconsideration, and must be supported by any pertinent precedent decisions to establish that the decision was based on an incorrect application of law or policy, and that the decision was incorrect based on the evidence of record at the time of the initial decision.[28]

There is no special form for a motion to reopen or motion to reconsider, but advocates should check the *BIA Practice Manual* or the *Immigration Court Practice Man-*

---

[21] *See* INS Memorandum, B. Cooper, "Motions to Reopen for Consideration of Adjustment of Status," (May 17, 2001), *published on* AILA InfoNet at Doc. No. 01070333 (*posted* Jul. 3, 2001).

[22] 8 CFR §§1003.2(d), 1003.23(b)(1); *see also Matter of Armendarez-Mendez*, 24 I&N Dec. 646 (BIA 2008).

[23] *William v. Gonzales*, 499 F.3d 329 (4th Cir. 2007).

[24] *See, e.g., Lin v. Gonzales*, 473 F.3d 979 (9th Cir. 2007); *Contreras-Rodriguez v. AG*, 462 F.3d 1314 (11th Cir. 2006); *Cardoso-Tlaseca v. Gonzales*, 460 F.3d 1102 (9th Cir. 2006); *Singh v. Gonzales*, 412 F.3d 1117 (9th Cir. 2005). For an excellent discussion of the post-departure bar on motions to reopen or reconsider and strategies, see R. Rosenbloom and P. Whitworth, "Filing Post-Departure Motions to Reopen or Reconsider," (Center for Human Rights and International Justice, Boston College, Post-Deportation Human Rights Project), *available at www.bc.edu/postdeportation*.

[25] 8 CFR §§1003.2(c), 1003.23(b)(3).

[26] *Id.*

[27] 8 CFR §§1003.2(c)(1), 1003.23(b)(3).

[28] 8 CFR §§1003.2(b), 1003.23(b)(2).

ual for any special requirements. Both motions should be supported by a brief or memorandum of law.

Both motions to reconsider and motions to reopen should be in the form of a motion and include the following:

- Fee or fee waiver request;

- A statement as to whether the validity of the unfavorable decision has been or is the subject of any judicial proceeding and, if so, the court, nature, date, and status of the proceeding;

- A statement as to whether the applicant is also the subject of any pending criminal proceeding under the Immigration and Nationality Act (INA) and, if so, the current status of that proceeding

- Proof of service on all other parties;

- Form EOIR 27 (Notice of Appearance before the BIA) or Form EOIR 28 (Notice of Appearance before the Immigration Court); and

- A copy of the underlying order.[29]

The filing of a motion to reopen or a motion to reconsider does NOT stay deportation or the execution of any decision in a case. The only motions to reopen that have an automatic stay are VAWA[30] motions to reopen.[31] There is also an automatic stay for motions to rescind in absentia removal orders filed within 180 days of the removal order and where there were exceptional circumstances why the individual did not attend, including the individual having received no notice[32] (See below for a discussion of in absentia removal orders). A stay must be requested specifically, preferably by written motion, from the entity with whom the motion to reopen or reconsider is filed. ICE also may be able to grant a stay.[33]

The BIA has set out the procedure for requesting a stay in its practice manual. The BIA categorizes stay requests into two categories—emergency and non-emergency. Emergency motions may be filed only by an individual in custody who is facing imminent removal, deportation, or exclusion. The BIA instructs persons in such situations, or their advocates, to call (703) 306-0093[34] on weekdays from 9:00 am to 5:30 pm EST, for further instructions requesting an emergency stay. The BIA does not rule immediately on non-emergency stay requests, but instead, considers the request during the normal course of adjudication. A non-emergency stay request may be sup-

---

[29] 8 CFR §§1003.2, 1003.23.

[30] VAWA, *supra* note 20.

[31] INA §240(c)(7)(C)(iv).

[32] INA §240(b)(5)(C).

[33] 8 CFR §1003.2(f).

[34] This telephone number is for emergency stay requests only.

plemented by an emergency stay request, however, if circumstances change so that the person is facing imminent removal, deportation, or exclusion.[35]

Motions to Reopen in Absentia Removal Orders

There are special provisions for reopening in absentia removal cases for the purpose of overturning orders of removal issued in those proceedings.

Under INA §240(b)(5), an IJ must order that the respondent be removed—even if the respondent is absent from the hearing (in absentia)—if ICE establishes by clear, unequivocal, and convincing evidence that:

- The respondent was given written notice of the hearing;
- The respondent is removable; and
- The respondent has been given certain information in writing.

This information, set out at INA §239(a), includes a notice that the respondent must advise ICE and the immigration court in writing of his or her current address and any address changes, and a notice that the court may order the respondent removed in absentia if he or she does not appear for the hearing. If those requirements have not been given in writing to the respondent, then the requirements for an in absentia removal order are not met. These warnings are given in the notice to appear (NTA), the charging document for removal proceedings. A respondent may be removed in absentia even absent the INA §§239(a)(1) or (2) written notices if he or she has not provided the immigration court, (as well as ICE), with his or her address, as required under INA §239(a)(l)(F).[36]

Respondents ordered deported in absentia, other than because of exceptional circumstances, are ineligible for various forms of relief for a period of five years after the date of the final deportation order. These forms of relief are voluntary departure, cancellation of removal, registry, and adjustment or change of status.[37]

Because of these drastic consequences of a failure to appear, counsel must emphasize to each *individual* that he or she must keep USCIS, ICE, the immigration court, the BIA (if the case is on appeal), and counsel apprised of his or her current address. Notices of change of address should be in writing, on Form EOIR-33, and sent to the immigration court or, if the matter is on appeal, the BIA, by certified mail, return receipt requested. A copy also must be sent to the ICE associate district counsel.

The order of removal in absentia can be rescinded only:

- Upon a motion to reopen filed within 180 days of the date of the order of removal, if the individual demonstrates that the failure to appear was because of exceptional circumstances (*e.g.*, serious illness or death of the individual, or his or her spouse, parent, or child); or

---

[35] *See EOIR Immigration Court Practice Manual* (effective July 1, 2008), ch. 8—a short chapter on stays and the format required for a discretionary stay request.

[36] INA §240(b)(5)(B).

[37] INA §240(b)(7).

- Upon a motion to reopen, filed at any time, demonstrating that the individual did not receive notice (as required under INA §§239(a)(1) or (2)), or that the individual was in federal or state custody and the failure to appear was through no fault of his or her own.[38]

In 2006, VAWA[39] added battery and extreme cruelty to the list of exceptional circumstances.

Partly because of historic USCIS delays in adjudicating certain types of administrative applications, it is not at all uncommon that an applicant for some sort of USCIS benefit (*e.g.*, asylum) may have moved to a new address by the time USCIS adjudicates the application. If the NTA is sent to that last address, the individual no longer may be living there and, thus, will not receive the NTA. The individual may be surprised and horrified to learn—perhaps through a Freedom of Information Act[40] request or other investigation by his or her advocate, or perhaps when he or she is picked up and deported by ICE—that he or she has a removal order, despite not being present at the hearing.

In this sort of situation, the advocate should investigate whether the in absentia proceedings may be reopened. In two precedent decisions, the BIA held that, if ICE elects to serve the NTA with its required warnings to the last address it has for the respondent, the service constitutes the required INA §239(a) notice if the respondent actually received the notice, or can be charged with receiving the notice. Furthermore, the respondent can be charged with receiving the notice if it is sent to the correct address, but fails to reach the respondent through some failure in the internal workings of the household. If the respondent actually received or can be charged with receiving the notice, then in absentia proceedings may be held.[41]

If the respondent did not actually receive the NTA and the notice of hearing it contains, and cannot be charged with receiving the notice, then the respondent cannot be on notice of either removal proceedings or the address obligations particular to removal proceedings. In this case, the entry of an in absentia order is precluded.[42] If the respondent who fails to appear for a hearing, however, does not argue that the notice was sent to the incorrect address, or that the postal service did not deliver it, service of the NTA to the last address provided is sufficient to satisfy the INA §239(a) notice requirements.[43] The government in *Matter of G–Y–R–*[44] argued that

---

[38] INA §240(b)(5)(C).

[39] VAWA, *supra* note 20.

[40] Freedom of Information Act, 5 USC §552, as amended by Pub. L. No. 104-231, 110 Stat. 3048.

[41] *Matter of G–Y–R–*, 23 I&N Dec. 181 (BIA 2001); *Matter of M–D–*, 23 I&N Dec. 540 (BIA 2002).

[42] *Matter of G–Y–R–*, *supra* note 41 (NTA sent to address given by respondent in an asylum application that was several years old and in which the INS took some 16 years after filing the application before sending a notice of the asylum interview).

[43] *Matter of M–D–*, *supra* note 41 (NTA sent by certified mail, which was not claimed by respondent; no argument that address was incorrect or that postal service did not notify him that he had a certified letter).

[44] *Matter of G–Y–R–*, *supra* note 41.

the INA §265(a) requirement of notification to the attorney general of address changes meant that an NTA sent to the last address provided by the individual supports an in absentia removal order. The BIA did not agree, noting that an in absentia removal order is not one of the penalties imposed for failure to comply with that registration requirement.

In *Matter of M–R–A–*,[45] the BIA held that a respondent did not receive proper notice of his hearing. The BIA held that because notices of hearing need not be sent by certified mail, there was a weak presumption of delivery of the notice, which the respondent overcame. The BIA distinguished its holding in *Matter of Grijalva*[46] and *Matter of M–D–*;[47] stating that these cases were decided when all notices of hearings were required to be sent by certified mail, which created a stronger presumption of delivery. The BIA in *Matter of M–R–A–*[48] held that a respondent can rebut the weaker presumption of delivery by regular mail by presenting evidence, which could include, but was not limited, to the following:

- Respondent's affidavit;

- Affidavits from family members or others knowledgeable about the facts relevant to whether notice was received;

- Respondent's actions upon learning of the in absentia order and whether due diligence was exercised to redress the situation;

- Any prior affirmative application for relief, indicating that respondent had an incentive to appear;

- Any prior application for relief filed with the immigration court or prima facie evidence of eligibility for such relief;

- Respondent's previous attendance at immigration court hearings, if applicable; and

- Any other circumstances or evidence indicating possible nonreceipt of notice.

Advocates who wish to reopen an in absentia removal order should read carefully the BIA's decision in *Matter of M–R–A–*[49] and follow the BIA's suggestions on how to overcome any presumption that the respondent received notice of his hearing.

Importantly, the stringent requirements for a motion to reopen an in absentia order do not need to be met in cases where an individual did not receive oral warnings as to the consequences of a failure to appear at his or her hearing, and is now eligible for a form of relief that was unavailable at time of the hearing in which the in absentia order was entered.[50] In such cases, an individual can move to reopen his or her case

---

[45] *Matter of M–R–A–*, 24 I&N Dec. 665 (BIA 2008).

[46] *Matter of Grijalva*, 21 I&N Dec. 27 (BIA 1995).

[47] *Matter of M–D–*, *supra* note 41.

[48] *Matter of M–R–A–*, *supra* note 45.

[49] *Id.*

[50] *See Matter of M–S–*, 22 I&N Dec. 349 (BIA 1998); *see also* INA §240(b)(7).

under the regular motion to reopen rules, though a joint motion may be required if it is beyond the 90-day time limit for regular motions to reopen.

Conclusion

Appeals to the BIA, motions to reopen, and motions to reconsider provide three important means of administrative review. Advocates must be careful to comply with the number, timing, and content requirements of each.

JUDICIAL REVIEW OF REMOVAL ORDERS

Individuals who receive final orders of removal often wish to seek judicial review of these orders in federal court. Unfortunately, the Anti-Terrorism and Effective Death Penalty Act of 1996 (AEDPA),[1] the Illegal Immigration Reform and Immigrant Responsibility Act of 1996 (IIRAIRA),[2] and, most recently, the REAL ID Act of 2005 (REAL ID),[3] have severely restricted judicial review of deportation and removal cases. Judicial review of deportation and removal orders is an extremely complex area of the law. With the recent passage of REAL ID, there are many questions regarding what types of cases may receive judicial review. Litigation to interpret REAL ID no doubt will make its way through the courts for years to come. For this reason, the immigration practitioner must thoroughly research the current case law in the particular circuit where an individual seeks review of a final order or other government decision or action.

The purpose of this final chapter is to update the immigration practitioner on some basic developments in this area and to provide a framework for analyzing what remedies may remain for individuals in the federal courts. Due to the complexity of this area of the law and unresolved questions about how REAL ID will be interpreted and implemented, it is advisable to consult with experienced practitioners when considering a federal court challenge.[4]

Judicial Review Before 1996 Changes

Until passage of IIRAIRA,[5] §106 of the Immigration and Nationality Act (INA)[6] had been the *sole and exclusive* procedure for judicial review of deportation and exclusion orders since 1961. The purpose of this provision was to minimize delays in deportation cases by replacing district court review of BIA decisions with review before the appropriate U.S. court of appeals. Orders of exclusion, however, still were reviewed in habeas corpus proceedings in district court. Furthermore, if the noncitizen was in custody, he or she could seek judicial review of the deportation order by

---

[1] Antiterrorism and Effective Death Penalty Act of 1996, (AEDPA) Pub. L. No. 104-132, 110 Stat. 1214.

[2] Illegal Immigration Reform and Immigrant Responsibility Act of 1996 (IIRAIRA), Pub. L. No. 104-208, div. C, 110 Stat. 3009, 3009-546 to 3009-724.

[3] REAL ID Act of 2005, Pub. L. No. 109-13, div. B, 119 Stat. 231, 302–23.

[4] For more information on REAL ID's impact on judicial review, *see* the American Immigration Law Foundation's (AILF) Legal Action Center at *www.ailf.org/lac/lac_pa_topics.shtml*.

[5] IIRAIRA, *supra* note 2.

[6] Immigration and Nationality Act of 1952 (INA), Pub. L. No. 82-414, 66 Stat. 163, (codified as amended at 8 USC §§1101 *et seq.*).

filing a petition for habeas corpus (which literally translates as "having body") in district court.

Judicial Review Under the Transitional Rules

Although INA §106 was repealed by IIRAIRA,[7] it remained in effect for certain *transitional cases*. Transitional cases were generally deportation and exclusion cases that commenced prior to April 1, 1997—the effective date of IIRAIRA. These cases were subject to the *transitional rules*.[8]

Transitional rules instituted a number of dramatic new provisions, including:

- Direct review of exclusion orders in the court of appeals, and resulting shortened 30-day filing deadline;

- A requirement that cases be filed in the circuit where immigration court proceedings were completed;

- Discretionary decisions barred from judicial review;

- Service of the petition for review no long stayed the noncitizen's deportation without a separate order to that effect;

- Appeal not permitted for noncitizens inadmissible or deportable for having committed certain crimes;

- The court of appeals could not order the taking of additional evidence; and

- The noncitizen's departure from the United States would result in the federal court losing jurisdiction of the case.

Judicial Review of Removal Orders After Passage of REAL ID

Overview

REAL ID was signed into law on May 11, 2005, and became effective on that date. The provisions of REAL ID apply to final orders of removal, deportation, and exclusion issued before, on, or after the enactment date. Thus, REAL ID modifies the transitional rules for cases—commenced prior to April 1, 1997—resulting in final orders, and directs that habeas petitions filed under the transitional rules *shall* be treated as if filed as a petition for review under REAL ID.

Judicial review occurs in one of two levels of courts—either the federal district court or the circuit court of appeals. REAL ID changes prior law by eliminating habeas corpus review of final orders in the district court, and transferring jurisdiction directly to the circuit court of appeals, thereby eliminating one step in the review process. It expands judicial review somewhat, by allowing a petition for review in circuit court of some previously non-reviewable cases and issues (*i.e.,* asylum denials based on the one-year filing deadline). It completely eliminates judicial review of some types of cases—*e.g.*, certain mandamus or *all writs* actions.

---

[7] IIRAIRA, *supra* note 2.

[8] INA §106 as amended by IIRAIRA §309(c).

Habeas Corpus in District Courts

Habeas Corpus Prior to REAL ID

According to 28 USC §2241, a district court in habeas proceedings has jurisdiction to review whether a person is "in custody in violation of the Constitution or laws or treaties of the United States." The suspension clause of the Constitution states that "[t]he Privilege of the Writ of Habeas Corpus shall not be suspended, unless when in Cases of Rebellion or Invasion the public Safety may require it." Historically, the writ of habeas corpus has been a means of reviewing the legality of detention by the executive branch of government. Going back as far as the case of *Ex parte Yerger*,[9] federal courts were required by the Constitution to grant habeas review of all cases "not plainly excepted by law."

The passage of IIRAIRA[10] and AEDPA[11] in 1996 appeared to preclude habeas corpus review of removal orders based on criminal grounds (under INA §242), although review of questions of law, and questions of mixed law and fact, was, arguably, still available. Subsequently, the U.S. Supreme Court decided in the cases of *INS v. St. Cyr*[12] and *Calcano-Martinez v. INS*[13] that the 1996 laws did not preclude habeas corpus review of removal orders based on prior aggravated felony convictions. This led to a flurry of federal cases and an eventual split in the circuit courts over the scope of review and the types of issues reviewable for removal orders based on criminal grounds.

REAL ID purports to moot the question of habeas availability under IIRAIRA and AEDPA by eliminating specifically *all* habeas corpus review (under 28 USC §2241) of final orders of removal, deportation, and exclusion. Congress amended seven subsections of INA §242 to include an explicit restriction on review by habeas corpus. Congress left alone, however, habeas corpus review challenging the actual detention of a noncitizen.

Habeas Petitions Pending Prior to REAL ID

Persons who filed habeas petitions under 28 USC §2241 in district court, prior to the enactment of REAL ID, will have their cases transferred to the court of appeals for the circuit in which a petition for review could have been filed (*i.e.,* the circuit having jurisdiction over the place the IJ completed proceedings). Section 106(c) of the uncodified provisions of REAL ID states that the district court shall transfer such cases (or the part of such cases) that challenge a final order of removal, deportation, or exclusion. Likewise, habeas petition cases that were filed under the prior INA §106(a) pursuant to the old transitional rules will be treated as if filed as a petition for review under amended INA §242.

---

[9] *Ex parte Yerger*, 8 Wall 85, 102 (1869).

[10] IIRAIRA, *supra* note 2.

[11] AEDPA, *supra* note 1.

[12] *INS v. St. Cyr*, 533 U.S. 289 (2001).

[13] *Calcano-Martinez v. INS*, 533 U.S. 348 (2001).

The court of appeals must treat the transferred case as if it was filed as a petition for review, with one exception: the requirement that a petition for review must be filed within 30 days of the final removal order does not apply to these transferred cases. This means that a habeas petition that challenged a final order pending prior to REAL ID will be transferred to the court of appeals, even if the habeas petition was not filed within 30 days of the final removal order. However, the 30-day deadline applies to all petitions for review challenging post–REAL ID final orders. For cases not pending prior to REAL ID, failure to file a petition for review within 30 days of the final removal order will result in the inability to obtain any judicial review.[14]

Habeas petitions that do not challenge a final order should remain in the district court. This would include, for example, a case challenging detention alone. Other pending habeas cases may involve review of the legality of both a final order and of the person's detention. In these cases, only the part of the case challenging the final order should be transferred.

Habeas Challenges to Detention

REAL ID does not address detention challenges. The legislative history of REAL ID provides that the habeas jurisdiction-stripping provisions were not intended to apply to challenges to detention that are independent of challenges to removal orders. In *INS v. St. Cyr*,[15] the Supreme Court stated that "[t]he writ of habeas corpus has always been available to review the legality of executive detention." Several circuit courts have ruled that REAL ID did not eliminate habeas jurisdiction of challenges to detention.[16] Therefore, practitioners should continue to pursue habeas challenges to unlawful detention.

Petitions for Review in the Courts of Appeals

Petitions for Review After REAL ID

REAL ID amendments require that all challenges to final orders of removal, deportation, or exclusion must be filed in the appropriate court of appeals via a petition for review. The Act adds a new section, INA §242(a)(5), which states that a petition for review "shall be the sole and exclusive means for judicial review of an order of removal." The only exception pertains to review of an order of expedited removal under INA§242(e), which permits only a very narrow scope of review in habeas corpus proceedings. REAL ID expands court of appeals jurisdiction to cover most of the habeas review that it eliminates. For example, new INA §242(a)(4) eliminates habeas review of claims under the Convention Against Torture and Other Cruel, Inhuman or

---

[14] *See Ruiz-Martinez v. Mukasey*, 516 F.3d 102 (2d Cir. 2008); *Kolkevich v. AG*, 501 F.3d 323 (3d Cir. 2007).

[15] *INS v. St. Cyr, supra* note 12.

[16] *Nnadika v. AG*, 484 F.3d 626 (3d Cir. 2007); *Kellici v. Gonzales*, 472 F.3d 416 (6th Cir. 2006); *Nadarajah v. Gonzales*, 443 F.3d 1069 (9th Cir. 2006); *Hernandez v. Gonzales*, 424 F. 3d 42 (1st Cir. 2005).

Degrading Treatment or Punishment (CAT)[17] and states that a petition for review is now the exclusive means for reviewing a CAT claim. REAL ID also expands court of appeals review to include review of all constitutional claims or questions of law as stated in new INA §242(a)(2)(D). Practitioners should note, when dealing with questions of law, that there is a strong argument, based on the legislative history of REAL ID, that cases involving both a question of law and a question of fact (*i.e.,* whether a person has sufficient "continuous residence" for cancellation of removal eligibility) may still be heard pursuant to a petition for review. REAL ID changed the term "*pure* questions of law" to state merely "questions of law" in INA §242(a)(2)(D). Thus, it can be argued that Congress intended mixed questions of law and fact to be subject to judicial review in the courts of appeals.

Practitioners should carefully research the relevant case law regarding what constitutes a *question of law* before seeking review in the courts of appeals. In addition, all cases that would have been reviewed by a petition for review prior to REAL ID will continue to be reviewed by a petition for review. This includes review by the court of appeals over whether the court has jurisdiction of the case. Such jurisdictional questions may include:

- Whether petitioner has been charged with and found deportable for a criminal offense;

- Whether the offense constitutes an aggravated felony or a crime involving moral turpitude (CMT); and

- Whether petitioner meets certain non-discretionary statutory eligibility requirements for discretionary relief.[18]

Bars to Judicial Review in the Court of Appeals

The same bars to judicial review that existed under INA §242 prior to the passage of REAL ID remain:

- Determinations made relating to INA §235(b)(1) for *arriving aliens*;

- Denials of discretionary relief under INA §§212(h), 212(i), 240A, 240B, or 245, or any other discretionary decision (other than the granting of asylum);

- Orders of removal based on the criminal grounds of inadmissibility or deportation; and

- Decisions or actions by the attorney general (AG) to commence proceedings, adjudicate cases, or execute removal orders.

---

[17] Convention Against Torture and Other Cruel, Inhuman or Degrading Treatment or Punishment (CAT), Dec. 10, 1984, 1465 U.N.T.S. 85 (entered into force June 26, 1987).

[18] For an excellent discussion of what types of decisions have been found to be reviewable on a petition for review, see AILF's "Federal Court Jurisdiction Over Discretionary Decisions after REAL ID: Mandamus, Other Affirmative Suits and Petitions for Review," (April 5, 2006), *available at www.ailf.org/lac/lac_pa_topics.shtml.*

REAL ID actually expands the jurisdiction of the courts of appeals so that they may review certain issues previously precluded by IIRAIRA.[19] A new INA §242(a)(2)(D) states that nothing in the INA "which limits or eliminates judicial review, shall be construed as precluding review of constitutional claims or questions of law raised upon a petition for review filed with the appropriate court in accordance with this section."

Thus, the courts of appeals now have jurisdiction to review *all* constitutional issues and questions of law related to a final order of removal, deportation, or exclusion. Accordingly, the bars to judicial review listed above only apply to non-constitutional questions and issues that do not involve questions of law. As a result of REAL ID amendments, *all* constitutional claims or questions of law related to final orders based on a criminal offense or a discretionary decision now will be in the court of appeals rather than in the district court by habeas corpus. Consequently, while habeas review has been eliminated, review over most—if not all—of the issues that would have been available in habeas proceedings under IIRAIRA now should be available via petition for review in the courts of appeals.

Denials of Discretionary Relief and the Special Case of Asylum. Under INA §242(a)(2)(B)(i), as amended by IIRAIRA and REAL ID, there is no judicial review of any *discretionary* decision relating to the following:

- Waivers of inadmissibility under INA §212(h) (for criminal grounds of inadmissibility);

- Waivers of fraud or misrepresentation under INA §212(i);

- Cancellation of removal under INA §240A;

- Voluntary departure under INA §240B;

- Adjustment of status under INA §245; and

- Any other decision specified under Title II of the INA to be discretionary.

To determine whether a bar applies, it is important to analyze whether the issue actually involves the exercise of discretion. Courts have reached different results regarding what constitutes discretion, so it is important to review the most current applicable law.

REAL ID expands the scope of the provision above, stating that judicial review is eliminated "regardless of whether the judgment, decision, or action is made in removal proceedings." This means that circuit courts likely will not review issues of law or constitutional issues unless they arise out of a removal order.[20] However, as stated above, where the Department of Homeland Security (DHS) or an immigration court denies relief on other than discretionary grounds, the bar to judicial review does not apply. In addition, the bar to review does not apply to benefits not specifically described in this provision. Thus, for example, a federal court may review decisions regarding S, T, and U visas or naturalization, even if the issue involves a question of

---

[19] IIRAIRA, *supra* note 2.

[20] *See, e.g., Nnadika v. AG,* 484 F.3d 626 (3d Cir. 2007); *Madu v. AG,* 470 F.3d 1362 (11th Cir. 2006).

the exercise of discretion, since these benefits do not appear in Title II of the INA, but rather in Titles I and III.

Asylum cases are the special exception to this bar. INA §242(a)(2)(B)(ii) permits judicial review of the exercise of discretion in the case of asylum determinations under INA §208(a). Thus, asylum-seekers may file a petition for review in the court of appeals in the circuit where the immigration judge (IJ) completed removal proceedings to challenge the exercise of discretion in denying asylum. However, the standard for review for discretionary denials is extremely high. The AG's denial of asylum "shall be conclusive unless manifestly contrary to law and an abuse of discretion."[21] In addition, INA §208(a) precludes judicial review of decisions in asylum cases relating to the one-year deadline, the safe third country bar, and whether a previous asylum application was filed in the respondent's case.

Orders Against Criminal Foreign Nationals. INA §242(a)(2)(C) states that there shall be no judicial review of any final order of removal against an individual who is removable for having committed a criminal offense covered by one of the following grounds:

- Criminal Grounds of Inadmissibility:[22]
  - CMTs
  - controlled substance violations
  - multiple criminal convictions
  - prostitution and commercialized vice
  - individuals asserting immunity from prosecution;
- Aggravated felony conviction;[23]
- Controlled substance convictions and drug abusers or addicts;[24]
- Firearms Offenses;[25]
- Miscellaneous crimes[26] such as espionage, sabotage, treason, etc.; and
- Multiple criminal convictions[27] (CMT convictions after admission to United States).

Just as in the case of discretionary decisions, although there is a general bar to any review (including habeas review) of removal orders based on certain criminal convictions, REAL ID amendments now permit the courts of appeals to review constitutional claims and questions of law in such cases. Soon after the passage of REAL ID,

---

[21] INA §242(b)(4)(D).

[22] INA §212(a)(2).

[23] INA §237(a)(2)(A)(iii).

[24] INA §237(a)(2)(B).

[25] INA §237(a)(2)(C).

[26] INA §237(a)(2)(D).

[27] INA §237(a)(2)(A)(ii).

the U.S. Court of Appeals for the Fifth Circuit ruled that it had jurisdiction over a pre–REAL ID Act habeas petition, notwithstanding the judicial bar against criminal foreign nationals, since the act permitted review of legal and constitutional questions.[28]

Decisions to commence proceedings, adjudicate cases, or execute removal orders. INA §242(g) precludes judicial review of a decision by the AG to:

- Commence proceedings;
- Adjudicate cases; and
- Execute removal orders.

INA §242(g) applies, under IIRAIRA §306(c)(1), to all *past or pending* deportation proceedings. After the passage of IIRAIRA, the government took the position that INA §242(g) precluded judicial review in all deportation or removal cases, except as provided otherwise by INA §242.

The Supreme Court rejected this interpretation in *Reno v. American-Arab Anti-Discrimination Committee,*[29] a case in which the plaintiffs asserted that the government selectively had targeted them for deportation because of their affiliation with the Popular Front for the Liberation of Palestine. The Supreme Court held that INA §242(g) was not a *broad, catch-all* clause precluding judicial review in all deportation and removal cases, but only applied to the three specific actions provided for in the statute. Where, however, the plaintiffs were seeking judicial review of the AG's decision to *commence proceedings*, jurisdiction ceased upon passage of IIRAIRA. The Court indicated, however, that the plaintiffs might be able to bring a selective enforcement challenge to the AG's decision to commence proceedings if the government had acted in a particularly outrageous manner.

REAL ID amends INA §242(g) to eliminate habeas review of decisions to commence proceedings, adjudicate cases, or execute removal or deportation orders. However, the new INA §242(a)(2)(D) leaves open the possibility of seeking judicial review by petition for review in the court of appeals when the issue involves a question of law or review of constitutional claims.

Procedural Rules Regarding Petitions for Review

The general rules regarding when and where to file the petition for review remain unchanged by REAL ID. The only exception, as mentioned above, is that cases filed under IIRAIRA's transitional rules will be treated as if they had been filed under INA §242 as amended by REAL ID. Thus, the 30-day deadline will not apply to those cases.

- **Filing Deadlines.** *All* petitions for review must be filed no later than 30 days after the date of the final order of removal (prior to IIRAIRA, INA §106 allowed 90 days in most cases, 60 days for *in absentia* orders, and 30 days for

---

[28] *Rosales v. BICE*, 426 F.3d 733 (5th Cir. 2005).

[29] *Reno v. American-Arab Anti-Discrimination Committee*, 525 U.S. 471 (1999).

aggravated felons). Habeas petitions in district court have no filing deadline. Thus, REAL ID results in a greatly accelerated filing deadline for those cases that previously would have proceeded as habeas challenges, but now must be filed as a petition for review. As stated above, habeas petitions filed before enactment of REAL ID will be *grandfathered* and transferred to the appropriate court of appeals:

– *Petitioner's brief* must be served and filed no later than 40 days after the date on which the administrative record is available. DHS must file the certified administrative record within 40 days of service of the petition for review. Most courts do not rely on the timeframe in the statute, but rather, issue a schedule setting out due dates for filing the administrative record and the briefs. Also, it is common for counsel on either side to move to extend the briefing schedule.

– *Petitioner's reply brief* must be served and filed no later than 14 days after service of the brief of the AG.

– The court may not extend these deadlines except upon good cause shown.

– If the petitioner fails to file a brief within the time provided, the court "shall" dismiss the appeal unless "manifest injustice" would result.

▪ **No Forum Shopping.** The petition for review must be filed with the court of appeals for the circuit in which the IJ completed removal proceedings;

▪ **Respondent is the AG.** Respondent in a petition for review is the AG. The petition shall be served on the AG and on the DHS officer in charge of the district in which the final order of removal was entered (ICE field office director for detention and removal);

▪ **No Automatic Stay.** Service of the petition for review does not stay the noncitizen's removal, unless the court orders otherwise. ICE may remove an individual before the 30-day deadline expires. Therefore, the petitioner may want to file a separate stay of the removal order and, if applicable, a stay of the voluntary departure period, pending the petition for review;

▪ **Facts Limited to Administrative Record.** The court of appeals will decide the petition only on the administrative record on which the order of removal is based;

▪ **Administrative Findings are Conclusive**. The administrative findings of fact are conclusive unless "any reasonable adjudicator would be compelled to conclude to the contrary." A decision that a noncitizen is not eligible for admission is conclusive unless "manifestly contrary to law." Similarly, the AG's discretionary judgment in asylum decisions is conclusive unless "manifestly contrary to law and an abuse of discretion."

In INA §242(b)(4)(D), REAL ID amends the provision regarding review of discretion in asylum decisions by stating that no court shall reverse such determinations on the availability of corroborating evidence unless the court finds that a reasonable trier of fact is "compelled to conclude that such corroborating evidence is unavailable;"

- **Petition Requirements.** A petition for review or for habeas corpus of a removal order must attach a copy of the order of removal, and state whether a court has upheld the order's validity. If the order's validity has been upheld, state the name of the court, date of the ruling, and kind of proceeding;

- **No Previous Federal Court Action.** No judicial review is allowed if another federal court has decided the validity of the administrative order unless:

  - The petition for review presents grounds that could not have been presented in the earlier proceedings; or

  - The remedy provided in that proceeding was inadequate or ineffective to test the validity of the administrative order;

- **No Loss of Jurisdiction.** The federal court does not lose jurisdiction if the foreign national is removed;

- **Consolidation of Petitions for Review.** Review of the order of removal is to be consolidated with review of any motion to reopen or reconsider that has been filed. Thus, the noncitizen must file two separate petitions for review in such instances, both within 30 days of the removal order;

- **Exhaustion of Remedies.** A federal court may review a final administrative order of removal only if the noncitizen has exhausted all administrative remedies; and

- **Post-Judgment Review**. A petition for rehearing may be filed within 45 days after entry of judgment.

Judicial Review of Particular Types of Removal Orders

Expedited Removal of Aliens Arriving at Ports of Entry

The INA §235, as amended by IIRAIRA,[30] includes provisions for the expedited removal of *inadmissible* individuals arriving in the United States. If the immigration officer determines that the noncitizen does not have the proper documentation or has made a misrepresentation in attempting to enter the United States, the immigration officer has broad authority to order the noncitizen removed without any hearing or review, unless the noncitizen indicates intent to apply for asylum or a fear of persecution.[31] Such an order bars the noncitizen from re-entering the United States for five years.[32]

IIRAIRA severely restricts judicial review of expedited removal decisions. It provides that no court shall have jurisdiction to review any individual determination un-

---

[30] IIRAIRA, *supra* note 2.

[31] INA §235(b)(1).

[32] INA §212(a)(9).

der the summary removal provision.[33] It specifically removes any federal jurisdiction "to entertain any other cause or claim arising from or relating to the implementation or operation of an order of removal" under the summary removal provisions. REAL ID amends INA §242(a)(2)(A) to prohibit specifically such challenges pursuant to habeas corpus in district court.

REAL ID leaves unchanged, however, INA §242(e)(2), which permits review of expedited orders of removal on a writ of habeas corpus filed in district court where review is limited to determinations of:

- Whether the petitioner is an alien;

- Whether the petitioner was ordered removed under the summary removal provision; and

- Whether the petitioner can prove by a preponderance of the evidence that he or she is an individual lawfully admitted for permanent residence or has been granted refugee or asylee status.

If the district court determines that the petitioner has demonstrated by a preponderance of the evidence that he or she is a lawful permanent resident (LPR), has been admitted as a refugee under INA §207, or has been granted asylum under INA §208, the court may order that the petitioner be provided a removal hearing under INA §240, but may not order any other remedy or relief.[34]

Treatment of Nationality Claims

REAL ID also leaves unchanged the former provisions regarding claims to U.S. nationality by persons with removal orders. Under INA §242(b)(5)(A), the court of appeals decides nationality claims if it finds from the pleadings and affidavits that no genuine issue of material fact is presented regarding the petitioner's nationality. Where, however, the court of appeals finds that a genuine issue of material fact regarding the petitioner's nationality is presented, the court must transfer the proceedings to the U.S. district court for the judicial district where the petitioner resides for a new hearing on the nationality claim, pursuant to 28 USC §2201.[35]

Challenges to the Validity of Removal Orders in Criminal Proceedings

The INA, as amended by IIRAIRA,[36] imposes criminal penalties under title 18 of the U.S. Code for any noncitizen who fails to depart after a final order of removal is issued. If a noncitizen is in criminal proceedings after having been charged with failure to depart under new INA §243(a), and the validity of the order of removal has not been decided previously by a federal court, he or she may challenge the original order of removal by filing a separate pre-trial motion in the criminal proceedings.[37] The

---

[33] INA §242(a)(2)(A).

[34] INA §242(e)(4).

[35] INA §242(b)(5)(B).

[36] IIRAIRA, *supra* note 2.

[37] INA §242(b)(7)(A).

district court judge, before trial and without a jury, will decide the motion regarding the removal order's validity. If, however, the validity of the order of removal has been decided previously by a federal court, the noncitizen cannot challenge its validity in criminal proceedings.

If a defendant is charged with violating INA §243(a) and claims in the pre-trial motion to be a U.S. national, the district court must determine whether a genuine issue of material fact exists. If the district court finds that no genuine issue of material fact about the defendant's nationality is presented, the court must decide the nationality claim only on the administrative record on which the removal order was based. The administrative findings of fact are conclusive "if supported by reasonable, substantial, and probative evidence on the record considered as a whole." If the district court finds that a genuine issue of material fact regarding the defendant's nationality is presented, the court must hold an new hearing on the nationality claim and decide that claim pursuant to 28 USC §2201.

REAL ID did not change any of the provisions regarding raising pre-trial claims of U.S. nationality or challenging underlying removal orders in criminal proceedings under INA §243(a).

Judicial Review of Certain Administrative Removal Orders

INA §238(b), as amended by IIRAIRA,[38] gives DHS the authority to order administratively the removal of a non-LPR or conditional permanent resident[39] who has been convicted of an aggravated felony. Under this provision, the DHS officer issues a notice of intent to issue a final removal order. The noncitizen must be given reasonable notice of the charges and an opportunity to present a written rebuttal. The final order of removal is not adjudicated by the same person who issues the charges. Although INA §238(b) allows DHS to bypass removal proceedings under INA §240, judicial review of this final administrative order is available before a federal circuit court of appeals.[40]

Judicial Review of Judicial Orders of Removal

Under IIRAIRA,[41] a U.S. district court has jurisdiction to enter a judicial order of removal at the time of sentencing against a noncitizen who is deportable if the order has been requested by the U.S. attorney, with the concurrence of the Immigration and Naturalization Services (legacy INS) Commissioner.[42] A person ordered removed under this provision may appeal the order of removal to the court of appeals in which the district court is located.[43]

---

[38] IIRAIRA, *supra* note 2.

[39] INA §216.

[40] INA §238(c).

[41] IIRAIRA, *supra* note 2.

[42] INA §238(c)(1).

[43] INA §238(c)(3).

Mandamus and Other Types of Petitions

REAL ID purports to eliminate federal court jurisdiction under the mandamus statute[44] and the *all writs* statute[45] in all of the sub-sections of INA §242 where habeas jurisdiction has been eliminated. The mandamus statute has been used effectively in the past to get a district court to order an officer or employee of the U.S. government (*i.e.,* DHS) to perform a ministerial act or mandatory duty owed to the person seeking the writ. Where such jurisdiction previously existed with respect to final orders, jurisdiction now will be by petition for review in the court of appeals. In non-removal cases (*i.e.,* to compel USCIS to adjudicate a long-delayed application, such as naturalization), practitioners should continue to seek a writ of mandamus.

---

[44] 28 USC §1361.

[45] 28 USC §1651.

APPENDICES

Appendix 1: Notice to Appear 313

Appendix 2: Order to Show Cause...317

Appendix 3: Sample I-122 323

Appendix 4: Criminal Record Check..325

Appendix 5: Court Instructions..327

Appendix 6: Summary Order of Removal 329

Appendix 7: Order of Expedited Removal.....................................331

Appendix 8: Administrative Order of Removal..............................335

Appendix 9: Naturalization Charts..337

Appendix 10: Motion to Suppress Evidence..................................349

APPENDIX 1
NOTICE TO APPEAR

U.S. Department of Justice
Immigration and Naturalization Service

Notice to Appear

In removal proceedings under section 240 of the Immigration and Nationality Act

File No: A0~~~~~~~~
Case No: BOS0706000264

In the Matter of: JOHN SMITH

Respondent: ~~~~~~ currently residing at:

ESSEX COUNTY HOC 20 MANNING AVE
MIDDLETON MASSACHUSETTS 01949   (978)750-1900
                                   (Number, street, city state and ZIP code)   (Area code and phone number)

☐ 1. You are an arriving alien.
☐ 2. You are an alien present in the United States who has not been admitted or paroled.
☒ 3. You have been admitted to the United States, but are deportable for the reasons stated below.

X 451

The Service alleges that you:

D -

20 44 25,00

        See Continuation Page Made a Part Hereof

On the basis of the foregoing, it is charged that you are subject to removal from the United States pursuant to the following provision(s) of law:

        See Continuation Page Made a Part Hereof

☐ This notice is being issued after an asylum officer has found that the respondent has demonstrated a credible fear of persecution or torture.

☐ Section 235(b)(1) order was vacated pursuant to: ☐ 8 CFR 208.30(f)(2)   ☐ 8 CFR 235.3(b)(5)(iv)

YOU ARE ORDERED to appear before an immigration judge of the United States Department of Justice at: _____
JFK Federal Building 15 New Sudbury Street Room 320 Boston MASSACHUSETTS US 0220
                                   (Complete Address of Immigration Court, Including Room Number, if any)
On __a date to be set__   at __a time to be set__ to show why you should not be removed from the United States based on the
   (Date)   (Time)
charge(s) set forth above.

MELINDA LULL
SUPERVISORY DEPORTATION OFFICER
(Signature and Title of Issuing Officer)

Date: June 14, 2007

Boston, MA
(City and State)

617-

See reverse for important information

Form I-862 (Rev. 1/22/99)N

313

Notice to Respondent

Warning: Any statement you make may be used against you in removal proceedings.

Alien Registration: This copy of the Notice to Appear served upon you is evidence of your alien registration while you are under removal proceedings. You are required to carry it with you at all times.

Representation: If you so choose, you may be represented in this proceeding, at no expense to the Government, by an attorney or other individual authorized and qualified to represent persons before the Executive Office for Immigration Review, pursuant to 8 CFR 3.16. Unless you so request, no hearing will be scheduled earlier than ten days from the date of this notice to allow you sufficient time to secure counsel. A list of qualified attorneys and organizations who may be available to represent you at no cost will be provided with this Notice.

Conduct of the hearing: At the time of your hearing, you should bring with you any affidavits or other documents which you desire to have considered in connection with your case. If any document is in a foreign language, you must bring the original and a certified English translation of the document. If you wish to have the testimony of any witnesses considered, you should arrange to have such witnesses present at the hearing.

At your hearing you will be given the opportunity to admit or deny any or all of the allegations in the Notice to Appear and that you are inadmissible or deportable on the charges contained in the Notice to Appear. You will have an opportunity to present evidence on your own behalf, to examine any evidence presented by the Government, to object, on proper legal grounds, to the receipt of evidence and to cross examine any witnesses presented by the Government. At the conclusion of your hearing, you have a right to appeal an adverse decision by the immigration judge.

You will be advised by the immigration judge before whom you appear, of any relief from removal for which you may appear eligible including the privilege of departing voluntarily. You will be given a reasonable opportunity to make any such application to the immigration judge.

Failure to appear: You are required to provide the INS, in writing, with your full mailing address and telephone number. You must notify the Immigration Court immediately by using Form EOIR-33 whenever you change your address or telephone number during the course of this proceeding. You will be provided with a copy of this form. Notices of hearing will be mailed to this address. If you do not submit Form EOIR-33 and do not otherwise provide an address at which you may be reached during proceedings, then the Government shall not be required to provide you with written notice of your hearing. If you fail to attend the hearing at the time and place designated on this notice, or any date and time later directed by the Immigration Court, a removal order may be made by the immigration judge in your absence, and you may be arrested and detained by the INS.

Request for Prompt Hearing

To expedite a determination in my case, I request an immediate hearing. I waive my right to have a 10-day period prior to appearing before an immigration judge.

_____
(Signature of Respondent)

Before:

_____   Date: _____
(Signature and Title of INS Officer)

Certificate of Service

This Notice to Appear was served on the respondent by me on _____, in the following manner and in
(Date)
compliance with section 239(a)(1)(F) of the Act:

[X] in person   [ ] by certified mail, return receipt requested   [ ] by regular mail

[ ] Attached is a credible fear worksheet.

[ ] Attached is a list of organizations and attorneys which provide free legal services.

The alien was provided oral notice in the _____ language of the time and place of his or her hearing and of the consequences of failure to appear as provided in section 240(b)(7) of the Act.

KEVIN M. WILLIAMS
IMMIGRATION ENFORCEMENT AGENT
_____   _____
(Signature of Respondent if Personally Served)   (Signature and Title of Officer)

Form I-862 (Rev. 3/22/99)N

U.S. Department of Justice

Immigration and Naturalization Service

Notice of Rights and Request for Disposition

FIN #:

Case No:
File No:

Name:

NOTICE OF RIGHTS

You have been arrested because immigration officers believe that you are illegally in the United States. You have the right to a hearing before the Immigration Court to determine whether you may remain in the United States. If you request a hearing, you may be detained in custody or you may be eligible to be released on bond, until your hearing date. In the alternative, you may request to return to your country as soon as possible, without a hearing.

You have the right to contact an attorney or other legal representative to represent you at your hearing, or to answer any questions regarding your legal rights in the United States. Upon your request, the officer who gave you this notice will provide you with a list of legal organizations that may represent you for free or for a small fee. You have the right to communicate with the consular or diplomatic officers from your country. You may use a telephone to call a lawyer, other legal representative, or consular officer at any time prior to your departure from the United States.

REQUEST FOR DISPOSITION

_____ ☒ I request a hearing before the Immigration Court to determine whether or not I may remain in the
Initials   United States.

_____ ☐ I believe I face harm if I return to my country. My case will be referred to the Immigration Court
Initials   for a hearing.

_____ ☐ I admit that I am in the United States illegally, and I believe I do not face harm if I return to my
Initials   country. I give up my right to a hearing before the Immigration Court. I wish to return to my
              country as soon as arrangements can be made to effect my departure. I understand that I may be
              held in detention until my departure.

_____   _____
Signature of Subject   Date

CERTIFICATION OF SERVICE

☒ Notice read by subject

☒ Notice read to subject by **KEVIN M. WILLIAMS**_____ , in the_____ language.

KEVIN M. WILLIAMS_____   _____
Name of Service Officer (Print)   Name of Interpreter (Print)

_____   _____
Signature of Officer   Date and Time of Service

		June 14, 2007

The Service alleges that you:

1) You are not a citizen or national of the United States;

2) You are a native of TRINIDAD AND TOBAGO and a citizen of TRINIDAD AND TOBAGO;

3) You were admitted to the United States at MIAMI, FL on or about   March 22, 1995 as a IMMIGRANT;

4) You were, on April16, 2001, convicted in the Natick District Court at Natick Massachusetts, for the offense of Larceny Over $250.00, in violation of Massachusetts General Law, Chapter 266, Section 30;

5) You were, on May 3, 2007, convicted in the Peabody District Court at Peabody Massachusetts for the offense of Forgery of a Document, in violation of Massachusetts General Law, Chapter 267, Section 1(A);

6) These crimes did not arise out of a single scheme of criminal misconduct.

On the basis of the foregoing, it is charged that you are subject to removal from the United States pursuant to the following provision(s) of law:

Section 237(a)(2)(A)(ii) of the Immigration and Nationality Act, as amended, in that, at any time after admission, you have been convicted of two crimes involving moral turpitude not arising out of a single scheme of criminal misconduct.

Signature	Title
MELINDA LULL	SUPERVISORY DEPORTATION OFFICER

_3_ of _3_ Pages

Form I-831 Continuation Page (Rev. 6/12/92)

APPENDIX 2
ORDER TO SHOW CAUSE

epartment of Justice
on and Naturalization Service

Order to Show Cause and Notice of Hearing

ORDER TO SHOW CAUSE AND NOTICE OF HEARING
(RDEN DE PRESENTAR MOTIVOS JUSTIFICANTES Y AVISO DE AUDIENCIA)

...tation Proceedings under section 242 of the Immigration and Nationality Act.
...rámites de deportación a tenor de la sección 242 de la Ley de Inmigración y Nacionalidad.)

ed States of America:
ados Unidos de América:)

File No: A12 _____
(No. de registro)

Dated   3/21/93
(Fechada)

matter of
...sunto de)
s
...ón)

Sergio _____

In Service Custody

(Respondent)
(Demandado)

one No. (Area Code)   415/255-1998
te teléfono y código de área)

...on inquiry conducted by the Immigration and Naturalization Service, it is alleged that:
...egún las indagaciones realizadas por el Servicio de Inmigración y Naturalización, se alega que:)

...u are not a citizen or national of the United States:
...d. no es ciudadano o nacional de los Estados Unidos.)

...u are a native of _____ Colombia _____ and a citizen of Colombia _____ ;
...d. es nativo de)   (y ciudadano de)

...ou entered the United States at or near San Isidro, CA _____ on or about 9/2/86 _____ ;
...d. entró a los Estados Unidos en o cerca de)   (el día o hacia esa fecha)

You were then admitted as an immigrant.

You were on November 20, 1992 convicted in the Superior Court of the State
of California of the County of San Mateo for the offense of POSSESSION
FOR SALE OF COCAINE, in violation of section 11378 of the California
Health and Safety Code.

u are required to be present at your deportation
aring prepared to proceed. If you fail to appear at
 hearing after having been given written notice of the
 m, time and location of your hearing, you will be
 dered deported *in your absence*, if it is established that
 u are deportable and you have been provided the
 propriate notice of the hearing.

u are required by law to provide immediately in writing
 address (and telephone number, if any) where you can
 · contacted. You are required to provide written notice,
 than five (5) days, of any change in your address or
 lephone number to the office of the Immigration Judge
 ted in this notice. Any notices will be mailed only to the
 st address provided by you. If you are represented,
 oce will be sent to your representative. If you fail to
 ppear at the scheduled deportation hearing, you will be
 dered deported *in your absence* if it is established that
 u are deportable and you have been provided the
 ppropriate notice of the hearing.

 you are ordered deported *in your absence*, you cannot
 ek to have that order rescinded except that: (a) you
 ay file a motion to reopen the hearing within 180 days
 er the date of the order if you are able to show that
 ur failure to appear was because of exceptional
 rcumstances, or (b) you may file a motion to reopen at
 y time after the date of the order if you can show that
 ou did not receive written notice of your hearing and you
 d provided your address and telephone number (or any
 anges of your address or telephone number) as
 quired, or that you were incarcerated and did not appear
 : your hearing through no fault of your own. If you
 oose to seek judicial review of a deportation order
 ntered *in your absence*, you must file the petition for
 eview within 60 days (30 days if you are convicted of an
 ggravated felony) after the date of the final order, and the
 eview shall be confined to the issues of validity of the
 otice provided to you, the reasons for your failure to
 ppear at your hearing, and whether the government
 stablished that you are deportable.

 n addition to the above, if you are ordered deported *in
 your absence*, you are ineligible for five (5) years from
 the date of the final order for the following relief from
 deportation: voluntary departure under section 242 (b) of
 the Immigration and Nationality Act (INA); suspension of
 deportation or voluntary departure under section 244 of
 the INA; and adjustment of status under sections 245,
 248, and 249 of the INA.

The copy of this Order to Show Cause served upon
 you is evidence of your alien registration while you
 are under deportation proceedings. The law requires
 that you carry it with you at all times.

Está obligado a asistir a la audiencia de deportación
y de estar preparado para ella. Si no asiste a
cualquiera de las audiencias después de haber sido
notificado por escrito de la fecha, hora y lugar de la
audiencia, se ordenará su deportación en su ausencia, si
se establece que puede ser deportado y que recibió los
avisos correspondientes.

La ley le obliga a informar inmediatamente por escrito de
su domicilio (y número de teléfono, de haberlo) donde
pueda ser localizado. Tiene la obligación de notificar por
escrito, en el plazo de cinco (5) días, cualquier cambio de
domicilio o de teléfono a la oficina del juez de inmigración
que aparece en este aviso. Los avisos se enviarán
solamente a la última dirección facilitada por Ud. Si ha
decidido tener un representante, se enviarán los avisos a
dicha persona. Si no asiste a cualquiera de las audiencias
después de haber sido notificado por escrito de la fecha,
hora y lugar de las mismas, se ordenará su deportación
en su ausencia, si se establece que puede ser
deportado y que recibió el aviso de la audiencia.

Si se ordena su deportación en su ausencia, no podrá
solicitar la anulación de esa orden salvo que: a) pueda
presentar un pedimento para tener otra audiencia en el
plazo de 180 días después de la fecha de la orden si
puede demostrar que no compareció debido a
circunstancias excepcionales, o b) puede presentar un
pedimento para tener otra audiencia en cualquier
momento después de la fecha de la orden si puede
demostrar que no recibió el aviso de la audiencia por
escrito y que había facilitado su dirección y número de
teléfono (o notificado los cambios de dirección o número
de teléfono) según lo previsto, o que estaba encarcelado
y no compareció a la audiencia por motivos ajenos a su
voluntad. Si decide solicitar una revisión judicial de la
orden de deportación en su ausencia, debe presentar la
solicitud de revisión en el plazo de 60 días (30 días si ha
sido condenado por un delito grave con agravantes) a
partir de la fecha de la orden definitiva, y la revisión se
limitará a decidir si el aviso que recibió es válido, las
razones por las cuales no compareció a la audiencia y si
el gobierno demostró que puede ser deportado.

Además de lo anterior, si se ordena su deportación en su
ausencia, no podrá, en el plazo de cinco años después
de la fecha de la orden definitiva, tener derecho a los
siguientes recursos: salida voluntaria según la sección 242
(b) de la ley de Inmigración y Nacionalidad (INA);
suspensión de la deportación o de la salida voluntaria
según la sección 244 de la INA, y ajuste de condición
según las secciones 245, 248, y 249 de la INA.

Esta copia de la Orden de Presentar Motivos
Justificantes que le ha sido notificada constituye la
prueba de su registro de extranjero mientras se llevan
a cabo los trámites para su deportación. La ley le
exige que la lleve consigo en todo momento.

U.S. Department of Justice
~gration and Naturalization Service

Order to Show Cause and Notice of Hearing

Continuation Sheet
(Hoja complementaria)

Dated (Fechada) 3/22/93

Respondent (Demandado) Sergio: ~~~~~~~~

File No. (No. de registro) ~~A12~~

AND on the basis of the foregoing allegations, it is charged that you are subject to deportation pursuant to the following provision(s) of law:

(Y según los alegatos anteriores, se le acusa de estar sujeto a deportación de acuerdo con la(s) siguiente(s) disposición(es) de la ley:)

Section 241(a)(12)(A)(iii) of the Immigration and Nationality Act in that at any time after entry you have been convicted of an aggravated felony, to wit: POSSESSION FOR SALE OF COCAINE.

Section 241(a)(2)(B)(i) of the Immigration and Nationality Act in that at any time after entry you were convicted of a violation of a law of the United States relating to a controlled substance.

WHEREFORE, YOU ARE ORDERED to appear for a hearing before an Immigration Judge of the Executive Office for Immigration Review of the United States Department of Justice at:

(POR LO CUAL, SE LE ORDENA comparecer ante un juez de inmigración de la Oficina Ejecutiva de Revisión de Inmigración del Departamento de Justicia de los Estados Unidos en:)

Address (Dirección) Date, time, and place to be scheduled by the Immigration Judge

On (Fecha) _____ At (Hora) _____ A m

and show cause why you should not be deported from the United States on the charge(s) set forth above.

(y mostrar motivos justificantes por cual no debena ser deportado de los Estados Unidos por los cargos expresa... anteriormente.)

Dated (Fechada) 3-22-93

Signature of Issuing Officer (Firma del funcionario que la expide) Lucinda Vincent

City and State of Issuance (Ciudad y Estado donde se expide) San Francisco, Ca

Title of Issuing Officer (Titulo del funcionario que la expide) Deputy District Director

J.S. Department of Justice
nmigration and Naturalization Service

Order to Show Cause and Notice of Hearing

JOTICE OF RIGHTS AND CONSEQUENCES

The Immigration and Naturalization Service believes that you are an alien not lawfully entitled to be in or o remain in the United States. Read this notice carefully and ask questions about anything In this notice you do not understand. This notice identifies your rights as an alien In deportation proceedings, and your obligations and the conditions with which you must comply In order to protect your eligibility to be considered for certain benefits.

Any statement you make before an Immigration Officer may be used against you in any immigration or administrative proceeding.

You may be represented, at no expense to the United States government, by an attorney or other individual who is authorized and qualified to represent persons in these proceedings. You will be given a list of organizations, attorneys and other persons who have indicated their availability to represent aliens in these proceedings. Some of these persons may represent you free of charge or for a nominal fee. You may also be represented by a friend, relative, or other person having a pre-existing relationship with you, provided his or her appearance is permitted by the immigration judge.

You will have a hearing before an immigration judge, scheduled no sooner than 14 days from the date you are served with this Order to Show Cause (unless you request in writing an earlier hearing date). The fourteen-day period is to allow you to seek an attorney or representative, if you desire to be represented. At your hearing, you will be given the opportunity to admit or deny any or all of the allegations in this Order to Show Cause, and whether you are deportable on the charges set forth herein. You will have an opportunity to present evidence and/or witnesses on your own behalf, to examine evidence presented by the government, to object, on proper legal grounds, to the receipt of evidence and to cross examine any witnesses presented by the government. Any document that you present that is in a foreign language must be accompanied by a certified English translation. It is your responsibility to ensure that any witnesses you wish to present on your own behalf be present at the hearing.

The immigration judge will advise you regarding relief from deportation for which you may be eligible. You will be given a reasonable opportunity to make an application for any such relief. If you are not satisfied with the decision of the immigration judge, you have the right to appeal. The immigration judge will provide you with your appeal rights.

AVISO DE DERECHOS Y CONSECUENCIAS

El Servicio de Inmigración y Naturalización opina que Ud. es un extranjero sin derecho legal a estar o permanecer en los Estados Unidos. Lea este aviso cuidadosamente y pregunte acerca de cualquier parte del mismo que no entienda. Este aviso le explica los derechos que tiene como extranjero en los trámites de deportación, y las obligaciones y condiciones que debe cumplir con el fin de proteger su derecho a que se le considere para recibir ciertos beneficios.

Las declaraciones que haga ante un funcionario del Servicio de Inmigración podrán usarse en su contra en cualquier trámite administrativo o de inmigración.

Ud. puede ser representado, sin costo alguno para el gobierno de los Estados Unidos, por un abogado o otra persona autorizada y calificada para representar personas en estos trámites. Ud. recibirá una lista de las entidades, abogados y demás personas dispuestas a representar a extranjeros en estos trámites. Algunas de esas personas pueden representarle gratuitamente o por honorarios nominales. También puede representarle un amigo, familiar o otra persona con la que tenga una relación establecida, siempre que el juez de inmigración permita su comparecencia.

Ud. tendrá una audiencia ante un juez de inmigración, fijada con un mínimo de 14 días a partir de la fecha que se le expidió esta Orden (a menos que Ud. solicite por escrito una audiencia en plazo aún menor). El plazo de catorce días le permitirá conseguir los servicios de un abogado o representante, si lo desea. En la audiencia se le dará la oportunidad de admitir o negar cualquiera de los alegatos de esta Orden o todos ellos, y se le informará si está sujeto a deportación por los cargos expresados en la misma. Ud. tendrá la oportunidad de presentar pruebas y testigos a favor suyo, de examinar las pruebas presentadas por el gobierno, de oponerse, con base en los razonamientos legales pertinentes, a la admisión de pruebas y de interrogar a cualquier testigo del gobierno. Todo documento que presente en un idioma extranjero debe ir acompañado de una traducción certificada al inglés. Será responsabilidad suya asegurarse de que cualquier testigo suyo comparesca a la audiencia.

El juez de inmigración le informará sobre los recursos de deportación a los que tenga derecho y se le dará una oportunidad adecuada para solicitarlos. Si no está de acuerdo con la decisión del juez, puede apelarla. El juez de inmigración le informará acerca de sus derechos de apelación.

Form I-221 (Rev. 6/92763) N

his Order to Show Cause shall be filed with the Immigration Judge of the Executive Office for Immigration Review at the address provided below. You must report any changes of your address or telephone number in writing to this office:

Debe presentar esta Orden de Presentar Motivos Justificantes a la Oficina Ejecutiva de Revisión de Inmigración en la siguiente dirección. Debe notificar cualquier cambio de su domicilio o número de teléfono por escrito a:

The Office of the Immigration Judge

55 E. Monroe
Chicago IL 60603

Certificate of Translation and Oral Notice

This Order to Show Cause ☒ was ☐ was not read to the named alien in the Spanish _____ language, which is his/her native language or a language which he/she understands.

March 21, 1993
Date _____ Signature _____

Nancy Cordero, Clerk
Printed Name and Title of Translator

Address of Translator (if other than as employee) or office and division (if INS employee)

(If oral notice was not provided please explain)

Manner of Service	Alien's Right Thumb Print
☒ Personal Service to Alien	
☐ Certified Mail - Return Receipt Requested	
☐ Alien	
☐ Counsel of Record	

Certificate of Service

This Order to Show Cause was served by me at Chicago, IL on March 21 1993. at 10:00 A.M. _____ m.

S. Jones   Sam Jones   Investigations Officer, Chicago, ILL.
Officer's Signature   Printed Name   Title   Office

Alien's Signature (acknowledgment/receipt of this form)
(Firma de extranjero/acuse de recibo)

Request for Prompt Hearing and Waiver of 14-Day Minimum Period
(Solicitud de audiencia inmediata y renuncia al plazo mínimo de 14 días)

To expedite determination of my case, I request an immediate hearing, and waive my right to the 14 day notice.
(Para agilizar la decisión sobre mi caso, solicito una audiencia inmediata y renuncio a mi derecho a un plazo mínimo de 14 días.)

Signature of Respondent
(Firma de demandado)

Date
(Fecha)

Form I-221 (Rev. 6-1-92) N

10-A-5

Pag. ?

Advocates' Guide 3/01

APPENDIX 3
SAMPLE I-122

NOTICE TO APPLICANT FOR ADMISSION DEFERRED/DEFERRED FOR HEARING
BEFORE IMMIGRATION JUDGE

To: _____ Juan Doe _____   Date: _____ 1/14/97 _____

A12-345-678

PLEASE TAKE NOTICE THAT:

You do not appear to me to be clearly and beyond a doubt entitled to enter the United States as you may come within the exclusion provisions of Section 212 (a) (7) (A) (i) I of the Immigration and Nationality Act, as amended, in that (see item checked below)

YOU APPEAR TO HAVE WILLFULLY MISREPRESENTED A MATERIAL FACT IN ORDER TO GAIN ADMISSION TO THE UNITED STATES. YOU APPEAR TO BE AN IMMIGRANT, NOT IN POSSESSION OF A VALID, UNEXPIRED IMMIGRANT VISA AND YOU ARE NOT EXEMPT THE PRESENTATION OF THE SAME.

YOU ARE NOT IN POSSESSION OF A VALID, UNEXPIRED NONIMMIGRANT VISA AND YOU ARE NOT EXEMPT THE PRESENTATION OF THE SAME.

[X] YOU APPEAR TO BE AN IMMIGRANT, NOT IN POSSESSION OF A VALID, UNEXPIRED IMMIGRANT VISA AND YOU ARE NOT EXEMPT THE PRESENTATION OF THE SAME.

[] YOU ARE NOT IN POSSESSION OF A VALID, UNEXPIRED TRAVEL DOCUMENT AND YOU ARE NOT EXEMPT THE PRESENTATION OF THE SAME.

Therefore you are detained/deferred under the provisions of Section 235 (b) of the Immigration and Nationality Act, as amended, for a hearing before an Immigration Judge to determine whether or not you are entitled to enter the United States or whether you shall be excluded and deported. During such hearing you will have the right to be represented by counsel and to have a friend or relative present.

AT THE HEARING BEFORE THE IMMIGRATION JUDGE YOU MUST ESTABLISH THAT YOU ARE ADMISSIBLE TO THE UNITED STATES UNDER ALL PROVISIONS OF THE UNITED STATES IMMIGRATION LAWS.

The hearing:

[ ] will be scheduled and you will be notified as to time and place. Notice of the hearing will be sent to you at the WESTWAY MOTEL, Jamaica, New York.

[ ] will be scheduled and you will be notified as to time and place. Notice of the hearing will be sent to you at US INS SPC - 201 Varick STREET, NY, NY.

[X] will be scheduled and you will be notified as to time and place. It is understood that you want the notice of hearing to be sent to you at the following address:

77   Mockingird Lane,   NY,   NY   10022   (212) 555-5555
(Street and Number)   (Apt. No.)   (City)   (State) (Zip Code)   (Phone-NO.)

The hearing will be held at US INS, 26 Federal Plaza, Corner of Duane Street and Broadway, IN Section - 13th floor, New York, NY 10278. If you have not been contacted within 30 days please phone (212) 264-5916. PLEASE DO NOT CALL JFK AIRPORT.

LEGAL LIST
PROVIDED

X _____ Charles Smith _____
(United States Immigration Officer)

CERTIFICATE OF SERVICE

Original of this notice was delivered to the above-named applicant by the undersigned on 1/14/97 and the alien has been advised of communication privileges pursuant to 8 CFR 242.1(c).

_____ Charles Smith _____
(United States Immigration Officer)

Form I-122
(Rev. 3-1-79)N
ITY 05/06/98

APPENDIX 4
CRIMINAL RECORD CHECK

JUSTICE FOR OUR NEIGHBORS
2418 "E" St.
Omaha, NE 68107
(402) 898-9862 ext. 106

A project of the Iowa and Nebraska Conferences of the United Methodist Church, the United Methodist Committee on Relief and the General Board of Global Ministries.

January 3, 2002

Federal Bureau of Investigation
US Department of Justice
CJIS Division
1000 Custer Hollow Road
Clarksburg, WV 26306

RE: Record Request for:
DOB:

To Whom It May Concern:

Our client is requesting a copy of his criminal record from the FBI. Enclosed please find a completed fingerprint chart and a money order for $18.00. A signed release appears below.

Please send your response to: Justice For Our Neighbors
                                     2418 E. Street
                                     Omaha, NE 68107

Thank you for your assistance.

Sincerely,

Alison Brown
Regional Attorney

RELEASE OF INFORMATION

I give permission for the FBI to send a copy of my criminal record to my representative at the Justice For Our Neighbors immigration clinic.

Signed: _____   Dated: _____

OBTAINING AN FBI BACKGROUND CHECK

<u>Send the following documents:</u>

A brief cover letter stating the reason you need the background check. A good reason to include is "for personal reasons." It is suggested not to give immigration as a reason. Include the requester's name and date and place of birth and the address to which the response should be sent.

If the FBI response is to be sent to someone other than the individual whose record is being checked, include a notarized release authorizing the FBI to send the response to a specific individual. The FBI has no specific form for this.

A fingerprint card. There is no requirement that the fingerprints be on a specific form. Any form used by the organization taking the fingerprints will do.

A money order for $18.00, made payable to the U.S. Treasury.

<u>Send the documents to:</u>

FBI, Attention FCU
1000 Custer Hollow Road
Clarksburg, West Virginia 26306

<u>For information, call the FBI at 304-625-3878.</u>

APPENDIX 5
COURT INSTRUCTIONS

INSTRUCTIONS FOR SUBMITTING CERTAIN APPLICATIONS IN IMMIGRATION COURT AND FOR PROVIDING BIOMETRIC AND BIOGRAPHIC INFORMATION TO U.S. CITIZENSHIP AND IMMIGRATION SERVICES

If you are filing both an I-589 Form and any additional forms (such as I-485, EOIR-40, EOIR-42A, EOIR-42B, or I-881), you must follow BOTH INSTRUCTIONS A & B.

☐ **A. Instructions for Form I-589 (Asylum and for Withholding of Removal)***

In addition to filing your application for asylum and supporting documents with the Immigration Court, you **must complete the following requirements** before the Immigration Judge can grant asylum relief or protection in your case:

SEND these 3 items to the address below:

(1) A clear copy of the **first three pages** of your completed Form I-589 (Application for Asylum and for Withholding of Removal) that you will be filing or have filed with the Immigration Court, which must include your **full name, your current mailing address, and your alien number (A number)**. (Do Not submit any documents other than the first three pages of the completed I-589),

(2) A copy of Form EOIR-28 (Notice of Entry of Appearance as Attorney or Representative Before the Immigration Court) if you are represented, and

(3) A copy of these instructions.

> **USCIS Nebraska Service Center**
> **Defensive Asylum Application With Immigration Court**
> **P.O. Box 87589**
> **Lincoln, NE 68501-7589**

Please note that there is **no filing fee required** for your asylum application.

After the 3 items are received at USCIS Nebraska Service Center, **you will receive:**

- A **USCIS receipt notice** in the mail indicating that USCIS has received your asylum application, and

- An **ASC notice** for you, and separate Application Support Center (ASC) notices for each dependent included in your application. Each ASC notice will indicate the individual's unique receipt number and will provide instructions for each person to appear for an appointment at a nearby ASC for collection of biometrics (such as your photograph, fingerprints, and signature). If you do not receive this notice in 3 weeks, call (800) 375-5283. If you also mail applications under Instructions B, you will receive 2 notices with different receipt numbers. You must wait for and take **both scheduling notices to your ASC appointment.**

You (and your dependents) must then:

- **Attend** the biometrics appointment at the ASC, and obtain a **biometrics confirmation** document before leaving the ASC, and

- **Retain** your ASC **biometrics confirmation** as proof that your biometrics were taken, and bring it to your future Immigration Court hearings.

☐ **B. Instructions for Form(s) I-485, EOIR-40, EOIR-42A, EOIR-42B, or I-881***

You **must complete the following requirements** before the Immigration Judge can grant relief in your case:

SEND these 5 items to the address below:

(1) A clear copy of the entire application form that you will be filing or have filed with the Immigration Court. (Do not submit any documents other than the completed form itself),

(2) The appropriate application fee. (The fee can be found in the instructions with the application, the regulations, and at www.uscis.gov or for the EOIR forms, at www.usdoj.gov/eoir).

(3) The \$70 USCIS biometrics fee,

(4) A copy of Form EOIR-28 (Notice of Entry of Appearance as Attorney or Representative Before the Immigration Court) if you are represented, and

(5) A copy of these instructions.

> **USCIS Texas Service Center**
> **P.O. Box 852463**
> **Mesquite, Texas 75185-2463**

Both fees must be submitted in the form of a check or a money order (or 2 separate checks/money orders) and be made out to: "Department of Homeland Security."

After the 5 items are received at the USCIS Texas Service Center, **you will receive:**

- A **USCIS notice** with your USCIS receipt number and **with instructions** to appear for an appointment at a nearby Application Support Center (ASC) for collection of your biometrics (such as your photographs, fingerprints, and signature). Your dependents will receive separate notices if they are required to provide biometrics. If you do not receive this notice in 3 weeks, call (800) 375-5283. If you also apply for asylum, take **both** scheduling notices to your ASC appointment (*see side A*).

You (and your dependents) must then:

- **Attend** this biometrics appointment at the ASC, and obtain a **biometrics confirmation** document from the ASC,

- **File** the following with the Immigration Court within the time period directed by the Immigration Judge: (1) the original **application Form**, (2) all **supporting documentation**, and (3) the USCIS **notice** that instructs you to appear for an appointment at the ASC, and serves as a receipt for your filing fees, and

- **Retain** your ASC **biometrics confirmation** as proof that your biometrics were taken, and bring it to your future Immigration Court hearings.

IMPORTANT: Failure to complete these actions and to follow any additional instructions that the Immigration Judge has given you could result in a delay in deciding your application or in your application being deemed abandoned and dismissed by the court.

(Eff. Date 4/1/05)

APPENDIX 6
SUMMARY ORDER OF REMOVAL

IMMIGRATION COURT
55 EAST MONROE STREET, SUITE 1900
CHICAGO, IL 60603

In the Matter of:

Respondent   A _____

                                        IN REMOVAL PROCEEDINGS

ORDER OF THE IMMIGRATION JUDGE

This is a summary of oral decision entered on _____June 1, 2001_____. This memorandum is solely for the convenience of the parties. If the proceedings should be appealed or reopened, the oral decision will become the official opinion in the case.

[ ]   The respondent was ordered removed from the United States to_____.
[ ]   Respondent's application for voluntary departure was denied and respondent was ordered removed to _____ alternative to _____.
[ ]   Respondent's application for voluntary departure was granted until_____ upon posting a bond in the amount of $_____ with an alternative order of removal to _____
[X]   Respondent's application for asylum was (X) granted ( ) denied ( ) withdrawn.
[X]   Respondent's application for withholding of removal was ( ) granted (X) denied ( ) withdrawn.
[ ]   Respondent's application for cancellation of removal under Section 240A(a) was ( ) granted ( ) denied ( ) withdrawn.
[ ]   Respondent's application for cancellation of removal under Section 240(b) was ( ) granted ( ) denied ( ) withdrawn. If granted, it was ordered that the respondent be issued all appropriate documents necessary to give effect to this order.
[ ]   Respondent's application for a waiver under Section ____ of the INA was ( ) granted ( ) denied ( ) withdrawn ( ) other.
[ ]   Respondent's application for adjustment of status under Section ____ of the INA was ( ) granted ( ) denied ( ) withdrawn. If granted, it was ordered that respondent be issued all appropriate documents necessary to give effect to this order.
[ ]   Respondent's status was rescinded under Section 246.
[ ]   Respondent is admitted to the United States as a _____ until _____.
[ ]   As a condition of admission, respondent is to post a $_____ bond.
[ ]   Respondent knowingly filed a frivolous asylum application after proper notice.
[ ]   Respondent was advised of the limitation on discretionary relief for failure to appear as ordered in the Immigration Judge's oral decision.
[ ]   Proceedings were terminated.
[ ]   Other:_____.

Date: 6-1-01
Appeal: (WAIVED) RESERVED (A/I/B)
APPEAL DUE BY: _____

                                        James R. Fujimoto
                                        Immigration Judge

APPENDIX 7
ORDER OF EXPEDITED REMOVAL

Department of Justice
Immigration and Naturalization Service

Notice and Order of Expedited Removal

DETERMINATION OF INADMISSIBILITY

File No: A77 ____
Date: ____/1999

In the Matter of: ____

Pursuant to section 235(b)(1) of the Immigration and Nationality Act (Act), (8 U.S.C. 1225(b)(1)), the Immigration and Naturalization Service has determined that you are inadmissible to the United States under section(s) 212(a) ☒(6)(C)(i); ☐(6)(C)(ii); ☒(7)(A)(i)(I); ☐(7)(A)(i)(II); ☐(7)(B)(i)(I); and/or ☐(7)(B)(i)(II) the Act, as amended, and therefore are subject to removal, in that:

You are ineligible for admission to the United States because you, by fraud or by willfully misrepresenting a material fact, seek to procure (or have sought to procure or have procured) a visa, other documentation, or admission into the United States or other benefit provided under the Immigration and Nationality Act.

Continued on form I-831 attached.

TAM O'NEIL
SENIOR IMMIGRATION INSP
Name and Title of Immigration Officer (Print)

Signature of Immigration Officer

ORDER OF REMOVAL
UNDER SECTION 235(b)(1) OF THE ACT

Based upon the determination set forth above and evidence presented during inspection or examination pursuant to section 235 of the Act, and by the authority contained in section 235(b)(1) of the Act, you are found to be inadmissible as charged and ordered removed from the United States.

Name and Title of Immigration Officer (Print)

Signature of Immigration Officer

Name and Title of Supervisor (Print)

Signature of Supervisor, if available

Check here if supervisory concurrence was obtained by telephone or other means (no supervisor on duty).

CERTIFICATE OF SERVICE

I personally served the original of this notice upon the above named person on ____ (Date)

Signature of Immigration Officer

Form I-860 (Rev 04-01-97)

Department of Justice
igration and Naturalization Service

Continuation Page for Form ____I-860____

s Name	File Number A72▉▉▉▉	Date ▉▉▉/1999
▉▉▉▉▉▉▉		

You are subject to removal, in that: (con't.)

You are ineleigible for admission to the United States because:

At the time of your application for admission to the United States you wore not in possession of a valid unexpired immigrant visa, reentry permit, border crossing card, or other valid entry document required by the Immigration and Nationality Act and/or

At the time of your application for admission, you were not in possession of a valid unexpired passport, or other suitable travel document, or document of identity and nationality.

Signature LIAM O'NEILL	Title SENIOR IMMIGRATION INSP

____2____ of ____7____ Pages

Form I-S31 Continuation Page (Rev.6/12/92)

Department of Justice
ration and Naturalization Service

Notice to Alien Ordered Removed/Departure Verification

File No: A77⬛⬛⬛⬛

Date: ⬛⬛⬛⬛0, 1999

is full name ⬛⬛⬛⬛

have been found to be inadmissible to the United States under the provisions of section 212(a) of the Immigration and
nality Act (Act) or deportable under the provisions of section 237 of the Act as a Visa Waiver Pilot Program violator. In
dance with the provisions of section 212(a)(9) of the Act, you are prohibited from entering, attempting to enter, or being in the
d States:

for a period of 5 years from the date of your departure from the United States as a consequence of your having been found
inadmissible as an arriving alien in proceedings under section 235(b)(1) or 240 of the Act.

for a period of 10 years from the date of your departure from the United States as a consequence of your having been
ordered removed in proceedings under any section of the Act other than section 235(b)(1) or 240, or of your having been
ordered excluded under section 236 of the Act in proceedings commenced prior to April 1, 1997.

for a period of 20 years from the date of your departure from the United States as a consequence of your having been found
inadmissible and of your having been previously excluded, deported, or removed from the United States.

at any time because in addition to having been found inadmissible, you have been convicted of a crime designated as an
aggravated felony.

your deportation or removal has been effected, if you desire to reenter the United States within the period during which you are
ed, you must request and obtain permission from the Attorney General to reapply for admission into the United States. You must
in such permission prior to commencing your travel to the United States. Application forms for requesting such permission may be
ed by contacting any United States Consulate or office of the United States Immigration and Naturalization Service.

ARNING: Title 8 United States Code, Section 1326 provides that it is a crime for an alien who has been removed from the
ited States to enter, attempt to enter, or be found in the United States without the Attorney General's express consent.
y alien who violates this section of law is subject to prosecution for a felony. Depending on the circumstances of the
moval, conviction could result in a sentence of imprisonment for a period of from 2 to 20 years and/or a fine of up to
0,000.

(Signature of officer serving warning)	SRI (Title of officer)	CA GO (Location of INS office)

Verification of Removal
(Complete this section for file copy only)

rture date	Port of departure		Manner of departure
ature of verifying officer		Title of officer	

Photograph of alien removed

Right index fingerprint
of alien removed

(Signature of alien whose fingerprint and photograph appear above)

(Signature of official taking fingerprint)

Form I-296 (Rev. 6-1-97)N

APPENDIX 8
ADMINISTRATIVE ORDER OF REMOVAL

FEB 07 2002 11:14AM HP LASERJET 3200

p. 2

U.S. Department of Justice
Immigration and Naturalization Service

Final Administrative Removal Order

FINAL ADMINISTRATIVE REMOVAL ORDER
UNDER SECTION 238(b) OF THE
IMMIGRATION AND NATIONALITY ACT

BOP No.: ▮▮▮▮▮▮
File No: ▮▮▮▮▮▮
Date: 10/27/99

To: ▮▮▮▮▮▮
Address: BOP ALLENWOOD LOW FCI LSCI-ALLENWOOD PO BOX 1500 WHITE DEER PA 17887
(Number, street, city, state and ZIP code)

Telephone: N/A
(Area code and phone number)

ORDER

Based upon the allegations set forth in the Notice of Intent to Issue a Final Administrative Removal Order and evidence contained in the administrative record, I, the undersigned Deciding Service Officer of the Immigration and Naturalization Service, make the following findings of fact and conclusions of law. I find that you are not a citizen or national of the United States and that you were not lawfully admitted for permanent residence. I further find that you have a final conviction of an aggravated felony as defined in section 101(a)(43) of the Act, 8 U.S.C. 1101(a)(43), and are ineligible for any relief from removal that the Attorney General may grant in an exercise of discretion. I further find that the administrative record established by clear, convincing, and unequivocal evidence that you are deportable as an alien convicted of an aggravated felony pursuant to section 237(a)(2)(A)(iii) of the Act, 8 U.S.C. 1227(a)(2)(A)(iii). By the power and authority vested in the Attorney General and in me as the Attorney General's delegate under the laws of the United States, I find you deportable as charged and order that you be removed from the United States to

_____Colombia_____ or to any alternate country prescribed in section 241 of the Act.

(Signature of Authorized INS Official)

District Director
(Title of official)

Philadelphia, PA 10/27/99
(Date and office location)

Petition for review: ☐ Waived by respondent.
                      ☐ Reserved by respondent.

Certificate of Service

I served this FINAL ADMINISTRATIVE REMOVAL ORDER upon the above named individual

11/16/1999   Allenwood, PA; US Mail / Personal Service   12:00 ↵
(Date, time, place and manner of service)

STREETE, Damian IHP Officer
(Signature and title of officer)

Form I-851A (Rev. 4/1/97)P

07 2002 11:14AM   HP LASERJET 3200

Attachment to Final Administrative Removal Order (I-851A)

Re:

I have considered all the information related to the Administrative Removal proceedings in your case, including responses submitted by yourself and your attorney on your behalf.

In recognizing your request for relief under the Convention Against Torture Act and section 241(b)(3)(B) of the INA [restriction on removal], your case will be referred to an Asylum Officer for adjudication of your claim. Nevertheless, I find that your alienage and the charge of removeability under section 237(a)(2)(A)(iii) of the INA have been sustained by clear, convincing and unequivocal evidence.

<u>Accordingly, this Administrative Order is deemed to be final.</u>

APPENDIX 9
NATURALIZATION CHARTS

AUTOMATIC ACQUISITION OF CITIZENSHIP
UNDER THE CHILD CITIZENSHIP ACT OF 2000

Effective Date of Act*	Eligibility Requirements**	Age Limit	Date of Automatic Acquisition	Law Applicable
2/27/01	At least one parent is U.S. citizen by birth or naturalization. Child residing in U.S. in the legal and physical custody of citizen parent pursuant to a lawful admission for permanent residence.	Under 18	Date last condition fulfilled	INA §320, as amended by P.L. 106-395

*   Law is not retroactive, *i.e.*, acquisition can only occur on or after 2/27/01 and only for children under 18 after 2/27/01.

**   Applies to adopted child if child has met requirements applicable to adopted children under INA §101(b)(1)(E) or (F).

EXPEDITED NATURALIZATION OF CHILDREN

Effective Date of Act*	Eligibility Requirements	Age Limit	Date of Acquisition	Law Applicable
2/27/01	At least one parent is U.S. citizen by birth or naturalization at time of filing N-600K. If citizen parent deceased during preceding 5 years, citizen grandparent or citizen legal guardian may file N-600K. Prior to filing, citizen parent has been physically present in U.S. for at least 5 years, at least 2 after age 14, or citizen parent has a citizen parent who has been physically present in U.S. for 5 years, at least 2 after age 14. Child is currently residing outside U.S. in legal and physical custody of citizen parent, or if citizen parent deceased, an individual who does not object to the application. Child is temporarily present in U.S. pursuant to a lawful admission and maintaining lawful status.	Under 18	Date of Issuance of Certificate	INA §322, as amended by P.L. 106-395 & by P. L. 107-273

*   Applies to adopted children under 18 if child has met requirements applicable to adopted children under INA §101(b)(1)(E) or (F)

AUTOMATIC ACQUISITION OF CITIZENSHIP
THROUGH NATURALIZATION OF PARENT(S)

Date Parent(s) Naturalized	Who Naturalized	Age Limit*	Date of Automatic Acquisition		Law Applicable
			If Residing in U.S.	**If Residing Abroad**	
Prior to 3/2/07	Either parent	Under 21	Date of naturalization of parent	Date child lawfully admitted U.S. for permanent residence	§2172, R.S. (Act 4/14/1802)
3/2/07 to noon EST, 5/24/34	Either parent	Under 21	Date of naturalization of parent	Date child lawfully admitted U.S. for permanent residence	§2172, R.S. Sec. 5, Act 3/2/07
noon EST, 5/24/34, to 1/13/41	One parent, other remaining alien	Under 21 when admitted U.S.	Upon completion 5 yrs. residence in U.S. including residence completed after age 21 and after 1/13/41		§5, Act 3/2/07, as amended by Sec. 2 Act 5/24/34
	Alien parent (other being citizen); surviving parent; or parent having custody in divorce	Under 21	Date of naturalization of parent	Date child lawfully admitted U.S. for permanent residence	§2172, R.S.
1/13/41 to 12/24/52	Alien parent other being citizen from child's birth	Under 18	Date of naturalization of parent	Date child lawfully admitted U.S. for permanent residence	§313, 1940 Act
	Both parents; surviving parent; or parent having custody in legal separation	Under 18	Date of naturalization of parent	Date child lawfully admitted U.S. for permanent residence	§314, 1940 Act
Subsequent to 12/24/52 but before 2/27/01	**Alien parent, other being citizen from child's birth	Under 18	Date last condition fulfilled	Date child lawfully admitted U.S. for permanent residence	INA §320, as amended by P.L. 95-417. Repealed by P.L. 106-395
	**Both parents; surviving parent; parent having custody in legal separation; or mother of child out of wedlock	Under 18	Date last condition fulfilled	Date child lawfully admitted U.S. for permanent residence	INA §321, as amended by P.L. 95-417. Repealed by P.L. 106-395

*   The date of the parent(s) naturalization and the date of the lawful admittance of the child must occur before the age shown in the age limit column.

**   Applies to an adopted child if the child is residing in the U.S. at the time of naturalization of such adopted parent or parents, in the custody of his adoptive parent or parents, pursuant to a lawful admission for permanent residence.

**ADJUDICATING CITIZENSHIP BASED ON
BIRTH OUT OF WEDLOCK TO A U.S. FATHER**

Determining Whether to Use "New" or "Old" INA §309(a)

Date of Birth	Applicable Statute	Age Before Which "Legitimation" Must Occur*	Date Before Which "Legitimation" Must Occur*	Statement of Support Required?
Before **Nov. 14, 1968**	Old Section 309(a)	21	11/14/89	No
On or after **Nov. 14, 1968**	Old Section 309(a)	21	11/14/92	No
but before **Nov. 14, 1971**	New Section 309(a)	18	11/14/89	Yes
On or after **Nov. 14, 1971**	Old Section 309(a)	15	11/14/86	No
but before **Nov. 14, 1986**	New Section 309(a)	18	11/14/04	Yes
On or after **Nov. 14, 1986**	New Section 309(a)	18	None	Yes

* Note that under **New Section 309(a),** the citizen father can, in lieu of legitimation, acknowledge paternity in writing and under oath, or paternity of the child can be established by adjudication of a competent court. Any one of the three methods of establishing paternity must occur before the child's 18th birthday.

Tables of Transmission Requirements Over Time
for Citizenship for Certain Individuals Born Abroad

Note—Governing Statute: Acquisition of U.S. citizenship **at birth abroad** to a U.S. citizen parent(s) is governed by federal statute. The governing law in the case of a person born abroad who claims U.S. citizenship through a U.S. citizen parent(s) is **the law in effect on the date of the claimant's birth,** unless a subsequent law specifically by its language in the statute applies retroactively to persons who had not already become citizens by the provisions of the prior law. At times, a new law will merely renumber an old law without changing the requirements or provisions. As such, it will read, *e.g.,* "§301(a)(7), now §301(g) INA."

When pertinent law requires specific conditions on the part of the U.S. citizen parent(s), the conditions must be met prior to the child's birth unless otherwise stated in the statute.

Residence or physical presence transmission requirements can be met while the transmitting parent is not a citizen.

Birth Abroad to U.S. Citizen Parent and Alien Parent

Date of Birth	Transmission Requirements	Reference	Retention Requirements	Reference
Before **May 24, 1934** (noon EST)*	Either U.S. citizen father or mother could transmit. U.S. citizen parent resided in U.S. before child's birth.	§1993, Revised Statutes (RS); 7 FAM 1135; §301(h) INA; P.L. 103-416.	None	
On or after **May 24, 1934** (noon EST),* *but before* **Jan. 13, 1941**	Either U.S. citizen father or mother could transmit. U.S. citizen parent resided in U.S. before child's birth.	§1993, RS as amended in 1934; 7 FAM 1135.1, 11.35.2.	Persons failing to fulfill below requirements may have citizenship restored upon taking oath of allegiance. (1) 5 years residence between the ages 13-21 if begun before 12/24/52; or (2) 2 years continuous physical presence between ages 14–28;[1] or (3) 5 years continuous physical presence between ages 14–28 if begun before 10/27/72.[2] (4) None if parent employed certain occupation.[3] (5) None if alien parent naturalized and child began to reside permanently in U.S. while under age 18.	§324(d)(1) Immigration and Nationality Act of 1952 (INA), §101 P.L. 103-416; 7 FAM 1133.5-15. (1) §201(g) and (h) Nationality Act of 1940 (NA), 54 Stat. 1137; 7 FAM 1134.6-3 (2) Former §301(b), (c) INA; 7 FAM 1133.5-7, 5-8 (3) Former §301(b), (d) INA; 7 FAM 1133.5-2, 1133.5–9 (4) §201(g) INA; 7 FAM 1134.6-2 (5) Former §301(b) INA; 7 FAM 1133.5-7, 1133.5-11

* *Sic.* The statute refers to "Eastern Standard Time"; however, Daylight Savings Time was in effect on May 24, 1934.
[1] Absences of less than 60 days in aggregate during 2 year period do not break continuity.
[2] Absences of less than one year in aggregate during 5 year period do not break continuity.
[3] U.S. Government, American education, scientific, philanthropic, religious, commercial, or financial organization or an International Agency in which the U.S. takes part. Note: residence or physical presence of parent must take place *before* child's birth.

Date of Birth	Transmission Requirements	Reference	Retention Requirements	Reference
On or after **Jan. 13, 1941,** *but before* **Dec. 24, 1952**	Citizen parent resided in U.S. or possession 10 years prior to child's birth, five of which after the age of 16.	§201(g) NA; 7 FAM 1134.2, 1134.3	Persons failing to fulfill below requirements may have citizenship restored upon taking oath of allegiance. (1) 2 years continuous physical presence between ages 14-28;[1] or (2) 5 years continuous physical presence between ages 14-28 if begun before 10/27/72.[2] (3) None if parent employed in certain occupation.[3] (4) None if child born on or after 10/10/52; (5) None if alien parent naturalized and child began to reside permanently in U.S. while under age 18.	§324(d)(1) INA, §101 P.L. 103-416; 7 FAM 1133.5-15 (1) Former §301(b), (c) INA; 7 FAM 1133.5-7, 5-8 (2) Former §301(b), (d) INA; 7 FAM 1133.5-2, 1133.5-9 (3) §201(g) NA; 7 FAM 1134.6-2 (4) P.L. 95-432; 7 FAM 1133.5-13 (5) Former §301(b) INA; 7 FAM 1133.5-7, 1133.5-11
	Citizen parent in U.S. military 12/7/41 to 12/31/46 and resided in U.S. or possession 10 years prior to child's birth, five of which after age 12.	§201(i) NA; 7 FAM 1134.2, 1134.4	Persons failing to fulfill below requirements may have citizenship restored upon taking oath of allegiance. (1) 2 years continuous physical presence between ages 14-28;[1] or (2) 5 years continuous physical presence between ages 14-28 if begun before 10/27/72.[2] (3) None if child born on or after 10/10/52. (4) None if alien parent naturalized and child began to reside permanently in U.S. while under age 18.	§324(d)(1) INA, §101 P.L. 103-416; 7 FAM 1133.5-15 (1) Former §301(b) INA; 7 FAM 1134.4e, 1133.5 (2) Former §301(b), (d) INA; 7 FAM 1133.5-2, 1133.5-9 (3) P.L. 95-432; 7 FAM 1133.5-15 (4) Former §301(b) INA; 7 FAM 1133.5-7, 1133.5-11

[1] Absences of less than 60 days in aggregate during 2 year period do not break continuity.

[2] Absences of less than one year in aggregate during 5 year period do not break continuity.

[3] U.S. Government, American education, scientific, philanthropic, religious, commercial, or financial organization or an International Agency in which the U.S. takes part. Note: residence or physical presence of parent must take place *before* child's birth.

Date of Birth	Transmission Requirements	Reference	Retention Requirements	Reference
(on or after Jan 13, 1941, but before Dec. 24, 1952— cont'd)	Citizen parent in U.S. military 1/1/47 to 12/24/52 and physically present in U.S. or possession 10 years prior to child's birth, five of which after age 14, and who did not qualify under either provision above.	§301(a)(7), now §301(g) INA; 7 FAM 1134.4f	Persons failing to fulfill below requirements may have citizenship restored upon taking oath of allegiance. (1) 2 years continuous physical presence between ages 14–28;[1] or (2) 5 years continuous physical presence between ages 14–28 if begun before 10/27/72.[2] (3) None if child born on or after 10/10/52. (4) None if alien parent naturalized and child began to reside permanently in U.S. while under age 18.	§324(d)(1) INA; P.L. 103–416; 7 FAM 1133.5-15 (1) Former §301(b) INA; 7 FAM 1133.5-7, 5-8 (2) Former §301(b), (d) INA; 7 FAM 1133.5-2, 1133.5-9 (3) P.L. 95-432; 7 FAM 1133.5-13 (4) Former §301(b) INA; 7 FAM 1133.5-7, 1133.5-11
On or after **Dec. 24, 1952**, but before **Nov. 14, 1986**	Citizen parent physically present in U.S. or possession 10 years prior to child's birth, five of which after age 14. Honorable U.S. military service, employment with U.S. government or intergovernmental international organization, or as dependent unmarried son or daughter and member of the household of a parent in such service or employment, may be included.	§301(a)(7), now §301(g) INA; 7 FAM 1133.2-2, 1133.3-3	None	
On or after **Nov. 14, 1986**	Citizen parent physically present in U.S. or possession 5 years prior to child's birth, two of which after age 14. Honorable U.S. military service, employment with U.S. government or intergovernmental international organization, or as dependent unmarried son or daughter and member of the household of a parent in such service or employment, may be included.	§301(g) INA; P.L. 99-655; P.L. 100-525; 7 FAM 1133.2-1	None	

[1] Absences of less than 60 days in aggregate during 2 year period do not break continuity.

[2] Absences of less than one year in aggregate during 5 year period do not break continuity.

[3] U.S. Government, American education, scientific, philanthropic, religious, commercial, or financial organization or an International Agency in which the U.S. takes part. Note: residence or physical presence of parent must take place *before* child's birth.

Birth Abroad to Two U.S. Citizen Parents

Date of Birth	Transmission Requirements (Parents' Residence)	Applicable Laws	Reference
Before May 24, 1934 (noon, EST)*	One parent resided in the U.S.	§1993, Revised Statutes (RS); §301(h) INA; §101 P.L. 103-416	7 FAM 1135.1
On or after May 24, 1934 (noon, EST),* *but before* Jan. 13, 1941	One parent resided in the U.S.	§1993, RS as amended by Act of 5/24/34	7 FAM 1135.6-1
On or after Jan. 13, 1941, *but before* Dec. 24, 1952	One parent resided in the U.S. or possession.	§201(c) NA	7 FAM 1134.2, 1134.3-1, 1134.3-2
On or after Dec. 24, 1952	One parent resided in the U.S. or possession.	§301(a)(3), now §301(c) INA	7 FAM 1133.2-1a, 1133.3-1a

Notes: (1) In all cases, residence must take place prior to the child's birth; (2) the law does not define how long residence must be; and (3) children born to two U.S. citizen parents never had retention requirements.

Child Born Out of Wedlock to U.S. Citizen Mother

Date of Birth	Transmission Requirements (Parents' Residence)	Applicable Laws	Reference
Before May 24, 1934 (noon, EST)*	Mother resided in the U.S. or possession prior to child's birth; child not legitimated by alien father before 1/13/41.	§205, paragraph 2, NA	7 FAM 1135.3-2
On or after May 24, 1934 (noon, EST),* *but before* Jan. 13, 1941	Mother resided in U.S. or possession prior to child's birth.	§1993, RS as amended by Act of 5/24/34; §205, paragraph 2, NA	7 FAM 1135.7-2
On or after Jan. 13, 1941, *but before* Dec. 24, 1952	Mother resided in U.S. or possession prior to child's birth.	§205, paragraph 2, NA	7 FAM 1134.5-4
On or after Dec. 24, 1952	Mother physically present in U.S. or possession continuously 12 months prior to child's birth.	§309(c), INA	7 FAM 1133.4-3

Note: Children born out of wedlock to a U.S. citizen mother never had retention requirements.

Child Born Out of Wedlock to U.S. Citizen Father and Alien Mother

Date of Birth	Transmission and Legal Relationship Requirements	Reference	Retention Requirements	Reference
Before May 24, 1934 (noon, EST)*	Legitimated under law of father's U.S. or foreign domicile. Father resided in U.S. before child's birth.	§1993, RS; 7 FAM 1135.3-1	None	
On or after May 24, 1934 (noon EST),* *but before* Jan. 13, 1941	Legitimated under law of father's U.S. or foreign domicile. Father resided in U.S. before child's birth.	§1993, RS as amended in 1934; 7 FAM 1135.7-1	Persons failing to fulfill below requirements may have citizenship restored upon taking oath of allegiance. (1) 5 years residence between ages 13-21 if begun before 12/24/52; or (2) 2 years continuous physical presence between ages 14-28;[1] or (3) 5 years continuous physical presence between ages 14-28 if begun before 10/27/72.[2] (4) None if parent employed certain occupation.[3] (5) None if alien parent naturalized and child began to reside permanently in U.S. while under age 18.	§324(d)(1) INA; §101 P.L. 103-416 1133.5-15 (1) §201(g) and (h) NA; 7 FAM1133.6-3 (2) Former §301(b), (c) INA; 7 FAM 1133.5-7, 1133.5-8 (3) Former §301(b), (d) INA; 7 FAM 1133.5-2, 1133.5-9 (4) §201(g) NA; 7 FAM 1134.6-2 (5) Former §301(b) INA; 7 FAM 1133.5-7, 1133.5-11

* *Sic.* The statute refers to "Eastern Standard Time"; however, Daylight Savings Time was in effect on May 24, 1934.

[1] Absences of less than 60 days in aggregate during 2 year period do not break continuity.

[2] Absences of less than one year in aggregate during 5 year period do not break continuity.

[3] U.S. government, American educational, scientific, philanthropic, religious, commercial, or financial organization or an international agency in which the U.S. takes part.

Note: Residence or physical presences of parent must take place before child's birth. Section 301(h) of INA took effect Oct. 25, 1994, and is retroactive to 1790. Section 324(d) of INA took effect March 1, 1995, and is applicable to anyone who failed to retain citizenship regardless of date citizenship ceased.

Date of Birth	Transmission Requirements	Reference	Retention Requirements	Reference
On or after **Jan. 13, 1941,** *but before* **Dec. 24, 1952**	(1a) Father physically present in U.S. or possession 10 years prior to child's birth, 5 of which after the age of 14. Honor-able U.S. military service, employment with U.S. government or intergovernmental international organization, or as dependent unmarried son or daughter and member of the household of a parent in such service or employment may be included; and	§301(a)(7) INA; 7 FAM 1133.3-3	Persons failing to fulfill below requirements may have citizenship restored upon taking oath of allegiance. (1) 2 years continuous physical presence between ages 14-18;[1] (2) 5 years continuous physical presence between ages 14-28 if begun before 10/27/72.[2] (3) None if parent employed in certain occupation.[3] (4) None if child born on or after 10/10/52. (5) None if alien parent naturalized and child began to reside permanently in U.S. while under age 18.	§324(d)(1) INA; §101 P.L. 103-416; 7 FAM 1133.5-15 (1) Former §301(b), (c) INA; 7 FAM 1133.5-7, 5-8 (2) Former §301(b), (d) INA; 7 FAM 1133.5-2, 1133.5-9 (3) §201(g) NA; 7 FAM 1134.6-2 (4) P.L. 95-432; 7 FAM 1133.5-13 (5) Former §301(b) INA; 7 FAM 1133.5-7, 1133.5-11
	(1b) Paternity established fore age 21 by the legitimation law of father's or child's residence/domicile; *or*	§309(b) INA		
	(2a) Father resided in U.S. or possession 10 years prior to child's birth, five of which after the age of 16 years; and	§201(g) NA		
	(2b) Paternity established during minority by legitimation or court adjudication before 12/24/52.	§205 NA; 7 FAM 1134.5-2		
On or after **Dec. 24, 1952,** *through* **Nov. 14, 1968**	(1) Father physically present in U.S. or possession 10 years prior to child's birth, five of which after age 14. Honorable U.S. military service, employment with U.S. government or intergovernmental international organization, or as dependent unmarried son or daughter and member of the household of a parent in such service or employment, may be included; and	§301(a)(7) INA	None	
	(2) Paternity established under age 21 by legitimation law of father's or child's residence/domicile.	§309(a) INA as originally enacted		

Note: INA §301(h) took effect 10/25/94 and is retroactive to 1790. INA §324(d) took effect 3/1/95 and is applicable to anyone who failed to retain citizenship regardless of date citizenship ceased.

[1] Absences of less than 60 days in aggregate during 2 year period do not break continuity.

[2] Absences of less than one year in aggregate during 5 year period do not break continuity.

[3] U.S. government, American educational, scientific, philanthropic, religious, commercial, or financial organization or an international agency in which the U.S. takes part.

Note: Residence or physical presences of parent must take place before child's birth. Section 301(h) of INA took effect Oct. 25, 1994, and is retroactive to 1790. Section 324(d) of INA took effect March 1, 1995, and is applicable to anyone who failed to retain citizenship regardless of date citizenship ceased.

Date of Birth	Transmission Requirements	Reference	Retention Requirements	Reference
After Nov. 14, 1968, *through* Nov. 14, 1971	(1) Father physically present in U.S. or possession 10 years prior to child's birth, five of which after age 14. Honorable U.S. military service, employment with U.S. government or intergovernmental international organization, or as dependent unmarried son or daughter and member of the household of a parent in such service or employment, may be included; and	§301(a)(7) INA	None	
	(2a) Blood relationship established between father and child, father a U.S. citizen at time of child's birth, father (unless deceased) agrees in writing to support child until 18 years, and while child is under 18 years: (i) child is legitimated, (ii) father acknowledges paternity, or (iii) paternity established by court adjudication, or	§309(a) INA as amended 11/14/86, 102 Stat. 2619; 7 FAM 1133.4-2		
	(2b) Paternity is established under age 21 by the legitimation law of father's or child's residence/domicile.	§309(a) INA, as originally enacted		

[1] Absences of less than 60 days in aggregate during 2 year period do not break continuity.
[2] Absences of less than one year in aggregate during 5 year period do not break continuity.
[3] U.S. government, American educational, scientific, philanthropic, religious, commercial, or financial organization or an international agency in which the U.S. takes part.
Note: Residence or physical presences of parent must take place before child's birth. Section 301(h) of INA took effect Oct. 25, 1994, and is retroactive to 1790. Section 324(d) of INA took effect March 1, 1995, and is applicable to anyone who failed to retain citizenship regardless of date citizenship ceased.

Date of Birth	Transmission Requirements	Reference	Retention Requirements	Reference
After Nov. 11, 1971, but before Nov. 14, 1986	(1) Father physically present in U.S. or possession 10 years prior to child's birth, five of which after age 14. Honorable U.S. military service, employment with U.S. government or intergovernmental international organization, or as dependent unmarried son or daughter and member of the household of a parent in such service or employment, may be included; and (2) Blood relationship established between father and child, father a U.S. citizen at time of child's birth, father (unless deceased) agrees in writing to support child until 18 years, and while child is under 18 years: (i) child is legitimated, (ii) father acknowledges paternity, or (iii) paternity established by court adjudication.	§301(a)(7) INA §309(a) INA, as amended 11/14/86; 102 Stat. 2619; 7 FAM 1133.4-2	None	
On or after Nov. 14, 1986	(1) Father physically present in U.S. or possession five years prior to child's birth, two of which after age 14. Honorable U.S. military service, employment with U.S. government or intergovernmental international organization, or as dependent unmarried son or daughter and member of the household of a parent in such service or employment, may be included; and (2) Blood relationship established between father and child, father a U.S. citizen at time of child's birth, father (unless deceased) agrees in writing to support child until 18 years, and while child is under 18 years: (i) child is legitimated, (ii) father acknowledges paternity, or (iii) paternity established by court adjudication.	§301(g) INA; 7 FAM 1133.3-3 §309(a) INA as amended 11/14/86; 102 Stat. 2619; 7 FAM 1133.4-2		

[1] Absences of less than 60 days in aggregate during 2 year period do not break continuity.

[2] Absences of less than one year in aggregate during 5 year period do not break continuity.

[3] U.S. government, American educational, scientific, philanthropic, religious, commercial, or financial organization or an international agency in which the U.S. takes part.

Note: Residence or physical presences of parent must take place before child's birth. Section 301(h) of INA took effect Oct. 25, 1994, and is retroactive to 1790. Section 324(d) of INA took effect March 1, 1995, and is applicable to anyone who failed to retain citizenship regardless of date citizenship ceased.

APPENDIX 10
MOTION TO SUPPRESS EVIDENCE

UNITED STATES DEPARTMENT OF JUSTICE
EXECUTIVE OFFICE FOR IMMIGRATION REVIEW
OFFICE OF THE IMMIGRATION JUDGE
CHICAGO, ILLINOIS

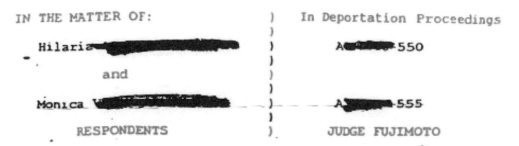

IN THE MATTER OF:)   In Deportation Proceedings
)
   Hilaria ▮▮▮▮▮▮▮▮▮▮▮▮▮   )   A▮▮▮▮▮550
)
          and   )
)
   Monica ▮▮▮▮▮▮▮▮▮▮▮▮   )   A▮▮▮▮▮555
)
      RESPONDENTS   )   JUDGE FUJIMOTO

RESPONDENTS' MOTION TO SUPPRESS EVIDENCE

Respondents, Hilaria A▮▮▮▮▮▮▮▮▮▮ and Monica V▮▮▮▮▮

▮▮▮▮▮, through their legal representative, Travelers &

Immigrants Aid of Chicago, hereby move for the suppression and

exclusion of all evidence, physical and testimonial, obtained

derived from or through or as a result of the unlawful detention,

arrest, and interrogation of Respondents on March 16, 1994 by

officers of the Immigration & Naturalization Service ("INS").

Specifically, Respondents move for the suppression and exclusion

of the following:

A.   INS forms I-213, I-214, or any other statements or forms

     completed from information that may have been given to the

     INS as a result of the unlawful arrest of the Respondents,

     and any forms signed by the Respondents on or about March

     16, 1994, including forms completed from information that

     may have been given to INS as a result of the unlawful

     arrest of Respondents which the Respondents refused to sign

B.   Any statements by the Respondents on Form I-215B or any other statement made by the Respondents, signed or unsigned.

C.   Any and all other property, papers, information, or testimony pertaining to the Respondents, obtained or taken by the agents of the INS, or by any other person acting in concert with them, on or about March 16, 1994.

D.   Any and all other property, papers, information, or testimony pertaining to the Respondents obtained from INS files, or any other source as the fruit of the illegal detention, arrest, and interrogation that occurred on or about March 16, 1994.

In support of this Motion, the Respondents state as follows:

1.   On March 15, 1994, Respondents ██████████████████████ and her daughter, Monica V████████████, flew from Phoenix, Arizona to Chicago, Illinois on America West Airlines flight 333. Also travelling with the Respondents were family members Antonio V█████████, husband of Respondent Hilaria A███████████ and father of Respondent █████ V████████████, and Maria Dolores V████████████, age 12, and Adriana V█████████████, age 9, the two youngest

children of the Vasquez family.

2. The Respondents' flight arrived at O'Hare International
   - Airport in Chicago at approximately 12:00 a.m. on March 16,
   1944. Along with other passengers on the plane, the
   Respondents disembarked from the aircraft and began walking
   through the tunnel connecting the plane with the terminal.
   At the end of the tunnel they saw three men blocking the
   entrance to the terminal. As the Respondents approached the
   end of the tunnel the men blocking the entrance showed the
   Respondents INS badges and said they were INS officers.
   Respondents, along with other disembarking passengers, were
   ordered to step to one side if they did not have documents.

3. As Respondents and their family walked around the officers
   to enter the terminal, they were immediately approached by
   another man who identified himself an an INS officer and
   asked them if they had documents. After his questions were
   answered, the INS officer moved on. Respondents were not
   free to leave the area, which was being patrolled by
   several INS officers.

4. While the Respondents were in the terminal, they also
   observed the INS officers standing at the entrance to the
   terminal only appeared to be detaining and questioning

passengers of Latino appearance; passengers who appeared "anglo" or "American" were allowed to enter the terminal without questioning.

5. As the INS officers stopped and questioned passengers of Latino appearance, more individuals were detained in the area with the Respondents. After all the passengers disembarked, a group of approximately 30 passengers of Latino appearance, including the Respondents, were ordered to follow the INS officers to a bus, which they were then directed to board. The Repondents were not shown a warrant for their arrests.

6. The bus carrying the Respondents and the other passengers was driven to another location approximately ten minutes away which was not clearly identified to the Respondents. There the Respondents were directed to empty their pockets and have their bags ready to be searched. They were then told to remain in a waiting room until they were called. After approximately two or three hours an INS officer called them for questioning. They were questioned in the general waiting area, and were not advised of their rights to make a telephone call or consult with an attorney prior to questioning. Finally, at approximately 5:00 a.m., after being questioned, fingerprinted, and photographed, the

Respondents were each served with an Order to Show Cause, and released on their own recognizance.

7.   Based on the above, the detention, arrest, and interrogation of the Respondents by the INS officers on or about March 16, 1994 were conducted in violation of the Fourth and Fifth Amendments of the U.S. Constitution, and in violation of 8 C.F.R. Sections 242.1, 242.2, 287.3, and the settlement directives of Lopez v. INS, in that:

   A.   INS officers had no valid warrant authorizing them to arrest the Respondents;

   B.   INS officers had no reasonable suspicion based on specific articulable facts that the Respondents were aliens unlawfully in the country in order to detain and arrest, as their detention and arrest was based solely on their appearance;

   C.   INS officers did not inform the Respondents of the reasons for their arrests, did not advise them of their right to counsel and their right to contact counsel, and id not advise them that statements they made could be used against them;

D.   The circumstances of the Respondents' arrests,
     detention, and interrogation were such that any
     statements taken as a result of their unlawful arrest
     were coerced and involuntary in violation of the Fifth
     Amendment of the U.S. Constitution;

E.   The circumstances asserted in A, B, C, and D were such
     that any statements or evidence taken were coerced
     involuntarily in violation of 8 C.F.R. and the
     settlement directives of Lopez v. INS;

F.   The egregious circumstances asserted in A, B, C, and D
     above were such that fundamental fairness was violated.

WHEREFORE, the Respondents respectfully move that all such
evidence be suppressed and excluded from deportation
proceedings against them.

Respectfully submitted,

Delia Seeberg
Accredited Representative
Travelers & Immigrants Aid
208 S. LaSalle Street, Suite 1818
Chicago, Illinois 60604
(312) 629-1960

TABLE OF DECISIONS

A

A– and Z–, Matter of, A72 793 219 (IJ Arlington, VA. Dec. 20, 1994) 247

Abdelqadar v. Gonzales, 413 F.3d 668 (7th Cir. 2005) 35, 46, 47

Abebe v. Mukasey, No. 05-76201, U.S. App. LEXIS 23859 (9th Cir. Nov. 20, 2008) 191

Abel v. United States, 362 U.S. 217 (1960) 115

Abiodun v. Gonzales, 461 F.3d 1210 (10th Cir. 2006) 42, 109

Acosta, Matter of, 19 I&N Dec. 211 (BIA 1985) 239, 244, 250

Acosta Hidalgo, Matter of, 24 I&N Dec. 103 (BIA 2007) 102, 279, 281, 282, 283

Adams v. Baker, 909 F.2d 643 (1st Cir. 1990) 73

Adeniji, Matter of, 22 I&N Dec. 1102 (BIA 1999) 12

Adetiba, Matter of, 20 I&N Dec. 506 (BIA 1992) 35, 44, 47

A–G–, Matter of, 19 I&N Dec. 502 (BIA 1987), *aff'd sub nom. M.A. v. INS,* 899 F.2d 304
    (4th Cir. 1990) 240

A–H–, Matter of, 23 I&N Dec. 774 (A.G. 2005) 253

A–K–, Matter of, 24 I&N Dec. 275 (BIA 2007) 247

Akindemowo v. INS, 61 F.3d 282 (4th Cir. 1995) 47

Alaka v. Attorney Gen., 456 F.3d 88 (3d Cir. 2006) 256, 257

Alarcon-Serrano v. INS, 220 F.3d 1116 (9th Cir. 2000) 73

Albillo-DeLeon v. Gonzales, 410 F.3d 1090 (9th Cir. 2005) 229

Albrekton; United States v., 151 F.3d 951 (9th Cir. 1998) 116

Aldebesheh, Matter of, 22 I&N Dec. 983 (BIA 1999) 71, 109

Ali v. Mukasey, 525 F.3d 497 (7th Cir. 2008) 110

A–M–, Matter of, 7 I&N Dec. 322 (1965) 98

A–M–, Matter of, 23 I&N Dec. 737 (BIA 2005) 274

Amaya-Saenz, Matter of, A90-897-254, (BIA Aug. 12, 2005) 105

American Baptist Churches (ABC) v. Thornburgh, 760 F. Supp. 796 (1991) 196, 218

Andazola, Matter of, 23 I&N Dec. 319 (BIA 2002) 206, 207

Anderson, Matter of, 16 I&N Dec. 596 (BIA 1978) 157, 158, 216

Andrasian v. INS, 180 F.3d 1033 (9th Cir. 1999) 255

Arai, Matter of, 13 I&N Dec. 494 (BIA 1970) 137

Arellano-Garcia v. Gonzales, 429 F.3d 1183 (8th Cir. 2005) 11

Aremu v. DHS, 450 F.3d 578 (4th Cir. 2006) 35, 46

Arguelles, Matter of, 22 I&N Dec. 811 (BIA 1999) 270

Armendariz-Montoya v. Sonchik, 291 F.3d 1116 (9th Cir. 2002) 192

Arthur, Matter of, 20 I&N Dec. 475 (BIA 1992) 133, 134

Artigas, Matter of, 23 I&N Dec. 99 (BIA 2001) 127, 153

A–T–, Matter of, 24 I&N Dec. 296 (BIA 2007) 246

A–T–, Matter of, 24 I&N Dec. 617 (A.G. 2008) 247

Ateka v. Ashcroft, 384 F.3d 954 (8th Cir. 2004) 86

Atkinson v. Attorney Gen., 479 F.3d 222 (3d Cir. 2007) 192

Avilez-Nava, Matter of, 23 I&N Dec. 799 (BIA 2005) 204

Azarte v. Ashcroft, 394 F.3d 1278 (9th Cir. 2005) 275
Azurin, Matter of, 23 I&N Dec. 695 (BIA 2005) 191

B

Babaisakov, Matter of, 24 I&N Dec. 306 (BIA 2007) 110
Bah v. Mukasey, 529 F.3d 99 (2d Cir. 2008) 246, 247
Baires-Larios, Matter of, 24 I&N Dec. 467 (BIA 2008) 99
Balao, Matter of, 20 I&N Dec. 440 (BIA 1992) 155
Balogun v. INS, 31 F.3d 8 (1st Cir. 1994) 47
Banda-Ortiz v. Gonzales, 445 F.3d 387 (5th Cir. 2006) 276
Barcenas, Matter of, 19 I&N Dec. 609 (BIA 1988) 111, 120
Barranza-Rivera v. INS, 913 F.2d 1443 (9th Cir. 1990) 244
Barrios v. Attorney General, 399 F.3d 272 (3rd Cir. 2005) 276
Barroso v. Gonzales, 429 F.3d 1195 (9th Cir. 2005) 275
Bautista-Gomez, Matter of, 23 I&N Dec. 893 (BIA 2006) 202
Beato, Matter of, 10 I&N Dec. 740 (BIA 1964) 44
Beck v. Ohio, 379 U.S. 89 (1964) 117
Bejjani v. INS, 271 F.3d 670 (6th Cir. 2001) 31
Benitez, Matter of, 19 I&N Dec. 173 (BIA 1984) 121
Bilokumsky v. Tod, 263 U.S. 149 (1923) 122
Blake, Matter of, 23 I&N Dec. 722 (BIA 2005) 190, 191, 285
Blake v. Carbone, 489 F.3d 88 (2nd Cir. 2007) 191
Blancas-Lara, Matter of, 23 I&N Dec. 458 (BIA 2002) 180
Bona v. Gonzales, 425 F.3d 663 (9th Cir. 2005) 127
Brieva, Matter of, 23 I&N Dec. 766 (BIA 2005) 191
Brignoni-Ponce; United States v., 422 U.S. 873 (1975) 115, 120
Buitrago-Cuesta v. INS, 7 F.3d 291 (2d Cir. 1993) 189
Bull v. INS, 790 F.2d 869 (11th Cir. 1986) 135
Burgos, Matter of, 15 I&N Dec. 278 (BIA 1975) 120

C

C–A–, Matter of, 23 I&N Dec. 951 (BIA 2006) 244
Cabrera, Matter of, 24 I&N Dec. 459 (BIA 2008) 42
Calcano-Martinez v. INS, 533 U.S. 348 (2001) 299
Camins v. Gonzales, 500 F.3d 872 (9th Cir. 2007) 15
Campos-Torres, Matter of, 22 I&N Dec. 1289 (BIA 2000) 181
Canas-Segovia v. INS, 902 F.2d 717 (9th Cir. 1990) 244
Cardoso-Tlaseca v. Gonzales, 460 F.3d 1102 (9th Cir. 2006) 291
Caroleo v. Gonzales, 476 F.3d 158 (3d Cir. 2007) 191
Castro-Cruz v. INS, 239 F.3d 1037 (9th Cir. 2001) 31
Cavazos v. Moore, No. M-03-347 (S.D. Tex. Jan. 07, 2005) 13
Cervantes, Matter of, 22 I&N Dec. 560 (BIA 1999) 157, 158, 168
C–H–, Matter of, 9 I&N Dec. 265 (Reg'l Comm'r 1961) 127

Chambers v. Reno, 307 F.3d 284 (4th Cir. 2002) 192
Chang, Matter of, 20 I&N Dec. 38 (BIA 1989) 240, 241
Chapman v. United States, 365 U.S. 610 (1961) 116
Chedad v. Gonzales, 497 F.3d 57 (1st Cir. 2007) 276
Chen, Matter of, 20 I&N Dec. 16 (BIA 1989) 237
Chun, Matter of, A45 246 969 (BIA 2005) 11
Cisneros-Gonzalez, Matter of, 23 I&N Dec. 668 (BIA 2004) 182, 204
Colorado v. Connelly, 479 U.S. 157 (1986) 116
Compean, Matter of, 24 I&N Dec. 710 (A.G. 2009) 9
Contreras-Rodriguez v. Attorney Gen., 462 F.3d 1314 (11th Cir. 2006) 291
Corea, Matter of, 19 I&N Dec. 130 (BIA 1984) 159
Cota-Vargas, Matter of, 23 I&N Dec. 849 (BIA 2005) 112, 185
Cox v. Monica, No. 1:07-CV-0534, 2007 U.S. Dist. LEXIS 44660 (M.D. Pa.
    June 20, 2007) 13
C–V–T–, Matter of, 22 I&N Dec. 7 (BIA 1998) 157, 180, 185, 186
C–Y–Z, Matter of, 21 I&N Dec. 915 (BIA 1997) 241

D

Dada v. Mukasey, 128 S. Ct. 2307 (2008) 274, 275, 276
Daryousch, Matter of, 18 I&N Dec. 352 (BIA 1982) 16
Da Silva v. Ashcroft, 394 F.3d 1 (1st. Cir. 2006) 240
Davis, Matter of, 20 I&N Dec. 536 (BIA 1992) 73
Deanda-Romo, Matter of, 23 I&N Dec. 597 (BIA 2003) 181, 203
De Cardenas v. Reno, 278 F. Supp. 2d 284 (D. Conn. 2003) 189
Dekoladenu v. Gonzales, 459 F.3d 500 (4th Cir. 2006) 276
Delgado; INS v., 466 U.S. 210 (1984) 119
Delgado v. Mukasey, 516 F.3d 65 (2d Cir. 2008) 32, 90, 173
Del Risco, Matter of, 20 I&N Dec. 109 (BIA 1989) 72
Demore v. Kim, 538 U.S. 510 (2003) 13
Desai v. Mukasey, 520 F.3d 762 (7th Cir. 2008) 72
Desir v. Ilchert, 840 F.2d 723 (9th Cir. 1988) 242
Devison, Matter of, 22 I&N Dec. 1362 (BIA 2000) 43, 109
Diomande v. Wrona, No. 05-73290, 2005 WL 3369498 (E.D. Mich., Dec. 12, 2005) 13
D–J–, Matter of, 23 I&N Dec. 572 (AG 2003) 15, 16
D–L– & A–M–, Matter of, 20 I&N Dec. 409 (BIA 1991) 84
Ducret, Matter of, 15 I&N Dec. 620 (BIA 1976) 173
Duran-Gonzales v. DHS, 508 F.3d 1227 (9th Cir. 2007) 32, 90, 173

E

E–A–G–, Matter of, 24 I&N Dec. 591 (BIA 2008) 245
Elias Zacarias v. INS, 502 U.S. 478 (1992) 249
Enriquez-Alvarado v. Ashcroft, 371 F.3d 246 (5th Cir. 2004) 229
Eslamizar, Matter of, 23 I&N Dec. 684 (BIA 2004) 43

Esponda v. United States A.G., 453 F.3d 1319 (11th Cir. 2006) 288
Esposito, Matter of, 21 I&N Dec. 1 (BIA 1995) 190
Esqueda, Matter of, 20 I&N Dec. 850 (BIA 1994) 72
Ex parte. See name of party

F

Faiz-Mohammed v. Ashcroft, 395 F.3d 799 (7th Cir. 2005) 32
Fatin v. INS, 12 F.3d 1233 (3d Cir. 1994) 245
Fedorenko, Matter of, 19 I&N Dec. 57 (BIA 1984) 105
Fernandez-Vargas v. Gonzales, 548 U.S. 30 (2006) 31, 32, 90
Fisher v. INS, 37 F.3d 1371 (9th Cir. 1994), *amended* 61 F.3d 1366 (9th Cir. 1995),
    decided de novo 79 F.3d 955 (9th Cir. 1996) 246
Fong Yue Ting v. U.S., 149 U.S. 698 (1893) 2
Franklin, Matter of, 20 I&N Dec. 867 (BIA 1994) 43
Frentescu, Matter of, 18 I&N Dec. 244 (BIA 1982) 44, 256
Fualaau, Matter of, 21 I&N Dec. 475 (BIA 1996) 44

G

G–A–, Matter of, 23 I&N Dec. 366 (BIA 2002) 263
Gao v. Gonzales, 440 F.3d 62 (2d Cir. 2006) 247
Garcia, Matter of, 16 I&N Dec. 653 (BIA 1978) 132, 133
Garcia, Matter of, 17 I&N 325 (BIA 1980) 11
Garcia v. INS, 239 F.3d 409 (1st Cir. 2001) 43
Garcia-Hernandez, Matter of, 23 I&N Dec. 590 (BIA 2003) 71, 181, 203
G–C–L–, Matter of, 23 I&N Dec. 359 (BIA 2002) 241
Gebremichael v. INS, 10 F.3d 28 (1st Cir. 1993) 244
Gertsenshteyn, Matter of, 24 I&N Dec. 111 (BIA 2007) 110
Gertsenshteyn v. Mukasey, 544 F.3d 137 (2d Cir. 2008) 110
G–M–, Matter of, 7 I&N Dec. 40 (BIA 1955) 69
Gomes v. Ashcroft, 311 F.3d 43 (1st Cir. 2002) 189
Gonzales v. Duenas-Alvarez, 548 U.S. 183 (2007) 51
Gonzales v. Thomas, 547 U.S. 183 (2007) 247
Gonzales-Silva, Matter of, 24 I&N Dec. 218 (BIA 2007) 54
Gonzalez, Matter of, 16 I&N Dec. 44 (BIA 1976) 121
Gonzalez-Sandoval v. INS, 910 F.2d 614 (9th Cir. 1990) 47
Gooch; United States v., 6 F.3d 673 (9th Cir. 1993) 116
Granados, Matter of, 16 I&N Dec. 726 (BIA 1979) 181
Grijalva, Matter of, 21 I&N Dec. 27 (BIA 1995) 24, 295
Guang Li Fu, Matter of, 23 I&N Dec. 985 (BIA 2006) 175
Guerra, Matter of, 24 I&N Dec. 237 (BIA 2006) 15
Guevara, Matter of, 20 I&N Dec. 238 (BIA 1991) 122
Gutierrez, Matter of, 21 I&N Dec. 479 (BIA 1996) 102
G–Y–R–, Matter of, 23 I&N Dec. 181 (BIA 2001) 16, 23, 24, 83, 294

American Immigration Lawyers Association

H

H–, Matter of, 6 I&N Dec. 358 (BIA 1954) 44
H–, Matter of, 21 I&N Dec. 337 (BIA 1996) 244
H–A–, Matter of, 22 I&N Dec. 728 (BIA 1999) 134
Harrison, Matter of, 13 I&N Dec. 540 (Dist. Dir. 1970) 147
Hartman v. Elwood, 255 F. Supp. 2d 510 (E.D.P.A. 2003) 189
Hem v. Mauerer, 458 F.3d 1185 (10th Cir. 2006) 192
Hernandez v. Ashcroft, 345 F.3d 824 (9th Cir. 2004) 211
Hernandez v. Gonzales, 424 F. 3d 42 (1st Cir. 2005) 300
Hernandez-Castillo v. Moore, 436 F.3d 516 (5th Cir. 2006) 192
Hernandez de Anderson v. Gonzales, 497 F.3d 927 (9th Cir. 2007) 279
Hernandez-Ponce, Matter of, 19 I&N Dec. 613 (BIA 1988) 72
H–N–, Matter of, 22 I&N Dec. 1039 (BIA 1999) 169
Huang, Matter of, 19 I&N Dec. 749 (BIA 1988) 8, 14, 82, 105
Hy v. Gillen, No. 08-11699-JLT, 2008 WL 5077820 (D. Mass. Dec. 3, 2008) 13

I

Ige, Matter of, 20 I&N Dec. 880 (BIA 1994) 159
In re. See name of party
Iredia v. INS, 981 F.2d 847 (5th Cir. 1993) 47

J

Jara Riero, Matter of, 24 I&N Dec. 267 (BIA 2007) 131
J–B–N– & S–M–, Matter of, 24 I&N Dec. 208 (BIA 2007) 238
J–E–, Matter of, 23 I&N Dec. 291 (BIA 2002) 261, 263
Jean, Matter of, 23 I&N Dec. 373 (A.G. 2002) 170, 252, 253
Jean-Pierre v. Attorney Gen., 500 F.3d 1315 (11th Cir. 2007) 263
J–F–F–, Matter of, 23 I&N Dec. 912 (BIA 2006) 264
Joseph, Matter of, 22 I&N Dec. 799 (BIA 1999) 14
Jurado, Matter of, 24 I&N Dec. 29 (BIA 2006) 44, 180
J–Y–C–, Matter of, 24 I&N Dec. 260 (BIA 2007) 239

K

K–, Matter of, 7 I&N Dec. 594 (BIA 1957) 69
Kanivets v. Gonzales, 424 F.3d 330 (3d Cir. 2005) 276
Kao and Lin, Matter of, 23 I&N Dec. 45 (BIA 2001) 158, 200
Kasinga, Matter of, 21 I&N Dec. 357 (BIA 1996) 246, 249
Katebi v. Ashcroft, 396 F.3d 463 (1st Cir. 2005) 8, 62, 105
Kellici v. Gonzales, 472 F.3d 416 (6th Cir. 2006) 300

Khodagholian v. Ashcroft, 335 F.3d 1003 (9th Cir. 2003) 8, 62, 105
Kim, Matter of, 15 I&N Dec. 88 (BIA 1974) 159
Kim v. Gonzales, 468 F.3d 58 (1st Cir. 2006) 191
Kirong v. Mukasey, 529 F.3d 800 (8th Cir. 2008) 86
Kleindienst v. Mandel, 408 U.S. 753 (1972) 2
Kochlani, Matter of, 24 I&N Dec. 128 (BIA 2007) 44
Kolkevich v. Attorney Gen., 501 F.3d 323 (3d Cir. 2007) 300
Koloamatangi, Matter of, 23 I&N Dec. 548 (BIA 2003) 180
Kotliar, Matter of, 24 I&N Dec. 124 (BIA 2007) 12

L

L–, Matter of, 6 I&N Dec. 349 (BIA 1954) 58
Laduke v. Nelson, 762 F.2d 1318 (9th Cir. 1985) 116
Landon v. Plasencia, 459 U.S. 21 (1982) 8, 11, 62, 105
Lavira v. Attorney Gen., 478 F.3d 158 (3d Cir. 2007) 263
Lee, Matter of, 17 I&N Dec. 275 (BIA 1978) 172
Leocal v. Ashcroft, 542 U.S. 1 (2004) 51
Lettman, Matter of, 11 I&N Dec. 878 (Reg. Comm'r 1966) 147
Leyva, Matter of, 16 I&N Dec. 118 (BIA 1977) 98
Liadov, Matter of, 23 I&N Dec. 990 (BIA 2006) 287
Lin v. Gonzales, 473 F.3d 979 (9th Cir. 2007) 291
Lino v. Gonzales, 467 F.3d 1077 (7th Cir. 2006) 32, 90, 173
L–O–G–, Matter of, 21 I&N Dec. 413 (BIA 1996) 157, 158, 159
Logan, Matter of, 17 I&N Dec. 367 (BIA 1980) 44
Lopez v. Gonzales, 549 U.S. 47 (2006) 51
Lopez-Mendoza; INS v., 468 U.S. 1032 (1984) 11, 115
Lopez-Meza, Matter of, 22 I&N Dec. 1188 (BIA 1999) 44
Lopez-Molina v. Ashcroft, 368 F.3d 1206 (9th Cir. 2004) 73
Lozada, Matter of, 19 I&N Dec. 637 (BIA 1988) 9
Lujan-Almendariz v. INS, 222 F.3d 728 (9th Cir. 2000) 72, 112
Luna Rubio, In re, A74 317 521 (BIA Index May 24, 2000) 62
Ly v. Hansen, 351 F.3d 263 (6th Cir. 2003) 13

M

M–, Matter of, 7 I&N Dec. 51 (BIA 1956) 212
M.A. v. INS, 899 F.2d 304 (4th Cir. 1990) 240
Madu v. Attorney Gen., 470 F.3d 1362 (11th Cir. 2006) 302
Marekegn Asfaw Tamenut v. Mukasey, 521 F.3d 1000 (8th Cir. 2008) 230
Marin, Matter of, 16 I&N Dec. 581 (BIA 1978) 157, 185, 192
Martinez v. Mukasey, 519 F.3d 532 (5th Cir. 2008) 166
Martinez-Lopez, Matter of, 10 I&N Dec. 409 (AG 1964) 80
Matovski v. Gonzales, 492 F.3d 722 (6th Cir. 2007) 126
Matter of. See name of party

M–D–, Matter of, 23 I&N Dec. 540 (BIA 2002) 11, 23, 24, 83, 294, 295
Medina, Matter of, 15 I&N Dec. 611 (BIA 1976) 44
Mei v. Ashcroft, 393 F.3d 737 (7th Cir. 2004) 44
Mendenhall; United States v., 446 U.S. 544 (1980) 114, 118
Mendez, Matter of, 21 I&N Dec. 296 (BIA 1996) 126, 157, 167
Mendoza-Sandino, Matter of, 22 I&N Dec. 1236 (BIA 2000) 182
Meza, Matter of, 20 I&N Dec. 257 (BIA 1991) 190
Mohammed v. Gonzales, 400 F.3d 785 (9th Cir. 2005) 246
Momin v. Gonzales, 447 F.3d 447 (5th Cir. 2006) 127
Monreal, Matter of, 23 I&N Dec. 56 (BIA 2001) 159, 162, 205, 206, 207
Montenegro v. Ashcroft, 355 F.3d 1035 (7th Cir. 2004) 42, 109
Moosa v. INS, 171 F.3d 994 (5th Cir. 1999) 42, 109
Morales-Morales v. Ashcroft, 384 F.3d 418 (7th Cir. 2004) 204
Mouelle v. Gonzales, 416 F.3d 923 (8th Cir. 2005) 127
M–R–A–, Matter of, 24 I&N Dec. 665 (BIA 2008) 24, 29, 83, 295
M–S–, Matter of, 22 I&N Dec. 349 (BIA 1998) 295
M–U–, Matter of, 2 I&N Dec. 92 (BIA 1944) 43
Murphy v. INS, 54 F.3d 605 (9th Cir. 1995) 98

N

Nadarajah v. Gonzales, 443 F.3d 1069 (9th Cir. 2006) 300
N–A–M–, Matter of, 24 I&N Dec. 336 (BIA 2007) 256, 257
Ng, Matter of, 17 I&N Dec. 536 (BIA 1980) 84
Nguyen v. INS, 991 F.2d 621 (10th Cir. 1993) 47
N–J–B–, Matter of, 21 I&N Dec. 812 (BIA 1997) 196, 198
Nnadika v. Attorney Gen., 484 F.3d 626 (3d Cir. 2007) 300, 302

O

O–J–O–, Matter of, 21 I&N Dec. 381 (BIA 1996) 157, 158, 159, 216
Okeke v. Gonzales, 407 F.3d 585 (3d Cir. 2005) 182, 204
Olatunji v. Ashcroft, 387 F.3d 383 (4th Cir. 2004) 14
Olquin, Matter of, 23 I&N Dec. 896 44
Ortega-Cabrera, Matter of, 23 I&N Dec. 793 (BIA 2005) 202, 212

P

Parlak v. Baker, 374 F. Supp. 2d 551 (E.D. Mich. 2005) 13
Patel, Matter of, 15 I&N Dec. 666 (BIA 1976) 16
Patel, Matter of, 19 I&N Dec. 394 (BIA 1986) 274
Payton v. United States, 445 U.S. 573 (1980) 116, 117
Perez, Matter of, 22 I&N Dec. 689 (BIA 1999) 180, 182
Perez-Gonzalez v. Ashcroft, 379 F.3d 783 (9th Cir. 2004) 32, 90, 173

Perez-Vargas, Matter of, 23 I&N Dec. 829 (BIA 2005) 126
Perez-Vargas v. Gonzales, 478 F.3d 191 (4th Cir. 2007) 126
Pickering, Matter of, 23 I&N Dec. 621 (BIA 2003) 43, 112
Pierre v. Attorney Gen., 528 F.3d 180 (3d Cir. 2008) 263
Pierre v. Gonzales, 502 F.3d 109 (2d Cir. 2007) 263
Pilch, Matter of, 21 I&N Dec. 627 (BIA 1996) 157, 158, 159, 216
Pino v. Landon, 349 U.S. 901 (1955) 42, 108
Ponnapula v. Ashcroft, 373 F.3d 480 (3d Cir. 2004) 192
Puello v. BCIS, 511 F.3d 324 (2d Cir. 2007) 42, 109
Pula, Matter of, 19 I&N Dec. 467 (BIA 1987) 251, 255

Q

Quezada-Bucios v. Ridge, 317 F. Supp. 2d 1221 (W. D. Wash. 2004) 13
Qutin, Matter of, 14 I&N Dec. 6 (BIA 1972) 148

R

R–A–, Matter of, 22 I&N Dec. 906 (BIA 1999) 248, 250, 251
Rainford, Matter of, 20 I&N Dec. 598 (BIA 1992) 126
Ramirez-Rivero, Matter of, 18 I&N Dec. 135 (BIA 1981) 43, 109
Ramirez-Sanchez, Matter of, 17 I&N Dec. 503 (BIA 1980) 121
Ramos; United States v., 12 F.3d 1019 (11th Cir. 1994) 116
Recinas, Matter of, 23 I&N Dec. 467 (BIA 2002) 206
Reno v. American-Arab Anti-Discrimination Comm., 525 U.S. 471 (1999) 304
Restrepo v. McElroy, 369 F.3d 627 (2d Cir. 2004) 192
Reyes-Oropesa; United States v., 596 F.2d 399 (9th Cir. 1979) 118
R–H–, Matter of, 7 I&N Dec. 675 (BIA 1958) 73
Rico, Matter of, 16 I&N Dec. 181 (BIA 1977) 73
Rodriguez Galicia v. Gonzales, 422 F.3d 529 (7th Cir. 2005) 11
Rodriguez-Tejedor, Matter of, 23 I&N Dec. 153 (BIA 2001) 99
Rohas Paredes v. Attorney Gen., 528 F.3d 196 (3d Cir. 2008) 42
Rojas, Matter of, 23 I&N Dec. 117 (BIA 2001) 13
Roldan, Matter of, 22 I&N Dec. 512 (BIA 1999) 72, 112
Romalez, Matter of, 23 I&N Dec. 423 (BIA 2002) 203, 204
Rosales v. BICE, 426 F.3d 733 (5th Cir. 2005) 304
Rosas, Matter of, 22 I&N Dec. 616 (BIA 1999) 35, 46
R–R–, Matter of, 20 I&N Dec. 547 (BIA 1992) 243
Ruiz-Martinez v. Mukasey, 516 F.3d 102 (2d Cir. 2008) 300

S

S–, Matter of, 3 I&N Dec. 617 (BIA 1949) 44
S–, Matter of, 8 I&N Dec. 344 (BIA 1959) 181
Saba-Bakare v. Chertoff, 507 F.3d 337 (5th Cir. 2007) 280

Sadowski v. Mukasey, No. 07-1020-ag, 2008 WL 731245 (2d Cir. Mar 18, 2008) 279
Safaie v. INS, 25 F.3d 636 (8th Cir. 1994) 245
St. Cyr; INS v., 533 U.S. 289 (2001) 179, 187, 191, 299, 300
S–A–K and H–A–H–, Matter of, 24 I&N Dec. 464 (BIA 2008) 247
Sanchez-Linn, Matter of, 20 I&N Dec. 362 (BIA 1991) 148
Sanchez Trujillo v. INS, 801 F.2d 1572 (9th Cir. 1986) 251
S and B–C–, Matter of, 9 I&N Dec. 436 (AG 1960) 84
Saysana, Matter of, 24 I&N Dec. 602 (BIA 2008) 13
Saysana v. Gillen, No. 08-11749-RGS (D. Mass. Dec. 1, 2008) 13
Scheerer v. United States, 445 F.3d 1311 (11th Cir. 2006) 127
Seda, Matter of, 17 I&N Dec. 550 (BIA 1980) 69
See v. City of Seattle, 387 U.S. 541 (1967) 116
S–E–G–, Matter of, 24 I&N Dec. 579 (BIA 2008) 245
Sejas, Matter of, 24 I&N Dec. 236 (BIA 2007) 44
Sepulveda v. Attorney General, 378 F.3d 1260 (11th Cir. 2005) 240
Shaar, Matter of, 21 I&N Dec. 541 (BIA 1996) 134, 275
Shanu, Matter of, 23 I&N Dec. 754 (BIA 2005) 35, 45, 46
Shirdel, Matter of, 19 I&N Dec. 33 (BIA 1984) 84
Shivaraman v. Ashcroft, 360 F.3d 1142 (9th Cir. 2004) 35, 46
Short, Matter of, 20 I&N Dec. 136 (BIA 1989) 44, 45, 110
Sidikhouya v. Gonzalez, 407 F.3d 950 (8th Cir. 2005) 276
Silva-Trevino, Matter of, 24 I&N Dec. 687 (A.G. 2008) 45, 110, 111
Singh v. Gonzales, 412 F.3d 1117 (9th Cir. 2005) 291
Singh v. Gonzales, 432 F.3d 533 (3d Cir. 2006) 11
Singh v. Moschorak, 53 F.3d 1031 (9th Cir. 1995) 240
S–K–, Matter of, 23 I&N Dec. 936 (BIA 2006) 77, 78, 254
S–K–, Matter of, 24 I&N Dec. 475 (BIA 2008) 255
S–L–L, Matter of, 24 I&N Dec. 1 (BIA 2006) 241
Soriano, Matter of, 21 I&N Dec. 516 (BIA 1996) 187, 190
S–P–, Matter of, 21 I&N Dec. 486 (BIA 1996) 242
Succar v. Ashcroft, 294 F.3d 8 (1st Cir. 2005) 127
Sullivan; United States v., 128 F.3d 126 (4th Cir. 1998) 114
Sung v. Keisler, 505 F.3d 372 (5th Cir. 2007) 126
S–V–, Matter of, 22 I&N Dec. 1306 (BIA 2000) 261

T

Tandia v. Gonzales, 437 F.3d 245 (2d Cir. 2006) 255
Terry v. Ohio, 392 U.S. 1 (1968) 114, 117
Terzich, In re, 153 F. Supp. 651 (W.D.Pa. 1957) 286
Thom v. Ashcroft, 369 F.3d 158 (2d Cir. 2004), *cert. denied,* 126 S. Ct. 40 (2005) 192
Thomas, Matter of, 21 I&N Dec. 20 (BIA 1995) 42, 108
Thomas v. Hogan, No. 1:08-CV-0417, 2008 U.S. Dist. LEXIS 88169 (M.D. Pa. Oct. 31, 2008) 13
Tijam, Matter of, 22 I&N Dec. 408 (BIA 1998) 84, 168

Tijani v. Willis, 430 F.3d 1241 (9th Cir. 2005) 13
Tin, Matter of, 14 I&N Dec. 371 (Reg'l Comm'r 1971) 172, 173
Toboso-Alfonso, Matter of, 20 I&N Dec. 819 (BIA 1990) 244
Toia v. Fasano, 334 F.3d 917 (9th Cir. 2003) 189
Toro, Matter of, 17 I&N Dec. 340 (BIA 1980) 11, 115
Torres-Garcia, Matter of, 23 I&N Dec. 866 (BIA 2006) 89, 173
Torres-Varela, Matter of, 23 I&N Dec. 78 (BIA 2001) 44
Tran, Matter of, 21 I&N Dec. 291 (BIA 1996) 44, 54
T–Z–, Matter of, 24 I&N Dec. 163 (BIA 2007) 239

U

Ugokwe v. United States, 453 F.3d 1325 (11th Cir. 2006) 276
U–H–, Matter of, 23 I&N Dec. 355 (BIA 2002) 73, 254
United States v. See name of opposing party
Uritsky v. Gonzales, 399 F.3d 728 (6th Cir. 2005) 43

V

Valere v. Gonzales, 473 F.3d 757 (7th Cir. 2007) 191
Velarde, Matter of, 23 I&N Dec. 253 (BIA 2002) 134, 135, 275
Velazquez-Herrera, Matter of, 24 I&N Dec. 503 (BIA 2008) 45, 110
Villarreal-Zuniga, Matter of, 23 I&N Dec. 886 (BIA 2006) 126, 191
Vo v. Attorney Gen., 482 F.3d 363 (5th Cir. 2007) 191
Vue v. Gonzales, 496 F.3d 858 (8th Cir. 2007) 191

W

Walcott v. Chertoff, 517 F.3d 149 (2d Cir. 2008) 192
Walter v. United States, 447 U.S. 649 (1980) 115
Wang; INS v., 450 U.S. 139 (1981) 158, 216
Welsh v. Wisconsin, 466 U.S. 740 (1984) 115, 117
West, Matter of, 22 I&N Dec. 1405 (BIA 2000) 13
William v. Gonzales, 49 F.3d 329 (4th Cir. 2007) 192
William v. Gonzales, 499 F.3d 329 (4th Cir. 2007) 291
Winsor; United States v., 846 F.2d 1569 (9th Cir. 1988) 114, 117
Winter, Matter of, 12 I&N Dec. 638 (BIA 1968) 69
Woodby v. INS, 385 U.S. 276 (1966) 9, 35, 62, 98, 106

X

X–G–W–, Matter of, 22 I&N Dec. 71 (BIA 1998) 241
X–K–, Matter of, 23 I&N Dec. 731 (BIA 2005) 15

American Immigration Lawyers Association

Y

Y–C–, Matter of, 23 I&N Dec. 286 (BIA 2002) 236

Yerger, Ex parte, 8 Wall 85 (1869) 299

Yeung v. INS, 76 F.3d 337 (11th Cir. 1995) 155

Y–G–, Matter of, 20 I&N Dec. 794 (BIA 1994) 84

Y–L–, A–G–, and R–S–R–, Matter of, 23 I&N Dec. 270 (A.G. 2002) 257

Y–T–L–, Matter of, 23 I&N Dec. 601 (BIA 2003) 246

Yusupov v. Attorney Gen., 518 F.3d 185 (3d Cir. 2008) 73

Z

Zabadi v. Chertoff, No. C 05-03335 WHA, 2005 WL 3157377 (N.D. Cal. Nov. 22, 2005) .. 13

Zhang v. Mukasey, 509 F.3d 313 (6th Cir. 2007) 35, 46

Zheng v. Ashcroft, 332 F.3d 1186 (9th Cir. 2003) 261

Zheng v. Gonzales, 422 F.3d 98 (3d Cir. 2005) 127

INDEX

Alphabetization is word-by-word (e.g., "R visas" precedes "REAL ID Act")

A

***ABC* class members**
  asylum applications under NACARA, 221, 225

Abuse. *See* **Battered spouse or child**

Address change. *See* **Change of address**

Adjustment of status
  generally, 125–54
  arriving aliens, 126–27
  asylees and refugees, 125
  CAA, 125, 153–54, 170
  conditional residence, removal of, 137–39
  family-based immigrants, 129–37
    assertion of defense, 132
    benefits under §245(i), 130–31
    eligibility, 129
    filing application, 135–36
    merits hearing, 136–37
    motions to continue, 132–35
    prima facie eligibility, proof of, 135–36
    procedure, 131–32
  HRIFA, 125, 143–46
  IJ proceeding preferred over USCIS, 129
  LIFE Act, 143, 146
  motions to continue, 132–35
  motions to reopen, 134–35, 291
  NACARA, 125, 140–43, 170
  readjustment of status, 126
  registry provision, 146–50
  termination to proceed with before USCIS, 128–29
  T or U visas, 125

Administrative removal
  for aggravated felonies, 29–30
  Convention Against Torture and, 268
  order, 335

Administrative review of removal orders
  generally, 287–96
  appeals to BIA, 287–89
  judicial review, 308
  motions to reopen/reconsider, 289–96
    See also Motions to reopen/reconsider

AEDPA. *See* **Antiterrorism and Effective Death Penalty Act of 1996**

Affidavit for motion to suppress
  in removal proceedings, 120–21

Affirmance without opinion (AWO)
  regulations allowing, 288–89

After-acquired spouses and children
  adjustment of status, 131

Aggravated felonies
  administrative removal for, 29–30

cancellation of removal, 183–84
  defined under IIRAIRA, 183–84
  deportability, grounds for, 48–51
  inadmissibility for, 75–76
  naturalization, 280–81

Aging-out
  derivative status children, 234

Alienage
  establishing, 8–9

Aliens
  defined, 2
  smuggling of, 39–40

Antiterrorism and Effective Death Penalty Act of 1996 (AEDPA)
  criminal convictions, deportable or inadmissible, 47
  removal procedure, 187

Appeals
  See also Judicial review of removal orders
  to BIA, 287–89
  removal proceedings, 25
  voluntary departure, 274

Arrest
  mere questioning vs., 118–19
  warrants, 117–18

Arriving aliens
  See also Expedited removal
  adjustment in proceedings, 126–27
  CAT relief, 265–66
  credible fear of persecution, 259
  defined, 126

ineligibility for bond, 14–15
treatment of, 28–29
Assault
crime of moral turpitude (CMT), 44
Asylum seekers
adjustment of status, 125
CAT relief, 266
discretionary remedy, 251–53
evidence, 236–38
fear of persecution. *See* Persecution
firm resettlement, 255
inadmissibility, grounds for, 253–56
ineligibility, 253–58
internal relocation alternative, 240
NACARA. *See* Nicaraguan Adjustment and Central American Relief Act of 1997
safe third country, 255–56
standards of proof, 236–38
termination of asylum, 258–59
waivers, 169–70
withholding of removal vs., 233–36
Attorney representation. *See* Representation
Automatic stay of removal
during appeal to BIA, 287
judicial review, 305

B

Bars to cancellation of removal
NACARA, 228
Bars to suspension of deportation
NACARA, 226, 227–28

Battered spouse or child
cancellation of removal, 208–18
abused child, 209–10
background, 208
battery or extreme cruelty, 210–11
evidence, 216–17
extreme hardship, 215–16
good moral character, 212–14
inadmissible or deportable, 214–15
intake interview, 217
laws of other countries, 218
location of abuse, 212
marital relationship, 209
no residence with abuser, 212
self-petitions, 217–18
three-year continuous physical presence, 211–12
VAWA cap, 218
Battery or extreme cruelty
cancellation of removal, 210–11
exceptional circumstances to reopen, 294
BIA. *See* **Board of Immigration Appeals**
BIA Practice Manual
availability of, 288
Biometrics
removal proceedings, 23
Board of Immigration Appeals (BIA)
adjustment of status cases, 126
appeals to, 287–89
asylum, time of filing application for, 236
BIA Practice Manual, 288
CAT cases, 261–64

coercive family-planning programs as persecution, 241
credibility determination in asylum case, 239
exceptional and extremely unusual hardship cases, 205–7
female genital mutilation (FGM) cases, 246–47
motions to reopen, 274–76
Bonds
generally, 12–16
eligibility for, 15
hearings, 15–16
ineligibility for
arriving aliens, 14–15
mandatory detention, 12–14
public charge bonds, 82
Burden of proof
NACARA applicants, 230
removal proceedings, 8–9, 105–7

C

Cambodian nationals
adjustment of status, 150–53
Cancellation of removal
generally, 179–93
abused immigrant women and children, 208–18
See also Battered spouse or child
bars to cancellation eligibility, 183–85
discretionary factors, 185–86
LPR status, 53, 179–201
See also Lawful permanent residents

NACARA requirements, 222–25
See also Nicaraguan Adjustment and Central American Relief Act of 1997
ten-year bars, 228
non-LPRs, 201–8
annual cap of 4,000 foreign nationals, 208
continuous residence or physical presence, 202–4
eligibility, 202
exceptional and extremely unusual hardship, 204–7
grounds of ineligibility, 207–8
proposed repapering rule, 193, 198–99
relief under §212(c), 186–92
VAWA provisions, 208–18
See also Battered spouse or child
where and how to file, 186
CAT. *See* **Convention Against Torture**
Change of address
deportability for failure to register, 55
notice to Immigration Court, 8, 25
Change of venue
motion for, 17
Child abduction
inadmissibility/deportability, grounds of, 95

Child abuse. *See* **Battered spouse or child**
Child Citizenship Act of 2000
derivative citizenship, 59
Child custody disputes
hardship factor, 160
Child pornography
crime of moral turpitude (CMT), 44
Children
abuse. *See* Battered spouse or child
aging out, 234
removal proceedings, 11
representation of, 11
special immigrant juveniles, waivers for, 170
Child Status Protection Act of 2002 (CSPA)
generally, 234
Citizenship
See also Naturalization
certificate of, obtaining, 99
defense to removal, 97–100
falsely claiming, 56, 85–86
ineligible for, 87–88
CMT. *See* **Crimes of moral turpitude**
Coercive population control
as persecution, 240–41
Communicable diseases
inadmissibility, grounds for, 64–65
waiver, 163–64
Communist party members
inadmissibility of, 78–79
Conditional residence
denial of joint petition or waiver application, 138–39
failure to comply with procedural requirements, 138

jurisdiction of immigration court, 139
of refugees, 252
removal of, 137–39
termination of, 38–39
Congressional power
deportation and, 2
Conscription
as type of persecution, 243–44
Consent to reapply for admission
Form I-212, 172–75
Consolidated Appropriations Act of 2005
Vietnam, Cambodia, and Laos, adjustment of status for foreign nationals from, 150
Constitutional rights
in removal proceedings, 112–22
Consulates
detained foreign national may contact, 10
Continuances
motion to continue hearing date, 17
motion to continue in adjustment of status cases, 132–35
Continuous residence or physical presence
cancellation of removal battered spouse or child, 211–12
LPRs, 180–82
non-LPRs, 202–4
NACARA cases, 220, 222–23
evidence, 230
suspension of deportation, 197–98

Controlled substances offenses
 See Drug offenses
Convention Against Torture (CAT)
 generally, 260–68
 administrative removal, 268
 arriving at port of entry, 265–66
 asylum seekers, 266
 burden of proof, 264
 definition of torture, 260–64
 diplomatic assurances and, 268
 establishing eligibility, 264–65
 motion to reopen, 290
 pending cases on or before March 22, 1999, 266–67
 procedures, 265–68
 reinstatement of removal, 267
 removal proceedings, persons in, 266
 withholding and deferral of removal under, 30, 264–65, 266
Convictions. *See* **Criminal convictions**
Credible fear. *See* **Persecution**
Crime of moral turpitude (CMT)
 defined, 43–44
 deportability, grounds for, 41–47
 evidence for removal proceedings, 110–11
 inadmissability, grounds for, 70
  exceptions to, 70–91
  petty offense exception, 70–71
  "under 18" exception, 70

  sentence of one year or longer, 46
 time of CMT within 5 years of admission, 45–46
Criminal convictions
 See also Aggravated felonies
 constitutional rights and violations, 112–22
 controlled substances. *See* Drug offenses
 conviction for immigration purposes, 108–9
 defined, 69, 184
 deportability, grounds for, 41–54
 drug offenses, 52
 evidence for removal proceedings, 107–12
 expungement, 72, 111–12
 firearms violations, 53
 high-speed flight, 51
 inadmissibility, grounds for, 68–70
 judicial review of removal orders for, 303–4
 loss to victim, amount of, 109
 miscellaneous crimes, 53
 multiple convictions, 47, 71
 outcomes not constituting conviction under immigration law, 42–43
 pardons, 111–12
 petty offense exception, 70–71
 records to prove, 21, 69, 325
 sentence length, 46, 109
 serious crimes, 256, 257–58
 sex offender, failure to register as, 51

 standards of proof, 68–69
 term of imprisonment, 42
 time of CMT within 5 years of admission, 45–46
 waiver of inadmissibility, 165–67
 warrants. *See* Warrants
Criminal record checks
 FBI, 21, 325
Cuban Adjustment Act of 1966 (CAA)
 adjustment of status, 125, 153–54, 170
 spouses and children of Cubans, 154
Customs and Border Protection (CBP)
 creation and role of, 1

D

Deceit. *See* **Fraud**
Deferral of removal
 under Convention Against Torture, 30, 264–65
De novo hearings
 asylum applicants, 221
Department of ___. *See* name of specific department
Departure from U.S.
 suspension of deportation and, 223
Deportability, grounds of
 generally, 5–6, 35–59
 citizenship, falsely claiming, 56
 convictions. *See* Criminal convictions
 document-related grounds, 55–56
 economic grounds, 57–58
 failure to maintain status, 38

IIRAIRA provisions, 2–3, 37
immigration law violations, 37–38
inadmissible aliens, 36–37
security and foreign-policy grounds, 56–58
termination of conditional permanent residence, 38–39
terrorist activities, 57
voting offenses, 58–59
waivers, 175–77
Deportation hearings. *See* **Removal proceedings**
Depositions
motions for, 18
Derivative status
defined, 233
Detention
habeas review, 300
mandatory detention
bonds, ineligibility for, 12–14
Joseph hearings, 14
for questioning, 119–20
DHS. *See* **Homeland Security Department**
Diplomatic assurances
Convention Against Torture and, 268
Disabled persons
waiver of inadmissibility based on physical disorders, 164
Discovery
removal proceedings, 18–21
Discretion
asylum, 251–53
exercise of, 156–57
factors for cancellation of removal, 185–86
suspension of deportation, 201

Discretionary denials
judicial review, 302–3
Document and presentation fraud
deportability, grounds for, 55–56
inadmissibility, grounds for, 86–87
Documentation. *See* **Supporting documentation**
Domestic violence
See also Battered spouse or child
deportability for, 54
waiver, 176–77
as persecution, 247–48
Driving under the influence
crime of moral turpitude (CMT), 44
Drug addiction
defined, 67
Drug offenses
deportability of drug abusers, 52
illicit trafficking, inadmissibility for, 73
inadmissibility of drug abusers, 67–68, 71–72
inadmissibility of drug traffickers, 72–73
section 212(c) relief, 190
as serious crimes, 257
Due process
protections of, 2, 11, 115

E

Economic grounds
deportability for, 57–58
inadmissibility for, 80–82
bonds, 82
public charge standard, 80–82
refugee, 239
waivers for, 152

Election offenses
deportability, grounds of, 58–59
inadmissibility/deportability, grounds of, 95
EOIR. *See* **Executive Office for Immigration Review**
Espionage
deportability for, 53, 56–57
inadmissibility for, 76–77
Evidence
See also Standard of proof
asylum and withholding proceedings, 236–38
criminal ground of inadmissibility/deportability, 107–12
NACARA applicants, 230–31
removal proceedings, 22
right to present, examine, and object to, 10
suppression of, 11, 113, 120–21
Exclusionary rule
in removal proceedings, 114–15
Exclusion hearings. *See* **Removal proceedings**
Executive Office for Immigration Review (EOIR)
forms. *See* Forms
jurisdiction of NACARA cases, 222
procedural rules, 103
role of, 2
Expedited removal
See also Habeas corpus
for arriving aliens, 28–29
expedited order, 331
judicial review, 306–7

summary order of removal, 329

Expungement
conviction for purposes of immigration, 72, 111–12

Extension. See specific type of visa

Extreme cruelty. See Battery or extreme cruelty

Extreme hardship
cancellation of removal
battered spouse or child, 215–16
of non-LPRs, 204–7
defined, 157–60
documenting, 161–62
NACARA cases, 220, 224–26
evidence, 230–31
suspension of deportation, 200–201
waivers of inadmissibility/deportability based on, 157–62, 166

F

Failure to appear
NACARA
bar from cancellation of removal, 228
bar from suspension of deportation, 228
removal proceedings, 83

False statements. See Fraud

Family-sponsored immigration
adjustment of status, 129–37

Fear of persecution. See Persecution

Federal Bureau of Investigation (FBI)
criminal record checks, 21, 325

Federal First Offender Act
conviction dismissed under, 72

Felonies. See Aggravated felonies; Criminal convictions

Female genital mutilation (FGM)
as persecution, 246–47

Fifth Amendment
protections of, 2, 11, 112, 115
right to remain silent, 121–22

Filing procedures
motion to extend time for, 17

Firearms offenses
deportability for, 53
section 212(c) relief, 190

Firm resettlement
grounds for asylum, 255

Forced abortion, sterilization, or other pregnancy control methods
seeking asylum due to, 240–41

Forced marriage
as persecution, 247

Foreign Agents Registration Act
deportability for conviction under, 55

Foreign Operations Appropriations Act of 2001 (FOAA)
adjustment of status, 150

Foreign policy considerations
as grounds for deportability, 57

Foreign politicians
exception to grounds of inadmissibility for, 78

Form EOIR-27
Notice of Entry of Appearance as Attorney or Representative, 287

Form EOIR-33
Change of Address notice, 8, 25

Form EOIR-42A
cancellation of removal applicant to file, 186

Form I-122
commencement of exclusion proceedings, 7, 323

Form I-130
adjustment of status also filed, 132–33

Form I-212
consent to reapply for admission, 172–75
supporting documentation, 174–75

Form I-601
waiver of grounds of inadmissibility, 171–72

Form I-862. See Notice To Appear (NTA)

Former Soviet bloc countries
NACARA eligibility, 219–20

Fourth Amendment
protections, 113–17, 119

Fraud
crime of moral turpitude (CMT), 44
crimes that subject clients to inadmissibility, 36–37, 83–84
waivers, 167–68
crimes that subject clients to removal, 36–37, 40, 55–56
waivers, 175–76
document and presentation fraud, 55–56, 86, 87
marriage fraud, deportability for, 40

Freedom of Information Act (FOIA)
discovery method, 18–21
Fruit of the poisonous tree
in removal proceedings, 114–15

G

Geneva Convention
Relative to the Treatment of Civilian Persons in Time of War, 243–44
Genocide, participation in
as grounds for deportability, 57
as grounds for inadmissibility, 79–80
Global Leadership Against HIV/AIDS, Tuberculosis and Malaria Reauthorization Act
communicable diseases as grounds for inadmissibility, 64–65
Good moral character
cancellation of removal, battered spouse or child, 212–14
NACARA cases, 220, 223–24
evidence, 230
naturalization, 280
registry applicants, 148
suspension of deportation, 199–200
Grounds of persecution
race, religion, nationality, political views, or group membership. *See individual treatment of each topic*

Guatemalans
NACARA eligibility, 219, 221
See also Nicaraguan Adjustment and Central American Relief Act of 1997
Guilty pleas
inadmissibility, grounds for, 69
Gun offenses. *See* Firearms offenses

H

Habeas corpus
detention challenges, 300
in district court, 299–300
prior to REAL ID, 299
Haitian Refugee Immigration Fairness Act of 1998 (HRIFA)
adjustment of status, 125, 143–46
reinstatement of removal and, 31
Hardship. *See* Extreme hardship
Health-related grounds
deportability, 38
inadmissibility, 63–68
waivers, 163–65
Hearings. *See* Removal proceedings
High-speed flight
conviction of, 51
Homeland Security Act of 2002
reorganization by, 1
Homeland Security Department (DHS)
creation and role of, 1
Humanitarian relief
parole and, 152
waivers for LPRs who assist family member

to enter illegally, 39
Human trafficking
deportability for, 39–40
inadmissibility for, 75

I

ICE. *See* Immigration and Customs Enforcement
Illegal Immigration Reform and Immigrant Responsibility Act of 1996 (IIRAIRA)
aggravated felonies, definition of, 183
asylum applications, time for filing, 234
coercive family-planning and asylum status, 240–41
deportability, grounds for, 54
grounds of inadmissibility/deportability, 2–3
LPRs returning to U.S., 6
motions to continue, 132
refugee, defined, 241
students, five-year bar, 87
suspension of deportation, 195–96
Immigration Act of 1990 (IMMACT 90)
voluntary departure, 273
Immigration and Customs Enforcement (ICE)
creation and role of, 1–2
termination to proceed with adjustment before USCIS, 128–29
Immigration court procedures
removal. *See* Removal proceedings

Immigration law violations
deportability, grounds of, 37–38
inadmissibility, grounds of, 82–87

Immigration Marriage Fraud Amendments of 1986 (IMFA)
conditional resident status for spouses and children, 137

Immunity from prosecution
inadmissibility, grounds for, 74

Imputed political opinion
persecution due to, 242–43

In absentia hearings
motions to reopen removal orders, 293–96
removal hearings, 23–25

Inadmissibility, grounds of
generally, 5–6, 61–95
categories of, 63–70
communicable diseases, 64–65
waiver, 163–64
Communist party members, 78–79
convictions. *See* Criminal convictions
document and presentation fraud, 86–87
drug abusers, 67–68
drug offenses including trafficking, 71–72
economic grounds, 80–82
evaluating charges of inadmissibility, 62–63
false claim to citizenship, 85–86
fraud and willful misrepresentation, 36–37, 83–84
health-related grounds, 38, 63–68
waiver, 163–65

IIRAIRA provisions, 2–3
immigration law violations, 82–87
immunity from prosecution, 74
moral grounds, 70
national security grounds, 76–80
physical or mental disorders, 66
security and foreign-policy grounds, 76–80
smugglers and encouragers of unlawful entry, 86
stowaways, 86
terrorist activities, 77–78
unlawful presence, 90–91
vaccination, lack of, 65–66
waivers, 148–49, 155–75
criminal grounds, 165–67
economic grounds, 152
extreme hardship, 157–62
FOAA applications for adjustment, 150–51
Form I-601, 171–72
fraud, 167–68
health-related grounds, 163–65
nonimmigrant waiver, 169
refugees and asylees, 169–70
registry applicants, 148–49
section 212(c) relief, 190–91
strategy and procedure, 171–72
vaccination, 65–66, 164–65
VAWA, 169
visa fraud, 36–37

Internal relocation
as asylum alternative, 240

J

***Joseph* hearings**
mandatory detention, challenge to, 14

Judicial review of removal orders
generally, 297–309
of administrative removal orders, 308
bar in court of appeals, 301–4
criminal conviction and, 303–4
deference, 305
discretionary decisions, 302–3
of expedited removal process, 306–7
filing deadlines, 304–5
of judicial removal orders, 308
jurisdiction, 306
matters not reviewable, 304–6
nationality claims, 307
petitions, 306
pre-IIRAIRA, 297–98
procedural rules, 304–6
REAL ID and, 298–306
transitional rules on, 298
validity of orders in criminal proceedings, 307–8

Jurisdiction
conditional status, 139
judicial review of removal orders, 306
NACARA cases, 221–22
removal proceedings, 25–26

Juvenile delinquency adjudications
conviction for purposes of immigration, 43
"under 18" exception to inadmissibility, 70
Juveniles. *See* **Children**

L

Laotian nationals
adjustment of status, 150–53
Lawful permanent residents (LPRs)
cancellation of removal, 53, 179–93
residing in U.S. as LPR for 5 years, 180
seven years continuous residence after lawful admission, 180–82
deportability and, 39, 55
repapering rule (proposed), 193
returning, 6, 8
Legal Immigration and Family Equity Act of 2000 (LIFE Act)
adjustment of status, 143, 146
reinstatement of removal, 231
Legal services
availability of, 10
Loss of citizenship. *See* **Citizenship**
LPRs. *See* **Lawful permanent residents**

M

Mandamus
as legal remedy, 309
Mandatory detention
bond, ineligibility for, 12–14
Joseph hearings to challenge, 14
Marriage
forced marriage, 247
fraud, deportability for, 40
Master calendar hearings
removal proceedings, 21–23
Medical examinations
admissibility determination, 38
Membership in particular social group
for refugee status, 244–49
Mental disabilities
waiver of inadmissibility based on, 164
Merits hearings
removal proceedings, 22
Military Selective Service Act
deportability for conviction under, 53
Minors. *See* **Children**
Money laundering crimes
inadmissibility for, 75
Moral turpitude. *See* **Crime of moral turpitude (CMT)**
Motions
pre-hearing, 16–18
for termination of removal proceedings, 18, 102–3
Motions to reopen/reconsider
generally, 289–96
adjustment of status cases, 134–35, 291
contents of motion, 291–93

Convention Against Torture cases, 290
filing requirements, 291–93
in absentia order, 293–96
NACARA eligible individuals, 229–30
number limits for, 289–91
purpose of, 289
section 212(c) relief, 191
time limit for filing, 289–91
voluntary departure, 274–76
Motions to suppress
in removal proceedings, 11, 113, 120–21, 349

N

NACARA. *See* **Nicaraguan Adjustment and Central American Relief Act of 1997**
Nationality
treatment of nationality claims on review, 307
National security-related cases
See also Terrorism
inadmissibility, grounds for, 76–80
treason and sedition as grounds for deportability, 53, 56–57
Naturalization
generally, 279–86
aggravated felony convictions, 280–81
charts, 337
as defense to removal, 281–86
deportability, final finding of, 286
good moral character, 280

prima facie eligibility,
279–80
procedure, 281–86
prosecutorial discretion,
282–83
termination of removal
proceedings under
8 CFR §1239.2(f),
283–85
**Nazi persecutions, participants
in**
inadmissibil-
ity/deportability of,
57
inadmissibility of, 79–80
Nebraska Service Center (NSC)
jurisdiction over HRIFA
adjustment of
status, 145
Neutrality
in political opinion, 242–
43
**Nicaraguan Adjustment and
Central American Relief Act
of 1997 (NACARA)**
adjustment of status, 125,
140–43, 170
application in removal
proceedings, 228–
29
deadline for, 231
beneficiaries of, 219–21
burden of proof, 230
cancellation of removal,
222–25
bar to, 226–27
continuous presence, 220,
222–23
evidence, 230
departures, 223
dependent spouses and
children, 220
jurisdiction, 222
eligibility to apply, 219
evidence, 230–31

extreme hardship, 220,
224–26
evidence, 230–31
failure to comply with
immigration pro-
ceedings, bars re-
lating to, 227
good moral character, 220,
223–24
evidence, 230
immigration violations,
bars to, 226–27
jurisdiction of application,
221–22
motions to reopen, 229–30
reinstatement of removal,
31, 231
statutory bars to, 226–28
suspension of deportation,
bars to, 226, 227–
28
unmarried sons and daugh-
ters, 220
application in removal
proceedings,
229
Nonimmigrants
waiver, 169
Notice requirements
address change, 8
Notice to Appear (NTA)
challenging, 104–5
removal proceedings, 6–7,
313
service, 8

O

Order to show cause
removal proceedings, 7,
317
service, 8

P

Pardons
conviction for purposes of
immigration, 111–
12
Parole
See also Humanitarian
relief
arriving aliens, 127
humanitarian parole, 152
unlawful presence of pa-
rolees, 82–83
Passports
obtaining, 99
PATRIOT Act
removal proceedings and,
3
Penalties
removal order, noncompli-
ance with, 26
Permanent residency. *See* **Lawful permanent residents
(LPRs)**
Persecution
coercive family-planning
programs, 240–41
credible fear, 259
arriving aliens, 259
domestic violence as, 247–
48
economic harm, 239
elements of, 239–51
female genital mutilation
as, 246–47
forced marriage as, 247
by groups that government
cannot control,
239–40
internal relocation alternative, 240
proposed regulations, 249–
51
prosecution vs., 240
social group membership
as grounds for,
249–51

standard for withholding
of removal, 234
totality of circumstances
test, 239
well-founded, 234
**Persecutors of others for reli-
gious beliefs**
inadmissibility, grounds
for, 74–75
Petty offense exception
criminal convictions that
mandate inadmissi-
bility or deportabil-
ity, 70–71
Physical presence. *See* **Continuous residence or physical
presence**
Political opinion
imputed, 242–43
inadmissibility, grounds
for, 78
neutrality, 242–43
Polygamy
inadmissibility, grounds
for, 95
Pre-hearing conference
motion for, 18
Pre-hearing statement
removal proceedings, 21
Prior removal orders
inadmissibility, grounds
for, 88–89
Prosecution
vs. persecution, 240
Prosecutorial discretion
naturalization proceedings,
282–83
removal proceedings, 100–
103
Prostitution
inadmissibil-
ity/deportability,
grounds for, 73–74
waivers, 166
Protective orders
hardship factor, 160

violations of, as grounds
for deportability,
54
waiver, 176–77
Public charge, likely to become.
See **Economic grounds**

Q

Questioning
detentive questioning,
119–20
mere questioning, 118–19
right to remain silent, 121–
22

R

REAL ID Act of 2005
asylum, 238–39
on credibility determina-
tion, 239
on judicial review of re-
moval orders, 298–
306
petitions for review after,
300–301
removal proceedings and,
3
Reconsideration, motions for.
See **Motions to re-
open/reconsider**
**Re-entering after deportation or
removal**
See also Reinstatement of
removal
entry without authoriza-
tion, 94–95
Refugees
See also Asylum seekers
defined, 241
fear of persecution. *See*
Persecution
waivers, 169–70

Registry
adjustment of status, 146–
50
application process, 149–
50
discretionary remedy, 149
eligibility requirements,
146–47
good moral character, 148
grounds of inadmissibility,
148–49
not ineligible to citizenship, 148
residence, 147–48
Reinstatement of removal
generally, 31–32
Convention Against Tor-
ture and, 267
NACARA, 31, 231
Relocation
internal relocation alternative, 240
Removal proceedings
See also Expedited re-
moval
generally, 1–34
adjustment of status as
defense to, 125
administrative removal
orders for aggra-
vated felons, 29–30
appeals, 25
bar to reentry, 88–89
biometrics, 23
bonds, 12–16
burden of proof, 8–9, 105–
7
CAT relief, 266
charging documents, 6–7
citizenship, 97–100
commencement of, 6–8
consequences of, 25–26
contesting, 97–123
crimes that subject clients
to, 107–12
decision and order, 25

types of orders, 28–30
decision to concede or contest, 103–4
defined, 1
deportability as basis of, 106–7
DHS identification of individuals for, 3–5
discovery, 18–21
due process rights, 11
evidence, 22
  right to present, examine, and object to, 10
failure to appear, consequences of, 83
Fifth Amendment privilege. *See* Fifth Amendment
IIRAIRA procedure, 2–3
in absentia hearings, 23–25
individual hearings, 21–23
judicial removal order, 30
jurisdiction, 25–26
master calendar hearings, 21–23
merits hearing, 22
motions to close administratively, 102
motions to terminate, 18, 102–3
Notice to Appear (NTA), 6–7, 313
  challenging, 104–5
  service, 8
order to show cause, 7
  service, 8
penalties for noncompliance with court orders, 26
practice tips for non-court advocates, 32–34
pre-hearing motions, 16–18

pre-hearing procedures, 12–21
pre-hearing statement, 21
prior removal orders, 88–89
prosecutorial discretion, 100–103
recording of, 22–23
reinstatement of, 31–32
relief from, right to be advised of eligibility for, 11
representation, right to, 9–10
sample case scenario, 27
service, 8
standard of proof, 105–7
termination of
  motion for, 18
  naturalization application under 8 CFR §1239.2(f), 283–85
translation, right to, 10
types of orders, 28–30
videoconferenced or telephonic hearing, 23

Reopen, motions to
  See **Motions to reopen/reconsider**
Repapering rule
  proposed, 193, 198–99
Representation
  of children, 11
  right to, 9–10
Residency requirements. *See* **Continuous residence or physical presence**
Restriction on removal. *See* **Withholding of removal**
Returning lawful permanent residents (LPRs)
  treatment of, 6, 8

S

Safe third country
  asylum denial, grounds for, 255–56
St. Cyr case (2001)
  availability of §212(c) relief, 187–88
Salvadorans
  NACARA eligibility, 219, 221
  See also Nicaraguan Adjustment and Central American Relief Act of 1997
Search and seizure
  protection against unreasonable, 113–14
  warrants, 115–17
Section 212(c) relief
  application for, 191–92
  cancellation of removal, 186–92
  motions to reopen, 191
  persons not covered, 192
  St. Cyr case on availability of, 187–88
Security grounds for deportability
  threats against president, espionage, sabotage, or sedition, 53
Security grounds for inadmissibility
  generally, 76–80
  asylum seekers, 253–56
Sedition
  inadmissibility for, 76–77
  security grounds for deportability, 53, 56–57
Self-incrimination privilege
  in removal proceedings, 112

Self-petitions
  battered spouse or child, for cancellation of removal, 217–18
Serious crimes, conviction of
  asylum denial, grounds for, 256
  withholding of removal denial, grounds for, 257–58
Service
  removal proceedings, 8
Sex offenders
  registration requirements, 51
Silence, right to
  Fifth Amendment protection, 121–22
Smuggling
  See also Human trafficking
  deportability for human smuggling, 39–40
  inadmissibility for human smuggling, 86
Special immigrant juveniles
  waivers for minors, 170
Spousal relationship
  marriage fraud, 40
Spouses
  derivative status, 233
Stalking
  deportability for, 54
  waiver, 176–77
Standard of proof
  asylum and withholding proceedings, 236–38
  criminal convictions, 68–69
  removal proceedings, 105–7
Stay of removal
  during appeal to BIA, 287
Stop time rule
  generally, 180–81, 182

Stowaways
  inadmissibility, grounds for, 86
Students
  five-year bar of inadmissibility, 87
Summary dismissal
  BIA appeals, 288
Summary removal. *See* Expedited removal
Supporting documentation
  extreme hardship, 161–62
  Form I-212, 174–75
Suppress, motions to
  in removal proceedings, 11, 113, 120–21, 349
Surviving spouse. *See* Widow(er)s
Suspension of deportation
  generally, 195–231
  continuous physical presence, 197–98
  current availability of, 196–201
  discretion, 201
  eligibility, 197
  extreme hardship, 200–201
  good moral character, 199–200
  IIRAIRA changes, 195–96
  NACARA, 222–25
    bars to, 226, 227–28
  pre-IIRAIRA, 195–201

T

T visas
  adjustment of status, 125
  waiver of inadmissibility for, 170
Tax evasion
  inadmissibility, grounds of, 95
Telephonic conference
  removal proceedings, 23

Temporary protected status (TPS)
  waiver of inadmissibility for, 170
Termination
  of asylum and withholding, 258–59
Termination of removal proceedings
  motions for, 18, 102–3
  naturalization application under 8 CFR §1239.2(f), 283–85
Terrorism
  deportability, grounds of, 57
  inadmissibility, grounds of, 77–78
  asylum seekers, 253–56
Texas Service Center (TSC)
  jurisdiction over NACARA adjustment of status, 142
Time limits
  asylum applications, filing of, 234
  motion to reopen/reconsider, 289–91
Torture
  See also Convention Against Torture (CAT)
  defined, 260–64
Totality of circumstances
  test for asylum, 239
TPS. *See* Temporary protected status
Trading with the Enemy Act
  deportability for conviction under, 53
Translation
  removal hearings, 10
Travel documents
  offenses as grounds for deportability, 53

Treason and sedition
 as grounds for deportability, 53, 56–57

U

U visas
 adjustment of status, 125
 waiver of inadmissibility
  for, 170, 173–74
Unlawful presence
 bars, 90–91
 parolees, 82–83
 periods of, calculation of,
  91–95
 three- and ten-year bars,
  90–91
 waiver for extreme hard-
  ship, 168–69
U.S. citizens. *See* **Citizenship**
**U.S. Citizenship and Immigra-
 tion Service (USCIS)**
 adjustment applications for
  arriving aliens who
  are parolees, adju-
  dication of, 127
 creation and role of, 1
 HRIFA adjustment of
  status, jurisdiction
  of Nebraska Ser-
  vice Center, 145
 NACARA adjustment of
  status, jurisdiction
  of Texas Service
  Center, 142
USA PATRIOT Act
 removal proceedings and,
  3

V

Vaccination
 lack of, as grounds for inadmissibility, 65–
  66

 waiver, 164–65
Venue
 motion to change, 17
Videoconferenced hearings
 removal proceedings, 23
**Vienna Convention on Consular
 Relations**
 applicability, 10
Vietnam nationals
 adjustment of status, 150–
  53
Violence, crimes of
 inadmissibil-
   ity/deportability
   for, 191
**Violence Against Women Act
 (VAWA)**
 adjustment of status, 125,
  143, 154
 cancellation of removal,
  208–18
  See also Battered
    spouse or child
 deportability for crimes of
  domestic violence,
  stalking, etc.,
  waiver of, 176–77
 I-212 waivers, 173
 inadmissibility, grounds
  under, 83, 95
 waiver, 166, 169
 removal proceedings and,
  3, 37
 voluntary departure, 272–
  73
Visas
 See also specific types
 invalid documents, inad-
  missibility for, 87
Voluntary departure
 generally, 269–77
 appeals, 274
 application for, 276
 arguments to avoid consequences of failure
  to depart, 274

 at conclusion of removal
  proceedings, 270–
  71
 establishing compliance
  with, 277
 failure to timely depart,
  271–74
 motions to reopen, 274–76
 NACARA
  bar from cancellation of
   removal, 228
  bar from suspension of
   deportation, 228
  post-9/11 detainees, 272
  prior to removal proceedings, 270
  requirements, 269–71
Voting offenses
 deportability, grounds of,
  58–59
 inadmissibility, grounds
  of, 95

W

Waivers
 conditional residence. *See*
  Conditional resi-
  dence
 of deportability, 175–77
  crimes of domestic vio-
   lence, stalking,
   or violation of
   protection order,
   176–77
  fraud, 175–76
 exercise of discretion,
  156–57
 for humanitarian reasons.
  See Humanitarian
  relief
 of inadmissibility, 155–75
  criminal grounds, 165–
   67
  economic grounds, 152

extreme hardship, 157–62

FOAA applications for adjustment, 150–51

Form I-601, 171–72

fraud, 167–68

health-related grounds, 163–65

nonimmigrant waiver, 169

refugees and asylees, 169–70

registry applicants, 148–49

strategy and procedure, 171–72

vaccination, 65–66, 164–65

VAWA, 169

visa fraud, 36–37

Warrants

arrest warrants, 117–18

search warrants, 115–17

Welfare benefits

deportability and, 58

Willful misrepresentation

crimes that subject clients to inadmissibility, 83–84

Withholding of removal

asylum vs., 233–36

under Convention Against Torture, 30, 264–65

evidence, 236–38

ineligibility for, 256–58

standard of proof, 236–38

termination of, 258–59

Women. *See* **Battered spouse or child; VAWA**